D1606254

DATE DUE

11-16-11			

Margaret Sanger's
Eugenic Legacy

Margaret Sanger's Eugenic Legacy

*The Control
of Female Fertility*

ANGELA FRANKS

McFarland & Company, Inc., Publishers
Jefferson, North Carolina, and London

LIBRARY OF CONGRESS CATALOGUING-IN-PUBLICATION DATA

Franks, Angela, 1971–
    Margaret Sanger's eugenic legacy : the control of female
fertility / Angela Franks.
        p.   cm.
    Includes bibliographical references and index.

    ISBN-13: 978-0-7864-2011-7
    softcover : 50# alkaline paper ∞

    1. Sanger, Margaret, 1879–1966.   2. Birth control — United
States.   3. Eugenics— United States.   4. Sterilization (Birth
control) — United States.   5. Women social reformers— United
States.   I. Title.
HQ766.5.U5F67   2005
363.9'2 — dc22   2004029008

British Library cataloguing data are available

On the cover: Margaret Sanger in 1922 (*Library of Congress*);
background ©2005 Artville

Manufactured in the United States of America

McFarland & Company, Inc., Publishers
  Box 611, Jefferson, North Carolina 28640
  www.mcfarlandpub.com

To my firstborn child, my daughter,
whose coming changed my life.

In memory of all those women
who have been robbed of their fertility,
their children, their lives.

Contents

Preface and Acknowledgments 1

INTRODUCTION: Taking Sanger Seriously 5

ONE: Woman and the New Race 21

TWO: Eugenics as the Control of Births 65

THREE: Eugenicists, Coworkers, Friends 98

FOUR: Quality, Not Quantity:
Population Control and Eugenics 127

FIVE: Money Means Power: The Rich Have Their Say 150

SIX: "Sterilize All the Unfit!" 179

SEVEN: Selling Out the Sisterhood 203

EIGHT: Beyond Control: Toward a New Feminism 237

APPENDIX 1: List of Abbreviations 253

APPENDIX 2: Chronology 256

Chapter Notes 259
Works Consulted 307
Index 337

Preface and
Acknowledgments

Another book about Margaret Sanger perhaps requires an explanation. Many historians have turned their attention to her, given her significance in the history of American reproductive politics. The resultant scholarship has varied depending on the standpoint of the scholar behind it: historians with a commitment to women's history have tended to canonize her (which requires explaining away her association with eugenics), while scholars of eugenics have tended to argue she was indeed connected, although somewhat peripherally, with the eugenics movement. Recently feminist researchers have begun to examine more seriously the eugenic involvement of the first generation of American feminists, and Sanger scholarship can only be improved as a result.

This book is part of that last general movement in feminist scholarship. Utilizing more than twenty-five manuscript sources (Sanger's own papers, the archives of her organizations, and manuscript collections related to her coworkers and institutions friendly to her cause), as well as transcripts of interviews with her colleagues, I argue that Sanger had a genuine commitment to the eugenic ideology. As this work will show, at no time did her belief in eugenics lag; she differed from the "professional" eugenicist only in her emphasis on birth control and her ambivalence regarding positive eugenics (namely, activities directed toward encouraging the eugenically "fit" to have more children). In addition, I will present the continuing life of these ideas in the organizations she founded by drawing on institutional documents and publications in order to show how her legacy — the control of female fertility — still inflicts suffering upon women. Other

1

books have alluded to her eugenic faith, but *Margaret Sanger's Eugenic Legacy* is the first scholarly, book-length work to treat the topic. This book will address Sanger's ideas concerning birth control, eugenics, population control, and sterilization against the backdrop of the larger eugenic context. In the introduction, I will address the general topic of Sanger's relationship with eugenics by analyzing other scholarly views on the question before summarizing her eugenic ideology of control and the way it compromises her feminism. I will then in chapter one look in detail at Sanger's eugenic beliefs as they were expressed in her published and unpublished writings from the beginning of her career as a birth-control activist up to the end of her life, as well as the perpetuation of her ideas in the organizations she founded. Chapter two will examine the eugenics movement as a whole in order to contextualize Sanger's beliefs and activities. In chapter three, I will recount the activities of some of her most significant coworkers and the centrality of their eugenic commitments to their professional and personal relationships with Sanger. Chapters four and five will present a history of the population-control movement, highlighting the continuity between the eugenicists and the population controllers. Lastly, in chapters six and seven, I will look directly at the mechanisms by which Sanger's control ideology has victimized vulnerable women. Chapter six is devoted to sterilization and chapter seven turns to other means by which a misogynist bureaucracy continued the institutionalization of the control of female fertility begun by Sanger. The book closes with a summary of Sanger's distorted feminism and argues for a revisioning of female embodiment and fertility. Many other topics could have been addressed more extensively, such as how Sanger's eugenic attitudes toward charitable assistance are reflected in current proposals on welfare reform, or what declassified documents reveal about the motivations of governments in establishing population control — but the constraints of writing a book of manageable size has forced me to limit myself.

Such an improbable book as the present one owes its genesis to many people. I must thank first of all the thinkers who inspired and helped me, either directly or without knowing it (though it should not be assumed that they would all agree with my analysis): the list includes Diane Paul, who provided personal encouragement and scholarly insights in equal proportion; Lisa Sowle Cahill, who commented on drafts and plowed through a great many pages of historical material; Germaine Greer, who opened my eyes to the experiences poor women have of their fertility and to the threat eugenics poses to feminism; Jean Bethke Elshtain, whose theoretical sophistication helped me better understand what Greer describes and who is a model of the feminist scholar; and the many feminist activists working to liberate women from the "controllers," such as the Boston Women's Health Book Collective, Dorothy Roberts, and others.

I also owe much to immensely skilled and often anonymous archivists at the various libraries I visited. I am especially grateful to Scott DeHaven at the American Philosophical Society Library for tracking down an important but obscure Frederick Osborn quote with great efficiency. In a class of his own is Tom Rosenbaum of the Rockefeller Archive Collection, who remains one of the best friends this book has had and, in addition, a friend of its author. Many people gave permission to quote from manuscript collections; of these, special mention must be made of Alexander Sanger, whose generous attitude was an unexpected delight.

Most of my colleagues deserve thanks simply for letting me rant periodically about this book's subject matter. On an institutional level, I owe thanks to the Boston College Department of Theology for benignly turning a blind eye to the non-dissertation activities of one of its doctoral students. In particular, my dissertation director Robert Imbelli and my readers Michael Waldstein and Matthew Lamb have my gratitude for providing understanding and the utmost minimum of gentle reminders that I ought to be writing something theological too.

On a personal level, I owe a huge debt (much of which could be quantified!) to my parents, who have never failed to provide support, child care, and insights. Likewise, my mother-in-law Dolores provided nourishment and baby care at frequent intervals. In addition, I must thank my erstwhile employers, David and especially Jacki, once my boss but always simply one of my best friends. This book would not be without her. I must also thank Randy and Laura for their expertise and encouragement. Both my siblings-in-law worked as the only research assistants I have ever had; I especially am grateful to Matt for lending a patient ear to my frequent declamations on all matters eugenic when he lived in our household, and I also owe much to Mary Anne's high-powered work in feminist philosophy. My own siblings, Tony (and his family) and Erika, contributed a sense of perspective and a sense of humor.

Lastly, regarding my immediate family, I can say without a touch of exaggeration that I would have never completed this book without the assistance of my husband. I simply cannot enumerate the many ways he contrived to facilitate the research and writing process. An indefatigable sounding board, a superb father, an ever-supportive husband, an excellent pasta cook and dishwasher, an enviably good editor, and the most committed feminist I have ever known: David, I am privileged to be building a life with you. To my children, the fruit of that life, I hope that I can give you as much as you have given me, not least of which is an experience of the power of female fertility, shared with mothers throughout the world. May this book do some part in making your world a better place for mothers and daughters, fathers and sons.

INTRODUCTION

Taking Sanger Seriously

"I see no wider meaning of family planning than control and as for restriction, there are definitely some families throughout the world where there is every indication ... that restriction should be an order as [well as] an ideal for the betterment of the family and the race."— Margaret Sanger, 1955[1]

"All the time women have been agitating for freedom and self-determination they have been coming more and more under a kind of control that they cannot even protest against."— Germaine Greer, 1999[2]

Sanger as Symbol and as Reality

Margaret Sanger, the American birth-control and population-control advocate who founded Planned Parenthood, stands like a giant among her contemporaries. With her dominating yet winning personality, she helped generate shifts of opinion on issues that were not even publicly discussed prior to her activism, while her leadership was arguably the single most important factor in achieving social and legislative victories that set the parameters for today's political discussion of family-planning funding, population-control aid, and even sex education. Sanger had a powerful and decisive mind that could grasp the big picture; as we will see in the eighth chapter, her compelling book *Woman and the New Race* lays out an imaginative and original synthesis of socialism, birth control, and feminist theory. Yet she was also a most capable administrator and detail-per-

5

son. She published a journal, ran clinics, organized conferences, wrote and edited books, kept up an active correspondence with friends and coworkers, spoke at venues throughout the world, founded and led several organizations, raised money, lobbied Congress, and held her own in a male-dominated world.

In light of these achievements, it is not surprising that she is viewed by many feminists as a paragon of female achievement against an oppressive order. In this light, Sanger represents the success possible in the struggle for the liberation of women from, for example, the suffocating confines of suburban housewifery, enabling entrance into the larger social, economic, and political sphere. So it would seem that Sanger's cry for freedom from motherhood opens up the larger world to women; such freedom would render women as unencumbered by their reproductive physiology as men seem to be. Today's feminists often see her as a promethean bringer of the kind of freedom that they enjoy now to a greater degree than ever before, a freedom built on the control of female fertility.

So it would seem. Yet can the *liberation* of women be built on the *control* of their bodies? Symptoms of an inherent instability become visible in the light of the fate of particular women and their bodies. Poor women, especially, can testify to being pressured into submitting to sterilization or to semi-permanent forms of chemical contraception. Many other women have been told by their boyfriends or husbands that contraception is a female responsibility, because male contraceptive methods interfere too much with a man's sexual pleasure.

Who is controlling whom? While women have felt the deleterious effects of sexism for as long as history can recall, how did misogynist attitudes infect the use of what is still almost universally considered a means of female liberation, namely, contraception? If contraceptive availability was initially promoted by women with feminist convictions, why does current contraceptive practice seem to be so unresponsive to female needs? The purpose of this book is precisely to investigate the history of the current situation and to ask, from a feminist perspective, the question: why? Is our present situation an accident of history, or does it have roots that can be traced to the attitudes and decisions of the early birth-control pioneers? In examining this history, I will eschew any false dichotomy of fact and value, of "is" and "ought." In other words, one can gain clearer historical insight into the nature of Sanger's commitments to the degree that one understands the ideologies at work and judges them in light of the concrete toll they take on women's lives.[3]

This book takes a different approach to Sanger than have most books about her: it takes her seriously. Too many writers who have studied her have succumbed to the temptation to censor aspects of her thought that do not seem consistent, at least to our way of thinking. How could a feminist advocate forced sterilization? Why did Sanger participate so extensively in the eugenics movement? Too many scholars have dealt with this aspect of her thought only by throwing up their hands and saying, "Well, maybe she didn't really mean it." In contrast, I will try to make sense of Sanger's thought as something that *she*, at least, considered internally consistent (and, as we will see, it *is* in fact consistent); whether or not it is actually rational or ethically acceptable is another question that I will address separately. In any case, Sanger of course assumed her views to be rational, even claiming their scientific necessity. This book, then, will not dismiss as peripheral themes that she herself from beginning to end insisted were central. That is, it will not assume that one can know *a priori* what she was about, according to contemporary definitions of feminism, or accede to some patronizing sense of what this woman must have *meant* despite what she *said*. That does not mean that I will not criticize Sanger; I consider it crucial to take her seriously precisely because she has been so influential and, I believe, dangerous.[4] My criticisms, however, will assume that she was acting out of an internally consistent set of convictions.

I contend that Sanger believed that birth control (and reproduction in general) was, simply put, a matter of power and that the solution to women's and humanity's problems was to add more powerful weapons to the arsenal targeting female fertility. Part of the problem lies in Sanger's conception of freedom; as I will show, Sanger's utopian vision of liberation was too severely infected with a mindset of oppressive control to be able to promote true female liberation. "Birth control" (a term she helped coin) was intended from the beginning to control the births of certain kinds of people, and this situation Sanger considered freedom, not oppression. As this book will explore, birth control has often been used to cement existing power imbalances or else to create new ones altogether, and Sanger remained all too often supportive of this new technological oppression. Part of the aim of this book is to demonstrate that contraception has been and is still being used as a means of control — often, contrary to feminist hopes, for misogynist purposes.

I will in fact argue that this pattern of controlling women through birth control was initiated and sedimented by Sanger herself. She was not naive concerning the coercive potential of birth control; in fact, she advocated the employment of this potential. As I will show, Sanger believed that certain classes of people should not be parents, and if they would not embrace a childless state voluntarily, it should be forced upon them.[5] In 1955, toward the end of Sanger's life, in a letter protesting a report that

argues that Planned Parenthood should "shift the emphasis from controlling restriction to the fuller and wider meaning of family planning," she
argues,

> To me that seems a very short-sighted view of the world situation. I see
> no wider meaning of family planning than control and as for restriction,
> there are definitely some families throughout the world where there is
> every indication ... that restriction should be an order as [well as] an ideal
> for the betterment of the family and the race.[6]

For Sanger, the control of female fertility through contraception ("family
planning") has "no wider meaning" than control. She had no delusions
about the fact that contraception was a means of power.[7]

What use can dwelling on this dark side of Sanger's motives have,
beyond satisfying historical curiosity? I will argue throughout this book
that it is essential for women who have admired this pioneer not to be
blindly uncritical of her faults and, even more, to realize that she championed an ideology that is much less benign than it first appears, an ideology ultimately destructive of the ideals of female liberation. Thus, my
concern here is not with contraception as such[8] (except insofar as I hope
to raise consciousness about the fact that it was developed, and has served,
as a tool of power) or with drawing an antiquarian portrait of Sanger.
Rather, I am ultimately concerned with the ideology that she powerfully
formulated and disseminated by means of her organizational genius,
effectively determining the contours of the birth-control and population-
control movements. This ideology of Sanger's I call "the ideology of control."

For Sanger, a constellation of three varieties of control was the center of her life's work: birth control, eugenic control, and population control; each of these aspects of the ideology was equally indispensable. This
ideology of control is not a matter of mere historical curiosity but an acute
contemporary concern, especially given that Planned Parenthood exercises such strong influence on many feminist activists. Many other, less
mainstream feminists have taken issue with population control's misogynist and controlling ideology, yet their opinions do not seem to be well-
known among most women. I hope to give these perspectives a fair hearing
by showing that Sanger's eugenic attitudes have been institutionalized and
thus perpetuated, although sometimes in an underground or quasi-uncon-
scious way, through the naive reception and reproduction of an ideology
that has not yet been subjected to critical analysis.[9]

I use the term "ideology" to indicate a worldview that obfuscates reality to such a degree that the person holding these beliefs is simply unable

to recognize what is really the case. Ideology obscures reality in the service of some vested interest, some political or social end — in the present case, the control of female fertility. The ideology diagnosed in this book is an ideology that renders a person incapable of making sense of female fertility. The ideology of control does not attempt to understand a woman's body in itself but only sees it as a symbol and a cipher: a symbol of chaotic reproductive forces threatening to swamp the world in sheer fecundity, and a cipher because, in the end, the female body is an abstraction, an "at-risk reproducer," perhaps an opportunity for pleasure, but not a concrete reality — a nothing. Thus, nothing really happens when, as I will describe in later chapters, a female body (or several of them) is mutilated or eliminated. Numbers shift in columns, but the tragic reality is not engaged, because the ideology protects one from that engagement.

If this seems like an unduly harsh assessment of a heroine who was nothing if not committed to promoting the pleasures inherent in inhabiting a female body, read on. As I will show, Sanger's ideology is a vaguely gnostic sensualism that allows for injustice to be performed on women because it cannot understand what real injustice is. Sanger's vision of female liberation was too truncated and too burdened by her romance with social-control mechanisms to be genuinely emancipatory. Unfortunately, her brand of the ideology of control lives on today in the organizations she founded.

I certainly do not mean to accuse individual supporters of Planned Parenthood today of being eugenicists; there is too little historical awareness for that to be the case. However, I am concerned with the lack of progress we have made in exorcizing some of the ideologies analyzed in this book, and I am even more troubled by the (un)ethical assumptions, sometimes leading to grotesque human rights violations, that various organizations devoted to birth control and population control still hold. I have found that a feminist hermeneutics, one that is consistently aware of the effects of sexism and coercion on disenfranchised women, sees the concrete, social effects of ideology with a clearer vision than do other perspectives. Thus, the rest of the book will, from this viewpoint, both explore Sanger's own control ideology and trace her continuing influence by analyzing current manifestations of this way of thinking, for the purpose of gaining precious clarity concerning our own ideas as feminists. I hope this clarity can enable us to purge from our belief systems any lingering elitist bigotry which does not do justice to the dignity of each human being and does not assist us in better protecting women and girls from violence.

Taking Ideology Seriously
(or, Maybe Sanger Meant What She Said)

Historians of eugenics have generally considered Sanger to be a eugenicist, but scholars specializing in women's history have tended to come to the opposite conclusion.[10] To a large degree, the divide is due to unfamiliarity with eugenic language and beliefs on the part of the latter camp. For example, it is common for a contemporary person to equate eugenics with racism and anti–Semitism, given the connection in the popular imagination between eugenics and Nazism, yet the one ideology did not and does not necessarily imply the other. Thus, it would be incorrect to assume that a person in the 1930s was not a eugenicist simply because that person does not appear to be a racist or anti–Semite.[11] I agree with the historians of eugenics concerning Sanger's eugenic commitments, but let us first briefly examine the arguments of those who believe Sanger was not a eugenicist.

Some biographers of Sanger have viewed her as a consistently radical leftist and have thus downplayed her eugenic connections. Ellen Chesler, for example, claims that eugenicists joined the birth-control movement late in the day, in the 1930s.[12] Historian James Reed sees Sanger as primarily a feminist emancipator, who embraced eugenic philosophies only partially and out of political prudence: "[O]pportunism, pragmatism, or plain dishonesty was characteristic of Sanger and accounts for the considerable confusion that exists concerning her positions on many issues, and especially her relationship to the eugenics movement, other feminists, and the medical establishment."[13] Reed also notes Sanger's opposition to positive eugenics (the belief that the eugenically "fit" should have more children) and thereby concludes that she opposed eugenics altogether.[14]

On all three counts, Chesler and Reed's conclusions do not hold up. Chesler overlooks the fact that, of the fifty clergymen, scientists, and physicians listed on the National Council of Sanger's American Birth Control League (ABCL) in the 1920s, at least twenty-three of them were involved at a prominent level in eugenics— either as members of the board of directors of the American Eugenics Society (AES) or by otherwise publicly supporting her eugenics agenda.[15] Thus, eugenicists were deeply involved with Sanger's organizations already a decade earlier than Chesler claims. With regard to Reed's contention, I will show in the next chapter that the negative eugenic position (the belief that the eugenically "unfit" should refrain from having children) was often held by committed eugenicists who did not believe in positive eugenics. Negative eugenics was a well-developed ideology of its own, with a complete legislative agenda including agitation for compulsory sterilization and immigration restriction.

But the most important claim concerns Sanger's motives: did she make eugenic statements just to win favor from the eugenic-minded elite?[16] Sanger was certainly capable of equivocation: indeed, with other issues Sanger acted as Chesler and Reed have claimed she did with eugenics, by saying one thing in public while confiding a quite different belief in private letters to her friends. Her opinion concerning abortion is a good example. Sanger advertised contraceptive services as the means of preventing recourse to abortion; her handbill for the first birth-control clinic in Brownsville, New York, reads, "Do not kill, do not take life, but prevent."[17] In addition, she vociferously denied in public that she was in the business of procuring abortions for women. Yet both Sanger's actions and her private letters belie any real opposition to abortion: there is evidence that her Birth Control Clinical Research Bureau referred at least seventy-five women for abortions, some for non-disabling or non-life-threatening conditions.[18] She also wrote in a letter concerning the situation of women in Japan, "Remember that the women of Japan did not have to fight the men for political equality or for Birth Control or even for the right to abortion."[19] That sort of rhetoric, which equates abortion with the (for her) unqualified good of birth control, not to mention suffrage, indicates that she had little, if any, moral problem with the practice. This whole pattern of pragmatic equivocation — apparent public opposition, combined with private support — is completely different from the pattern we see when it comes to Sanger and eugenics.

Let us take a 1939 letter from Sanger to the premier American eugenicist of the twentieth century, Frederick Osborn. In it, she comments on a recent booklet issued by the American Eugenics Society entitled "American Eugenics Today." She does disagree with the booklet, but not because she disagrees with eugenics; rather, she finds the brochure too moderate. Instead of calling for a more indirect approach, in the first paragraph she asserts, "It is essential that we take an unequivocal and courageous stand and present a clear-cut program. We know, without doubt, that certain groups should not reproduce themselves. Why not say so, as the English eugenists [*sic*] have done." She voices disappointment that sterilization is not mentioned and derides Osborn's reticence in categorizing certain classes as "unfit": "While we are investigating, thoroughly, the classes and individuals who are to be designated 'fit' or 'unfit' a continuous flood of what most of us consider 'unfit' is coming into being." She certainly recognizes the connected fates of the two movements: "I want to see the eugenics movement pushed ahead in this country and it is for this reason that I am telling you so frankly just what I think and feel about it.... Everything that advances the eugenic movement helps birth control as well." Yet she does not view the issue from a purely pragmatic perspective: "We cannot improve the race until we first cut down production of its least desirable members. If we really believe this, let us say so, plainly and bluntly. In the end such a policy will win more support than one less forthright." Sanger leaves no doubt as to what she herself believes.[20] She is so little inclined to dissemble about her eugenic position that she takes it upon herself to chastise the head of the American Eugenics Society for his lack of boldness in a letter that is sometimes barely polite.

Given the overwhelming evidence for Sanger's eugenic commitments, Carole McCann has recently taken an approach different from that of Chesler and Reed: she acknowledges that Sanger was a eugenicist but claims that her brand of eugenics was not really ethically troublesome.

> ... I argue that Sanger's actions and rhetoric derive their meaning from within the political terrain and discursive horizons of her time. This broader cultural-political terrain set the boundaries of meaning expressed in birth control politics.... Sanger sought to bend eugenics' scientific authority to birth control and, at the same time, resisted its more invidious aspects. Departing from previous interpretations of birth control's connection to eugenics, I argue that there were positive benefits to this otherwise problematic association.[21]

McCann admits that what she calls "racism" is woven into the American feminist movement's history but claims the eugenic discourse of Sanger and her followers was not any worse and was often much better than that of the dominant American culture. There are two problems with her approach. First, she refrains from making a clear judgment concerning the ethical responsibility of the Sanger camp, basically exculpating these advocates of an oppressive ideology on the grounds that that ideology was culturally pervasive.[22] Yet many people, mostly those *not* part of the social and economic elite, challenged eugenics at the time during which Sanger advocated it, making clear that it is indeed possible to resist the cultural drift. Would McCann also suggest that we not judge the Nazi eugenicists because their bigotry was popular and culturally conditioned?

The second problem with McCann's assertion about the benign character of Sanger's eugenic beliefs is that it is simply not historically accurate. She argues that Sanger "reworked" eugenics, stressing environmental influences more than hereditary factors, and she also claims that Sanger's residual hereditarian language was simply contradictory in light of her feminism.[23] For example, she cites Sanger's statement, "Children who are underfed, undernourished, crowded into badly ventilated and unsanitary homes, and chronically hungry cannot be expected to attain the mental development of children upon whom every advantage of intelligent and scientific care is bestowed."[24] McCann's analysis, however, is not based on a sufficiently broad understanding of the factions within the American eugenics movement. Many other eugenicists of the "reform" branch, including Frederick Osborn, argued against the racist elements within eugenics, in favor of a greater integration of environmental with hereditarian factors in eugenic understanding, and for a eugenics based on propaganda over coercion.[25] Yet Osborn, like Sanger, did not hesitate to recommend coercion as a last resort: if the eugenically "unfit" would not be persuaded, then they must be forced. Contrary to McCann's claims, eugenics is not synonymous with racism and extreme hereditarianism, and Sanger's own version of the ideology is consistent with that of the most prestigious American eugenicists of her day.[26]

In addition, Sanger's eugenics, as will be shown, was still firmly rooted in hereditarian assumptions: although she gave a nod to environmental factors, they played less of a role in her ideology than did the innate hereditary "stock" of each individual. For example, an unpublished paper entitled "Hereditary Factor" asks the question, "Which path shall we choose — Strength and Efficiency or Degeneration and Decay?" She explains the rationale behind this choice when she insists, "A Nation rises or sinks on the physical or mental quality of its citizens. It cannot thrive when its fundamental structure is based on defective stock, the increase of morons, feebleminded, psychopaths [*sic*], diseased slum populations." The phrase "defective stock" is a eugenic term referring to the hereditary heritage of the "unfit." She clarifies this point later:

> The unemployables, sick, diseased, may be more or less than our statistics quote, but the fact remains clear, and, all honest investigators will admit, that one-fourth of those who make up this Nation are physically or mentally unfit to carry on the heritage of our civilization. It is this group who [*sic*] combat and weigh down the advance of the nation.[27]

McCann's willingness to explain away this sort of rhetoric as a regrettable but perhaps necessary pragmatic concession to the larger culture[28] eviscerates feminism by taking away its noblest purpose, namely, the defense of the vulnerable. McCann's book takes a feminist position that is diametrically opposed to the one in this book, for I will argue that feminism can only be faithful to its purpose when it refuses to be compromised by any unjust ideologies.

Sanger's Brand of Feminism

If eugenic ideology is inconsistent with the truth of feminist liberation, then, given Sanger's deep commitment to eugenic ideology, how does
one explain the undeniable presence of feminist liberation language in her
writings and speeches? One must read these words in the context of her
whole work. My guiding assumption in this book is that Sanger's motivations for promoting birth control were internally consistent, even if they
seem (and perhaps are) irrational. In other words, even if her premises are
false, *she* at least believed that her rationale for her activity was coherent,
and we must try to understand that internal coherence if we are to do justice to her thought and the activism flowing from it. We must try to understand how feminist liberation and eugenics were interimplicated in Sanger's
mind.[29]

So when Sanger speaks in rhapsodic terms about the liberation of
woman from the burdens of reproduction, one must ask: what did she mean
by liberation? Was it a freedom *from* something or a freedom *for* something, or both? I do not think it is an accident that the title of Sanger's
foremost feminist text, *Woman and the New Race*, melds feminist concerns with eugenic utopianism. Of course, it was a different vision of
eugenics than that preached by many mainstream eugenicists in the United
States. Sanger was probably the foremost American representative of eugenic
sexology along the lines of that proposed by the Englishman Havelock
Ellis. She promoted a sexuality on the phallocentric model: pleasures without commitment. This is a sexuality with a very definite socio-economic
positioning, typified in the routines of upper-class adultery, shared with
the bohemians and members of the intelligentsia who are the hangers-on
of the decadent upper class. Sanger's commitment to this kind of sexuality is revealed in her life and words.[30] Unfortunately, connected to Sanger's
desire for this specific type of bourgeois sexuality is a belief that every
woman ought to make the same reproductive choices that she herself had
made. Now, this particular patterning of sexual behavior, romanticized
sex without committed relationship, harmonizes nicely with the goals of
negative eugenics, in that the kind of "freedom" at stake in this sexuality
necessitates the reduction of childbirth. More to the point, extension of
this specific kind of sexual behavior to the working classes through birth
control also advances the negative eugenic goal of reducing the reproduction of the poor. Thus the working classes are pressured to copy the particular reproductive choices of society's elite.[31]

This combination of eugenics with sexual free-thinking can be seen
in Sanger's essay, "The Need for Birth Control in America," published in

Birth Control: Facts and Responsibilities and edited by eugenicist and American Birth Control League National Council member Adolf Meyer. There she defines "what we mean by Birth Control today: *hygienic, scientific, and harmless control of procreative powers.* Thus comprehended, Birth Control places in our hands the key to that greatest of all human problems— how to reconcile individual freedom with the necessities of race hygiene."[32] In one sentence, Sanger links the two ideas—free sex and eugenics—that motivated her agenda, and ties them together with what makes both possible: birth control. Sanger's brilliance as a strategist reveals itself here: she saw clearly that if women could be made to internalize what she truly believed was sexual freedom (that is, the kind of sexuality described above), this introjected heteronomy would also further eugenic purposes. As we will see in the last chapter, Sanger argued that "liberated" motherhood would "instinctively" avoid "all those things which multiply racial handicaps."[33] Eugenic unfreedom would feel like liberation.

But what if "individual freedom" refused to be reconciled to the necessities of the race? That is, what if a woman preferred children over the pursuit of bourgeois sexual pleasure? This was indeed a central dilemma for Sanger, and she solved it by determining who was and was not worthy of "individual freedom" in light of the eugenic criterion of what conforms to the race's needs (bearing in mind that "race" for Sanger meant the human race). This is the fundamental point when it comes to Sanger's supposed "voluntarism" regarding contraceptive use: as a "controller" (as birth control advocates were called in Sanger's day by Marie Stopes, the English birth-control activist), she believed that a woman had a right to individual freedom only when she demonstrated that she was fit to use that freedom appropriately — and the test of fitness was whether or not she recognized her eugenic responsibility.[34] When she did not, more "rational" authorities had to step in.

For example, in *Woman and the New Race*, she argues that women incur a "debt to society" through their thoughtless reproducing, "unknowingly creating slums, filling asylums with insane, and institutions with other defectives."[35] In the 1925 essay we have already cited, "The Need for Birth Control in America," which drew on the eugenic studies of her day, she compares the "typical" small-family and large-family groups, concluding that the latter group "is correlated for the most part with poverty, distress, tuberculosis, delinquency, mental defect, and crime. Poverty and the large family generally go hand in hand." She concludes:

> Such parents swell the pathetic ranks of the unemployed. Feeble-mindedness perpetuates itself from the ranks of those who are blandly indifferent

to their racial responsibilities. And it is largely this *type of humanity* we are now drawing upon to populate our world for the generations to come. In this orgy of multiplying and replenishing the earth, this type is *pari passu* multiplying and perpetuating those direst evils which we must, if civilization is to survive, extirpate by the very roots.[36]

The phrase "this type of humanity" provides the key. A large family is the *sign* of being unfit. In Sanger's worldview, the poor are poor because they are unfit, and they have large families because they are unfit. In the June 1917 issue of the *Birth Control Review*, which she edited, she refers contemptuously to "the great horde of unwanted," which lacks the "courage to control its own destiny."[37] The real problem, she notes in her 1922 book, *Pivot of Civilization*, is when "the incurably defective are permitted to procreate and thus increase their numbers." At this point, the state should interfere, "either by force or persuasion." She acknowledges that personal liberty is important, but in the present emergency situation, society should not hesitate to run roughshod over human rights by segregating and sterilizing its undesirables. The "defective" must be controlled, even if, as Sanger insists, it requires "drastic and Spartan measures."[38] The "unfit" woman who cannot be persuaded to do what Sanger wishes must be controlled by more coercive means.

What does this mean for Sanger's feminism? It indicates, at least, that she had a eugenically vitiated view of woman's liberation, which did not mean the freedom for every woman to decide, without coercion, the number of children she desired to have; rather, it meant sexual freedom for the "fit," who seemed to be those who made the same reproductive decisions as Sanger. If a woman showed herself to be "unfit" by wanting a large family and by not responding to Sanger's propaganda, then her reproduction ought to be controlled by those who know better. Sanger viewed her "overbreeding" Catholic foes this way; as her niece Olive Byrne Richard once said, "She reacted with hating them with a bitter hatred.... I think she figured if the world is full of people like this they need birth control."[39] (Indeed, this antinatalist — that is, anti-reproductive — bias exists still among birth-control and population-control advocates today, as I will show in the seventh chapter concerning oppression of women in the name of demographic reduction.) For Sanger, "freedom" meant the liberty for her and her socialite friends to have as few children as they wished, as well as the freedom to control the reproduction of those who had different ideas and thereby "needed" birth control.

In the end, "freedom" meant the justification of a self-serving "bohemian" sexuality, which was not desired by many of those whom she claimed to serve. She probably was not dishonest in this respect; she *did* think it would be better for every woman to live as she did, with a long list of would-be intellectual lovers and little interaction with the few children who resulted.[40] The fact that her romantic, sexual ideal as well as her antinatalist bias were foreign to much of the working class whom she claimed to want to help, foreign both to their experience and to their values, was never considered. *Sanger* knew what was best for them, and their opinions were never solicited, as the aspirations and desires of poor women today are usually not considered when bureaucrats and population-control professionals discuss their fertility. Her self-assurance in knowing what was needed for other classes of people was so great that she refused even to consider Osborn's suggestion that not every poor individual was necessarily "unfit," insisting instead that eugenics must target whole classes: "I am frank to say that I do not see how it is possible to 'sort out individual values within each class' and make an 'individual selection' of those fit to reproduce, nor am I at all sure that such selection would be really eugenic."[41]

It would be one thing if Sanger's elitism with regard to the poor were just a theoretical matter. Unfortunately, her truncated idea of liberation has done much to exacerbate their problems. Sanger and her birth-control and population-control allies have always considered contraception to be the first (and often the only) solution to social problems. Such a fertility-obsessed feminism perpetuates unjust social structures by scapegoating the poor. If one buys the ideological obfuscation that the problems of the poor are due solely to their fertility, and not, say, to our greed and comfortable insouciance, then one is encouraged to feel that one's responsibility toward them is discharged simply by offering contraception. The astonishing success of Planned Parenthood in attracting corporate support might have something to do with the facile neatness of Sanger's ready-made solution to the problem of poverty.

The Mystification Continues

In spite of her curious view of liberation, Sanger believed that she was a feminist. Unfortunately, her influence was institutionalized in the organizations that she founded, as was her view of feminism. I write this book as a feminist who fears the ideologically compromised feminism which Sanger has bequeathed to America and, due to the great power that population controllers have around the world, to all women. Therefore, this book focuses on her eugenic convictions, because I believe that this element needs to be purged from feminism and from our ethical thinking.

Because the feminist establishment is so closely linked to Planned Parent-hood today, feminists fear to criticize it as much as they have done in the not-so-distant past, but feminism can never survive if it sells its soul — that is, a critically conscious commitment to opposing oppression — for political expediency. A feminism that allows oppression for the sake of a "greater good" has violated its own fundamental beliefs.

Feminism is, of course, a widely variegated movement, legitimately spoken of in the plural. I certainly do not mean to convict all feminisms and feminists with my assessment, nor will I engage in the (worthwhile) task of delineating which forms of feminism fall under my critique; that project would require its own book-length treatment that cannot obviously be undertaken here. My concern is with those kinds of feminism that most often filter down from academia to the popular level, which are commit-ted to projects for female emancipation often predicated on Sanger's trun-cated view of liberation understood as almost solely sexual liberation, with a heavy dose of social-control ideology undergirding this superficial free-dom. This sexual focus was historically promoted (long before the sixties!) by a few, often male, elites, who also tended to be eugenicists.

I also do not wish to give up too easily on the task of discerning what makes any given form of feminism a worthwhile project and not merely an academic exercise that produces a sufficient number of publications to guarantee tenure. Certainly it is not necessary for all feminisms to look the same, but any feminism worthy of the name should have a central core of commitment to the concrete liberation of women. This may seem like an unfashionable form of "victim feminism." It certainly is not. Women must not be compromised by a victim mentality that saps their sense of self-responsibility or their emancipatory potential. It is precisely my claim that feminism holds promise to be the premier liberation movement. Fem-inists must therefore *actively* resist oppressive ideologies, but this empow-erment depends on seeing those ideologies for what they are and for what they do to the minds and bodies of females.

Ultimately, this book is about the ever-present temptation to reduce a person to a number or a disease, a temptation to a utilitarian rationale that forcibly violates human dignity so long as some consequentialist cal-culus seems to indicate that a greater number will benefit. This temptation belongs intrinsically to what I call the ideology of control. Sanger's belief that she and others like her could and should control the reproduction of those lacking a proper sense of what they owe to the greater good still dri-ves one of the most historically effective forms of control ideology.

Such an ideology was professed by many eugenicists. Yet Sanger's influence on American society has far surpassed that of the prominent eugenicists of her day: what person on the street has ever heard of Frederick Osborn or Harry Laughlin, for example? The reason why this book centers on Sanger and not around Frederick Osborn is because Sanger succeeded in changing societal and cultural beliefs in a way in which the professional eugenicists could not, primarily through institutionalizing her own brand of eugenics within Planned Parenthood. The birth-control and population-control movement (which I will call collectively the "control movement") framed its agenda around her concerns. Knowingly or not, Planned Parenthood continues by its words and actions to perpetuate eugenic beliefs about the poor and about the disabled, albeit modulated to sound more sweetly to contemporary ears. These beliefs ought to be seen for what they are and to lead to a reconsideration of Planned Parenthood's position as a respectable charity.

I admit that I have a personal interest in the stories related in this book. At the age of eighteen, I spent a life-changing half-year or so in Harlem, living and working in a soup kitchen and homeless shelter. As I worked and walked and observed my surroundings, I learned a little of what it was like to be a woman born into poverty and facing the low expectations of the larger society. This enlightenment enabled me to see more clearly that the message given to the average Harlem woman is: "It's your fault." Your disenfranchisement and poverty are all due to your having so many kids, especially since you could (and should) just take a pill and make your reproductive potential disappear. Instead of examining the irresponsibility and sexism of the men involved and rather than scrutinizing the links between misogynism, racism, and economic injustice, well-meaning whites offer more condoms or more IUDs. To paraphrase one observer, the message is: your poverty is not due to our rapacity but to your fecundity.[42]

This response kindled into flame my innate feminism, and I began to think through these questions more carefully. This book is in part an intellectual distillation of those first stirrings of disgust with the eugenic attitudes that still exist. For some comfortable intellectuals, the ovaries and wombs of impoverished women are the unceasing source of the bulk of human suffering. This scapegoating is fundamentally anti-woman, because it implies that the female body is to be feared, that it is the cause of societal and environmental downfall and really just needs to be neutered. Thus the desire for eugenic control inevitably segues into the desire to control that most unruly of human forces, female fertility.

This book tells several stories, but they all revolve around one woman's single-minded pursuit of her mission, the promotion of birth control and population control. I will focus on Sanger and Planned Parenthood, yet I do not intend the examination to end there but rather to shed light on the whole through viewing the part, by critically presenting and analyzing the genealogy of one powerful component of the mechanism of oppression operative in our society, one that has coopted much of the feminist establishment. Thus, the approach will be primarily historical but will also address contemporary manifestations of the ideology of control — manifestations that are better camouflaged but for that reason all the more dangerous.[43]

Feminism ought to be the premier liberation movement. Yet with bedfellows like Planned Parenthood, feminism is threatened with incoherence. As Karl Barth said, with the horror of Nazism full in his mind, "No community whether family, village or state is really strong if it will not carry its weak and even its very weakest members.... On the other hand, a community which regards and treats its weak members as a hindrance, and even proceeds to their extermination, is on the verge of collapse."[44] The temptation to apply eugenic solutions to human problems is among the gravest threats to feminism today. The future of feminism as a vital and authentic emancipatory force depends on a critical examination of conscience.

CHAPTER ONE

Woman and
the New Race

"Natural law makes the female the expression and the conveyor of racial efficiency."— Margaret Sanger, Woman and the New Race, *1920*[1]

"The race hygiene discourse since the end of the nineteenth century deals with women much more than do most other social or political theories, since women have been hailed as 'mothers of the race,' or, in stark contrast, vilified, as the ones guilty of 'racial degeneration.'"— Gisela Bock, *"Racism and Sexism in Nazi Germany," 1983*[2]

As the introduction indicated, many historians of Sanger and the birth-control movement assume that Sanger embraced eugenics only pragmatically on behalf of her feminism, and thus that her feminism neutralizes her eugenics.[3] But this chapter will demonstrate that, in fact, her eugenics compromises her feminism.

In order to understand how this is possible, one must clearly recognize that paying attention to "women's issues" does not somehow in and of itself defuse a eugenic commitment. Indeed, eugenics tends to require such attention. In her studies of sexism in Nazi Germany, German scholar Gisela Bock has shown that eugenicists often viewed women as the primary bearers of eugenic fitness or unfitness, thereby placing on women the burden of maintaining the genetic health of society.[4] In Sanger's case, her vision of women's liberation makes that liberation inseparable from achieving eugenic aims. I will argue that her eugenic ideology prevented her from including all women in her vision of freedom, or, more precisely, it made her exclude women whose desired fertility ran counter to her preferences.[5]

Sanger's ideological aims can best be summarized by the slogan, "Quality, not Quantity." This statement, which appears often in the writings and speeches of the control movement, appeared in Latin as the motto for the British Neo-Malthusians.[6] In her 1922 book *The Pivot of Civilization*, Sanger emphasizes the importance of "a *qualitative* factor as opposed to a *quantitative* one" in population matters.[7] A desire to control the population's quality by decreasing its quantity ties together the seemingly disparate elements of eugenics, population control, and women's health that dominate Sanger's rhetoric. The organizations that Sanger founded echo her fundamental aim: "To contribute directly and effectively to raising the quality of our people in every walk of life — that is the great fundamental aim of the birth control movement."[8] Sanger's vision of the "qualitative" purpose of birth control was also shared by those whom she recruited as coworkers. For example, the editor of the *Birth Control Review*, Stella Hanau, said in 1932 that birth control and eugenics were not only "interdependent" but also shared "identical aims."[9]

As I will show, Sanger promoted a eugenically circumscribed version of women's health and rights, a vision determined by the interests of the "fit" woman. This chapter will first give a brief overview of Sanger's work as a birth-control organizer and provide an account of her wealthy, eugenicist supporters. I will then examine the eugenic views she expressed in the 1920s, 1930s, and during World War II and spend some time on the question of racism, before turning to her work in the International Planned Parenthood Federation (IPPF). After examining how the solid eugenic foundation that she laid was built upon by her Planned Parenthood Federation of America successor, Alan Guttmacher, I will close by summarizing the evidence of some disturbing eugenic trends manifest in Planned Parenthood today.

Sanger as Birth-Control Organizer

Margaret Louisa Higgins was born into an impoverished working-class family in Corning, New York, in 1879. Her father, Michael Higgins, was a free-thinking and outspoken socialist, who raised his children to have the same opinions and personality traits. Her mother Anne, on the other hand, was a believing Catholic who stood for everything that Margaret later rejected.[10] Anne had eleven children, "without spot or blemish," as Margaret noted with "eugenic pride" in her autobiography,[11] but died of consumption at the age of fifty.[12] Margaret blamed her mother's many pregnancies for her demise, although the profligacy of Michael Higgins that drove Anne to hard manual labor to support the family is at least as likely to blame.

While she was training to be a nurse, in 1902 Margaret married artist Bill Sanger, whose radical leanings were consonant with those of her socialist father. They moved to a community outside New York City. Margaret gave birth to three children, though she did not seem to have formed any profound maternal attachment to them. (Margaret depended on wet nurses and nannies and, later, extended family and boarding schools to provide her children with the bulk of the nurturance they received. Of course, this indicates that Bill for his part did not form any profound paternal attachment to the children.) The family moved from the suburbs to the city in 1910. This was a time of great social upheaval. The second industrial revolution of the last decades of the nineteenth century, with the emergence of the vertically integrated corporation and the mass-production and mass-consumption economy based on it, had been accompanied by explosive urbanization (including a massive influx of immigrants and large-scale entry of young unmarried women into the working world), the reform projects of Progressivism, and socialist and trade-union activism. Among other things, traditional attitudes toward sex and marriage were being challenged by novel patterns of urban life.

The Sangers were stepping into the center of this vortex when they moved to New York City. The Sangers became active Socialist Party members (though Margaret would leave the party for the direct-action agitation of the Industrial Workers of the World). She began to detach herself from her household, circulating in the bohemian Greenwich Village milieu and writing a column on sexuality for the socialist paper *The Call*. Bill soon recognized that the revolution Margaret was coming to desire had more to do with sex than with economics or politics; meanwhile, he remained devoted to his wife and to the straightforward socialist pursuit of economic and political reform.[13] In one of the many letters they exchanged, he wrote her desperately, "They call me conservative but if Revolution means promiscuity — they can call me a conservative and make the most of it."[14] In contrast, throughout her life Margaret remained convinced that sexual liberation was, especially for women, more fundamental than economic restructuring. Mabel Dodge, in a famous story, reminisced that Sanger was "the first person I ever knew who was openly an ardent propagandist for the joys of the flesh." Margaret "told us all about the possibilities in the body for 'sex expression'; and as she sat there, serene and quiet, and unfolded the mysteries and mightiness of physical love it seemed to us that we had never known it before as a sacred and at the same time a scientific reality."[15] In *Woman and the New Race,* Sanger details this vision of the union of the "mystical" and the "scientific" aspects of sexuality, made possible by the rational use of birth control to control reproduction.[16] At the time, the excitement over the introduction of the seemingly scientific into the realm of reproduction arose not only among birth-control advocates but also among eugenicists. It seemed as if the possibilities for progress were limitless.

According to her 1938 autobiography, in 1912, while working part-time as a visiting nurse to the tenements of New York's Lower East Side, she encountered Sadie and Jake Sachs, the parents of three children. Sadie had apparently fallen unconscious from septicemia stemming from a self-induced abortion. Sanger, and the doctor who called for her, were able to save Sadie. After three weeks, as Sanger prepares to take her leave, Sadie asks her, "Another baby will finish me, I suppose." Sanger alerts the doctor to Sadie's concern: "Mrs. Sachs is terribly worried about having another baby." The doctor replies, "She well may be. Any more such capers, young woman, and there'll be no need to send for me." One of the odd things about this telling of the story is that the exchange is based on a non sequitur: it is implied that childbirth is the threat to Sadie, when, in fact, it is abortion that threatens her life. Abortion seems to be taken as some kind of fate laid upon this impoverished woman should she get pregnant again. Given this fatalism, contraception appears to be the only solution, and Sadie asks the doctor to reveal the "secret" of how to keep her from getting pregnant. "Tell Jake to sleep on the roof," the doctor tells her. Of course, in a few months Sadie is pregnant again, and after performing the second fated self-induced abortion, she falls into a coma, dying within ten minutes of Sanger's arrival. Or so the story goes. Sanger's biographer Ellen Chesler acknowledges that the Sachs story may be "an imaginative, dramatic composite of Margaret's experience." In any case, Sanger repeatedly cited the story as the inspiration for leaving nursing and turning to activism for "fundamental social change."[17] Both Reed and Chesler highlight the problem of maternal mortality as a motivation for Sanger's work, but it is telling that her activist efforts were not directed toward improving childbirth conditions.[18] Nor, with regard to the Sachs problematic in particular, did she work for a transformation of social attitudes whereby male sexual desire might be conformed to the requirements of the female body and to the preferences of women — a truly feminist "fundamental social change." These would be more direct responses to the deeper problems epitomized in the Sachs story. But it was anathema to Sanger to limit sexual desire even if the concrete result of not doing so was the exploitation of women.

Instead, her vision of liberation demanded the ability to disconnect fertility from sexuality through birth control, to control female fertility instead of male desire.

Like Reed and Chesler, many commentators have asserted that Sanger's motivation to take up the cause of advancing birth control was primarily a feminist concern for women's health, as supposedly reflected in the Sachs story.[19] This implies that eugenics did not play a role in, at least, *initially* motivating Sanger, an implication crucial for those who would preserve birth control from being intrinsically tainted by eugenics. In this way, they hope to historically validate the possibility of a non-eugenic birth-control advocacy by pointing to a socialist and feminist Sanger who had not yet, in these prewar years, dabbled in eugenics.

In a related line of argument, Linda Gordon presents the birth-control movement as shifting from feminist and socialist commitments to eugenic ones as it became "professionalized" after World War I. Gordon's argument rests on two false moves. First, she incorrectly draws a sharp distinction between a nineteenth-century eugenics utilized by social reformers and a "new" eugenics of the early twentieth century advocated by "conservatives." Second, she occludes the centrality of Sanger for the birth-control movement. Connecting these two assumptions is a failure to appreciate adequately the depth of Sanger's own commitment to eugenics.[20]

The first stirrings of the organized birth-control movement in America are to be found in the Progressive Era, with its utopianism, scientism, and proclivity for elitist social engineering. And, given precisely those tendencies (inflected by social Darwinism of both right and left), this was also a time when eugenic ideas had general currency among elites. The only seemingly paradoxical conjunction of wealthy patronage, bohemia, and labor and political radicalism that was Sanger's Greenwich Village was but a late product of the Progressive Era.

Gordon minimizes but does not completely cover up the fact that eugenics had something to do with the beginnings of the birth-control movement. But to safeguard the movement from eugenic taint, Gordon implies that there was a basically benign eugenics current among nineteenth-century radicals, one that balanced environmentalism and hereditarianism. This would have been the kind of eugenics that had some share in the incipient birth-control movement. But this eugenics, according to Gordon, must be sharply distinguished from a eugenics that arose only with the scientific debunking of the theory of the inheritance of acquired characteristics (Lamarckism). In this telling, an inherently reactionary hardline hereditarianism transformed eugenics into an elitist, and right-wing, movement. However, Gordon's sharp distinction between an earlier leftist, feminist eugenics and a later right-wing eugenics is historically incorrect. Eugenic historiography of the last couple of decades has made clear that many on the left were committed to eugenics, even in its strict hereditarian form. The scientific case debunking Lamarckism was already being made in 1883 with the work of the German cytologist August Weismann. As Diane Paul notes, "Not every Lamarckian was democratic and egalitarian, nor every convert to Weismannism a reactionary. Indeed, Herbert Spencer, the leading proponent of Lamarckism in Britain, favored unrestrained capitalism, whereas Alfred Russel Wallace, its leading opponent, rejected capitalism in favor of a planned economy."[21]

There is a reason for Gordon's strained handling of the historical evidence on this point. Gordon is quite straightforward about the fact that she writes her birth-control history as a partisan of leftist politics, of feminism, and of birth control. She also recognizes that eugenics is unsavory. However, she acknowledges that eugenic themes were sounded by many reformers and radicals with whom she has political sympathies. Therefore, she must distinguish between a basically benign eugenics of the left and a basically sinister eugenics of the right. However, it is my contention that eugenics as such (provisionally defined as a preoccupation with the reproduction of certain types of people, as I will discuss in the next chapter) is invariably a threat to the powerless.

Gordon fails to recognize the per se danger of the eugenic attitude because she misunderstands the scope of elitism as a sociological phenomenon. Eugenics is advocated by members of a self-anointed elite, and thus eugenic ideology cuts across the political right and left, as the next chapter's discussion of the eugenics movement will explore. The middle class and the super-wealthy, bohemians, intellectuals— many among these groups consider themselves elites who know better than the rest and who ought to have the power to control society. Eugenic ideology is inherently elitist, whether it is of the right or left. Gordon's tendentious rhetorical tic of labeling every position to which she is opposed as "conservative" mystifies this fact.

But elitism infected much of feminism in this country from the beginning. And feminists who would truly be advocates for women, especially for the interests of the most powerless women and girls, must reject elitism root and branch. Now, there are those who espoused certain eugenic ideas who did not pose an immediate threat to the powerless: many suffragists, for example, did espouse such ideas. However, the trajectory of such ideas, whether completely traversed by a given exponent or not, always ends with assaults on the bodies and minds of the powerless.

More germane as far as this book goes than this strategy of distinguishing a benign and a sinister eugenics to preserve contraception from eugenic taint is Gordon's second strategy: she occludes Sanger's centrality for the birth-control movement in America. Gordon recognizes that Sanger espoused eugenic ideology. And, again, Gordon is rightly uncomfortable with eugenics. Given her deep commitment to birth control, therefore, Gordon must minimize Sanger's role in the birth-control movement. One of the moves Gordon makes to accomplish this is to emphasize anarchist sex radical Emma Goldman's undeniable formative influence on the shape of Sanger's thought, an influence that Sanger later tried to cover up. By doing so, however, Gordon unintentionally gives a clue indicating how profound the connections between eugenics and the birth-control movement were.

Goldman helped define bohemia, developing the profile of the "new woman." She was no small part of the ferment in New York City when Sanger arrived there in 1910. Goldman had a broad social agenda, encompassing anarchism, Neo-Malthusianism, contraception, free speech, sex education, and sexual revolution. She also had a remarkable range of intellectual interests, including the philosophy of Nietzsche, the then-new theories of Freud, and modern literature, especially drama.

Masterfully surveying nineteenth-century sex radicalism, Gordon points out that in Goldman converged the streams of influence conducive to birth control. She called for radical sexual liberation, going beyond the arguments of the free lovers, who were opponents of marriage as a legal institution but who were generally committed to defending monogamy and motherhood. Goldman belonged to the fin-de-siècle radicalization of the free-love movement, her arguments shading into a rejection of the inherent superiority of monogamy and motherhood. This line of thought, which had almost no currency among feminists of the age (who rightly saw that it basically submitted women to a deformed masculine desire), was crucial for the advancement of birth control because it rejected outright any intrinsic connection between sex and reproduction.

This sex radicalism was bolstered by certain renegade doctors who argued that "indulgence" was physiologically preferable to "continence," a view nicely coinciding with the newly emerging mass-consumption economy. The most important of these doctors, whose crucial role in gaining an intellectual foothold for birth control in the United States should not be underestimated, was William Josephus Robinson. He had a single-minded devotion to the cause of birth control, and Emma Goldman was quite familiar with his work.

Goldman agitated for birth control, giving lectures on the topic, including one on the "birth strike." This was a transposition of the anarcho-syndicalist theme of the general strike into the realm of reproduction: the machinery of capitalism and of imperialism would grind to a halt should the working class refuse to provide sufficient human numbers to keep it going. Along with her lover Benjamin Reitman, Goldman distributed the pamphlet *Why and How the Poor Should Not Have Many Children,* which provided contraceptive information. She thus transferred birth-control advocacy from the pages of certain journals into the wider public sphere. Gordon notes, "American sex radicals, despite their militant rhetoric, had not so far defied law and convention by publishing such explicit contraceptive advice."

Clearly, Gordon is right to point out the importance of Goldman for the beginning of the birth-control movement in America. But insofar as this move is meant to insulate the movement from eugenic taint by minimizing Sanger's importance, it is a failure, for Gordon glosses over the fact that Goldman herself had taken up eugenics in those heady pre–World War I days, including lectures on the topic in her speaking tours across the country. Goldman's journal *Mother Earth* even published books on eugenics written by free-love anarchist Moses Harman, editor of the *American Journal of Eugenics.*[22] Goldman used eugenic arguments to bolster her anti-capitalist variant of free-love arguments against marriage. Her sentimental romanticism concerning sexual love maintained that the "fewer and better" children born of romantic love would escape the fate of becoming the drudges of the capitalist machine.

So, by pointing out the undeniable importance of Goldman for the beginning of the American birth-control movement, Gordon in fact helps us see how inseparable eugenic ideology and birth control were historically. And, when it comes to Sanger in particular, this indicates that she likely began embracing eugenics even before the war, precisely given Goldman's influence on her.

In 1913 the Sanger family traveled to France, and there Margaret experienced for herself the French syndicalism that Goldman had introduced her to, which combined birth-control agitation with eugenic ideas. Gordon notes that Goldman, in 1900, "…had attended the secret conference of Neo-Malthusians in Paris and had even smuggled some contraceptive devices into the United States," but fails to make clear the eugenic nature of late nineteenth-century Neo-Malthusianism and its embrace by many on the European left.[23] As I will discuss in more detail, Neo-Malthusianism insisted on the eugenic and economic necessity of getting the poor to limit their fertility through the use of contraceptive devices. It was an ideology that blended eugenics, birth-control advocacy, sexual radicalism, and population control. Goldman helped bring that synthesis to America, and now Sanger was motivated by her direct experience of it in France to found her own paper, *The Woman Rebel*, when she returned to the States. The magazine was to be "dedicated to the interests of working women," modeled after Goldman's approach. Sanger employed the anti-capitalist rhetoric of a militant syndicalism, but the focus was on revolutionizing sexual life, in part by challenging restrictions on the dissemination of sex-educational material and by presenting an anarchist vision of the development of personality. It is clear at this point that birth control is but one, albeit important, part of a multi-faceted radical program: "I believe that woman is enslaved by the world machine, by sex conventions, by motherhood and its present necessary childrearing, by wage-slavery, by middle-class morality, by customs, laws and superstitions."[24]

The focus on sexual revolution was reflected in Sanger's life; she took up with an old lover after returning to New York from France and demanded to be released from her marriage vows: the death-blow to her marriage. Contraception, a vital component of the revolution in sexual life that Sanger was advocating, needed a new name. At a gathering of friends in her new flat far uptown, Sanger weighed different suggestions. An acquaintance, Otto Bobsein, suggested "birth control," after "population control" and "race control" as well as others failed to satisfy.[25] But the idea of *control* had to be present — the eugenic restructuring of family life through the rational control of the supposedly erratic process of female fertility. Instead of Neo-Malthusianism, which was too focused on economic reasons for contraception, Sanger was aiming for something more profound: the revolutionizing of intimacy.

The first issue of Sanger's magazine declared the intention of its editor and chief writer: "To look the world in the face with a go-to-hell look in the eyes; to have an idea; to speak and act in defiance of convention."[26] In the last issues, Sanger clearly supported the assassination of John D. Rockefeller, Jr., who, ironically, would become her greatest financial supporter about ten years later. A criminal charge of inciting assassination was brought against her, as well as charges of violating the federal Comstock laws, which forbade the mailing of indecent materials by post. She fled to England toward the end of 1914 under a false name.

Up to this point, Sanger and Goldman must be treated together. However, this does not mean that Gordon is right to make Goldman out to be the true initiator of the American birth-control movement. For neither Goldman nor Sanger was contraception the primary focus at this time. It was Sanger who was to have the breakthrough theoretical insight into the centrality of birth control; Sanger, not Goldman, was indeed the initiator of the birth-control movement in America.

Sanger's single-minded focus on birth control crystallized only after her flight to England in late 1914. This was the time when her faith in eugenic population control was solidified due to the influence of Havelock Ellis, and her commitment to eugenics was constant from then until her death. The conversion to birth control, in other words, as *the* means of promoting her ideology of control was prompted not by Sadie Sachs or even Emma Goldman but by Havelock Ellis and the British Neo-Malthusians.

Judging from the change in Sanger's rhetoric after her return from England, one recognizes that her sojourn there laid the foundations of her later work. During her stay, she learned enough about contraception to decide to focus her considerable energies, which had up to that time been diffused upon all sorts of issues concerned with sexual liberation, upon birth control. James Reed has called her year in Europe a "turning point in her career."[27] She settled in London under the tutelage of sexologist and eugenicist Henry Havelock Ellis and the other British Neo-Malthusians (who advocated both birth and population control), such as Alice Vickery. Sanger always called Ellis "the king." According to her son Grant Sanger, there was "no doubt" that Ellis was the person with the deepest influence on Margaret. In describing her time in England, Grant stresses the role that Ellis played: "She had Havelock Ellis for a tutor and the Reading Room of the British Museum for her library. And she stayed there for a year, and said, 'This is where I was educated.'"[28]

Ellis was one of the pioneering eugenicists in England. With Vickery and other Neo-Malthusians, he assisted in the founding of the Eugenic Education Society (EES), and he also served as a member of the EES Council.[29] As he wrote in an article published in Sanger's *Birth Control Review*, Ellis believed that eugenics consisted of the "sound breeding of the race. Here we touch the highest ground, and are concerned with our best hopes for the future of the world."[30] Ellis was also not averse to using control language. In the same article, he argues that humanity should develop "a social order which in the sphere of procreation could not be reached or maintained except by the systematic control of offspring."[31] Ellis realized that the "dysgenic" would not voluntarily refrain from parenting, but that with the advent of birth control and sterilization, practical eugenics had nonetheless become possible.[32] These eugenic rationales for birth control were, for him, the primary reason to support contraception.[33]

Ellis himself did not believe that birth control was itself the only solution to societal difficulties, and his biographer believes that he supported birth control primarily because of its value to eugenics.[34] Ellis was, like Sanger, dubious about the prospects of positive eugenics (encouraging the "fit" to breed more) and insisted that the one thing necessary was to encourage the "lowest social stratum of all" to use contraception or else to sterilize them: "The rational method of meeting this situation is not a propaganda in favour of procreation — a truly imbecile propaganda, since it is only carried out and only likely to be carried out, by the very class which we wish to sterilise — but by a wise policy of regulative eugenics."[35] This policy would be, of course, the promotion of contraception and sterilization to the poor and disabled, and it would be "wise" because "the very best classes," people such as himself, would carry it out.

Ellis was also the primary Neo-Malthusian influence in Sanger's life.[36] The Neo-Malthusians, who based their philosophy on the works of the nineteenth-century political economist Thomas Malthus, were among the earliest supporters of population control. They often decried the fact that the poor had greater fertility than the wealthier members of society, a phenomenon they termed "differential reproduction," and they encouraged the distribution of birth control to the poor as the solution. Thus, the Neo-Malthusian League promoted the distribution of contraceptives "at hospitals, institutions, welfare centres, etc., where the sick, the very poor, or less fit members of society apply for public assistance in various ways...."[37] This denigration and targeting of the poor would be repeated later by Sanger and by the organizations she founded. For example, the Birth Control Federation of America would later say that, due to the great fertility of the poor, 37 percent of Americans born are "wholly or partially wasted.... This means that only 63% of the babies born in the United States in 1940 will be healthy, normal boys and girls able to become independent, productive citizens of the state and nation." In case the point about "waste" had not been sufficiently made, the copy continues under the heading "WASTED LIVES — WASTED DOLLARS" to note, "In the nation, therefore, thousands and thousands of lives are thus being wasted while billions of dollars are spent for various types of 'palliative' relief, while omitting to include essential steps to remove or to reduce some of the major causes of death, disease, delinquency and dependency."[38]

Besides espousing eugenic and Neo-Malthusian beliefs, Ellis was, by profession, one of the first sexologists. He believed sexuality was "an inborn drive that could only become repressed or distorted by culture," according to Ellen Chesler, and thus he advocated the liberalization of societal sexual mores.[39] In this aversion to placing limits on sexual desire, his philosophy was amenable to, and provided highbrow support for, Sanger's own understanding of the necessity of sexual freedom. Her view is reflected in an anecdote (perhaps told to her by Ellis) published in 1925. Sanger tells the story of a social worker who informed a husband that his wife should not get pregnant again for health reasons and thus the husband should "exercise self-control." The results, however, were awful: the previously gentle, responsible husband became a brute! After decrying the loafing, child abuse, and generally disreputable behavior of the new version of the man, the story concludes: "That husband had been thrust back into the primitive stage of development from which mutual love had lifted him. Deprived of that love in the home, futilely attempting to suppress his own passions, he had, with the most lamentable results, driven his emotions underground."[40] This, to say the least, improbable story serves the purpose of reinforcing the ideology of bourgeois sexuality: according to this ideology, what she elsewhere calls the "sex force" is "one of the strongest forces in Nature — an instinct by no means less powerful than the instinct of Hunger."[41] Simply put, the sexual drive could not be controlled without danger; a far better policy, according to her, was to control fertility.

Ellis was simply one of the more prominent representatives of a kind of progressive, sexology-oriented brand of eugenics. These "sex reformers," as they are sometimes called, united a concern for rational reproduction (a eugenic goal) with a belief in the liberating power of sexual freedom, a belief they thought was supported by a scientific examination of human relationships and sexuality. (The Weimar Republic had many of these eugenically oriented progressives.[42]) Frequently professing some variety of Freudianism, they often counseled couples and advocated the repeal of restrictions on birth control (and, sometimes, abortion). Sanger would easily become the most influential of these eugenicists, promoting a vision of eugenic liberation that has had a far greater reach than that of the more staid and scientific American Eugenics Society.

Having deeply imbibed Ellis's brand of eugenic philosophy by the time of her departure from England, Sanger wrote that his "unparalleled service to the world" consisted in helping each woman "to lift herself above the level of a subservient breeder of undesired and unfit children...."[43] Here all the strands of Sanger's ideology of control coalesce: free-sex ideology, Neo-Malthusianism, and eugenics, all made possible by the one mechanism of birth control. At this point, thanks to Ellis and his colleagues, Sanger's worldview has crystallized, and it will not significantly change until her death. James W. Reed has perceptively noted that, while Sanger absorbed this kind of philosophy in incipient form from her socialist friends, it was Ellis who taught her to be prudent and scientific: less the "woman rebel" and more the focused and savvy activist who used the latest sexological research to make a well-rounded case for contraception, appealing as much to the upper class as to the workers. Given this change in emphasis, Sanger biographer Ellen Chesler has said, "It is virtually impossible to overestimate the impact Ellis would have on Margaret."[44] Probably his lover and certainly his pupil, she said of him, "I have never felt about any other person as I do about Havelock Ellis."[45] She annually dedicated the February issue of the *Birth Control Review* to him, and she probably kept alive his fame in America longer than it would have otherwise survived.[46]

After her immersion in British leftist elite views on contraception and population policy, Sanger returned to the U.S. in 1915 (the *Woman Rebel* charges against her were eventually dropped), and followed the Neo-Malthusian plan of action by setting up the first American birth-control clinic in the poor Brownsville section of Brooklyn (inhabited mostly by immigrant Jews and Italians) in 1916.[47] Planned Parenthood dates its founding from the establishment of this clinic, thus legitimizing its claim to being the oldest reproductive-rights organization in America. The clinic was quickly closed down, and its various workers, including Sanger and her sister Ethel, were charged with distributing contraceptive information and maintaining a public nuisance (i.e., the clinic). While in jail, Ethel achieved much publicity for the cause by going on a hunger strike, and Margaret occupied herself by gathering together the Committee of One Hundred, a group of society women who drew up to the courtroom in their limousines and provided the birth controllers with social respectability.[48] Sanger was given a thirty-day stint in the workhouse and, upon her release, was greeted by a crowd of supporters, including representatives of the Committee of One Hundred. One of these well-heeled ladies referred to the occasion as "Margaret's coming-out party."[49]

Sanger began publishing the *Birth Control Review* in 1917 and commenced a busy schedule of birth-control activism, speaking often and organizing several national and international conferences on birth control and population issues. While she was an effective organizer, her main talents were her rhetorical skill and her ability to generate controversy. Many people attended her public appearances expecting a wild-eyed rabble-rouser, and instead they got a petite and altogether demure spokeswoman for birth control. Several of her supporters, such as her second husband J. Noah Slee and Ellen Watamull, were drawn to her cause and to her person after viewing one of her public appearances.[50]

Drawing on the support that her high-profile imprisonment had generated, Sanger founded the American Birth Control League (ABCL) in 1921.[51] From the beginning, the ABCL was motivated by eugenic concerns as explicitly set forth in its official documents. Among the "principles and aims" of the ABCL were the convictions that the "healthy" classes bore the costs of "those who should never have been born" and that the sterilization of the insane and feebleminded ought to be encouraged.[52] An early draft of the pamphlet "What We Stand For" (probably published in 1921) laid out the problem.

> The complex problems now confronting America as the result of the practice of reckless procreation are fast threatening to grow beyond human control. Everywhere we see poverty and large families going hand in hand. Those least fit to carry on the race are increasing most rapidly. People who cannot support their own offspring are encouraged by Church and State to produce large families. Many of the children thus begotten are diseased or feeble-minded; many become criminals. The burden of supporting these unwanted types has to be borne by the healthy elements of the nation. Funds that should be used to raise the standard of our civilization are diverted to the maintenance of those who should never have been born.[53]

Here at the beginning of Sanger's career of institutional leadership we find a summary of the concerns that would preoccupy her for the rest of her life, as well as the organizations she founded. Human procreation, instead of being rationally controlled, was random and "reckless," leading to the births of many ill and disabled people who, according to Sanger, should not have been born in the first place. This dysgenic situation was bad enough for the future of the race, but even worse for the taxpayer and the economic health of the nation. By reproducing themselves more rapidly than the wealthy, the poor (that is, the unfit) caused a huge economic drain on the rest of the nation compelled to support them. From the very beginning of the existence of the ABCL (later to become Planned Parenthood), we find a firm, official commitment to eugenics.

Under the auspices of the ABCL, Sanger organized many conferences. For example, in 1923 she sponsored the Middle Western States Birth Control Conference. According to a letter sent out to solicit support for the conference, the latter's purpose was as follows: "The population problem is one of the most important now confronting civilization. It is the aim of the American Birth Control League to arouse, enlighten and direct public opinion to the menace of uncontrolled population, *both from the quantitative and qualitative standpoint.*"[54] Accordingly, among the "chief purposes" of the conference were "to consider practical and feasible methods of decreasing dependency and delinquency" and "to awaken social workers, physicians and the public at large to their racial responsibility."[55] The program noted, "Because the self-supporting, self-respecting members of society must shoulder the burden of the defective, delinquent and dependent ... to ameliorate social evils is not enough. WE MUST PREVENT THEM!"[56] Among the proposed speakers were eugenicists Professor Leon

Cole, speaking on "Animal Aristocracy and Human Democracy" (presumably the former was preferable to the latter), and Adolphus Knopf, describing "What Scientific and Judicious Birth Regulation may mean in the Progress of Mankind."[57]

However, Sanger's leadership of the organization lasted less than a decade. She never worked well with others in the birth-control movement unless it was understood that she was in charge. After her trip to Europe for the 1927 World Population Conference, she returned to New York to find that the ABCL board had been running things fairly comfortably without her under the leadership of Eleanor Dwight Jones. By June of 1928 she had turned in her resignation, and by January 1929 she surrendered the *Birth Control Review* to the ABCL leadership. Thereupon, she broadened her focus to include political activism alongside the direct approach of distributing contraception through a clinic system, with the Birth Control Clinical Research Bureau (BCCRB), her Manhattan clinic, as the flagship.[58]

The lobbying effort was organized through the National Committee for Federal Legislation of Birth Control (NCFLBC), which worked out of Washington to change the federal laws to make it legal to distribute birth control. The articles of incorporation for the NCFLBC show that its purposes included the attempt to "educate the public concerning the social, economic, *eugenic* and ethical importance of birth control."[59] Although she generated much publicity for the cause, in part because of the famous people connected with her campaign (such as Katharine Houghton Hepburn, the mother of the more famous actress, hailing from Sanger's hometown but from Corning's wealthy side of the tracks), ultimately her goal was achieved not through the legislature but through the courts. Contraceptives were not allowed to be imported into the country under the Comstock laws, so Sanger and her lawyer Morris Ernst set out to complete the judicial redefining of the Comstock laws that had already begun. Accordingly, in 1932, when a package of cervical caps was seized by customs officials, her clinic doctor Hannah Stone became the claimant in a case humorously named *United States v. One Package Containing 120, more or less, Rubber Pessaries to Prevent Conception.* The case went to the Second Circuit Court of Appeals in New York, where a panel of judges, including Augustus and Learned Hand, heard the case. The latter was the father of Frances Hand Ferguson, a birth-control activist who later served as president of PPFA from 1953 to 1956, vice president of IPPF from 1959 to 1962, and board member of the American Eugenics Society (1957–63), the Euthanasia Society of America (1955–62), the Association for Voluntary Sterilization (1956–95), and the Association for the Study of Abortion (1967–70).[60] IPPF recognized her over 40 years of service on its board of directors by giving her an award in 1992.[61] Ferguson was preoccupied with slowing the birth rate, saying, "I think if we don't stop the numbers multiplying in the world the way they are, there can be no salvation. I think it's at the root of everything."[62] This demographic emphasis meant that reducing the numbers was much more important than the individuals being "served": "I'd rather do less good service to more people, than perfect service to fewer people."[63]

In the matter of the pessaries, the panel of judges found in favor of Sanger's side. Indeed, the ruling basically rewrote the Comstock Act, arguing that those materials considered offensive and obscene in 1873 (such as contraception) were no longer so considered in 1936.[64] The result was to legalize completely the mailing and importing of contraceptives. Claiming victory, even though the NCFLBC had achieved little in Congress, Sanger dissolved the organization in the summer of 1937.

Not one to keep still for long, Sanger began to focus more and more on securing governmental funding of contraceptives, especially through public-health programs. In order to increase organizational effectiveness and fund-raising efficiency, Sanger's Clinical Research Bureau was reunited to the ABCL in 1939 to form a third entity, the Birth Control Federation of America (BCFA). But after this organizational triumph, she found herself marginalized by the leadership, especially by the BCFA's professional director, D. Kenneth Rose, hired from the consulting firm John Price Jones, which had done some work for Sanger in the past. Rose managed to alienate Sanger by pursuing an agenda that was less confrontational in its approach, which included changing the name of the BCFA to the Planned Parenthood Federation of America (PPFA) in 1942. Mary Lasker, who served on PPFA's executive committee as well as terms as secretary and vice president, claimed that her husband Albert, a wealthy advertising executive, came up with the new name. "The words 'Planned Parenthood' were more acceptable, he felt, to men than birth control, which he felt advocated continence, an unpopular idea among the male population."[65] The name change, in other words, was one of many attempts by Planned Parenthood to encourage wealthy men to accept and promote contraception and population control.

Ellen Chesler has claimed that Sanger was alienated from PPFA because of her feminist disillusionment with PPFA's emphasis on recruiting male leadership, but I would argue instead that Sanger shared with Rose the belief that male leadership was important for the birth-control movement's fund-raising and general success.[66] A letter from Sanger to an old coworker at the NCFLBC acknowledges as much: in it she says, "It is good that you are pushing Birth Control over your state and I agree that it is important to get men to to [*sic*] talk to men in order to raise funds. [Eugenicist Frederick] Osborn is a good name and perhaps you should plan now for next winters' [*sic*] speakers."[67] Chesler's theory ignores the fact that Sanger herself encouraged the election of a male to the presidency of the new BCFA, her only other requirements being that he must understand eugenics and population control.[68] It seems more likely that Sanger was mostly upset by the soft-pedaling approach of the new organization, whose caution led to the switch from the name "birth control," her preferred term because of the power that it designated, to the significantly more neutral "planned parenthood" or "family planning." She never wavered from her commitment to birth *control* as necessary to master the previously untrammeled "reproductive power," as she argues in *The Pivot of Civilization*.[69] Her niece, Olive Byrne Richard, complained that "family planning" did not properly describe what was being planned: "Family planning for what, for summer vacations?" Sanger is quoted as asking.[70] The recognition that families might have their own reproductive preferences introduced an unwarranted distraction from the central issue of control.

Wealthy Eugenicists Target the Poor

Sanger's eugenic ideas were especially attractive to the rich, who often perceived their wealth as a demonstration of their innate genetic superiority.[71] For example, the Rockefellers generously funded Sanger, despite her earlier death threats against the family's patriarch. In the 1920s, John D. Rockefeller, Jr., was a liberal, albeit anonymous, contributor, sometimes giving as much as $15,000 a year from his own fortune and foundations, and his son John D. Rockefeller 3rd continued the trend: the total Rockefeller support of Sanger and PPFA between 1940 and 1955 alone was estimated to be $396,000.[72]

Sanger's eagerness to get birth control to the lower classes was a large part of her appeal to the Rockefellers. The family knew that eugenics and birth control were a package deal. In an internal memo noting a $10,000 donation to the ABCL, one of Rockefeller's staffers summarized the state of the birth-control/eugenics movement.

> The birth control problem is undoubtedly one of the most important and at the same time one of the most contentious with which the world is faced. The movement has the support of many of the best and most intelligent people in the world and it also has the support of some people whose mental balance is not the best. In between these two classes, we find the people who hold debatable opinions, the most capable group being the Eugenists....[73]

This memo illustrates the extensive overlap between the eugenics and birth-control movements and shows to what degree many philanthropic supporters of Sanger were committed to her cause as an outgrowth of their eugenic philosophy. (By and large, Sanger was funded by large donations from the wealthy, as opposed to small donations from the less well-off.)

The American Eugenics Society (AES) was also a beneficiary of the Rockefellers' eugenic commitment, and in 1925 the group sent a letter to Rockefeller, Jr., requesting his membership on a committee. His response is telling: he highlighted the part of the letter that read, "[T]he people make the slums; moral people are born, not made; the criminal is a defective human, also born, not made; the intelligent will be successful anyway…."[74] He then wrote an internal memo to one person on his staff, noting, "The matter of which the letter speaks is, I believe, a profoundly important one to the future of this country…. I should like to be helpful in the field, but could not take any personal part."[75] His reticence was perhaps due to what one PPFA leader later would candidly summarize as a public-relations problem: "Certainly the Rockefellers didn't want to be known as a family who was telling little brown Indians not to have babies."[76]

Unfortunately for the Rockefellers' public image, one of the family's foundations supported such unattractive groups as the German "race-hygiene" (i.e., eugenic) institutions. Indeed, the Rockefeller Foundation was a supporter of eugenic research in Germany in the crucial decade of the 1920s, supporting, among other projects, the Kaiser Wilhelm Institute for Psychiatry and the Kaiser Wilhelm Institute for Anthropology, Eugenics, and Human Heredity. Among the eugenicists behind these projects were Emil Kraepelin, Eugen Fischer, Fritz Lenz, and Ernst Rüdin, and without these men and their institutions, the scientific development and acceptance of Nazi eugenics would have been greatly impeded. Worse, the Rockefeller Foundation continued to support these eugenic projects in Germany even after the Nazis came to power.[77] The family was not alone among American eugenicists in their blindness to the dangers of Nazism; Leon F. Whitney of the American Eugenics Society, speaking of the Nazi sterilization law, said in 1934 that "many far-sighted men and women in both England and America have long been working earnestly toward something very like what Hitler has now made compulsory."[78]

The Rockefellers' eugenic support of both the American Eugenics Society and Margaret Sanger continued through the 1930s, in part perpetuated by the strongly pro-eugenics staff that the Rockefellers had hired to work in their foundations. One of them, Arthur W. Packard, who served as the Rockefeller point man for birth control and eugenics, believed that the AES was a "constructive propaganda agency" that understood that "contraceptive knowledge must be available to all families, but not all families at all times should use it, though some families at all times should use it."[79] Packard's eugenic commitment did not diminish even after World War II; in 1947, he complained to Rockefeller, Jr., that "we have in America today a population differential between different social and cultural groupings which from the eugenic point of view tends to make the practice of birth control a disgenic [*sic*] factor in American life...."[80] It is no coincidence that the memo in which this complaint appeared was written for the purpose of encouraging Rockefeller, Jr., to contribute to a new Planned Parenthood campaign that would target low-income people.

The Rockefellers were not Sanger's only source of largesse; she also married into wealth. Her second husband, J. Noah Slee, was the head of the Three-in-One Oil Company and became, somewhat unwillingly, a major financial supporter of birth-control propaganda. The juxtaposition of a supposedly radical feminist agenda with the needs of a prominent industrial company led to some strange results, such as the surreal sight of a full-page ad (complete with happy housewife) for Three-in-One Oil inside almost every back cover of the *Birth Control Review* while it was under Sanger's editorship.

Sanger's cause was also financially aided to a great degree by her courting of the upper-class society ladies of Manhattan. These women became her core supporters, both financially and personally. Dorothy Brush, one close friend, recalled that "Margaret was rather like a lion tamer. She kept us each on our boxes until she needed us—and then we jumped and jumped fast."[81] Grant Sanger, Margaret's second son, recalled how important and powerful these women were: "You thought they didn't have a brain in their head or an interest in anything at all, [and then] these women would gather themselves up with their furs and their chauffeurs and they'd go down and see the mayor of the city of New York. He'd have to see them because they were in such a position in town...."[82] Anyone whom the mayor of New York would "have" to see was a significant help to a cause that had once been centered around Greenwich Village bohemia. Indeed, the typical member of the ABCL was an upper-middle-class to upper-class, white, native-born Protestant female.[83] From this, Linda Gordon has concluded that the ABCL's organizing efforts centered around high-society groups, "drawing an unmistakable picture of a rich woman's organization."[84]

Likewise, feminist Bonnie Mass has observed that Sanger never really identified with working-class demands and needs, desiring if anything to escape from the stigma of being born on the wrong side of the tracks.[85] Sanger's niece, Olive Byrne Richard, recalled how her mother Ethel resented the migration of the birth-control movement—a movement for which Ethel also had suffered—from the socialists to the society crowd. Byrne Richard remembers, "You see, my mother was not a good 'uptown' person; she was a rebel—far more a rebel than Margaret ever was and she never was anything else."[86] As did Ethel, feminist Angela Y. Davis later would protest against the birth-control movement's elitist and consumerist attitudes.

> [T]his vision [of the birth controllers] was rigidly bound to the lifestyle enjoyed by the middle classes and the bourgeoisie. The aspirations underlying the demand for "voluntary motherhood" did not reflect the conditions of working-class women, engaged as they were in a far more fundamental fight for economic survival.[87]

Instead of developing a sympathy for those women whose economic lot Margaret and Ethel as children had shared, Margaret remained to the end a "good uptown person." "What did [Margaret] want most?" Byrne Richard reminisced. "She wanted what she took; she wanted to go to Europe and do these things and have these love affairs and be important."[88]

Sanger as Eugenicist and the Question of Racism

We have seen that many of her donors were eugenicists, but we have not examined in much detail Sanger's own beliefs. This section will show that Sanger embraced the eugenics program in what at first seems an idiosyncratic manner. It is this that has led advocates of Sanger to assert that she was not a eugenicist.[89] I will show, however, that the evidence clearly points in the other direction: Sanger was a committed eugenicist, but she generally advocated only "negative" (or "preventive"), not "positive" (or "constructive") eugenics.[90] The distinction between negative and positive eugenics was made by eugenicists themselves in the early part of the movement. Positive eugenics entailed encouraging the "fit" to have more children and thus to perpetuate their good genes. Negative eugenics was concerned with limiting, either by persuasion or by force, the reproduction of the "unfit" and thus halting the perpetuation of their genes within the human gene pool. Eugenicists designated as "unfit" those they considered threats to the genetic integrity of humanity, including the poor, the physically disabled, the sickly, epileptics, alcoholics, those with impaired mental capacity, real or imagined (broadly designated the "feeble-minded," further distinguished as "idiots," "imbeciles," or "morons"). Sanger accepted these as categories of unfitness, as the rest of this book will show.

Though she generally rejected positive eugenics, she was a committed negative eugenicist.[91] To a reader unfamiliar with the internecine eugenic debates of the first half of the twentieth century, Sanger's rhetoric and that of Planned Parenthood may not seem to be explicitly eugenic, but such a reading would depend on a lack of historical awareness. An examination of the eugenics movement, its worldview, and the people whom it targeted clearly reveals that Sanger falls into the eugenics camp.[92] For example, when Sanger alluded to the need for stopping the "waste" of charitable giving that allowed the "feebleminded" to reproduce themselves, she was referencing a whole eugenic worldview with the use of a few code words, and her contemporaries would have easily recognized the ideology to which she was referring.

Part of the problem in recognizing Sanger's eugenic commitment these days arises from the current tendency to reduce eugenics to racism. It is important to recognize that, historically, not all eugenicists were racists. We must distinguish between, on the one hand, straightforward racism, which refuses to recognize the simple human dignity of persons of certain races, which sees them as inferior, *because of* their race, and, on the other hand, what I would call elitist bigotry.

The latter involves a self-anointed elite's rationalized disdain for supposedly inferior types of people, in which race as such is not understood to determine the inferiority. Though not directly racist, the sentiments of elitist bigotry are deeply prejudicial (for example, a preoccupation with the reproduction of those in the lower social classes), and, in the concrete, lead to the disproportionate victimization of marginalized races.[93] The eugenics movement as a whole evinces this elitist bigotry, but any given eugenicist is not necessarily imbued with straightforward racism — though many indeed were. ABCL National Council member and eugenicist Leon J. Cole, having received a letter from Sanger about whether or not the ABCL should endorse forced sterilization, demonstrates the casual bigotry of Sanger's coterie.

> ... I think you will see that to my mind there is fully as much necessity of giving attention to means of restriction of propagation in this lower irresponsible stratum of society as there is of providing a means of voluntarily reducing the numbers born in the better classes. (I use these terms such as "better classes" without definition as I know you will understand the way in which I intend them.)[94]

The "restrictive measures ... imposed by law" which the benevolent scientist recommends were "naturally sterilization and segregation."[95]

To summarize the distinction between eugenics and racism: eugenics depends on a lethal elitism that can eventually lead to genocidal results, but many eugenicists would protest (and with some warrant) that they personally could not be called racists.[96]

The issue, in Sanger's case, is perhaps more subtle than partisans for or against her have thus far admitted. This is how the sides line up in the debate over Sanger's racism: the Planned Parenthood camp points to the absence of racist language in Sanger's writings and her friendships with such African-American leaders as Mary McLeod Bethune, while PPFA's opponents highlight her eugenic beliefs and her friendships with notorious racists, including Harry Laughlin (the sterilization advocate), Guy Irving Burch (the anti-immigration activist who later lobbied for Sanger in Washington), and Clarence Gamble.[97] The next chapter will discuss Burch's involvement with Sanger and his racist views, and the third chapter will discuss Gamble in more detail. Concerning Laughlin, it is sufficient to note that he, as the "Expert Eugenic Agent" for the House Committee on Immigration and Naturalization in the 1920s, worked to implement racial quotas that would keep out what he called the "dross in America's modern melting pot." (However, it must be said that eugenics was but one motivation among others that drove immigration restriction.)

> The logical conclusion is that the differences in institutional rations, by races and nativity groups ... represents real differences in social values, which represent, in turn, real differences in the inborn values of the family stocks from which the particular inmates have sprung. These degeneracies and hereditary handicaps are inherent in the blood.[98]

Through the platforms given by the Eugenics Research Organization and the *Eugenical News*, he promoted Nazism during the 1930s, approving of its racist laws and working (with Burch) to prevent Jews seeking asylum in the United States from receiving visas.[99]

In addition to these men, with whom Sanger worked closely, Lothrop Stoddard also participated in the American Birth Control League by serving on the largely honorary National Council, the fifteen-member board of directors, and the conference committee of the First American Birth Control Conference and by publishing eugenicist articles in the *Birth Control Review* (for example, in the December 1921 issue).[100] He was invited to join ABCL's National Council in 1920 after his book, *The Rising Tide of Color Against White World Supremacy*, became a best-seller. The text contained such inflammatory statements as the following: "'Finally perish!' That is the exact alternative which confronts the white race.... Just as we isolate bacterial invasions, and starve out the bacteria, by limiting the area and amount of their food supply, so we can compel an inferior race to remain in its native habitat...."[101] In an attempt to distance Sanger from this man, PPFA has implied that her involvement with Stoddard was limited to allowing a review of his book (the topic of which is innocuously described as "the international politics of race relations in the first decades of the century") to be published in *Birth Control Review*.[102] Such dishonest selectivity in the presentation of the facts is a hallmark of PPFA's approach to its founder.

Other less famous individuals involved with Sanger also displayed racism. For example, eugenicist C. C. Little, who served on the ABCL board of directors and National Council, complained in the August 1926 issue of the *Review* (still under Sanger's editorship) that while the racial problems were not "acute" where he worked in New England, they were quite formidable in New York, where there was, he claimed, "an immense diversity of racial elements.... I happen to be working in Maine, where the proportion of the old New England stock is very, very high.... I don't want to see that particular element in the situation [what he calls "Yankee stock"] mixed up or mauled up," he said. "I want to keep it the way a chemist would prize a store of chemically pure substances...."[103]

With Sanger surrounding herself with such unsavory men, was she a racist or not? Perhaps both sides get something right in this debate. Sanger does not seem to have been an overt racist; there is no evidence that she maintained the genetic superiority of whites over blacks, for example. Such eugenic criteria as poverty, intelligence, and disability were sufficient for her division of humanity into the "fit" and the "unfit."[104]

The most questionable statement concerning race comes in a letter to Clarence Gamble. Here she is discussing the fledgling "Negro Project," an attempt by the Birth Control Federation of America to promote contraceptive use among Southern blacks, arguing that there is a need to recruit African-American doctors and ministers to carry out the BCFA's plan.

> It seems to me from my experience where I have been in North Carolina, Georgia, Tennessee and Texas, that while the colored Negroes have great respect for white doctors they can get closer to their own members and more or less lay their cards on the table which means their ignorance, superstitions and doubts.... The ministers [*sic*] work is also important and also he should be trained, perhaps by the Federation as to our ideals and the goal that we hope to reach. We do not want word to go out that we want to exterminate the Negro population and the minister is the man who can straighten out that idea if it ever occurs to any of their more rebellious members.[105]

Some opponents of Sanger have argued that this letter reveals a sinister, genocidal intent, while her defenders have claimed that she is merely anticipating an objection in hyperbolic terms. Certainly, the reference to "ignorance, superstitions and doubts" reveals a patronizing attitude, but it is at most a kind of "soft" racism, able to coexist with, for example, her appreciation of colleague Florence Rose's "quality of humanness with none of the race prejudice that most white people dealing with Negroes have imbedded in their genes."[106] Based on statements such as this, Sanger clearly did not think of herself as having "race prejudice." The extermination statement is of course more serious. Was her insistence on bringing birth control to blacks founded on a conviction of their genetic inferiority, a conviction that she might have considered "scientific" and thus not a manifestation of "race prejudice" (which would consist of how one "deals with" blacks at an interpersonal level)? Or was she merely using hyperbole to describe a possible misconception? There is simply not enough evidence one way or the other to make a definitive judgment, though I find the latter reading more plausible.

What is clear is her determination to keep the Negro Project out of the hands of blacks. She wished for a black minister to spread the word, but only after he had been trained by her organization "as to *our* ideals and the goal that *we* hope to reach" (italics mine). In another letter to Gamble, she confides her hopes for the Project: "What I wish to see is the employment of an up and doing modern minister, colored, and an up and doing modern colored medical man, both to come to New York and train at the Clinic and at the Federation until they are oozing with birth control as well as population."[107] Again, Sanger envisions hiring black workers only if they are willing to present Sanger's ideology and not a homegrown vision of black advancement. "Oozing with birth control as well as population": the addition of the latter element indicates that Sanger had more than maternal health and women's rights in mind. One of the overriding goals of the Negro Project was the reduction of the number of blacks for at least eugenic, if not racist, reasons.

In any case, we must recognize that the ideology that she perpetuated, even if not explicitly racist, would be used to support racist outcomes because of its elitist bigotry with regard to marginalized classes. For example, there is some evidence that Sanger had considerable antipathy towards immigrants, but it is not clear that this bad feeling was racially motivated. It seems more likely that it arose from her distaste for the poverty and illiteracy under which immigrants invariably labored. Yet this eugenic belief led her to hold attitudes as dangerous to immigrants as attitudes straightforwardly motivated by racism. One reason why Sanger is vulnerable to charges of racism is that those who have large families and who appear "dysgenic" to the upper classes often come from poor minority groups (and here the question of anti–Catholicism joins the question of racism). Even if she did not attack racial minorities *because of* their race, her eugenic efforts nonetheless threatened them disproportionately. Thus, she noted with approval that immigration laws prevented the "unfit" from overrunning America. Though she clearly defines the problems of unfitness in eugenic-qualitative, not racial, terms, she nonetheless comes to deeply prejudicial conclusions.

> Anybody in this vast country is at perfect liberty to become a father or a mother! You may be diseased, you may be a mental defective, a moron, a pauper, a habitual criminal; you may be insane, irresponsible, with no knowledge of the laws of health, hygiene, or common decency; yet you may bring not merely one child into these United States. You are encouraged to bring a dozen…. I, for one, believe that it is high time to recognize that if it is not right to import into our country individuals from whom we must later protect ourselves, it is even more imperative to protect ourselves and to protect American society today and tomorrow from the procreation of such individuals within our gates.[108]

In addition, as we have seen, there were certainly racists in the power structures of her organizations; she attracted racist followers and published their statements, thereby making her responsible for encouraging and legitimating racism. Examining the issue, Edwin Black concludes, "Therefore, even though Sanger was not a racist or an anti–Semite herself, she openly welcomed the worst elements of both into the birth control movement."[109]

Sanger's tolerance of racist viewpoints was later copied by her followers. For example, in the 1970s Beatrice Blaire accepted money for a clinic in a predominantly black neighborhood in Rochester, knowing "damn well that many people, in their minds, made the connection, well, we're going to keep the blacks down." She "took the money anyway." Likewise, Lonny Myers raised money from racists in Chicago, rationalizing that "any cause has strange bedfellows."[110]

Most seriously, investigative reporters have brought to light the involvement of key International Planned Parenthood Federation players in Nazi Germany's eugenic politics. Hans Harmsen, a physician and Rockefeller-supported demographer in Germany, was an important scientific and academic supporter of Nazi policies. He supported the brutal 1933 sterilization law that mandated coercion and served in the East Frisian sterilization bureaucracy, responsible for eugenic sterilizations performed on the disabled.[111] A later report determined that he "supported forced sterilizations of the mentally handicapped and helped to carry them out in the Protestant Inner Mission institutions for which he was responsible."[112] After the war, given Harmsen's anti-socialist leanings, both Sanger and the Rockefeller Foundation supported him as the best candidate to lead the German birth-control movement. He became the president of the German Society for Demography and then president of Pro Familia, the German affiliate of IPPF, in 1952.[113] He continued to promote ostensibly "voluntary" eugenic sterilization and campaigned for a new law in the post–Nazi age. In 1980, after decades of leadership roles within Pro Familia, he was awarded an honorary presidency. But in 1984, new historiography and investigative reporting revealed Harmsen's Nazi collusion. He was forced to resign, still unrepentant.[114] Pro Familia later confessed, "The organization has to admit self-critically, that it was only forced to this confrontation with itself from the outside and had up till now evaded confronting its own past."[115] The Planned Parenthood movement as a whole has still successfully avoided such a confrontation with its own history, refusing to recognize the degree to which the movement has allowed prejudice and racism to flourish within its ranks.

So it seems as if Sanger was not an out-and-out racist but nevertheless tolerated racism in her coworkers. But if racism did not motivate Sanger to accept eugenics, what did? The answer lies in her fear of and distaste for the "breeding" of the "unfit." She showed how deeply she held the fundamental assumptions of eugenics in *The Pivot of Civilization* (1922), in which she distinguished positive and negative eugenics and explicitly advocated the aims of the latter.

> We should not minimize the great outstanding service of Eugenics for critical and diagnostic investigations.... This [genetic] degeneration has already begun. Eugenists demonstrate that two-thirds of our manhood of military age are physically too unfit to shoulder a rifle; that the feeble-minded, the syphilitic, the irresponsible and the defective breed unhindered; ... that the vicious circle of mental and physical defect, delinquency and beggary is encouraged, by the unseeing and unthinking sentimentality of our age, to populate the asylum, hospital and prison. All these things the Eugenicist sees and points out with a courage entirely admirable.[116]

Sanger's use of the third person in referring to "eugenists" should not lead the reader to believe that she was not in the eugenics camp. Rather, Sanger here refers to the professional eugenicist, the scientist who performs the "critical and diagnostic investigations." Her own promotion of negative eugenics is clear and reflected her discomfort regarding the reproduction of the lower classes: "But it is well to emphasize that we advocates of birth control are not so much disturbed by the stationary birth rate of the thinking classes, as by the reckless propagation of the ignorant."[117] She clarified her differences with positive eugenics in her autobiography: "The eugenists [*sic*] wanted to shift the birth control emphasis into less children for the poor to more children for the rich. We went back of that and sought first to stop the multiplication of the unfit. This appeared the most important and greatest step towards race betterment."[118]

In other words, Sanger believed that birth control served a great negative eugenic purpose by enabling the limitation of those "stocks" which should not be reproduced. In her 1920 book *Woman and the New Race*, Sanger calls birth control "nothing more or less than the facilitation of the process of weeding out the unfit, of preventing the birth of defectives or of those who will become defectives."[119] Among the "unfit" she included those with "inheritable disease" (mistakenly including such conditions as epilepsy), the "feeble-minded," people with syphilis, and anyone who had previously given birth to children who were "not normal," in an article tellingly entitled "Mrs. Sanger's Nine Reasons Children Should Not Be Born."[120] Accordingly, she called persons with disabilities "biological and racial mistakes."[121] Quite simply, birth control was the key to wiping out human evils, including hunger and crime, through wiping out the propagation of those people who suffered (but who, according to Sanger, also perpetuated) those evils.[122]

> Hap-hazard, uncontrolled parentage leads directly and inevitably to poverty, over-crowding, delinquency, defectiveness, child labor, infant mortality, international friction and war, and ... the development of more perfect contraceptive methods and the better understanding of the various problems of Birth Control are necessary if these evils are to be stamped out....[123]

Sanger's rhetoric, as extreme as it is, simply reflects her fundamental conviction that "the most urgent problem to-day is how to limit and discourage the over-fertility of the mentally and physically defective."[124] As I showed in the introduction, this "problem" justified coercive or outright forcible methods in Sanger's eyes; she hoped, in the end, that governments would "attempt to restrain, either by force or persuasion, the moron and the imbecile from producing his large family of feeble-minded offspring."[125] Sanger did not hesitate to advocate force, but she preferred, in general, to "persuade."

Other people within the control movement understood that the "unfit" could be "persuaded" to use birth control through intensive propaganda campaigns. Former PPFA president Frances Hand Ferguson once said that getting the poor to use birth control "doesn't happen by itself....

You've got to get to those people to motivate them, to make them under-stand what birth control is about." The whole process would require a huge propaganda system mobilizing the hegemonic forces of ideological dissemination, from academia to Madison Avenue: "But to motivate peo-ple, mass education, and so forth, you need psychologists, you need people who've been in the advertising business, you need all types of business-men, all kinds of people putting this puzzle together to make it effective."[126]

Whenever confronted by recalcitrant resistance, however, Sanger and others recognized that propaganda might have to give way to brute force: "Possibly drastic and Spartan methods may be forced upon society if it con-tinues complacently to encourage the chance and chaotic breeding that has resulted from our stupidly cruel sentimentalism."[127] In other words, if the "unfit" would continue to refuse Sanger's version of liberation, then they would have to be forced into it. Such is the "liberation" offered by the control ideology.

The frequent use of the word "breeding" to describe human repro-duction in Sanger's writings was another of her eugenic tics, serving to dehumanize the reproduction and family-rearing of the "unfit." Appro-priating the eugenic predilection for comparing human reproduction to the animal breeding of a stud farm, she often made use of agricultural analogies. For example, she referred to certain unfit persons as "human weeds."

> In his last book, Mr. [H. G.] Wells speaks of the meaningless, aimless lives which cram this world of ours, hordes of people who are born, who live, who die, yet who have done absolutely nothing to advance the race one iota. Their lives are hopeless repetitions. All that they have said has been said before; all that they have done has been done better before. Such human weeds clog up the path, drain up the energies and the resources of this little earth. We must clear the way for a better world; we must culti-vate our garden.[128]

She used the comparison to weeds more than once. For example, she wrote the following in a popular magazine, combining several eugenic meta-phors: "'Nature eliminates the weeds, but we turn them into parasites and allow them to reproduce.' Could any business maintain itself with the bur-den of such an 'overhead'? Could any breeder of livestock conduct his enterprise on such a basis? I do not think so."[129]

Over twenty years later, she had still not shaken the habit of deper-sonalizing her fellow human beings. In her opening speech to a population conference in 1948, she compares American migrant workers to voracious insects.

We are, moreover, becoming a nation of vast homeless, rootless, uprooted migrants, now sweeping onward toward the Pacific Coast ... like a scourge of locust, or a devastating flood of nomadic humanity. Can you imagine the impact of this vast scourge of human grasshoppers upon the settled communities which are not prepared to welcome them.[130]

In addition, the dehumanizing eugenic slogan, "To create a race of thoroughbreds," was used as a banner on the cover of the November 1921 issue of the *Birth Control Review*. The Planned Parenthood Federation of America today claims that the remark was pulled by Sanger from a paragraph written by Dr. Edward A. Kempf concerning the need for maternal and infant care clinics and "how environment may improve human excellence." According to Planned Parenthood, Sanger used the phrase with this more charitable intent in mind.[131] Yet this interpretation must simply ignore statements to be found throughout her writings (a mere sampling of which we have just looked at), as well as the history of eugenic rhetoric. Sanger often compared human reproduction to animal breeding. This particular metaphor was widely used among eugenicists, who often sponsored "human stock" contests at state fairs, with the prize going to the family who had most capitalized on the "science of human husbandry."[132] In an unpublished, pro-eugenic article or speech entitled "We Must Breed a Race of Thoroughbreds," Sanger advocated giving birth control to various categories of the "unfit," such as those with transmissible disease, "where the children already born are subnormal or feeble-minded."[133] Clearly, Sanger used this phrase with a hereditarian, eugenic intent.

Despite this evidence, Charles Valenza of Planned Parenthood and others have denied that Sanger was a eugenicist. PPFA's defense of Sanger on its web page quotes the 1919 *Birth Control Review* article, "Birth Control and Racial Betterment" (while neglecting to mention its eugenic title!), where Sanger says, "Eugenists imply or insist that a woman's first duty is to the state; we contend that her duty to herself is her first duty to the state."[134] This sentence, however, is taken out of context: the whole article clearly indicates that only the "fit" woman is deemed worthy of making reproductive decisions. The sentences immediately before the one quoted above indicate that Sanger is arguing against *positive* eugenics, not eugenics *tout court*, in this paragraph: "The eugenicist also believes that a woman should bear as many healthy children as possible as a duty to the state. We hold that the world is already over-populated."[135] In addition, she opens the article by praising eugenics, saying, "Like the advocates of Birth Control, the eugenists, for instance, are seeking to assist the race toward the elimination of the unfit. Both are seeking a single end but they lay emphasis upon different means."[136] What is evident is Sanger's desire to guarantee reproductive freedom to *some* women, those who (like herself) were "fit," while controlling the reproduction of the "unfit." She explicitly affirms the *negative* eugenic goal of eliminating the "unfit."

Surprisingly, it appears that even Sanger's criticism of positive eugenics faded by the later 1930s. When discussions began concerning the merger between the American Birth Control League and the Birth Control Clinical Research Bureau, Sanger argued that the most important factor in the merger was the goal ahead, a goal which would cause the eventual union of "eugenics, population, birth control and allied fields together." This would be served by electing as president a "man who knows eugenics, population, methods, research along biological lines."[137] In an undated memo she spelled out what the aims of the new entity should be.

1. To raise the general level of intelligence of the nation's population.
2. To improve the quality of life....
3. To raise the standards of health for mothers and children and to reduce the infant and maternal death rate.
4. To balance the dysgenic birth rate,
    a. by discouraging the increase of that strata of the population perpetuating inheritable or transmissible diseases as well as among the chronically indigent.
    b. by encouraging the increase of the birth rate where health, intelligence and favorable circumstances tend to promote desirable types or racial stock.[138]

What is most notable about this list, other than the fact that three out of the four objectives for the incipient BCFA are explicitly eugenic, is the introduction in the last item of *positive* eugenics into Sanger's rhetoric, one of the few times where she voices that belief.

Birth Control and World War II

Soon after the formation of the Birth Control Federation of America, the United States entered World War II. Sanger and her groups reframed the issue in ways to appeal to then-current concerns. During this time, the control movement became more overtly nationalistic than it had ever been before — a strong contrast to Sanger's *Woman Rebel* rhetoric. To prevent a disappearance of interest in the eugenic cause, the BCFA and its Citizens Committee published such statements as "Democracy Needs Quality" and stressed the importance of racial preparedness and health to the building of the national defense.

For example, one pamphlet cried out, "Race betterment can never wait till 'more propitious times'—it is a task which must be started now."[139] The rhetoric adopted a new — or perhaps different — tone of urgency: birth control was desperately needed to support the nation's ability to defend itself; otherwise the country would sink into unfitness and be defeated by the fascists. The Citizens Committee stressed, "Our democracy, in the face of the forces within, as well as without, which threaten its existence, can hope to endure only so long as the quality of our people is maintained. To contribute directly and effectively to raising the quality of our people in every walk of life — that is the great fundamental aim of the birth control movement."[140]

The close relationship between national defense and birth control on one hand and population control on the other was constantly reiterated during this time period. As one pamphlet put it, "WE CAN'T AFFORD WASTE NOW."[141] The copy in this brochure claims that more than 40 percent of American draftees were rejected for physical or mental unfitness. Painting an alarmist picture regarding the impoverished one-third of the American population who were having the most children, it concludes, "Two to three million people in America are so seriously defective in mind or body as a result of hereditary factors that they are burdens to themselves and the nation."[142]

It is often assumed that the revelations of horrific Nazi atrocities after the war brought eugenics into general disrepute. This may have been true at a popular level, but it was not true of Planned Parenthood operatives and other members of the control movement. Eugenicists did not suddenly give up their commitment to eugenic ideology after the war. Rather, they adapted to the new public-relations situation. The Nazi taint led them to make their case in terms of population control and to eschew public mention of "eugenics" per se. But the rhetoric and the reasoning remained intact. The eugenic motto of "quality, not quantity" was reiterated even more frequently, but the public emphasis came more and more to rest, as it were, on the *not quantity* part of the equation. We have seen how Sanger adopted this slogan; it perfectly summarizes the eugenic ideology and makes clear that its internal logic entails birth/population control. Before and during the war, the eugenic rationale was explicitly put forward for reproductive control. With the postwar disclosure of Nazi evils, population control was increasingly presented as an end in itself. Nevertheless, population control continued to be a matter of rendering the nation not just less numerous but more fit.

But both during and after the war, the case was made in terms of national defense, and this rhetoric was not relaxed to any considerable degree until the sixties, when Planned Parenthood's language was adapted to the War on Poverty. In the 1950s, the new threat to the American way of life was communism, and again birth control and population control were presented as essential instruments in the fight to keep the world safe for democracy. For example, Alan Valentine's 1952 address to the annual meeting of PPFA strikes all the same chords of fear and urgency as were struck during the war, while taking up the familiar eugenic refrain of "quality, not quantity." And, clearly, eugenic arguments were still explicitly rehearsed in-house.

> My own work in recent years has made me especially sympathetic with your concern about the quality as well as the quantity of individuals making up the human race, and whether decent opportunity is available to each. Our greatest internal danger is that through a distorted idea of democracy, we level down from mediocrity to mediocrity until we become too mediocre to survive — or to deserve to survive.[143]

Valentine proposed that the U.S. make its foreign aid contingent upon the adoption of population-control measures in foreign countries, a policy that has indeed been carried out in the decades since his talk.[144]

The International Planned Parenthood Federation and Sanger's Last Years

The prospect of international work, long a fascination for Sanger, led her to undertake a new organizational initiative, the first since her relinquishing of administrative involvement in the newly renamed Planned Parenthood. She had always had a special interest in birth-control and population-control work in the developing world, especially in India, which was to her, as she confided in a letter to Clarence Gamble, "a bottomless sink as there is no limit to the amount of money that you can put in there. They need birth control on a large scale and it should be continually prodded into a national consciousness daily, hourly, for at least five years. If I am not too old when this war is over, I should like to make my next epoch's work China and India."[145]

She managed to muster up the energy to continue to preach the control message abroad. A family-planning conference convened in Sweden in 1946 provided the opportunity for Sanger to return to active involvement in population control. Sanger decided to build on the momentum of this first conference, planned by her friend and coworker Elise Ottesen-Jensen, by holding another international conference in Cheltenham, England, in

1948, with the British Family Planning Association (FPA) serving as hosts. The FPA was deeply involved with the English Eugenics Society.[146] The second conference was partially funded by Sanger's longtime supporter, John D. Rockefeller 3rd, who was becoming more and more concerned with population growth. A press release for the conference noted that, among the talks to be given, "Dr. Clarence J. Gamble will discuss sterilization to help reduce the number of hopeless misfits, who drain our resources further, pathetic cyphers who fill our asylums & hospitals to overflowing."[147] Clearly, eugenic concerns would not be neglected in Sanger's international work.

The attendees resolved to form an International Planned Parenthood Committee, with a paid secretary ensconced in the Eugenics Society offices in London, and Dorothy Brush came up with $5,000 of seed money from her family's eugenic foundation.[148] C. P. Blacker, who would be very important to the establishment of Sanger's international organization, noted, "The International Committee is much concerned with the problems of the backward and overpopulated countries of South East Asia...."[149] This committee was later renamed the International Planned Parenthood Federation (IPPF) in 1952 at a conference in Bombay, India, one of those "backward" countries to which Blacker had referred.

IPPF's constitution, co-written by Harriet Pilpel and T. O. Griessemer, codified the eugenicism of Sanger, its founder. Among the aims of the new organization was the stimulation of research into "the biological, demographic, social, economic and eugenic implications of human fertility and control."[150] The explicit mention of eugenics was *added* to the last drafts of the constitution and remained in IPPF's constitution even after its revision in the 1970s.[151] As Sanger underlined in a letter on IPPF letterhead to eugenicist C. P. Blacker in 1953, "I appreciate that there is a difference of opinion as what [*sic*] a Planned Parenthood Federation should want or aim to do, but I do not see how we could leave out of its aims some of the eugenic principles that are basically sound in constructing a decent civilization."[152]

As an illustration of the continuing life of eugenic ideas within IPPF, one can consider a summary of a lecture by Dr. A. S. Parkes called "The Biological Control of Conception" printed by the Medical Committee of IPPF in a newsletter in 1961. The lecture was substantially about the development of a birth-control pill, which Parkes thought was needed to "solve" the population problem in the developing world. He noted that the mere numerical control of population would not settle the "practical, aesthetic and eugenic requirements" of intelligent population control.[153] The inclusion of this ideological piece within the supposedly "scientific" newsletter of the Medical Committee indicates the eugenic slant of even the most scientific subgroup of IPPF.

Sanger herself grew no more moderate in her last years. In 1950, she was awarded the Lasker Award, recognizing achievement in family planning, and she sent her son Grant to collect the award in New York and to read her statement. Even her biographer Ellen Chesler, an admirer, acknowledges, "It was not his mother's finest moment."[154] Sanger, citing increased population growth, complained, "The brains, initiative, thrift and progress of the self supporting, creative human being are called upon to support the ever increasing and numerous dependent, delinquent and unbalanced masses."[155] To respond to the crisis of "quantity without quality," she proposed two courses of action: first, placing emphasis on "quality as a prime essential in the birth and survival of our population"; second, "decreasing the progeny of those human beings afflicted with transmissible diseases and dysgenic qualities of body and mind," through the provision of a pension in return for the sterilization of "the feebleminded and the victims of transmissible, congenital diseases."[156] She suggested the pension as a way for the "present Federal Governmental Santa Clauses," who "have their hands in the taxpayer's pockets," at least to "be constructive … in their generous giving mood," instead of (presumably) spending more money on welfare programs.[157] Her frustration with those who would not accept her vision of a childless female freedom was evident in her concluding statement: "We cannot give them freedom on a silver platter but we can awaken in them the demand for a free, self disciplined life and consciously controlled birth rate and population."[158] She was never able to see why some women would not find her presentation of "freedom" freeing, saturated as it was with the eugenic ideal of control. To the end of her life, Sanger persisted in a eugenically compromised conception of freedom, which could not rid itself of the impulse to manipulate the marginalized.

As the unstable and resentful rhetoric of the Lasker speech indicates, Sanger was slipping further out of touch with reality in her last years. Her closest friends in the control movement, including the Neo-Malthusians whom she had known in England as well as her fellow travelers in America, were passing away.[159] In the last years of her life, she continued to travel and campaign for the promotion of birth control abroad, as the "population explosion" became big news, but her growing loneliness led to greater dependence on Demerol and alcohol. In 1961, the World Population Emergency Campaign, a population-control fund-raising organization initiated by businessman Hugh Moore, held an expensive fund-raising dinner honoring her. At this her last public appearance, the toll that her addictions had taken was reportedly evident.[160] Succumbing to arteriosclerosis, Margaret Sanger died on September 6, 1966, almost 88 years old.

Sanger's Successor Alan Guttmacher

Sanger's worldview, if not her particular style of leadership, was perpetuated by her less flamboyant followers in Planned Parenthood. As she had hoped, by the 1950s PPFA was increasingly emphasizing population control, due mostly to the fact that wealthy businessmen were becoming interested in the birth-control movement out of a concern for the supposed connection between population and economic stability.[161] One sign of PPFA's increased focus on population control was the hiring of William Vogt as national director in 1951. Vogt made his name with the best-selling book *Road to Survival* (1948), which argued for population control by utilizing Malthusian logic. Vogt's book exemplifies the close interaction between eugenics and population control. Among other proposals, he urged, "From the point of view of society, it would certainly be preferable to pay permanently indigent individuals, many of whom would be physically and psychologically marginal, $50 or $100 rather than support their hordes of offspring that, by both genetic and social inheritance, would tend to perpetuate their fecklessness."[162] Vogt backed up his words with action, serving on the Medical and Scientific Committee of the leading pro–eugenic-sterilization organization, the Human Betterment Association of America (HBAA).[163]

PPFA worker Frances Hand Ferguson would later insist, "Bill Vogt was a great scholar to my mind, and a great leader, and a shocker. I mean that *Road to Survival* was one of the first books that woke people up to the horrors of life." Among his antics, Ferguson recalled, "[H]e would say things that would shock people, like … to WHO [World Health Organization] physicians, 'Why are you trying to save the lives of children when you'll just doom them to starvation?' … Of course, when we got him, we thought he was the greatest catch we'd ever known.…"[164]

Despite Vogt's prestige, Ferguson recalled that, when physician Alan Guttmacher seemed to be interested in the job, "I think it was a choice between Bill and Alan, and Alan had much more … you realize that Alan was a much bigger catch for us than Bill Vogt."[165] Guttmacher served with Vogt on HBAA's Medical and Scientific Committee, and he was an even more active eugenicist than Vogt was. By 1956, Guttmacher was a vice president of the HBAA and the head of the medical committee.[166] He assumed the leadership of PPFA in 1962.

He was a longtime advocate of eugenic sterilization for the mentally disabled, advising parents with "a mentally retarded child who is approaching reproductive age and yet is not sufficiently abnormal to require hospitalization" that "it is a safeguard against unwanted pregnancy to have such a child sterilized, since he may lack either sufficient emotional control or intellectual insight to use the God-given power of reproduction properly."[167] He acknowledged in 1973, "I have done occasional sterilizations on adolescent females brought to me by their parents for sterilization because of serious mental retardation."[168]

In an essay in 1964, he summarized the "indications" for sterilization: "First of all, eugenic; second, therapeutic; third, socio-economic; and fourth, population control." Guttmacher also stated approvingly that "[t]he oldest indication for sterilization in this country is eugenic. We have 28 states with laws governing such sterilization in this country." His description of "socio-economic" sterilizations indicates that these reflected the old eugenic preoccupation with "pauperism": "At my own institution, The Mount Sinai Hospital, because of the type of ward patient living in the slums who attends our clinics, we decided some years ago that it was only humane to carry out a socio-economic program of sterilization."[169]

Guttmacher's positive view of eugenic sterilization, like his view of family planning as a whole, was rooted in his eugenic convictions and his contempt for the abilities of poor women to know what was best for their own families. In the *Eugenics Quarterly*, he wrote an article on treatment of diabetes, which noted, "The fecundity suddenly bestowed upon the diabetic in 1922 by the boon of insulin is not a pure blessing, certainly not a genetic blessing."[170] When the birth-control pill was first approved and proffered as a "solution" to differential fertility, he responded, "[F]or poorly motivated people sterilization is a much better technique than contraception. I know this from practical experience at The Mount Sinai Hospital.... [Puerto Rican women] refuse to be bothered by birth control techniques."[171] The question as to why such "poorly motivated" women should be pressured into using contraception at all, much less be permanently sterilized, is not addressed.

The Puerto Rican woman was the exemplar of "dysgenic" differential fertility, a eugenic "problem" with which Guttmacher was quite concerned. According to his wife,

> Alan actually got interested in family planning ... birth control ... when he first became an intern on the [Johns] Hopkins staff, because in those days the wards were separated, the black wards from the white wards and so forth, and he realized ... he saw the population explosion. We both did. We lived in the ghetto area right by the Hopkins then which was where all

the black people lived. He saw the ward patients, the poor blacks and poor whites....[172]

The interviewer inquired, "So it [his motivation] was differential fertility?" to which Mrs. Guttmacher assented.

As he told a BCFA conference in the 1940s, both positive and negative eugenic means were necessary to solve the problem of differential fertility.

> It is obvious from every study that parents in the upper intelligence brackets ... are not replacing themselves, and therefore the group is a gradually declining one. On the other hand the mentally retarded and the mentally defective are more than replacing themselves and bid fair to double their number each generation. Insidiously they are replacing the people of normal mentality. Many students of population are shouting their warnings; they have largely fallen on deaf ears.[173]

Guttmacher must have been pleased that he could say by 1963, as president of the Planned Parenthood Federation of America, that it was "evident that we are serving predominantly young parents of low or modest income."[174]

A concern with "motivation" seems to be behind Guttmacher's promotion of permanent and semi-permanent means of birth control over the pill, which must be taken every day to be effective. The IUD shared many of the same benefits as sterilization and was touted accordingly by Guttmacher while he was head of PPFA. The relative advantages of the IUD vis-à-vis the pill are clarified by him in a letter meant for PPFA donors, and it is evident that nowhere do concerns for women's health enter into the equation for either Guttmacher or his PPFA supporters: rather, it is all about the control of female fertility.

> The advantage of an IUD for the less conscientious, less motivated patient is that once it is in place, and it is not ejected, it requires no further action by the patient. I believe there is a real place for both pill and IUD. For most private patients and more highly motivated clinic patients, the pill may give the best protection. Where there is less motivation, the IUD is superior. In huge, national overseas programs, the price differential in favor of an IUD is very important.[175]

In other words, the IUD is the best contraceptive for the woman who does not really want contraception, because it does not allow her to discontinue the method whenever she desires.

Guttmacher was even more frank in 1964 with the president of G. D. Searle: the IUD had problems but not in the demographic arena.

IUD's have special application to underdeveloped areas where two things are lacking: one, money, and the other sustained motivation. No contraceptive could be cheaper, and also, once the damn thing is in, the patient cannot change her mind. In fact, we can hope she will forget that it is there and perhaps in several months wonder why she has not conceived. I do not believe the IUD's will cut into the competitive pill market materially in industrialized, more sophisticated regions. The big difference is that the IUD's are not as effective as the pill in preventing conception. If Mrs. Astorbilt, or Mrs. Searle or Mrs. Guttmacher gets pregnant while using an IUD, there is quite a stink — the thing is not good and a lot of people will hear about it. However if you reduce the birth rate of ... the Korean, Pakistanian or Indian population from 50 to 45 per 1,000 per year to 2, 3, or 5, this becomes an accomplishment to celebrate.[176]

With this motive in mind, Guttmacher became a prominent advocate of the Lippes Loop IUD.[177] He had desired a cheap contraceptive for a long time as a means of advancing the population-control efforts in poorer countries. Speaking of India's incentive program, he said, "Brave India is facing up to its population problem squarely, but it appears that its solution in the next few years is close to impossible. The mores of the masses are opposed to family planning." As a means of bypassing those moral objections that would be inflamed every time a woman took a pill, he hoped for "an inexpensive physiological method of contraception" that could be put in once and kept in for a long period of time. "[T]he urgency of its discovery becomes more imperative with each passing day that adds twenty thousand new persons to India's swarming throngs."[178]

All of his support and promotion of the IUD, however, did not negate his approval of the pill. In *Birth Control and Love* in 1969 he observed that, from his vantage point as president of PPFA, "I probably have the biggest pill practice in the world — almost 300,000 women in our Planned Parenthood Centers are now using the pill."[179] He was so adamant about "simple methods" of birth control that he disregarded warnings about their potential health dangers. Dr. Phillip Ball, trained at the Mayo Clinic, had hoped to discuss some worries that he had about the pill with Guttmacher at a professional meeting, yet, according to Ball, the president of PPFA was not interested in hearing anything that might put a cog in the population-control machinery. "I didn't attack him in the pulpit or anything like that. I just spoke to him before the meeting, told him my experiences. He was very irate. He just walked away from me."[180] In addition to the pill and the IUD, already by the 1940s he approved of the use of abortion; later he would openly profess that he believed in aborting a disabled fetus for "eugenic reasons."[181]

Despite these eugenic beliefs, Guttmacher stood out from the crowd of many hard-core population-control advocates such as Garrett Hardin by publicly insisting that contraception and sterilization remain "voluntary." His wife later recalled that Guttmacher's choice of words was always careful, always concerned to make birth-control use in developing countries appear as voluntary as possible: "There had been some abrasive people in the family planning movement who would go into the Far East or who would go to Europe and say, you know … what you need is population control. That kind of thing, which may have been true, of course. Alan never did that sort of thing."[182] Guttmacher, like Sanger, realized the importance of getting people to think that their contraceptive decisions were self-originated, not heteronomously shaped.

Yet, like Sanger, "voluntariness" did not preclude various forms of covert or outright pressure. In the end, "freedom" for Guttmacher was only the freedom to use contraception. His concept was expansive enough to include employing financial incentives and disincentives to pressure the poor into sterilization, including sterilization bonuses and tax-law revisions which would penalize large families, saying, "A thousand-rupee [sterilization] bonus would easily solve India's problem in a few years."[183] But, as various feminist authors have pointed out, offering money or food to a starving family is in fact coercive. In the late 1960s, Guttmacher put a limit on voluntarism: if we don't see a population decline by 1980, he said, "we'll have to get tough."[184] In the end, Guttmacher's embrace of "voluntarism" comfortably co-existed with the hope that "perhaps some day a way of enforcing compulsory birth control will be feasible."[185] Like Sanger, freedom was only for the "fit."

This form of "voluntarism" easily flowed from Guttmacher's eugenic commitment, which never waned. After he had served as a vice president of the American Eugenic Society in the 1950s, he wrote to Frederick Osborn, the president of that society, regarding Guttmacher's decision to take the presidency of PPFA instead of a leadership position at the Rockefeller-run Population Council. Guttmacher explained that it was a difficult choice, but he felt that the opportunities for activism at PPFA fit his personality better; yet, he added, "I am such an extravagant admirer of you that I believe if you had still been president of Population Council, I would have made a different choice."[186] Guttmacher's close ties with Osborn and his admiration for the foremost eugenicist in America at the time indicates the depth of cooperation between PPFA and the eugenics movement, well after Sanger's abdication of power. Evidently, Sanger had laid a firm foundation for Planned Parenthood's future eugenic activities.

Planned Parenthood Now:
Eugenics Gone Underground

According to its own self-description, Planned Parenthood's history as an organization dates back to the 1916 founding of Sanger's first clinic in Brownsville, New York.[187] The eugenic history of PPFA's predecessor organizations, all of them founded by Sanger (the American Birth Control League, the Clinical Research Bureau, the National Committee on Federal Legislation for Birth Control, and the Birth Control Federation of America), is not irrelevant to understanding Planned Parenthood today, because that history is indeed PPFA's past — even according to its own self-presentation. But to what degree does that history impinge on current Planned Parenthood activities? Is PPFA still complicit in the eugenic control ideology? It is the contention of this book that the lens through which Planned Parenthood views female fertility is largely eugenic, although the omnipresence of that lens tends to render it invisible to those who currently peer through it.

Or to use another metaphor, PPFA's entire control-based approach to female fertility flows from a eugenic deep-structure, whether or not current PPFA operatives are conscious of this reality. To deny this deep-structure is to deny Sanger's world-historical achievement: she succeeded in realizing eugenic goals to an arguably unparalleled degree.[188] To deny the continuing effectiveness of her eugenic vision is, in effect, to explain away Sanger's legacy, the true power of her organizational and systematic genius. For the Planned Parenthood of today to engage in such a public sanitizing of its founder's driving beliefs is to commit a singular act of spiritual matricide.[189] Besides, as we have seen, Sanger was hardly the last eugenicist to lead the organization. It should be borne in mind, for example, that Guttmacher headed the group until his death in 1974. The explicit eugenic commitment of PPFA's leadership thus lasts at least into the seventies. That is hardly ancient history. Despite cosmetic changes, nothing in the intervening years has materially disrupted the eugenic deep-structure so powerfully instituted by Margaret Sanger and carried on by Guttmacher and others.

Accordingly, in order to expose this deep-structure, much of the rest of this book will describe in detail the eugenic nature of population control, in order to demystify the ideology of control underlying Planned Parenthood's current activities. Population control as a strategy is frequently quite successful in camouflaging its eugenic genealogy.

Yet sometimes the deep-structure pokes through to the surface, and nakedly eugenic attitudes can be discerned with little probing. I will close this chapter with a sampling of such instances in the areas of coercion, poverty, and disability. These themes will recur throughout the book; let us simply look at a few examples of how Sanger's eugenic approach comes, as it were, to the surface in today's Planned Parenthood.

Contemporary Planned Parenthood rhetoric stresses individual free-dom to the point of being libertarian, yet (again) the "individual" in ques-tion is somewhat selectively defined. Regarding the question of Chinese women and their subjection to forced sterilization and forced abortion, for example, Planned Parenthood has remained silent, only insisting that IPPF's presence in China is ultimately beneficial to these women. PPFA's 1986 "Issues Manual," an in-house document that provides sound-bite answers to "hard questions," says lamely that "the People's Republic of China [has] more radical population policies than PPFA advocates," call-ing such policies "community involvement in deciding family size."[190] I doubt that Chinese women violated by coerced sterilization and forced abortion would recognize China's program to be simply a matter of "com-munity involvement" in family planning. And, despite whatever mild reservations PPFA might have, it has praised China's coercive activities as being "at the forefront of family planning."[191]

Advocates for persons with disabilities have found in Planned Par-enthood plenty of cause for concern. Already by the 1967 International Planned Parenthood Federation conference, with the ominous slogan "Planned Parenthood — a Duty and a Human Right," the organization was embracing genetic counseling, which, as I will show in the next chapter, was developed and promoted by eugenicists for eugenic reasons.[192]

This kind of preoccupation with disability has continued in more recent times. A session at a PPFA conference in 1983 examined the "Eth-ical Implications of New Technology for Reproductive Health Care," including genetic counseling (as well as abortion decisions based on the desired gender of the child). Concerning genetic counseling, the question was raised of how much pressure the counselor should bring to bear on the woman who is carrying a disabled fetus. A PPFA leader from Cincin-nati noted, "Our non-advocacy counseling has centered on the right of the individual and only the individual. I submit that this might have to change."[193] Another speaker raised the old eugenic nightmare of persons with disabilities reproducing themselves. Claiming that there was a dou-bling in the number of disabled children born in the previous twenty-five years, Al Moran from the influential New York City affiliate said that, in addition to mutations, a cause of this doubling was the "larger number of children born with genetic defects and who survive and who themselves bear children. We then begin to look at the fact that we need to be concerned with more issues than we are concerned about."[194]

The session came to few concrete conclusions regarding definite plans of action, but, as the moderator said, "For those who would say that 'this is not Planned Parenthood's business,' I would submit that if we truly wish to represent ourselves as responsible leaders in the reproductive health care area, we cannot sweep these questions under the rug."[195] In fact, PPFA was already encouraging genetic screening. By 1986, PPFA was reporting hopefully that chorionic villus biopsy would allow genetic testing of fetuses to be done even earlier than amniocentesis, noting that this method would allow for "earlier abortions."[196] (These techniques also determine a fetus's sex, thereby facilitating the possibility of abortions performed simply because of the gender of the fetus.)

PPFA's anti-disability bias affects adults as well. To reference recent anecdotal evidence (scholars do not have access to internal manuscript evidence for researching PPFA attitudes and activities during the past few decades), persons with diseases or disabilities who have taken jobs at Planned Parenthood have reported an uncomfortable work environment. One severely disabled woman, Barbara Faye Waxman, quit because she sensed that her colleagues were not comfortable with disability. She complained that they believed in the "need" to abort disabled fetuses. "There was a feeling that they were bad babies," she reported. "There was a strong eugenics mentality that exhibited disdain, discomfort, and ignorance toward disabled babies."[197]

Beyond its problems with persons with disabilities, the Planned Parenthood of today could also be accused of having a eugenic mentality toward the poor: the facts show that the poor here in America do not escape the ingrained eugenics of the control movement any more than do those in the developing world. In 1982, Pasadena Planned Parenthood was sued by Angelica Oliva, who charged that she was told that she could receive postpartum care only if she first signed a statement detailing which birth-control method she would promise to use. The city of Pasadena contracted its Medi-Cal (California's version of Medicare) postpartum services to the local Planned Parenthood clinic, in effect coercing the city's lower-income women into using some sort of postpartum contraception.[198] The Oliva case indicates the kind of eugenic outlook regarding the poor that is still in effect among Planned Parenthood affiliates.

A 1983 document by Planned Parenthood affiliates in New York, *Spending to Save*, shows that the attitude in Pasadena could be found on the other side of the country. The paper, essentially an argument for increasing state support of family planning, claims that family planning results in a "ratio of costs to benefits" of about 1 to 3: $3 are supposedly saved for every $1 spent on family planning for the poor.[199] In addition, the affiliates argued that genetic counseling was needed to detect birth defects and give women the option of aborting fetuses with disabilities when the latter would be "gravely defective."[200] The same attitude emanated from PPFA's national office recently, except that it has upped the ante: "Publicly funded family planning is cost-effective," PPFA claims. "Every dollar spent on publicly subsidized family planning services saves $4.40 on costs that would otherwise be spent on medical care, welfare benefits, and other social services to women who became pregnant and gave birth."[201] In reducing human persons to a utilitarian calculus, PPFA and its allies relentlessly ignore the evidence that children born to women on welfare return to the government in the form of taxes an average of 3.7 times the amount spent on them in the form of welfare assistance.[202] In other words, people (including those on welfare!) invariably prove to be a financial resource, not a burden, for society.

Conclusion

In her pursuit of reduction of quantity for the sake of eugenic quality, Sanger, because she considered woman "the conveyer of racial efficiency," sought specifically to control *women's* reproductive power (and especially that of socially marginalized women), making it subserve her eugenic ideology under the cover of libertarian rhetoric.[203] The pressure exerted on women to conform their reproductive desires to those of Planned Parenthood's is still present within PPFA, although usually expressed more subtly. Planned Parenthood's overarching antinatalist philosophy was adequately if crudely enunciated by an ad campaign that its Minnesota-South Dakota affiliate ran in 1996. Newspaper readers in the Midwest were confronted with the following statement, jumping out at them in white print against a black background: "BABIES ARE LOUD, SMELLY, AND EXPENSIVE. UNLESS YOU WANT ONE."[204] The ad copy expresses Planned Parenthood's distaste for uncontrolled female fertility: exaggerating the inconveniences of child rearing and overlooking its blessings, while strangely implying that the value and behavior (and smell!) of babies depends on the opinion of their parents. Even "wanted" babies (by which Planned Parenthood usually means "planned" ones that can be fit into a comfortable bourgeois lifestyle) sometimes cry. The ad indicates the distorted lens through which reproduction is viewed; only the uncomfortable elements are given prominence. What kind of a mother or father would first describe a child of theirs— even an unplanned one, which no inconsiderable number of us were — as "smelly"? The point of the ad is to dissuade people, especially the young, from wanting to become mothers and fathers, insinuating that having children is something exceptional rather than one of the most natural things in the world.

This general anti-child prejudice is only sharpened when the usual eugenic targets are in question. Here Sanger's insistence that being born into a large family marks a person out for social backwardness and economic destitution becomes relevant. PPFA's family-planning and genetic counselors have definite ideas about which babies can truly be wanted, and they counsel accordingly. A special target of messages such as the one in the newspaper ad are those people who still tend to view large families positively, namely, the poorer, especially minority, classes.[205] This is often cloaked as an altruistic campaign to stop "teen pregnancy," but however it is dressed up, this is a campaign that has, for example, contributed to the flatlining of the black population rate of this country. By contrast, some feminists such as Germaine Greer have passionately defended the validity of the poor's preference for children, arguing that opposition to this choice on the part of the wealthy is often guided by a eugenic rationale.[206]

As this chapter has shown, the ideology propping up Sanger's anti-natalist bias was consistently and thoroughly eugenic. Yet Planned Parenthood has protested weakly that, since Sanger has been dead for a while and cannot defend herself, it is a better policy to examine "what she did rather than ... why she did it."[207] But just because PPFA turns a blind eye to its founder's motivations does not mean that the rest of us, especially those poor women who are targeted, should also be uncritically accepting of the pernicious ideology that served as Planned Parenthood's foundation and that still shapes its activity. The point of this book is to resist the mystification concerning Sanger that PPFA urges upon us, because *why* someone does something has an effect on *what* is done and *how* it is done. If Sanger did act out of eugenic motives, as is unquestionably the case, the effects of that motivation will manifest themselves in concrete actions detrimental to human dignity.[208] The rest of this book will detail the anti-woman and anti-humanitarian effects of her web of eugenic motivations.

CHAPTER TWO

Eugenics as the Control of Births

"The campaign for Birth Control is not merely of eugenic value, but is practically identical in ideal with the final aims of Eugenics."—Margaret Sanger, "The Eugenic Value of Birth Control Propaganda," 1921[1]

"Birth control and abortion are turning out to be great eugenic advances of our time."— Frederick Osborn, American Eugenics Society, speech, 1974[2]

Eugenic historiography has generally been sounder than feminist scholarship in the matter of Margaret Sanger's relation to eugenics: the former tends to be less timid about describing the eugenic connection than is the latter, which sometimes is too close to its subject to have sufficient critical distance. Nevertheless, the tendency within eugenic scholarship is to minimize her role; Sanger receives a footnote or a chapter of coverage, but the real action, so historians tend to think, is played out on the scientific stage.[3] This stage is, not coincidentally, populated by men: scientists, but also wealthy philanthropists, foundation heads, and full-time eugenicists. It presents the history of eugenics as a drama written from the perspective of the American Eugenics Society and its sober male leaders, with many additional cranks and fools, like Harry Laughlin, spicing up the dramatic action. The occasionally outrageous activity of the birth controllers, while important and entertaining, is only a sideshow to what is happening on the main stage. Such a viewpoint is not simply wrong.

Indeed, we will have need to examine these male personages in more detail and to measure the scope of their influence.

But this perspective fails to grasp the true world-historical achievement of Margaret Sanger. Without her, eugenics itself would have become the sideshow, largely limited to the self-important musings and designs of academic societies and conferences. What I would argue — and what the Osborn quote cited at the beginning of this chapter indicates — is that Sanger hit on a eugenic strategy that worked where almost all the others failed. She brought an expansion of eugenics as an activist movement that was breathtaking. Before her, the practical reach of the eugenics movement had not gone beyond immigration restriction and sterilization of the disabled. Although hardly limited in scope and in human suffering, the tens of thousands of sterilizations would be dwarfed by the eugenic impact of Sanger's organizations. As we will see, the eugenics movement weathered the challenges of World War II and subsequent scientific discoveries by ultimately adopting — for the sake of self-preservation — Sanger's focus on negative eugenics, on the control of female fertility through birth control and population control. Further: Sanger *institutionalized* this eugenic ideology of control, which would allow the engines of eugenic progress to keep firing long after her death. But to recognize the centrality of eugenics for Sanger and her centrality in the history of eugenics, we must have some historical awareness of the larger eugenic context in which she worked.

The last chapter examined the importance of eugenics in Sanger's program for Planned Parenthood. This chapter will analyze some of the important groups and personages constituting the eugenics movement up to this day. Sanger relied on categories derived from eugenic science; her writings rehearse common negative eugenic catchphrases and ideas. Her originality as a eugenicist was pragmatic and systematic: it came in her reframing of the eugenic agenda, involving a disavowal of positive eugenics at least as a practical preoccupation, while directing the organized efforts of the eugenic cause to purely negative goals.[4] By drawing out the ideology of eugenic control as revealed in the history of eugenics, this chapter will present further evidence that Sanger's commitment to eugenics was not superficial but lay at the core of her activities and beliefs.

However, such an analysis of the history of eugenics requires that we make our concept of eugenics more precise. In the previous chapter, Sanger's beliefs and activities exemplified various aspects of eugenics, and the distinction between positive and negative eugenics helped to refine the matter. As a result, we have seen that the eugenic ideology involves advocacy of sterilization for the "unfit," a preoccupation with the fertility of the lower classes, and Malthusian concerns about over-population. Yet these features do not yet provide a definition of eugenics. In fact, as Diane B. Paul has pointed out, no scholarly consensus exists as to what precisely eugenics *is*.[5] The issue is not merely a matter of academic hairsplitting, for it is only by understanding what constitutes the eugenic ideology that we can attempt to discern whether, for example, contemporary genetics (most visibly exemplified in the Human Genome Project) and the biotech revolution it has engendered are admixed with the same motivations that inspired the earliest eugenicists. Indeed, we need to know what eugenics is before we can make a judgment about its ethical status.[6]

For example, if genetic counselors insist that they provide strictly non-directive, neutral counseling, merely making possible an informed choice, and that they would never encourage a woman to abort a disabled fetus, does that mean that genetic counseling is not eugenic in motivation?[7] Daniel Kevles, for one, argues that contemporary genetic advances and their practical application in genetic counseling are not eugenic in nature because contemporary geneticists are motivated by the desire to foster individual choice, not to control society's reproduction.[8] But Paul observes that "motivation" is a slippery thing to pin down, especially when the attitude in question (as with eugenics) is one that is somewhat discredited, at least in the popular mind, giving rise to the need for (perhaps unconscious) deception. This chapter will examine this question — to what degree is eugenics still alive?— in more depth in the last section. For now, the question concerning the eugenic status of contemporary science highlights the importance of understanding what eugenics is. I would like to propose a working definition of the basic eugenic attitude, a heuristic notion that will help us grasp the intelligibility of the history of eugenics, which this chapter will outline: eugenics is an ideology of control that views the human being more as a locus of genetic potential and peril than as a person with an innate and incalculable value and that, accordingly, seeks to shape decisions about who should reproduce or not and what kind of children are to be born or not.

Herbert Spencer Jennings (one of the "progressive" critics of much of the eugenic policy agenda who was nevertheless committed to the fundamental eugenic ideology) demonstrates this basic eugenic attitude with stark and threatening clarity.

> A defective gene — such a thing as produces diabetes, cretinism, feeble-mindedness— is a frightful thing; it is the embodiment, the material realization of a demon of evil; a living self-perpetuating creature, invisible, impalpable, that blasts the human being in bud or leaf. Such a thing must be stopped wherever it is recognized.[9]

The eugenic perspective reduces the person to a host of an evil gene: the eugenic magnifying glass makes the disease or the dysgenic trait loom so large that the person is blotted out by its ominous shadow. The abstract disease is made concrete, while the concrete person is reduced to the abstract, a member of some subset of dysgenesis: "feebleminded" or "wheelchair-bound" or "genetic underclass." The genetic parasite must be stopped, regardless of the cost to the human host. Unfortunately, this sort of dehumanization is just as present in the current "new eugenics" associated with the biotech revolution. Sociologist Barbara Katz Rothman has perceptively described our contemporary situation as fragmentation: "When you can fragment people into the traits and characteristics that are believed to be genetic, then genocide can be targeted not against a people, but against a characteristic: gene-ocide, destroying selectively."[10]

It should be noted at this point that the claim, often heard now, that eugenicists lacked scientific respectability and engaged only in "pseudoscience" is historically inaccurate. The large majority of the professionally trained geneticists of the early twentieth century — including some prominent scientific pioneers — were united in the belief that heredity determined most or all of the important facets of one's physical, mental, and intellectual makeup, including IQ, personality, inborn virtues and vices, and so forth.[11]

Why is this point of any interest? What is at stake is effective resistance to eugenics. Opponents of eugenics who rely upon the claim that it is simply scientific quackery make two mistakes: first, the claim is historically false — many eugenicists were quite good geneticists and experimental scientists; second, the claim is morally precarious—for what happens if today's serious scientific research were to support humbler, but still quite significant, claims of genetic determinism?[12] Indeed, some traits *are* genetically transmitted and perhaps could be greatly reduced through, say, compulsory birth control.[13] The feminist question that this book raises is whether such an action is *ethically*, not just scientifically, defensible, when one recognizes the dignity of all human beings and the duty to protect, not eliminate, those whom society has marginalized. Anything less than recourse to an ethical realism leaves the powerless open to control by the androcentric medical and scientific elite. We need the moral courage to refuse to commit acts that violate human dignity, even if done for the purpose of achieving seemingly desirable goals. With that in mind, let us turn to a history of the eugenics movement.

A Brief History of Eugenics

The Beginning of Eugenics

The word "eugenics" was coined by Francis Galton (1822–1911), a cousin of Charles Darwin and the founding father of eugenics. He wanted a word to express a scientific endeavor to improve the human stock, and he combined the prefix "eu," meaning "well" in Greek, with the root meaning "born." Thus the neologism means "well-born" and is intended to designate the inherent genetic worth of those individuals who were valued by society and who were duty-bound to produce more children for the good of the future race. According to Charles Benedict Davenport, who was the one principally responsible for transplanting the movement from England to the United States, eugenics was "the science of the improvement of the human race by better breeding."[14] For Galton and his followers, qualities such as intelligence, thriftiness, a predisposition to physical health, and sound morality were all hereditary; thus society ought to conform its breeding patterns to increase the amount of "good stock" in the human gene pool.

Galton typified in many ways the kind of eugenicists who would follow him: a well-off, educated male with a natural bias in favor of his own kind (Anglo-Saxon) and his own class (middle to upper).[15] His travels to Africa and other parts of the world developed in him the conviction of the inherent superiority of some races, with the white race at the top, and cousin Darwin's evolutionary theory gave Galton the idea that the human race could be improved through a rational program of procreation. Galton was also a positivistic rationalist, and he hoped that eugenics would provide a rational substitute for what he considered the superstition of institutional religion.[16] His ideas were developed in an 1869 book, *Hereditary Genius*, which purported to prove that the genius of prominent contemporaries was derived from their families' superior heredity.[17]

Galton's ideas took hold both in Europe and in America. Mendelian genetics was rediscovered in 1900, and the awareness followed that "traits" (soon to be called genes) occurred in pairs, one from each parent, and that one trait dominates the other "recessive" trait. As Mendelian genetics became more accepted, the belief became entrenched within the scientific community that certain dominant "unit characteristics" (features of a person controlled, it was thought, by a single gene) would unfailingly be passed down from parent to child. The characteristics bad for society — one of the most frequently quoted deleterious traits was "feeblemindedness," or low intelligence — could be stamped out by preventing those who

had the trait from reproducing. This project was called "negative eugenics."[18]

As we saw in the previous chapter, eugenic policies and programs
were divided between "positive" and "negative" eugenics, a delineation
that refined the eugenic political agenda. Reportedly coined by Caleb W.
Saleeby with Galton's approval, the terms indicated the two courses of
action endorsed by eugenics: positive eugenics encouraged more breeding among the "fit" or the "well-born," while negative eugenics aimed to
discourage or altogether prevent the "unfit" from reproducing.[19] Those
designated "unfit" included: the "idiots," the severely mentally disabled;
the "feebleminded," the borderline mentally disabled who could cope fairly
well with the demands of everyday life; all those with "hereditary diseases"
believed at that time to include even epilepsy; and the low-income, socially
disadvantaged in general, who supposedly genetically perpetuated such
traits as "criminality" and "pauperism."[20]

In England Galton emphasized positive eugenics, but Davenport, his
American counterpart, preferred to place the emphasis on negative eugenics.[21] Kevles has argued that "his negative eugenics expressed in biological language the native white Protestant's hostility to immigrants and the
conservative's bile over taxes and welfare."[22] This statement is true as far
as it goes, but, as Paul has shown, the eugenics movement crossed traditional political boundaries and incorporated many socialists and radical
leftists, including many Russian communists, who believed that eugenics
was consistent with the Bolshevik, technocratic approach to "scientific"
social control, although this faction was not the majority among eugenicists.[23] The political heterogeneity of eugenicists makes Sanger's support
of eugenics less surprising, because she also held other "progressive" social
beliefs. Though the eugenics movement in America included activists from
all different political persuasions, both conservative and radical birth-control supporters, they were nevertheless united in their support of most of
the negative eugenics program.

Although conceived in England, eugenics was really born in America, where a highly successful political and legal program was developed.[24]
Larson distinguishes four categories of negative eugenic laws: marriage
regulation, sexual segregation, involuntary sterilization, and limits on
immigration. A certain amount of legal success was achieved by the American eugenics movement in all of these areas; the first three policies constituted the agenda for state legislatures, while the last was achieved in
part by the passage of the federal immigration law of 1924.[25] One of the
standard eugenic textbooks of the day, Popenoe and Johnson's *Applied
Eugenics*, argued that any additional negative eugenic enactments would

not be that different from "existing measures and agencies" such as "voluntary restriction of conception, … surgical sterilization, [and] segregation."[26] Legalizing coercive measures might be necessary, according to the authors, because "a person who is lacking in intelligence, foresight, and self-control, is poor, is perhaps alcoholic, and is able to get more money from the county charities for every new baby, is unlikely to be successful in preventing childbearing."[27] The "problem" identified here — that the "unfit" who most "needed" negative eugenic measures would likely be the least likely to wish to utilize them — was a problem with which the eugenics and birth-control movements would have to deal continually. Sanger solved it by proposing propaganda for the many and coercion for the resisting few. Others would advocate different ratios of propaganda and coercion, but most eugenicists kept both weapons in their arsenal.

Popenoe and Johnson were not alone in their worry over the fertility of women dependent on private or governmental assistance: one important reason for radical negative eugenic measures was the concern over the perpetuation of the genes of "chronic pauper families."[28] Charles Davenport in particular was adept at finagling money from the wealthy for the fledgling eugenics movement in America by using the argument that eugenics provided a scientific and cost-effective way to improve the human race, in contrast to the old, dysgenic method of charitable assistance. "Vastly more effective than ten million dollars to 'charity' would be ten million dollars to eugenics," he explained.[29] Many rich patrons agreed with him, and he organized the well-funded Eugenic Record Office (ERO) in Cold Spring Harbor on Long Island's North Shore with their money.[30] Initially established in 1904 to be a biological research institution with funding from the Carnegie Institution, the ERO was further developed in 1910 to do human genetic research through fieldwork. Mrs. E. H. Harriman, heiress of her husband's railroad money and a primary donor, considered eugenics to be the human equivalent of the racehorse breeding in which her husband and father engaged. All in all, from 1910 to 1918, she contributed over half a million dollars to the ERO, a phenomenal sum at that time.[31] In addition to Harriman, the ERO received about another half million dollars from the Carnegie Foundation and additional funds from John D. Rockefeller, Jr. The ERO was not the only eugenic project funded by corporate money: John H. Kellogg, who made his money from cereal, sponsored the Battle Creek Race Betterment Foundation, and Ezra Gosney founded and funded the Human Betterment Foundation.[32] This money funded the work of eugenic fieldworkers and, through them, influenced the reception of eugenics as a scientific discipline. As Davenport wrote to Harriman, "What a fire you have kindled! It is going to be a purifying *conflagration* some day!"[33]

Yet the eugenic fieldwork that the ERO promoted was a strangely unscientific science. It called for the charting of family trees in order to demonstrate how certain characteristics (such as intelligence) had been passed down through generations. In this way, it attempted to show that certain phenotypes (the actual appearance in a person of certain characteristics) were genetically based or, in other words, signs of their respective genotypes. The accuracy of eugenic fieldwork was dubious for many reasons: it depended on hearsay and gossip concerning the alleged abilities or faults of previous generations; it was skewed by the prejudices of the fieldworkers themselves, often too enthusiastic about the eugenic social project to be objective observers; and it lacked truly scientific means to measure the real existence of many of the characteristics for which it was looking.[34] Nevertheless, the "data" obtained by fieldworkers were used as authoritative proof of the genetic basis of various human qualities, and many of the workers went on to institutional positions as professional eugenicists within government or academia, including state-run eugenic sterilization boards.[35]

It was believed by eugenicists such as Davenport that eugenic fieldworkers would be able to test scientifically the intelligence level of the people whom they were investigating through the recently developed intelligence tests. A person's "intelligence quotient," supposedly a quantitative measurement of native intelligence, was first tested by the Simon-Binet tests around the turn of the twentieth century. Henry H. Goddard, a psychologist and eugenicist, brought the test to America in 1908 and initiated a flurry of IQ testing. The World War I draft expanded the field of testing subjects, because the military wished to match potential soldiers with the job most suitable to them. Robert Yerkes, influenced by both Galton and Davenport, developed the tests that would be used by the military, but despite his claims of scientific objectivity, the tests were ridiculously biased in favor of those with some schooling and, even more important, cultural literacy of a most peculiar sort.[36] (Keep in mind that these tests were meant to measure intellectual *ability*, not intellectual *achievement*.) For example, one Army test included the following multiple-choice question: "The *Pierce Arrow car* is made in *Buffalo, Detroit, Toledo, [or] Flint*."[37] Despite these flaws, many eugenicists cited the results of such tests as proof that the nation's "racial" health was rapidly deteriorating. Sanger herself referred to the tests when she said, "Eugenists demonstrate that two-thirds of our manhood of military age are physically too unfit to shoulder a rifle."[38]

Sanger's facility in reciting the eugenic line on many issues indicates her familiarity with eugenic literature and her desire to be part of the eugenic mainstream. Despite Davenport's coldness toward her and her cause, due to his distaste of activist propagandizing, Sanger never ceased appealing for his involvement in her various conferences. The old guard did not recognize that it would be Sanger who would make eugenics into a world-historical force. She completed the turn toward negative eugenics begun by Davenport. The latter refused an invitation to serve on the board of the Birth Control League of Massachusetts, even though it came to him from the wife of his friend (and Sanger coworker) Edward East.[39] Undaunted by his refusals, Sanger invited him to participate in the Sixth International Neo-Malthusian and Birth Control Conference to be held in 1925 under the auspices of her American Birth Control League; the program she enclosed announced that the conference would be concerned with "all aspects of population problems in relation to birth control," defined as including "biological, eugenical, economic, political and industrial [aspects] and in relation to individual, public, and racial health."[40] As a result of her persistence, he agreed to serve on a roundtable discussion on eugenics and birth control.[41]

Sanger herself saw little difference, positive eugenics aside, between the goals of "professional" eugenicists and those of her own organizations. In 1921, she emphasized, "[T]he campaign for Birth Control is not merely of eugenic value, but is practically identical in ideal with the final aims of Eugenics." In case any doubt might be lingering in the mind of the reader, she added,

> [T]he most urgent problem today is how to limit and discourage the over-fertility of the mentally and physically defective.... Possibly drastic and Spartan methods may be forced upon society if it continues complacently to encourage the chance and chaotic breeding that has resulted from our stupidly cruel sentimentalism.[42]

Sanger was not the only one to make this assessment. Prominent eugenicist and Sanger supporter Henry Pratt Fairchild noted in 1940 that "birth control and eugenics, after some decades of misunderstanding and even friction, today find themselves working in harmony. Each recognizes the indispensability of the other for its own objectives."[43] The two had, according to Fairchild, "drawn so close together as to be almost indistinguishable."[44]

Fairchild's opinion was shared by the official eugenics organizations. In a pamphlet by the American Eugenics Society, the American Birth Control League is listed under the heading "Other Eugenical Organizations," while Sanger's *Birth Control Review* is favorably reviewed for its frequent articles on eugenics.[45] One funder of eugenic projects, the Rockefeller family and its various foundations, seemed to agree that eugenics and Sanger's program were substantially identical, as one internal memo by John D. Rockefeller, Jr.'s staff noted.

> During the last few years there has been a gratifying trend toward a better integration of the work of the [Birth Control] Federation [of America], the National Committee on Maternal Health, and the American Eugenics Society. While these three agencies are separate and distinct organizations, their programs are of such a complementary nature as to warrant some measure of consideration of Mr. Rockefeller Jr.'s interest in the whole group....[46]

People seeking grants from the Rockefellers also found it prudent to stress the connection between eugenics and contraception. In a letter to John D. Rockefeller 3rd, H. Curtis Wood, Jr., of the eugenic sterilization group Human Betterment Association of America, pointed out, "You will notice that many of the names on our letterhead are familiar as leaders in the Planned Parenthood movement, for the Human Betterment program merely extends Planned Parenthood's basic precept of control of conception by temporary means to include control of a permanent nature by surgical instances."[47]

The strangeness of the coexistence of PPFA's supposed feminism with a eugenics of Wood's variety is made somewhat more understandable when the extent of the involvement of women in eugenics is understood. Although not active in leadership at the national level, women were omnipresent within the movement.[48] They were considered by both Davenport and his British counterpart Karl Pearson to be the ideal eugenic fieldworkers, partly because they were willing to work for little pay and also because they were believed to have the special qualities, such as sympathy and intuition, that the "scientific" fieldwork required. In addition to fieldwork, women who agreed with the ideals of eugenics volunteered their time in organizational roles. They were an especially important presence in the local American groups and in Canada and England.[49] As one scholar explains, "Eugenics seemed a natural part of [the] wider movement to engage the state in new kinds of social reform."[50] As such, eugenics was believed to be consistent with the ideal of social improvement through female activism that the "cultural" feminism of the earlier part of the twentieth century advocated.[51] The presence of women within the elitist eugenic movement indicates the susceptibility of any idealistic enterprise (here, the feminism of the progressive era) to ideological cooptation by the dominant cultural views, and contemporary feminism can overlook this historical lesson only to its peril.[52]

The American Eugenics Society
and Its Activists

As eugenics grew in popularity and power, the need for an umbrella educational group became evident to the movement. Accordingly, the American Eugenics Society (AES) was founded shortly after the Second International Congress of Eugenics in New York City in 1921.[53] Henry Fairfield Osborn was elected president of the congress, while Harry Laughlin served as the chair of the Exhibits Committee.[54] Other driving forces behind the new organization included Irving Fisher and Leon Whitney, the latter acting as its field secretary. Whitney was especially sympathetic to Sanger's cause, seeking out greater cooperation with the American Birth Control League (ABCL) in 1928.[55]

Already by March 1923, the AES was powerful enough to lobby the New York state legislature against a bill that would provide increased educational assistance for mentally disabled children. Laughlin wrote a memo for the AES describing the proposed legislation as completely "anti-eugenic," in that it reduced the amount of money that could be spent on the intelligent. He suggested that the law be amended to ensure the sterilization of the mentally disabled instead. Despite AES maneuvering, the bill passed in its original form.[56]

Although the AES did not prevail in this matter, the 1920s were a flush decade for the group. Eight full-time paid workers staffed the office of the AES, and the society had a budget of $17,000 in 1925, with John D. Rockefeller, Jr., alone giving $10,000 between 1925 and 1926.[57] The eugenics movement's greatest legislative successes were achieved during this time, partly because, as Frederick Osborn later observed, the 1,260 members of the AES in 1930 made up "a veritable blue book of prominent and wealthy men and women...."[58] But by the 1930s, the Great Depression had taken its toll, and money was scarce. It was not until 1936, after the organization had been overhauled under Osborn's leadership, that membership and financial support began to climb again, a trend that continued until the World War II years.[59]

Among the AES-connected eugenicists whom Sanger actively recruited and involved in the early organizational work of her various projects were some of those whom Daniel J. Kevles calls the "eugenic priesthood," responsible for much of the research in eugenic science: Raymond Pearl (whose career will be examined in the next chapter); Clarence C. Little, who served actively in the ABCL as a member of the board of directors and of the consulting committee of the advisory board of the Clinical Research Bureau and as vice president and chairman of the advisory board of the Birth Control Federation of America (BCFA); Henry Pratt Fairchild; and Edward M. East, who was also on the advisory board of the Bureau.[60] In addition, out of the fifty clergymen, scientists, and physicians listed on the National Council of Sanger's ABCL in the 1920s, at least twenty-three were involved at a prominent level in eugenics, either as members of the board of directors of the AES or by otherwise publicly supporting Sanger's eugenics agenda. Among these were Leon J. Cole, Rev. Raymond B. Fosdick, Rabbi Louis L. Mann, Adolf Meyer, Stuart Mudd, and Lothrop Stoddard (who, as we have seen, wrote the inflammatory racist tract *The Rising Tide of Color Against White World Supremacy* and paid a visit to Nazi Germany to witness its Eugenic Supreme Court in action).[61] After the end of Sanger's active involvement with the Planned Parenthood Federation of America (PPFA), various PPFA operatives continued the long tradition of working closely with the AES. In 1958, future PPFA president Alan Guttmacher was the AES vice president, and on the AES board were the following people who were also actively involved with PPFA and/or the International Planned Parenthood Federation (IPPF), as well as population control: Dorothy Brush, Robert C. Cook, Frances Ferguson, Dudley Kirk, Clyde V. Kiser, Frank Lorimer, Emily H. Mudd, and Warren S. Thompson.[62]

Sociologist Henry Pratt Fairchild is an especially interesting case. He was one of the incorporators of the AES in 1926 and its president from 1929 to 1930; one scholar observes that he was "clearly part of the inner core of the Society's leadership."[63] He was also one of the strongest eugenic advocates for population control, his book *People: The Quantity and Quality of Population* typifying the ideology of those involved in promoting eugenics, population control, and contraception.[64] He attended Sanger's World Population Conference in Geneva in 1927 and co-founded the Population Association of America in 1931 before serving as its first president.[65] He was also quite active within Sanger's various organizations, especially within the BCFA and its later incarnation as PPFA, even acting as vice president from 1939 to 1948.[66] As we will see in the fourth chapter, Fairchild was as adept as Sanger in synthesizing the birth-control, population-control and eugenics movements.

In addition to individual activists such as these, the American Eugenics Society officially supported many of Sanger's activities, especially while she was lobbying Congress in the 1930s for a federal bill that would mandate birth-control instruction to all families on relief. By May 1932 the AES had officially endorsed her National Committee on Federal Legislation for Birth Control (NCFLBC), while they formally joined her lobbying efforts in 1933 by sending officers to testify at her hearings and pledging complete support of her efforts.[67] This support should come as no surprise, given that the AES's eight-member "Committee on Eugenics and Dysgenics of Birth Regulation" was made up of Sanger coworkers Robert L. Dickinson and Guy Irving Burch (a Sanger lobbyist), with the majority of the rest serving on her advisory committee. Regarding the eugenic testimony that she solicited, Sanger said once to Leon Whitney, "I very much want your organization represented at our hearing, for certainly the eugenic aspect must be brought out...."[68] Continuing on as a dues-paying member even when she was no longer active in the birth-control movement and when any need for maintaining pragmatic connections had long since passed, she remained committed to the American Eugenics Society to the end of her life.[69]

Eugenics Between the World Wars

The 1920s was perhaps the most fruitful decade of legislative activism for the eugenics cause. During this time, eugenicists took advantage of (and often fomented) nativist fears and prejudices in order to pass anti-immigration legislation, while the AES's Harry Laughlin worked feverishly to promote eugenic sterilization laws.[70] During the 1930s, the great human misery brought about by the Great Depression and the resulting increase in government spending on the poor inflamed resentment, with the result that eugenicists found an audience quite willing to reassure itself that the economic misfortune befalling others was due simply to bad heredity.[71] Since eugenicists began to have a growing awareness of the eugenic value of controlling population growth, they continued to work closely with both Sanger and also with population-control groups such as Fairchild's Population Association of America.[72]

Among the fears raised by the Great Depression was the specter of "relief babies," the product of welfare-dependent families with an above-average birthrate.[73] In order to call attention to this "differential birthrate," Sanger's National Committee for Federal Legislation for Birth Control hosted the "American Conference of Birth Control and National Recovery" in 1934. Among the presentations was "Sickness, Unemployment and Differential Fertility" by Edgar Sydenstricker and G. St. J. Perrott of the Milbank Memorial Fund, who stated that unemployment during the Depression was not so much a result of difficult economic times as it was a sign of an "inability to succeed in the severe competition for jobs brought about by the depression."[74] In other words, Sydenstricker and Perrott assume a social Darwinism: unemployment signals an innate inferiority rather than the vicissitudes of the market. They conclude that their findings support "the conclusion to which Margaret Sanger, as an observant social worker among the poor, came to years ago. For the families in the least fortunate, least efficient group of the population whose problems are aggravated by heedless fertility, birth control should take its proper place not only as a medical prescription but as an important social means...."[75] This conference was held at the time during which Sanger was lobbying to mandate birth-control instruction to all families receiving government assistance.

Reflecting similar anxiety over differential fertility was Guy Irving Burch, the eugenicist and anti-immigration activist, who worked for the NCFLBC while running the Population Reference Bureau (PRB) in Washington, D.C. Burch was not renowned for his own intelligence, as Arthur W. Packard, the Rockefeller Foundation's point man on contraception, population control, and eugenics, jotted down in an internal memo: "Burch, we understand to be a likeable, earnest individual of very limited intellectual capacity not outstanding as a population expert, and the Population Reference Bureau constitutes primarily a job for him. It is pretty much a one man show made to look more pretentious with names which are purely honorary in their relation."[76] Regardless of his own limited intelligence, Burch felt quite justified in viewing the intelligence of others as inferior based on their class, race, or nationality, and he explained that his interest in birth control was purely eugenic: on NCFLBC letterhead, he wrote that he had worked to prevent sound American stock from "being replaced by alien or negro stock, whether it be by immigration or by overly high birth rates among others in this country."[77] These types, he complained, were "poverty-stricken [and] rapidly-breeding people" whom he compared to a "cancerous growth that eats away the vital organs of its victim." He warned that "in three generations ... the descendants of the so-called 'have nots' will be sixteen times as numerous as the descendants of an equal number of so-called 'haves,'" and this differential was due, he believed, to the fact that the "have nots" did not have knowledge of birth control. Contraception was the answer to the problem of "human erosion" in the "health, intelligence, and possibly the heredity of the Nation...."[78] Warren Thompson, himself a demographer and eugenicist, thought that Burch was extreme even for a eugenicist, but Sanger herself supported him in setting up the Population Reference Bureau and also interceded with the Birth Control Federation of America to find him a job in 1939.[79]

Sentiments similar to Burch's were also found among the other bureaucrats within Sanger's organizations. D. Kenneth Rose, the national director of the BCFA, utilized comparable scare tactics in 1942, when he argued, "Planned Parenthood must be understood first, as a major health force, second as a vital contributor to social adjustment and security, and by reason of these two factors— it becomes a matter of tremendous economic significance to the family unit, the community and the nation."[80] Why, according to Rose, was PPFA of such economic importance? Because "one-third of our population — the ill-fed, ill-clothed, ill-housed [is] producing two thirds of all our children."[81] The solution, for Rose, was to increase outreach to "the Negro and our migrant population."[82]

Like Rose, many eugenicists advocated immigration control because of an ingrained racism that equated members of certain racial groups with the "unfit." Among these eugenicists were Madison Grant and Lothrop Stoddard, designated the nation's two most influential racists by one historian,[83] as well as David Starr Jordan, Robert DeCourcy Ward, and Prescott Hall of the Immigrant Restriction League. These eugenicists, helped by the tireless lobbying efforts of Sanger colleague Harry Laughlin, who was named the "Expert Eugenic Agent" of the House Committee on Immigration and Naturalization in the early 1920s, enabled the passage through Congress of the 1924 Immigration Act. This piece of legislation was designed, as one congressman put it, for the purpose of "purifying and keeping pure the blood of America."[84] The fact that Sanger tolerated the racism of Laughlin and Stoddard, as well as the fact that both Laughlin and Stoddard believed her cause to be eugenically beneficial, indicates that her ideology of control was not too far removed, at least in outcome, from the more outrageous racism of many eugenicists.[85]

In addition to immigration control, by the 1920s eugenicists were beginning to see that population control could be used to slow the reproduction of people with physical and cognitive disabilities.[86] For example, biologist Edward M. East and statistician Raymond Pearl were among those who advocated a eugenic examination of population growth, and they were both important academic resources for Sanger when she planned and convened the first conference devoted to population problems in 1927.[87] As we will see in the fourth and fifth chapters, this interest in population control would continue among eugenicists and be further refined with the growth of demography.

World War II and Its Aftermath

As we have seen in the last chapter, it is widely believed that eugenics died out as a result of the revelations of the Nazi atrocities. Yet historians of eugenics have found that the 1930s, not the late 1940s and 1950s, constituted the low point in eugenic research, since it was during the years

of the Great Depression that money dried up for eugenics, while many
geneticists came forward to criticize eugenics as it was then conceived.[88]
(However, this criticism has perhaps been exaggerated by scholars; Mehler
points out that the number of well-respected scientists on the AES Advisory Council *increased* between 1923 and 1935.)[89] By the late 1940s and
early 1950s, the general climate of the post–World War II culture reacted
strongly against eugenics, but there is little evidence that this caused any
change in the basic attitude of professional eugenicists, only curtailing
their public advocacy of the movement out of prudence. Indeed, eugenics continued to be popular among geneticists after World War II, so much
so that one scholar has emphasized that "'eugenics' in the 1950s still
retained positive connotations for many scientists and their sponsors."[90]
Any reduction in the popularity of the eugenic ideology immediately after
the war among scientists was counter-balanced by new enthusiasm for
genetics prompted by Watson and Crick's discovery in 1953 of DNA's dou-
ble-helix structure, as well as by the growing concern at the dawn of the
nuclear age over the deleterious effects of radiation upon humanity's
genetic heritage.[91]

As we have seen, Sanger's organizations utilized the occasion of the
war to rally eugenic support to their cause. In 1940, the Birth Control Federation of America held a forum entitled "Race Building in a Democracy."
The very title reflects Sanger's eugenic complaint, expressed much earlier
in her life, that democratic societies should not allow the unfit to vote:

> The danger of recruiting our numbers from the most "fertile stocks" is fur-
> ther emphasized when we recall that in a democracy like that of the United
> States every man and woman is permitted a vote in the government, and
> that it is the representatives of this grade of intelligence who may destroy
> our liberties, and who may thus be the most far-reaching peril to the future
> of civilization.[92]

Among other speakers, the forum featured eugenicists Henry Pratt
Fairchild and Frederick Osborn. Fairchild's talk, later reprinted as a pamphlet by the BCFA, called for "a drastic improvement in the human material itself with which society has to deal." This improvement had to entail
"not merely the elimination of the obviously unfit, mentally or emotion-
ally. The whole average of society must be lifted to a higher level."[93]

Two years later, it should be remembered, Alan Valentine broadened
the message of societal improvement through eugenics to include themes
specific to wartime. Postulating that victory in the war was for the purpose of supporting the "good life," he claims, "Americans have always conceived that good life in terms of health, intelligence, free opportunity and

domestic tranquility, and in terms of a more perfect union. These conceptions are to be realized through elevating the quality of American citizens, — all of them."[94] Yet such quality could not be attained, he argued, if society would not become efficient "in eliminating low quality by preventive measures. We have not attacked poor quality at its source." Before wasting billions of dollars in social support, Valentine argued, the nation must first work to "improve our citizens at their source."[95]

Elsewhere, the BCFA stated explicitly that eugenic improvement was necessary for the sake of democracy. One pamphlet featured the large heading "Democracy Needs Quality" and went on to make the following eugenic argument:

> Our democracy, in the face of the forces within, as well as without, which threaten its existence, can hope to endure only so long as the quality of our people is maintained. To contribute directly and effectively to raising the quality of our people *in every walk of life*— that is the great fundamental aim of the birth control movement.[96]

Clearly, eugenic ideals could be used to serve both fascist and "democratic" jingoism.

The aftermath of the war not only did not sway Sanger and her colleagues from their eugenic ideals, it actually allowed eugenicists to hide under the cloak of progressivism regarding race relations. The genocidal anti–Semitism of Nazism ultimately defined its form of eugenics. As a result, given the link in the public mind between eugenics and Nazism, there arose a significant amount of confusion about the true nature of eugenics— a simple conflation of eugenics and genocide — to such a degree that it is still assumed today that, if the latter is not present, then the former could not be present either.[97] In this way, Planned Parenthood has often succeeded in arguing that Sanger was not a eugenicist because she was not an anti–Semite. Yet, as we have seen, eugenics is not synonymous with anti–Semitism; indeed, many Jews were also eugenicists, both before and after World War II, including Sanger's clinic doctors, Hannah and Abraham Stone.[98]

As I have indicated, scholars have shown that, even in the 1950s, "*eugenics* was not yet a term of opprobrium among scientists and would not be until the 1960s."[99] One contemporary eugenicist, Richard Lynn, even argues eugenics did not peak until 1963, when several prominent, Nobel prize–winning geneticists argued for eugenics at the Ciba Conference. One of these, none other than Francis Crick, insisted that a system of licensing parents should be set up, so that only the "fit" reproduce, while a tax on children could be used effectively to discourage the "dysgenic" poor from becoming parents.[100] Clearly, scientific ability need not coexist with ethical sensitivity. Yet, if medical professionals and scientists did not reject the eugenic ideology, the general public was a different matter, given the revelations of the Nazi eugenic program. As a result, the standard legislative agenda of eugenic sterilization, immigration laws, and so forth was increasingly difficult to enact.

Scholars have noted that the more hostile post-war environment of the larger culture led eugenicists such as Frederick Osborn to cut their losses by purging the movement of its more virulently racist rhetoric and focusing its efforts on the promotion of birth control and genetic research.[101] One historian compares Osborn's leadership of the AES to the latter's prudence in business: "Osborn set out to turn a failing venture — the American eugenics movement — into a successful operation. This he did by making cosmetic changes ... and by spreading money around liberally to younger scholars of promise."[102] Any lingering concern on the part of positive eugenicists about the inadvisability of allowing the "fit" to have free access to contraception was countered by the awareness that, first, birth control was there to stay, and, second, other, more coercive means of eugenic control were slowly becoming less and less feasible as the public mood shifted inexorably away from anything resembling Nazi tactics. Mehler argues convincingly that the agenda of the "new" reformed eugenics was fundamentally continuous with that of the "old," with the exception that emphasis was placed on the propagandizing of eugenic principles rather than on imposing eugenic measures legislatively, so that people come to choose eugenic measures "freely" instead of being forced into them. Osborn remained committed, however, to such coercive eugenic measures as the sterilization of "hereditary defectives" (the AES had even endorsed the Nazi sterilization program in 1937).[103] Osborn also was unable to completely purge racism even from his own thinking, since he continued to fret about the high birthrates of Native Americans and Mexicans.[104]

While Osborn still promoted positive eugenics, the science of human genetics with its more professional and scholarly appearance allowed for an incremental, "negative" influence on the reproductive behavior of individuals, in that genetic data could be used in genetic counseling. As I will show later in this chapter, genetic counseling was initiated and practiced by eugenicists for eugenic reasons from the beginning, and it depended for its success upon the voluntary use of contraception and (later) abortion in order to prevent or eliminate any "unfit" offspring that might result. Thus, eugenics depended upon subterfuge for its survival: eugenic goals could be achieved without public outcry as long as the word "eugenics" did not appear in connection with eugenic activities. Over thirty years after this strategy was put into play, Osborn could look back on the preceding decades with some satisfaction and say, "Birth control and abortion are turning out to be great eugenic advances of our time. If they had been advanced for eugenic reasons it would have retarded or stopped their acceptance."[105]

Another very important means of effecting eugenic control was population control: if the public would not accept coerced sterilization on the grounds that it was eugenic, maybe they would accept it when it was done with another, more apocalyptic rationale, such as the imminent destruction of human society through population growth. Of course, this was just eugenics by another name. Population control had been connected with eugenics since the Neo-Malthusians, and this link was given a new justification after World War II with Hermann Muller's hypothesis of "genetic load." He argued that every animal carried a load of genetic mutations that occurred as a result of environmental influences. In modern times, the burden of the genetic load has become much heavier: at an earlier time, humans with an unusually high level of mutations (namely, the unfit) would die before reproducing, but now they tend to be able to survive longer and pass on their defective genes; in addition, the genetic load of mutations is now greater than before, due to radiation and other environmental problems. The answer was to reduce overall population in the hopes of preventing a continuing degradation of the race's genetic stock, while encouraging the intelligent to reproduce; in this way, the overall level of the race's genes could perhaps be raised. (As Daniel Kevles put it, the theory of genetic load "formed a central tenet in the reform-eugenic response to the population explosion."[106]) Muller called this approach "Germinal Choice."[107] A rather odd example of Muller's positive eugenic ideology was the "Sperm Bank," as it is commonly known, founded by Muller and by millionaire Robert K. Graham of California, which at first gathered only Nobel laureates' sperm. (Presumably the gametes of Nobel prize winners are more resistant to radioactive mutations.) Among the eugenicists who encouraged the Sperm Bank's formation were Frederick Osborn and Sanger coworker C. P. Blacker.[108] The Sperm Bank closed in 1999.

Whatever dip in popularity that eugenics might have suffered among scientists was clearly overcome by 1969, when scientists such as Robert Sinsheimer — later one of the first initiators of the Human Genome Project — claimed that a "new eugenics" had arisen due to increased scientific sophistication in genetics, soon to be accompanied by genetic engineering breakthroughs such as recombinant DNA technology.[109] He argued, "The old genetics was limited to a numerical enhancement of the best of our existing gene pool. The new eugenics would permit in principle the conversion of all the unfit to the highest genetic level."[110]

Quickly, a number of old eugenic ideas were given a new lease on life. Among the revived ideas was the old eugenic insistence on the primary role of heredity in intelligence; the foundation of this new eugenic focus on intelligence was the work of British eugenicist and psychologist Cyril Burt. In several studies of identical twins raised in different homes in the decades between 1940 and 1970, Burt claimed to have determined that, despite differences in environmental rearing, the twins showed a marked similarity in intelligence. These studies were quite influential, despite later proof that the data were substantially fabricated.[111] For example, in 1969, Arthur R. Jensen published an article based in large measure on Burt's work, arguing that differences in IQ between whites and blacks were largely determined by their respective genetic inheritance.[112] Jensen's work probably influenced Nobel prize–winning scientist William Shockley, who in 1969 called for research into "dysgenic" trends in America (meaning the higher birthrate of the poor) and in 1971 proposed a system of financial incentives for the sterilization of persons of low intelligence.[113] Jensen and Shockley were among the most prominent and controversial of the scientists who came out strongly in favor of old eugenic policies in the late 1960s and 1970s, yet even the sober National Academy of Sciences wrote a report in 1968 entitled *Biology and the Future of Man*, which closed with the rousing appeal: "Now he can guide his own evolution.... At last, he is Man. May he behave so!"[114]

The 1980s, 1990s, and the beginning of the new century have seen not only a resurgence of eugenic activity (as the last section of this chapter will show), but also a rehabilitation of the label "eugenics," which had previously been publicly taboo. As one correspondent to the *British Medical Journal* recently observed serenely, "Those who condemn eugenics may actually be a minority."[115] This turn of events may be partly due to the success of the Human Genome Project (HGP), shorthand for the astonishing project to identify the entire nucleotide sequence of human DNA. The HGP in America was a coordinated scientific effort organized by the National Institutes of Health's Office for Human Genome Research in 1988.[116] The project raised ethical questions, in part because, as C. Thomas Caskey puts it, "The genome project will significantly affect our ability to screen for diseases at birth, during pregnancy, and in all stages of adult life."[117] Among those who both recognized and supported the HGP's eugenic potential was Daniel Koshland, former editor of *Science*, who insisted, "The costs of mental illness, the difficult civil liberties problems they cause, the pain to the individual all cry out for an early solution that involves prevention, not caretaking."[118]

All in all, a noticeable shift in the acceptability of genetically deter-ministic explanations has been observed on the part of scientists.[119] Yet, as Evelyn Fox Keller has pointed out, scientific beliefs concerning these matters are as susceptible to socio-cultural influences as they are to labo-ratory results; scientists do not work in an ideological vacuum any more than do other professionals. Thus, the grandiose prediction of the National Academy of Sciences report of 1968 that humanity can now guide its future evolution did not arise from any known potential of molecular biology, a science that was still in its infancy at the time. Instead, what guided the Sinsheimers and Shockleys of the 1960s and 1970s was a prior commitment to a certain array of sociological, ethical, and philosophical beliefs con-cerning the role of science and the nature of "Man" (and, we might add, woman). These beliefs, in turn, served to influence the attitudes and research goals of later scientists, thereby setting up an entrenched eugenic ideology. Keller notes that visions of a genetic utopia "can be seen as expressions of a kind of intentionality; as such, they actively contributed to the construction of future scientific reality."[120]

This eugenic intentionality has had a ripple effect as it has been sim-plified and transmitted in the popular media. At the non-scientific level, eugenic vocabulary has become more prevalent. A "housewife and former nurse" recently told a survey collector in Great Britain, "Carriers [of genetic diseases] should not breed."[121] The best-selling book *The Bell Curve* liberally uses "eugenic" and "dysgenic" as though they were objective sci-entific terms.[122] A professor emeritus of psychology, Richard Lynn, wrote a popularizing book entitled *Dysgenics* that explicitly restates the old eugenic contention (uttered by Sanger and others) that contraceptive use is a sign of a person's superior intelligence, education, and character, not to mention his or her superior social class, and he claims that not only intel-ligence but also "conscientiousness" and other character traits are inher-ited.[123] These claims are to be found in a book published in 1996.

This resurgence of scientific eugenics has not been *directly* dependent on Sanger and Planned Parenthood, just as the older, scientific eugenics of the 1920s was not dependent on the birth-control "activists," and such eugenicists frequently put distance between themselves and Sanger. Yet Planned Parenthood bears much responsibility for the present state: its institutional power far exceeded (and exceeds) that of any other organi-zation of eugenic inspiration and kept eugenics alive during the leaner times by advancing eugenic goals and making them respectable. As the next chapter will show, many high-level coworkers of Margaret Sanger shared her commitment to the eugenic ideology and program, and she gave them a public platform, allowing them to form PPFA's agenda accordingly. By contributing to the perpetuation of the eugenic intentionality on the activist level and, more importantly, by encouraging and executing eugenic "solutions" to the problems of poverty, disability, and disease, Planned Parenthood did its part to keep eugenics alive. When later technology allowed for the selective elimination of the eugenically "unfit," PPFA was poised to supply the organizational machinery to carry out this activity. In this matter, Planned Parenthood is institutionally guilty.

Eugenics Today

The "new eugenics" claims to be different from the "old," oppressive eugenics in several ways: for example, one proponent has argued, "This eugenics will have several characteristics that the old eugenics did not have: the new eugenics will be benevolent and learned, painless and efficient."[124] Yet the old eugenics considered itself to have all of those qualities: it was supported by most of the best genetic scientists of the age; it advocated painless measures such as surgical sterilization; and it believed itself to be the kind and rational alternative to charity. Nevertheless, other apologists for the new eugenics naively insist, "The difference between the new eugenics and the eugenics of the Nazi era is that we do not brand individual lives as worthless because of genetic make-up, and our society continues to devote resources to the care of individuals born with inherited diseases." Their conclusion is that we can congratulate ourselves for living in such a "benevolent society."[125] Yet many people with disabilities and illnesses would strongly disagree with the breezy assumption that they receive adequate health care, as I will show.

These scientists assume that the "old" eugenics always looked like Nazism and therein lay its faults. Thus, the reasoning goes, if the "new" eugenics does not look like Nazism, it must not be ethically problematic.[126] Yet eugenics, especially in America, did not often involve obvious violence or outspoken hatred; indeed, some of the "feebleminded" women who were sterilized did not even know that the procedure had occurred (they were often told that another, medically necessary operation, such as an appendectomy, was being performed) until they discovered that they could not have children later in life. Was there any less real violation of these women's rights and dignity in such cases than if they had been rounded up into sterilization camps? In other words, the injustices perpetrated in the name of eugenics were and are often less spectacular than we might expect, but not for all that are they any less threatening to the powerless. Wearing a benevolent mask, they are in fact more insidious.

Conflating the old eugenics with Nazism serves the ideological function of immunizing the new eugenics from critical examination. But, of course, Nazi brutality hardly exhausts the ways of violating the powerless. Outright coercion did not generally characterize the eugenics movement of the first half of the twentieth century. That the "new" eugenics does not generally have recourse to outright coercion therefore does not settle the question of its ethical status. So, is there any significant material discontinuity between an old and new eugenics? To judge the case requires some substantive notion of what eugenics is, and this is where the heuristic definition proposed at the beginning of this chapter becomes clearly necessary: eugenics is an ideology of control that views the human individual more as a locus of genetic potential and peril than as a person worthy of respect. The threat posed by eugenics to the human rights of supposedly genetically problematic persons is just as real now as before. Ethical deficiency is inherent in the ideology. (I have also argued for the material continuity of the "old" and "new" eugenics by tracing the perduring institutional realization of Sanger's vision, especially in PPFA and IPPF.)

Part of the difficulty in seeing the threat posed by the "new" eugenics comes from an overly narrow understanding of coercion. One option that we will name "libertarian" is to see coercion only when there is active "interference" with a person's willed acts.[127] But a more critical perspective is also possible, one that refuses to view the willing person as a monadic island of choice insulated from larger environmental conditions. According to this understanding, a *situation* can be coercive, even when overt force is not applied.[128] It recognizes that social controls can exercise almost as powerful an influence as violent compulsion.[129] Whether the coercion be exercised through the withholding of economic resources for parents, especially single mothers, who wish to carry a child with disabilities to term or through subtle (or sometimes explicit) anti-child and anti-disability propaganda, the powerful, the elite, advances its interests through the deployment of social power, including the control of the conditions of knowledge production: what counts as obviously true, for example, about disability, about sex, about women, about children and convenience. Society bombards us with too many prejudiced value judgments concerning beauty, success, and worth for us to easily remain critically minded about these issues. The eugenics and population-control movements have always recognized this fact. Thus, groups such as Planned Parenthood frequently engage in million-dollar ad campaigns to sway public opinion; other population-control groups have hired musicians or filmmakers to propagandize for contraception in developing countries.[130] Thus, the coercive eugenic attitude is realized less by employment of overt force (although that is sometimes also present) than by strategies that seek to bend the "unfit" woman's will by disseminating messages about the undesirability of children and, often, providing monetary incentives to make the "right" decision.[131] Similarly, disability activists complain that genetic counselors usually focus much more on the burdens and hypothetical problems of raising children with disabilities than on the joys and concrete experiences of the disabled community.[132] Such counseling could count as "non-directive" only to a person in thrall to ideology.

The rest of this section will examine various manifestations of eugenics in contemporary society, focusing on eugenic attitudes toward genetic counseling and selective abortion.[133] I will show how eugenic rhetoric has made a resurgence, while technological advances have enabled the realization of the eugenic program to a degree only dreamed of by the early eugenicists.[134]

Persons with Disabilities and Genetic Counseling

It is to be hoped that we would have come a long way from the bigoted attitudes of earlier eugenicists regarding persons with disabilities. After all, the disability-rights movement has made significant progress in raising awareness about the dignity of the disabled, as well as the unnecessary societal difficulties imposed upon them. Yet it could be argued that the contemporary moment is as dangerous a time as ever to be disabled.

Eugenic attitudes toward the disabled persist. Among health and human services providers, with whom the disabled must often interact, research has shown endorsement of eugenic principles increases in proportion to the severity of mental disability in their clients.[135] There are scientists who complain about the fact that disabled people can now live long enough to have children, one geneticist calling it a "significant problem in genetic research."[136] This presentation of the reproductive activity of the disabled as genetically problematic echoes decades-old eugenic rhetoric; as Alan F. Guttmacher had put it, regarding diabetics, "The fecundity suddenly bestowed upon the diabetic in 1922 by the boon of insulin is not a pure blessing, certainly not a genetic blessing."[137]

As the last chapter showed, Dr. Guttmacher was never a friend of those eugenic targets, the disabled and the poor. The statement just quoted reveals the fundamental problem with his attitude and that of others in the control movements, especially physicians: they view disabled people as diseases, first and foremost, reducing their humanity and personhood to an afterthought.[138] We can recognize the basic attitude of eugenics here, given our heuristic definition. Against this lethal ideology stand those who defend the inherent dignity of the disabled. For example, disability advocate Kathleen O. Steel argues that the use of genetic screening to find and abort disabled fetuses does not qualify as preventive medicine, in that the abortions do not prevent the cause of the disease but the birth of the one suffering the disease. In other words, the individual is subsumed by the disease, so that death counts as a "cure"—but for whom? In arguing against this use of genetic counseling, she says, "It is difficult to feel that discrimination does not exist when a branch of medicine is intent on eradicating disabled people."[139] Steel's comment is harsh and seems extreme; after all, the motto of most genetic counseling services is "autonomy," through the expansion of the patient's reproductive choices. Yet, as is true with the "new eugenics" as a whole, the use of the rhetoric of autonomy does not guarantee truly free decision-making (quite aside from the question of the autonomy of the genetically impaired—or, shall we say, dysgenic—fetus).

In order to understand sufficiently the current state of genetic counseling, a brief examination of its origins is necessary. As was so often the case in the history of eugenics, it has its origins not in scientific creativity but in the prejudices of a few rich men. The first person to propose a genetic counseling center was James G. Eddy, who made his money in lumbering. Interested in plant genetics, he expanded his scientific curiosity to humans in 1939, when he approached the American Eugenics Society with the offer of funding a genetic counseling center. Osborn respected Eddy but decided that AES was not able to carry out the proposal.[140]

The AES, however, certainly approved of genetic counseling as a helpful eugenic activity. In a report describing the organization's program in the 1950s, as much is stated.

> Heredity counseling is laying the groundwork for public acceptance of the eugenic idea, and this gives it an importance even beyond its value to the individual couples to whom it is directed.[141]

Consequently, the AES held a conference on hereditary counseling in 1957.[142]

By this time, genetic counseling had already been established for seventeen years at the University of Minnesota by another wealthy man, physician Charles Fremont Dight. He wanted the clinic, later named the Dight Institute, to "promote biological race betterment," an aim which the clinic itself echoed in its institutional bulletin when it complained, "Very little is being done to protect our social system ... in respect to these dysgenic classes."[143] Not surprisingly, Dight was also involved with the Minnesota Birth Control League, an affiliate of Sanger's American Birth Control League. The first academic department of medical genetics in America, at the Bowman-Gray School of Medicine in North Carolina, was funded by another anti-immigrant eugenicist and population-controller, Wicliffe C. Draper (the founder of the Pioneer Fund), who made his fortune in New England in the textile industry.[144]

The eugenic ideals of the founders were reflected in those who worked in the clinics. One historian notes that "throughout the 1960s, most of the leading figures in medical genetics ... bluntly described their work as a form of eugenics."[145] The eugenic aim of heredity counseling led to overtly directive "counseling." For example, Lee R. Dice, the first director of the Dight Institute, insisted, "We must give due concern to the possibility of eliminating, or, perhaps, of perpetuating, undesirable or desirable genes. *We must not only be concerned with the particular family concerned but also with whether or not harmful heredity may be continued or spread in our population.*"[146]

The results of genetic screening have been manifold, many of them perhaps unforeseen. The original clinics could little more than guess at the likelihood of a certain couple bearing children with particular diseases. But once prenatal testing such as amniocentesis allowed an accurate assessment of a fetus's genetic state, selective abortion of disabled fetuses (sometimes called "search-and-destroy" abortions) could be done, ensuring that fewer children with disabilities would be born.[147] I will examine this procedure in the next section; here, I will present other, less well-known effects of a greater reliance upon genetic screening.

As one study notes, "Genetic discrimination exists and is manifested in many social institutions, especially in the health and life insurance industries."[148] "Genetic discrimination" has been defined as the "discrimination against an individual or against members of that individual's family solely because of real or perceived differences from the 'normal' genome in the genetic constitution of that individual."[149] What this definition concretely means can be illustrated by examining a few cases of genetic discrimination.

Problems usually arise when a genetic test done at some point in a person's life reveals a hereditary condition. The person concerned might not even have the disease; he or she might simply be a carrier of the gene. Yet the presence of any kind of genetic abnormality, whether affecting the carrier or not, can be enough to condemn the person involved to poverty; one study noted that all but two of the forty-one incidents of discrimination studied affected the victim's insurance or employment. Among the incidents reported: an unaffected carrier of Gaucher's disease was denied a government job; a man with Charcot-Marie-Tooth disease (which need not even cause serious disability) was denied auto insurance; a television newswoman in Los Angeles with ectrodactyly (the absence of some digits) was publicly criticized for getting pregnant, because she risked passing on her condition to her child; the United States Air Force used to prevent carriers of sickle-cell anemia from becoming pilots; and some insurance companies in New York State denied sickle-cell carriers health and life insurance.[150] (Here is another case of the concrete convergence of eugenics and racism.)

Soon genetic information might be made even more widely available, because one result of widespread genetic testing has been the development of DNA data banks. A scholar reports, "Information related to genetic labeling may enter large-scale data banks now used to store personal health-related information. Individuals' health profiles, which can include genetic conditions, are available privately and are generated in a manner similar to the ubiquitous credit checks encountered in business.... Genetic data on certain groups within our society are already being stored by governmental agencies."[151]

As the examples of insurers and employers show, one should not underestimate the role of economic motivations in the practices of those involved with genetic counseling. Among those who stand to gain financially from the decision to utilize genetic counseling include doctors, who hope to escape possible malpractice suits from upset parents of newborns with disabilities; biotechnology companies, which produce the testing equipment; and governments and insurance agencies, which have to pay for potentially expensive care for the disabled.[152] As always, economic motives have the potential to squash any ethical squeamishness, so that human life is submitted to some utilitarian calculus—inevitably lethal for marginalized persons.

"Search-and-Destroy" Abortions

The attitudes toward the disabled described above cannot but make their presence felt during the decision-making process of parents who are considering the abortion of a fetus with a disability.[153] "Treatment" for disability in these cases has come to be defined as the elimination of disabled fetuses, an approach that is seen as far more cost-effective than the expensive, lengthy process of caring for persons with disabilities or developing scientific cures.

The whole concept of "genetic disease" is a fairly recent one, and the idea has been embraced to provide a rationale for continuing to devote resources to genetic research and technology. However, as Keller has shown, the ability to use genetic technology for treatment is probably decades away. She says, "Thus, 'treatment' is at best a long-term goal, and 'prevention' means preventing the births of individuals diagnosed as genetically aberrant — in a word, it means abortion."[154] For example, the federal government's promotion of amniocentesis in the 1970s was motivated by an attitude that viewed search-and-destroy abortions as a primary means of "preventive" care. As Theodore Cooper, then assistant secretary of the Department of Health, Education, and Welfare, wrote in an internal report in 1975, "By focusing on prevention, we increase the resources available for other programs. Few advances compare with amniocentesis in their capability for prevention of disability."[155] Only the basic eugenic attitude could thus confuse prevention of a disability with the elimination of the disabled.

Many physicians and scientists have echoed Cooper's flawed reasoning, which equates the eradication of diseases with the eradication of the people who have those diseases. Walter Glannon has recently argued that "genetically defective" fetuses should be aborted, given that "severe disability" makes "their lives not worth living for them on the whole,"[156] eerily echoing the Nazi condemnation of "life unworthy of life." One doctor acknowledges, "The physician's role in genetic counseling is to insure the birth of unaffected children in those families which are at risk for genetic disease. Essentially, genetic counseling is the cornerstone of current genetic therapy...."[157] By admitting the degree to which his own biases affect counseling, with its *raison d'être* of disease "prevention," this doctor reveals that counseling's vaunted "non-directiveness" can never be guaranteed, especially if the individual counselor has his or her own eugenic axes to grind.

In fact, one commentator has noted that support is growing for explicitly directive — that is, manipulative — counseling in cases where a fetus is found to have a genetic disease. A recent British study indicates that many professionals in a counseling role often decide what would be in the pregnant woman's "best interest" and coerce their decision accordingly.[158] Indeed, the idea of clinics undergoing an audit of their "genetic services" has been floated. According to this proposal, a genetic clinic would lose its funding unless it shows that the number of births of individuals with a particular genetic disease is declining by means of increased abortions. In this vision of things, "success" means the increased abortion of fetuses with disabilities. The author sums up the situation by pointing out that "the notion [of counseling's aim] has now shifted to a cost-effective or utilitarian method." In other words, the field of genetic counseling is beginning to explicitly recognize what disabled activists have said all along, that its supposed "non-directiveness" really is motivated by the desire to save money or to eliminate "defective" genes through the elimination of persons with disabilities.[159]

Among all Americans, the acceptance of selective abortion of disabled fetuses in the first trimester ranges between 75 percent and 87 percent (although the percentage drops to only 10–20 percent when second-trimester abortions are at issue), a testament to the effective dissemination of eugenic ideology.[160] And some professional geneticists have moved from acceptance of to agitation for search-and-destroy abortions: Margery Shaw, a prominent geneticist and former head of the American Society of Human Genetics, states that a "defective fetus" should not "be allowed to be born," and she wants to put the power of the law behind her directive.[161] With regard to the non-treatment or even starvation of newborns with disabilities, Sir Douglas Black, past president of the Royal College of Physicians in Great Britain, said, "[I]t would be ethical to put a rejected child upon a course of management that would end in its death ... I say that it is ethical that a child suffering from Down's syndrome ... should not survive."[162] The common thread in all of these accounts is a lethal assumption about the quality of life of persons with disabilities: that it would be better not to be born than to live with a disability.

This situation puts a terrible burden on pregnant women. "With genetic selection, the mother becomes the quality control gatekeeper of the gene pool," observes Greg Worlbring, a biochemist and bioethicist. "This is not really choice, it's eugenics."[163] Rayna Rapp has also observed that many women have voluntarily taken on the role of genetic "gate-keeper," in that most genetic counselors are female. She theorizes that they are perhaps internalizing the unspoken paradigm that minding the race's future is "women's work."[164] As we saw in Sanger's groundbreaking account of the relation of "woman" to "the new race" (and as in Nazi Germany), the burden of eugenic responsibility falls squarely on the shoulders of women, and thus they become the target of both propaganda and direct coercion.

Conclusion

"New eugenics" is more eugenic than it is new. As we will see in the next chapter, the "revisionist" eugenicists, and Sanger coworkers, Frederick Osborn in America and C. P. Blacker in England spearheaded a transition from often overtly racist, "unscientific" eugenics to a subtler form that advocated primarily negative eugenics through "voluntary," although heavily propagandized and quietly coerced, choices for birth control, sterilization, and abortion. The basic eugenic attitude remains in place, an island of stability enduring through the tempests of scientific and cultural change.

The eugenics of our day threatens more women than just those with disabilities. The seventh chapter will deal with the elimination of females through abortion or infanticide that is occurring especially in India and China, but also in the United States. A 1991 study reported that 85 percent of genetic counselors in training were willing to participate in fetal sex-selection tests upon request.[165] In this case, as in the whole history of eugenics, the medical community has shown itself to be guided by motives other than a concern for women.

Certainly one central motive is financial. As Diane B. Paul puts it, "One clear lesson from the history of eugenics is this: what may be unthinkable when times are flush may come to seem only good common sense when they are not."[166] As we have seen again and again, the eugenics movement has used arguments based on cost-effectiveness with great success, thereby especially targeting the poor, the disabled, and anyone else who seems to be too financially burdensome in comparison to their projected productivity. Such arguments depend on the assumption made by the powerful and the comfortable that human worth is measured by balance sheets, and woe to that person who comes out in the red. Women have been especially endangered by this sort of rationale, because, in a world in which many women spend their time in "non-productive" household-based work or earn less for equal work outside the home, they invariably come up short in comparison with their more "valuable" male counterparts. This is especially so when reproduction in an antinatalist economy is taken to be antiproductive.

Besides the financial, yet another, deeper motive for eugenic activity lies in the pernicious devaluing of persons with disabilities just because they are disabled. On the January 15, 2001, episode of *Politically Incorrect*, host Bill Maher equated his two dogs with mentally disabled children. "I've often said if I had two retarded children, I'd be a hero, and yet the dogs, which are pretty much the same thing — what?" quipped Maher. Children with disabilities are "sweet," "loving," and "kind, but they don't mentally advance at all.… Dogs are like retarded children."

With greater polish but far more outrageously, Glenn McGee argues that sometimes parents have not just the option but also the *duty* to abort a fetus with severe disabilities,[167] while Peter Singer, awarded an endowed chair at Princeton in (ironically enough) Human Values, claims that parents have the right and even the responsibility to kill an *infant* with disabilities, if it is determined that the child would suffer "too much" and that the parents would have another, non-disabled child to replace the first.[168] What both McGee and Singer want is a revolution in the role of the physician. Whereas the old, Hippocratic tradition has seen the doctor as a healer before all else, the new quality-of-life ethics wants to make the doctor into eugenic gatekeeper, into judge, jury, and executioner, making judgments regarding the potential quality of life of another person. As a eugenicist said back in 1912, "The future physician must largely be an advisory functionary, rather than a dispenser of medicines. And his advice will be solicited not only for the individual and for the present, but for the race and for the future."[169]

With a technocratic mindset holding sway and a widespread acceptance of libertarianism and utilitarianism, how can the threat to the powerless posed by the eugenics of our day be resisted? Some feminists have advocated an extreme version of individualistic autonomy; for them, the way to oppose eugenic control is to assert an unfettered right to reproductive decision-making. The trouble with this libertarian logic is twofold. First, we have already noted that an uncritical concept of "autonomy" mistakenly assumes that freedom operates in splendid isolation, so that all that is necessary for its successful practice is the presentation of the relevant options. But human freedom does not work this way; its integrity can be compromised by various societal and cultural forces that may be quite inimical to the promotion of human rights.

Second, as a corollary, many disability rights activists have pointed out that the concrete exercise of "autonomy" quickly becomes a power play: the only ones who can exercise autonomy are those with institutional power. So, if a genetic counselor believes that a certain fetus should be aborted, the authority of the counselor's position makes it difficult to see through the subtle manipulation of the facts presented. "Autonomy" becomes the autonomy of institutions to decide the future of the marginalized.

Take, for example, the case made by prominent jurist and political philosopher Ronald Dworkin in favor of legal tolerance of increasingly comprehensive genetic testing and increasingly adventurous genetic experimentation and engineering. He takes his stand on the high-liberal principles of equality and autonomy: his "ethical individualism" holds that, on the one hand, we all have an interest in seeing that "any human life, once begun, succeed rather than fail — that the potential of that life be realized rather than wasted..." and that, on the other hand, each person has a "right to make the fundamental decisions that define, for him, what a successful life would be." Sounds innocuous enough. This defense of personal autonomy would seem to allow, say, the person with disabilities or with a low IQ to have the chance to experience her life as worthwhile. However, when Dworkin parses things out, we find that the first, the egalitarian, principle — that *we* have an interest in seeing every human life "succeed"— would, for example, indicate abortion should a genetic test reveal a fetus as having Down syndrome or as carrying the gene for Huntington's disease. Under the cover of liberalism's fundamental principles of equality and autonomy, a lethal elitism can work its dark will. The powerful get to decide when a fetus is too genetically imperfect, "when the life of the child, if carried to term, would be a frustrating one, in which the ambitions common to the full range of normal lives, which include freedom from pain, ample physical mobility, the capacity for an intellectual and emotional life, and the capacity to plan and execute projects, could be realized, if at all, only to a sharply reduced degree...." Cloaked in the authority of supposed experts, the ideological values of an elite determine which life is unworthy of life, who lives and who dies. Here eugenics is dressed up as compassion, while being made more lethal than ever. And eugenic abortion is but one component of a project to genetically reshape humanity, to decide "which kind of people, produced in which way, there are to be," or, as Dworkin actually puts it, to "play God." Dworkin derives an imperative to pursue this grandiose eugenic project from the core principles of liberalism and makes clear what "autonomy" amounts to when eugenically minded elites have sufficient power: the principle of autonomy entails the right of "scientists and doctors" to work to realize, without legal constraint, their elite vision of what counts as "success," what counts as a human life worthy of life.[170]

If one, with a demystifying gaze, takes note of the actual disposition of power relations in which "autonomy" gets exercised, it will become clear that the assertion of individualistic autonomy will not enable the powerless to resist the forces of eugenic control unleashed by the biotech revolution.

Clearly, this approach will protect no one but the elite. What patients need instead is a realization on the part of the medical community and the culture at large that the playing field of opposing autonomies is not level and that the purpose of rules and regulations should always primarily be to protect the powerless. As Keller has thoughtfully shown, genetic counseling's focus on "individual autonomy" is misplaced at a level even more basic than we have so far treated: rarely is the decision-maker's own health at issue, but rather it is the health of his or her offspring that is the concern, so that the individual is pressured to pass judgment on the worth of a human individual with disabilities, often in light of a utilitarian cost-benefit analysis helpfully provided by the counselor.[171] Yet this very approach sends the message that the appropriate context in which to judge the worth of human life is a quantitative or even financial one: another example of what Dorothy Nelkin has called our society's "actuarial mind-set," a by-product of a consumerist culture that in the end most values a safe profit margin, a lifestyle of ease and gratification, an image of success. Persons with disabilities threaten to disrupt such a social economy, but consumerist values should not be taken to trump the intrinsic dignity of any human individual — even one whose appearance, or existence, makes some of us uncomfortable.[172]

According to some people with disabilities, what is needed instead is the "normalization of vulnerability" — the recognition that all persons are vulnerable, and very likely have had, have now, or will have in the future some kind of disability. Rather than establishing a norm that is artificial, improbable, and downright unhealthy, our society must recognize that everyone is vulnerable and deserves compassionate care, and that the manifestations of vulnerability ought not be regarded as horrifying or even all that unusual.[173]

As opposed to a eugenic ethic of control and death, even if promulgated in the name of "autonomy," the poor and the marginalized require an ethic that stresses their personal dignity, especially the women and girls among them, given their constant disempowerment. Only such an ethic can stand against the basic eugenic attitude (the same today as decades before), so that a sick or disabled person is not seen primarily as a disease or a disability and only secondarily as a person. This an ethic of "individual autonomy" will not ensure. A historically informed, critical feminism should probe the degree to which the ideologies of the powerful and comfortable have blinded our consciences, thereby compromising the work of liberating all women and all the marginalized, including those with disabilities, from oppression. Only a critical perspective that eschews the dangerous naïveté of libertarian autonomy can hope to serve feminism's true end. Otherwise feminism will only end up carrying water for the same old eugenic ideology.

CHAPTER THREE

Eugenicists, Coworkers, Friends

"Margaret was rather like a lion tamer. She kept us each on our boxes until she needed us — and then we jumped and jumped fast."— Dorothy Brush[1]

Margaret Sanger accomplished as much as she did in promoting eugenic birth control and population control partly because she used her considerable charisma for the purposes of recruiting wealthy and powerful people to her cause. Sometimes she targeted upper-class women (such as Dorothy Brush), giving them a cause that promised a concrete way of solving social problems. Other times she convinced skeptical scientists and professionals to join her cause when their natural distaste for non-scientific "popularizers" and "activists" would have dictated otherwise.[2] As this chapter will show, many of the important personages with whom Sanger worked were also strongly committed to eugenics.

This chapter examines in some detail five important people within the birth-control movement whom Sanger recruited, encouraged, and defended.[3] As will be shown, these people were deeply committed to the eugenics movement, one piece of evidence indicating that Sanger's involvement with eugenics went beyond the pragmatic utilization of its rhetoric. She also created institutional ties with eugenic organizations. I will first examine the ideology of Frederick Osborn, the man synonymous with the American eugenics movement for almost fifty years. His involvement with Sanger was often cautious, due to his preference for "scientific," not "activist," approaches. Nevertheless he wholeheartedly endorsed birth control for eugenic purposes and frequently assisted Sanger in her propaganda efforts. Similarly, C. P. Blacker was a British eugenicist who attempted to "reform" eugenics in England in the same way and at the same time as Osborn. Blacker is also important to our study because of his heavy involvement in the International Planned Parenthood Federation. Next I examine the career of Robert Latou Dickinson, a physician and eugenicist, who encouraged the medical profession to support contraception, sterilization, and other eugenic measures. Part of his legacy derives from his providing an early home for maverick control propagandist Clarence Gamble, the fourth personage examined in this chapter. Gamble, besides being a millionaire, was a zealous eugenicist who spent his money and time agitating for increased birthrates among college graduates, forced sterilization for the "feebleminded" and otherwise "unfit" of the American South, and "simple methods" of birth control to be spread among the poor throughout the world. Another player on the international scene and the fifth and final Sanger coworker examined here, Dorothy Brush, served in various capacities for IPPF as well as on the board of her family foundation, the Brush Fund, which was dedicated to funding eugenic projects.

Sanger could not have achieved her ends— mass distribution of birth control to the poor through the federal government, heavily funded population-control programs, the institutionalization of medical eugenics— without the financial and strategic assistance of these important eugenicists. In addition, her endorsement of their eugenic activities indicates the depth of Sanger's complicity with the eugenic control ideology.

I. Frederick Osborn and the AES

The American Eugenics Society (AES) was single-handedly rescued from irrelevance by the work of Frederick Osborn. Christopher Tietze, the biostatistician who worked for Clarence Gamble and later for Osborn at the Population Council, noted that "Frederick Osborn ... was, in a way, a survivor of the eugenic debacle, you might say. He successfully made the transition from a discredited racist reactionary outlook to something that fitted more appropriately into the world at that time and he was eventually the one who established the Population Council."[4] As a sign of his respectability, the AES received grants under his tenure from the Dodge Foundation, the Population Council, the Draper Fund, and the Milbank Memorial Fund.[5]

Osborn and some of his family members were so important to the eugenics movement in America that historian Allan Chase has designated the AES an "Osborn fiefdom."[6] Osborn was born in 1889 into a wealthy family of bankers and businessmen; his great-uncle was J. Pierpont Morgan and his uncle the paleontologist and environmentalist Henry Fairfield Osborn, who helped to found the AES in 1923 and was a member of the board and advisory council for over a decade.[7] Frederick made enough money as CEO, bank partner, and president of the family railroad company in order to retire comfortably at the age of forty.[8] From 1928 to 1930, he studied eugenics and genetics full-time under his uncle Fairfield at the American Museum of Natural History, which influenced Frederick to sign on as an incorporator of the Eugenics Research Association in 1929.[9] He was nonetheless frustrated with the racist and unscientific bent of many of his colleagues, including Fairfield, and was determined to reform eugenics as it was then conceived.[10] His gentlemanly manner, organizational abilities, and quick mind, combined with his great personal commitment to eugenics and his many contacts in business and science, catapulted him into leadership positions within the eugenics movement. He was on the board of directors of the AES from 1928 to 1972, and by 1935, he had effectively taken over the AES, acting as its treasurer and functional director.[11] Leon Whitney, AES's field secretary at that time, complained, "Almost every one of our activities displeased him…. Preaching sermons was bad because 'we don't know enough about Eugenics.' That was his theme — We don't know enough about Eugenics."[12]

Striving to be a moderating force, Osborn objected to two aspects of the professional eugenics of his time: its straightforward racism and its grandiose claims regarding the heredity of traits.[13] (Recall that objecting to these very factors was highlighted by McCann as the reason why Sanger should *not* be considered a eugenicist. This logic would lead McCann to conclude that Osborn himself, the director of the American Eugenics Society, was not a eugenicist!) He argued instead that eugenic activity had to be made consistent with democracy and liberty, while urging eugenicists to allow for the role of environmental influences upon human traits.[14] Hoping that the American public would voluntarily take up eugenic practices, he formulated what he called the "eugenic hypothesis," which theorized that favorable environmental conditions and available birth control would lead the "fit" and "unfit" alike to gravitate toward their respective eugenic family sizes.[15] The same ideas can be found in Sanger, who insisted that most of the "unfit" could be persuaded, instead of forced, into birth-control use if enough propaganda was directed at them.

While Osborn's recognition of the importance of environmental factors could have served to mitigate the fatalistic determinism found within eugenics—that is, the belief that certain people were inevitably destined to turn out a certain way, either "fit" or "unfit"—in fact, it had the opposite effect. Osborn was willing to broaden the definition of eugenics, to move beyond simple biological determinants to environmental ones as well. In other words, he added environmental factors to the hereditary ones already present in the eugenic stew but maintained a deterministic attitude regarding all of these factors, so that he seemed to believe that environment could determine a person's development almost as surely as genes. Thus, he thought that "the white farmer of the Southern Appalachians is about as retarded as any one in this country," but he saw no indication that this farmer was biologically inferior; rather, Osborn believed that he was probably only culturally inferior.[16] Yet, he insisted, "we inherit our culture almost as surely as we inherit our genes," compounding one deterministic factor with another.[17] Therefore, Osborn's incorporation of environment and culture into the eugenic equation ends up meaning that the reproduction of those who are either genetically *or* environmentally "deficient" becomes a eugenic concern. As a result, Osborn casts a wider eugenic net of control: "There are social forces at work which, for good or for ill, are in the process of determining the ultimate future of our civilization. These forces are undoubtedly subject to social control and it is our responsibility that they be directed to useful ends."[18]

As the recurrence of the idea of control would indicate, Osborn was never so moderate that he refused to disallow the possibility of future eugenic coercion: "...we cannot rule out the possibility that any serious reduction in deleterious genes will not be possible by voluntary means alone," though he does go on to write, "It would probably take a grave and terrible increase in the proportion of people born with crippling genetic defects to bring about acceptance of compulsory limitation of childbearing by carriers."[19] He was willing, therefore, to countenance compulsory sterilization in the future, if only as a possibility, showing that his moderated eugenic ideology could potentially be as detrimental to the human rights of individual persons as that of the less subtle eugenicists. The problem with Osborn is that his hesitation in advocating coercive methods was based on the belief that such means were not *presently* necessary—but a per se ethical objection to coercion was absent. This kind of pragmatic approach does not fundamentally challenge the problematic ethical assumption embedded in all eugenic programs, namely, that a person's dignity is dependent upon his or her eugenic "fitness": an emergency situation could justify the suspension of the human rights of anyone judged to be dysgenic. Osborn's revision of eugenics enabled it to be placed on a more scientific footing, but he did not challenge its fundamental ideology.

His prettified version of eugenics no more abandoned the basic eugenic attitude (as summarized in the heuristic definition proposed at the beginning of chapter two) than does today's "new eugenics": it persists through all its avatars.

Despite (or perhaps because of) Osborn's fundamentally unreconstructed eugenics, he was admired so "extravagantly" by eugenicist Alan Guttmacher that the latter almost took over the reins of the Population Council after Osborn's retirement, though finally opting for the more activist and less professionally eugenic Planned Parenthood Federation of America. Part of Guttmacher's admiration must have been due to Osborn's aggressive promotion of birth control under the auspices of the AES: this promotion was an exercise of the social control necessary, according to the "eugenic hypothesis," to achieve eugenic ends.[20]

Osborn also used his position as president of the Population Council from 1952 to 1959 to promote eugenics, as we will see in the fifth chapter. He believed, he said, that the "quantitative aspect of population could not really be separated from the qualitative aspects."[21] He oversaw the establishment of Council fellowships in "medical genetics," which were given to graduate students interested in eugenics, thereby helping to maintain a eugenic presence within academia.[22] He also funded a eugenically oriented twin study with Population Council money. He gave all of his salary from the Population Council (as much as $10,000 a year in some years) to the American Eugenics Society, whose work, he believed, was "so closely related to the work of the Population Council."[23] Osborn's career makes clear that population control is fundamentally a eugenic ideology.

Osborn maintained contact with Margaret Sanger throughout, despite his reservations about the activist approach of PPFA.[24] He spoke at Planned Parenthood gatherings,[25] once on "Planned Parenthood's Contribution to the Future of America."[26] And, besides insisting that Sanger be involved in the Council on Population Policy, a proposed AES-American Birth Control League (ABCL) merger that will be examined in the next chapter, he made sure that she was on the Population Council's VIP list, even in her old age when she was marginalized within the birth-control movement. In the Sanger papers, a copy of the Population Council's annual report for 1958 is filed with a handwritten slip of paper, which reads, "To Mrs. Sanger, with warm and admiring regard, Fred Osborn."[27]

Osborn was the final redactor of an anonymous pamphlet on population control for Sanger's Birth Control Federation of America in the 1940s. Called *Our Human Resources*, it emphasized the link between eugenics and population control, as well as the role that birth control should play in relation to both. The first draft of the pamphlet, under the eugenic title "Birth Control's Opportunity to Strengthen our Human Resources— Our Population," played on wartime anxiety about the quality of America's population in the face of the threat to national security that Nazism posed. This draft was written by a group of eugenic demographers, including Henry Pratt Fairchild, P. K. Whelpton, Clyde Kiser, and others.[28] It boldly stated the need for eugenics within a democracy, a familiar theme during the war.

> Birth Control can contribute directly to national well-being…. The quality of democracy we have tomorrow, depends on the quality of babies born today. The dysgenic trend in the population of the United States has long been a cause for concern; the importance of correcting this trend becomes paramount as we strive to strengthen our nation from within. The problem is basically one of control or lack of control of the size of family in relation to health and income.[29]

Always cautious, Osborn toned the rhetoric down and suggested the removal of a paragraph calling for further study of coerced eugenic sterilization. The BCFA acquiesced, as it usually did, to his expertise.[30]

Osborn's reputation and scholarship were used by others within Sanger's organizations to provide the eugenic rationale for the control of births. For example, in a speech to the BCFA, Alan Guttmacher, later the head of the Planned Parenthood Federation of America, quoted eugenic studies done by Osborn in order to claim that a large population of Americans should never have been born.

> Osborn estimates that there are from 3 to 5 million people in the United States suffering from serious incapacities attributable in part, at least, to their genetic constitutions. Over half have such serious genetic handicaps that they are a tragedy to themselves and their families, and a heavy burden to a weary, already overburdened society. Acute diminution in the size of this future army of irredeemables is problem number one in preventive medicine. Where can prevention be better practiced than at the actual source of a disease? Treatment is the prevention of many such ill-starred conceptions, either through contraception or sterilization, whenever possible.[31]

Among the other scientific advances credited to Osborn's activism by another eugenicist was the "rapid development of such academic disciplines as medical genetics (especially genetic counseling) and demography."[32] (Note that both genetic counseling and demography are assumed to be eugenic disciplines, as indeed they are.)

Osborn succeeded in rehabilitating eugenics where many eugenicists before him had failed. Under his tenure, he could boast that the membership of the AES in 1960 "almost without exception" consisted of respected scientists and doctors.[33] He also led the charge to change the name of the AES to the Society for the Study of Social Biology (SSSB) in 1973. (Not coincidentally, the AES board of directors meeting that decided on the name change was held in the offices of the Population Council.[34]) His close contact with John D. Rockefeller 3rd, leading to his work for the Population Council, enabled organized eugenics in America to continue to achieve institutional respect, as we will see in the fifth chapter.[35] These and other savvy moves enabled the AES, kept afloat in part by the Population Council, to continue to inject eugenic ideology into academia, and from thence into the larger cultural sphere.[36]

Toward the end of his life in 1978, Osborn reminisced about his activities, especially his twenty-five years of support for the Population Council. He seemed to realize that the Council would prove to be the biggest project he had spearheaded, with a far greater reach than the more explicitly eugenic activities of the AES. Thinking about the "fire of those 25 years," he told John D. Rockefeller 3rd that "what you did [in founding the Population Council] will go down in history, as it is recognized today, as the first powerful injection of science in the study of human affairs with results which will endure."[37] Osborn's own activity was similarly significant for its legitimation of the control ideology as a valid ethical and scientific perspective. As Frank Notestein, always an admirer, said in 1981, "If a person of Frederick Osborn's insight and interest had been given a fund of say twenty million dollars to use in a decade, I think it probable that solid work in our field would have advanced considerably faster. But then, with minimal funds he did rather well as it was."[38]

II. C. P. Blacker and IPPF

The eugenics movement began in Great Britain with the work of Francis Galton, and continued through the work of the Eugenics Society, to which belonged many of Sanger's Neo-Malthusian friends. Many prominent British eugenicists assisted Sanger's work. During the 1940s and 1950s, Eugenics Society activist C. P. Blacker, involved in the International Planned Parenthood Federation (IPPF), was the main link between Sanger, Planned Parenthood, and the British eugenics movement.

We have seen how Sanger was intellectually formed by Neo-Malthusians in England around 1915: people such as Alice Vickery Drysdale and Havelock Ellis were essential to her education in the eugenic ideology. In the Neo-Malthusian tradition, the Eugenic Education Society — called later simply the Eugenics Society (ES) — was founded in 1907 by a group including Vickery Drysdale and Ellis "in order to modify public opinion and create a sense of responsibility ... [to] affect [*sic*] the improvement of the race."[39] Nearly 80 percent of the Society's initial membership was listed in the *Dictionary of National Biography*, an indication of their general level of education, wealth, and prestige.[40] Its earliest sorties against the fertility of the lower classes were conducted with the weapon of segregation (or compulsory institutionalization) of alcoholics, those with sexually transmitted diseases, and the "feeble-minded."[41] Among its more prominent members was the Anglican Dean Inge of St. Paul's, "one of the pauper class's most outspoken critics," as one scholar put it; the good clergyman was also published in Sanger's *Birth Control Review*.[42] Charles P. Blacker, known as just C. P. Blacker ("Pip" to his friends), took over as general secretary of the ES in 1931 and remained in that position until 1952, when he began to devote more and more time to IPPF (although he remained active in ES, partly because it had office space in the same building as did IPPF).

The English eugenics movement never achieved the kind of spectacular success that the Americans had with the passage of the 1924 immigration-restriction bill, partly because immigration was not an important issue for the English. But, as would be the case in the U.S., the sterilization of the poor would prove to be an initiative around which eugenicists could rally, and the ES began campaigning for "voluntary" eugenic sterilization in 1929 (though ultimately failing to get legislation passed). An editorial in a 1932 issue of *Eugenics Review* acknowledged that sterilization would be reserved for that portion of the unfit who were too "stupid, lazy or shiftless" to use birth control.[43] (Like the Americans, the British were also inclined to label as "unfit" those who refused to use birth control.) The "voluntary" aspect was disingenuous, in that Blacker himself attempted to build legal loopholes into the law that would allow for involuntary sterilization for the "feebleminded" and other "defectives." Clarence Gamble related the strategy in a letter to his mentor, Robert L. Dickinson.

> I had an interesting evening with Dr. C. P. Blacker, sec [*sic*] of the Eugenics Society. He says in Britain ops [operations] on the insane or fm [feebleminded] are illegal because you can't get their consent, and attempts on Parliament have shown the catholics [*sic*] are too strong. So their hope now is to get an opinion that a consent of a normal person is adequate and to arrange a series of sterilizations for hereditary defects.[44]

In other words, the eugenicists hoped for "voluntary" sterilization — by proxy.

The campaign for sterilization based some of its propaganda on statistical studies done by eugenicist Ernst Rüdin, who worked in Munich. Rüdin would later be notorious for his involvement with the Nazi sterilization law, a version of which he reportedly had prepared even before the Nazis took power.[45] Rüdin emphasized the need for sterilizing psychotic patients, but in England the attention remained fixed on the "social problem group."[46] The ES went so far as to set up a Social Problem Investigation Committee that would examine the question of differential fertility more closely.[47] The project of sterilization remained of central concern for Blacker even in his population-control activities: at the Sixth International Conference on Planned Parenthood in New Delhi, India, in 1959, Blacker chaired a study group on the subject (though one activist noted that "most Western scientists shied away from the whole subject"). Blacker insisted that sterilization was very important for India because of its high rate of fertility, especially among the poor. The unanimous resolution passed by the group not only supported sterilization but called it a "better method" than other contraceptive methods, given its permanence, a statement that seemed to be reflective of an imperialist antinatalism. Accordingly, delegates from the Third World protested the resolution, but to no avail.[48]

Historian Richard A. Soloway has observed that birth control and eugenics were completely intertwined within the ES and in the mind of the English people in general by 1930, to such an extent that the positive eugenic agenda received only lip service as the negative eugenic means of birth control and sterilization became the overriding concern and as research into population control became more and more important throughout the 1930s (the ES had more financial stability than its American counterpart during the Depression).[49] Yet the ES was mistrusted in the post–World War II climate, which was hostile not only for sterilization but also for all eugenic projects.[50] Blacker confronted the same postwar difficulties for eugenics as did Osborn and responded in a similar way: he attempted to bring respected academics into the fold and also tried to mitigate the elitist rhetoric of the Society by suggesting that the reproduction of the lower class was not entirely dysgenic (though the criteria he gave for the revised definition of "unfitness" remained substantially similar to the old criteria).[51] Blacker did not neglect to encourage, at least verbally, some traditional eugenic activities, even using the forum of an early IPPF conference to promote positive eugenic policies that were recognizably similar to those of Osborn.[52]

Blacker also showed the same breadth as Osborn in picking his eugenic targets: both were concerned about the fertility not only of the poor at home but also of the poor abroad. As with the earlier Neo-Malthusians, Blacker's eugenic commitment naturally extended to population control. As Soloway has pointed out, "post-Malthusian ideas of population control" were of central importance in transforming eugenics from a fringe Victorian intellectual club to "an important facet of biological thinking prominent in educated middle- and upper-class circles."[53] In the obituary for Sanger that he wrote in the *Eugenics Review*, Blacker was especially appreciative of her role in the international arena, for, as he states, "birth control for American women led on to the concept of population control."[54] His commitment to population control led him to IPPF.

Sanger was delighted that Blacker was willing to help in the formation of IPPF, so much so that she urged him to take the reins from her when she wanted to retire. Blacker shared Sanger's preoccupation with the fertility of Indians, especially those of the poorer classes. He said in 1952: "The International Committee is much concerned with the problems of the backward and overpopulated countries of South East Asia."[55] Blacker was to serve IPPF in various capacities, including as a member of the governing body and the executive committee, as vice-chairman, and as administrative chairman.

Blacker's Eugenics Society helped IPPF with resources as well as personnel. It funded Blacker's participation in IPPF conferences.[56] The treasurer and chairman of the Eugenics Society in the 1950s, G. Aird Whyte (who also served as treasurer and as a member of the governing body and the executive committee of IPPF), observed to Sanger in 1955 that the Eugenics Society funded a considerable part of the IPPF budget; this monetary support included an annual subsidy and office accommodation of three rooms in the ES building, free of rent.[57] Even an IPPF apologist who wrote a hagiographic history of the organization freely acknowledges, "Many of IPPF's leaders and supporters were also interested in eugenics, and the British Eugenics Society was one of the main groups giving support to both the local F.P.A. [Family Planning Association] and the IPPF in the early years of both organizations."[58]

By 1968, the Eugenics Society's *Eugenics Review* had to be discontinued due to lack of support. Prefiguring the name change that the AES would make a few years later (to the Society for the Study of Social Biology), Blacker changed the publication's name to the *Journal of Biosocial Science*, with a focus on demography. Pauline Mazumdar notes that the more things change, the more they stay the same, for, in the new journal, "the informed observer might discern shadows of its former concerns with differential fertility, social problems and intelligence, now often set in the Third World."[59]

III. Sanger's Coworker Robert Latou Dickinson

Blacker and Osborn bridged the worlds of "scientific" eugenics and birth-control advocacy; Robert Latou Dickinson (1861–1950), on the other hand, was the most important mediator between Margaret Sanger and the medical community. As a doctor and well-off gentleman, he exuded an aura of respectability and genial good humor, far removed from the scrappier image of Sanger. As head of the National Committee on Maternal Health, he fostered the publication of many scientific papers on contraception, which helped to bring about the medical establishment's acceptance of the practice. He was also responsible for bringing people like Clarence Gamble (to be discussed in the next section) and demographer Christopher Tietze into the birth-control fold. Like most of the active workers within the control movement, he was a committed eugenicist, serving on the boards of various eugenics groups and encouraging the use of birth control for eugenic purposes. Birth control was the answer to the question he posed to the members of his profession: "Is there a simple method of preventing propagation among women who are idiots, epileptic, hopelessly insane or incurably criminal?"[60]

Dickinson was born to a prosperous Brooklyn factory owner and moved in the community's better circles. James Reed notes, "The best society was Dickinson's natural milieu."[61] After finishing the three-year medical program at Long Island College Hospital in 1882 at the age of twenty-one, he was able to establish a flourishing obstetric-gynecological practice among the well-off ladies of Brooklyn. (It should be remembered that, at that time, a college degree was not a prerequisite for entering medical school, and it was by no means guaranteed that doctors even had much background in basic science.)[62] By the early 1920s, he had saved up enough money to be able to quit his active practice and devote himself full-time to his hobby: sexology and birth control. Dickinson's socioeconomic position reveals something essential about the class interests of the birth-control movement: he not only moved in the best society, he also depended on the funding of many wealthy female socialites, including Sanger supporter Gertrude Minturn Pinchot.[63]

Dickinson began his activism in 1923 by founding the Committee on Maternal Health (CMH), renamed the National Committee on Maternal Health (NCMH) in 1930. The CMH was intended to be a respectable, physician-run alternative to Sanger's lay-managed organization and clinic. Mary Steichen Calderone, the Planned Parenthood Federation of America's medical director from 1953 to 1964, recalled that Sanger's group was mostly a female organization. It was looked upon as a do-good, women's movement, certainly sparked by that great but very human woman, Margaret Sanger. And it depended a great deal on the largesse and concern of many highly placed, prominent society women who again had to run the gauntlet of people's scorn and ridicule themselves.... Now, Margaret Sanger herself had left a legacy to this struggling organization: She disliked physicians.[64]

Calderone, herself a physician, was a student of Haven Emerson, a medical eugenicist who was also involved in Dickinson's NCMH. Her statement indicates the mistrust and sometimes even hostility that once existed between the birth-control movement and much of the organized medical establishment, which was trying at the time to establish its professional and scientific credentials in contrast to much of the quackery that was promoted in the name of medicine in the nineteenth century.

Dickinson initially believed he would be able to provide birth-control counseling on an outpatient basis in hospitals, for strictly medical reasons. He had been elected president of the American Gynecological Society in 1920 and began to agitate for studies to be done on birth control distributed in a clinical setting.[65] Sanger's clinic in New York City, operating without a license but with a female doctor (Dorothy Bocker, at that point), was considered slipshod, due to its personnel — women doctors were not well-respected — and to the scientific work it produced.[66] Dickinson intended to work through various Manhattan hospitals to secure patients, but the protocol which he established, intended to be irreproachably scientific, proved to be too cumbersome as well as legally risky for reputable doctors, given that it would require their authorization of birth-control use, at least on a case-by-case basis. In addition, Dickinson could not get the needed contraband contraceptives except through one source — Margaret Sanger, who sold them to him at several times their production cost.[67] In the end, he could not get enough data for a scientific study and had to rely on Sanger for this also.

By 1928, the CMH realized that it would have to leave the clinical work to Sanger and the other freestanding, lay-run birth-control clinics. It decided instead to focus exclusively on evangelizing the medical profession, especially through the publication of scientific articles.[68] Part of Dickinson's rejection of the clinical route derived from his disillusionment with the clinical approach. In his correspondence with one financial backer, John D. Rockefeller 3rd, Dickinson expressed concern about the slow spread of birth control among the eugenically "unfit": "The present clinic methods are good. But half those taught reject them. They are impossible for mountain whites, Southern negroes, miners, China, India."[69]

The bureaucrats of the Rockefeller Foundation also shared Dickinson's concerns, and they correctly identified the central preoccupation of Dickinson's birth-control organization: eugenics, with its concomitant targeted population control.

> [The National Committee on Maternal Health] must look for a measure of its success in the numerical strength and biologic quality of a coming generation…. The quality of the biologic inheritance of coming generations is of no less importance [than numbers]…. A second objective of the Committee must then be the investigation of measures which will assure the fertility of the great mass of Americans who are possessed of a sound genetic inheritance, as well as of means by which the child bearing of the manifestly subnormal or inferior might be discouraged.[70]

In the 1930s, Dickinson served as chairman of the AES's committee on "Eugenics and Dysgenics of Birth Regulation," which undertook to determine the eugenic value of contraception. The committee promoted studies concerning "differential fecundity between 'superior' and 'inferior' stocks; eugenical sterilization of the insane, feebleminded, etc…. An important phase of the Committee's investigations is the question as to how much the practice of birth control is eugenic and how much it is dysgenic."[71] Among Dickinson's coworkers in the AES was Alan Guttmacher, who, as we have seen, was himself deeply involved with both Planned Parenthood and eugenics. Other eugenicists involved with Dickinson at the NCMH included Edward East, Adolf Meyer, and Raymond Pearl.

The research focus of the AES committee was consistent with a perennial concern of Dickinson himself, as the NCMH's publication of a study in 1930 by Caroline Hadley Robinson (for which Dickinson wrote the forward) indicates. The book, entitled *Seventy Birth Control Clinics: A Survey and Analysis Including the General Effects of Control on Size and Quantity of Population*, focuses on the relation between the promotion of birth control and the furthering of eugenic goals. Under the heading "Reaching the Poor [is] the Main Object," Robinson notes that poor women have less information regarding contraceptive methods than the rich; this observation segues into a delineation of the kinds of recommended birth-control outreach, listed under the heading "How [to] Increase Service to the Less Fit?" In other words, the poor were equivalent to the "less fit." The clinical method is still recommended, with Sanger's Clinical Research Bureau given as an example, with the proviso that "it will reach many unfit, but many fit as well…."[72] From the example of the Illinois Birth Control League, the study argues that, by increasing clinics among the poor, especially for "colored people," "the work will continue to become more eugenic."[73]

Unfortunately for Robinson, there remains a certain group that manages—with bewildering skill, as it presumably consists of "feebleminded" people — to evade all attempts to succumb to eugenic contraceptive propaganda.

> Mrs. Sanger, Mrs. Fuller, Mrs. Carpenter and others agree that there is a class which cannot be trusted to use the methods taught by the clinics. For instance, there is the affectionate, unreflecting type known to housing experts, who, though living in one room with several children, will keep a St. Bernard dog. Such people will relax birth control at times.[74]

Despite the discouraging resistance that met some eugenic propaganda disguised as birth-control instruction, Dickinson carried on his eugenic work. He was one of many eugenicists present at the founding of the Population Association of America (PAA), which occurred at a meeting that coincided with the annual meeting of the AES in 1931.[75] Margaret Sanger had been among the original thirteen people who met about six months before to suggest the founding of the organization, along with Harry Laughlin, the eugenicist and anti-immigrant racist.[76] For the 1931 meeting "[a] full range of eugenicists was invited, from the unrestrained to the temperate."[77] The meeting reflects the interimplication of eugenics and population control, a subject to be studied in the next chapter. For now it suffices to indicate how comfortably both Dickinson and Sanger moved in eugenic circles, and how closely their birth-control activism was tied to eugenics.

Population control was not the only manifestation of Dickinson's eugenic interests: he was also actively involved at a leadership level in the eugenic sterilization movement. In 1943, Marian S. Norton Olden founded Birthright, a pro-sterilization organization that took its name from a statement by a 1930 White House Conference on Child Health and Protection, which declared, "There should be no child in America that has not the complete birthright of a sound mind in a sound body, and that has not been born under proper conditions." Birthright used the term to mean that each child born should have a birthright of good genes, and if certain persons would not be able to provide that eugenic "birthright" for their children, they should be sterilized. The organization's constitution stated its eugenic purpose in a straightforward manner: "The purpose of this organization is to foster all reliable and scientific means for improving the human race."[78]

Dickinson already had agitated for eugenic sterilization in 1928, when he lectured the American Medical Association in favor of it.[79] In the 1940s, Dickinson attempted to convince the more conservative board of PPFA to change their long-standing sterilization policy, which was to not have a policy. Dickinson (who ultimately failed in his quest, despite the support of PPFA president Richard N. Pierson, M.D.) was commended in the Birthright minutes.[80] In his promotion of eugenic sterilization, as in that of eugenic birth control, Dickinson served as the medical liaison, couching eugenic propaganda in appropriately medical terms and presenting the issue as a dispassionately scientific one. Ultimately, on this issue, as in so many other instances, the predominately male medical community would not have the critical ability nor the ethical will to resist a program that would turn out to be a violent, misogynistic experiment in social control.[81]

Sanger had an up-and-down relationship with Dickinson throughout their careers, partly because she felt that he was trying to steal the limelight. Yet they got along in the end, partly because Dickinson was a diplomat and also because their goals were so similar. Sanger's organizations made use of his willingness to get involved: Dickinson served as vice president of PPFA, as well as on its board of directors, among other positions, and the program of the annual meeting of Planned Parenthood in 1945 notes that Dickinson received that year's Lasker Award, which honored outstanding achievement in the field of birth-control promotion. Evidently Dickinson's eugenic orientation caused no concern among the higher-ups within Planned Parenthood.[82]

IV. Clarence Gamble, Millionaire Eugenicist

A friend of Dickinson, Clarence James Gamble (1894–1966) was by turns an organizer, funder, and gadfly within the birth-control movement. An heir to some of the Procter and Gamble fortune, he did not need to work for a living and was able to dedicate his insatiable appetite for letter-writing and organizational activity to full-time birth-control and eugenics work. Sanger recognized the value both of his deep pockets and of his unorthodox style, which inspired, alienated, and exasperated his coworkers in turn. Most of all, however, she recognized in Gamble a kindred spirit who understood the issues at stake with birth- and population-control and who was willing to weather all sorts of displeasure in order to further his goals.

Gamble was introduced to eugenics by his Princeton biology teacher, Edwin Grant Conklin, a disciple of Francis Galton.[83] While at Princeton, Gamble made the acquaintance of Stuart Mudd, who later, with his wife Emily, directed the Pennsylvania branch of the American Birth Control

League, as did Gamble himself from 1933 to 1936. Stuart became a physician, and Emily was one of the first marriage counselors in the country, and they both later served on the board of the Pathfinder Fund, the population-control organization that Gamble founded. In reminiscing about Gamble after his death, Stuart Mudd recalled that Gamble became preoccupied with the differential birthrate while at Princeton, due to the influence of Conklin, the teacher of them both.[84]

Perhaps this interest contributed to Gamble's desire to go into medicine. He graduated from Harvard Medical School in 1920, the second in his class. He chose not to work with patients, preferring instead to do medical research, obtaining a non-salaried post with clinical pharmacologist Alfred N. Richards at the University of Pennsylvania, scheduled to begin in the fall of 1922.[85] But a catastrophic airplane accident badly injured Gamble.[86] He went to Philadelphia seven months later than planned. Partly due to the accident but also due to his psychological makeup, he found that he did not have the patience for sustained scientific research. He hung around the university and did some cardiac research when he was able until he moved to Massachusetts in 1937.[87]

While he was in Pennsylvania, he became involved with the state birth-control organization. The Mudds had known Margaret Sanger while they were in New York in the 1920s, and when they moved to Pennsylvania they founded the first birth-control committee and clinic in the state in 1929.[88] Gamble was elected president of the Pennsylvania Birth Control Federation in 1933 and served as the Pennsylvania representative on the board of the ABCL and then of PPFA from 1933 to 1946. In fact, he served as a member of the PPFA executive committee from 1939 to 1942.[89]

Gamble was also involved with Dickinson's National Committee on Maternal Health. He first met Dickinson in 1925, when the latter indicated that he would soon be too old to continue active work within the contraceptive field. Through the NCMH Gamble developed standardized tests for determining the efficacy of various contraceptives.[90] He also worked for Sanger under the auspices of her Birth Control Clinical Research Bureau, through which Gamble paid for fieldworkers in North Carolina.[91] The two of them also teamed up for a field test of "simple" contraceptives in rural America around 1950.[92] The Pennsylvania Birth Control Federation under his leadership emphasized the dysgenic effects of the new federal welfare programs in its organizational and educational literature, claiming that only by preventing the reproduction of the poor would the problem of poverty be attacked at its roots.[93] Poverty, in other words, had its source not in socioeconomic forces and interest but rather in the genes of those who were poor.

Gamble advocated both positive and negative eugenics. After he married Sarah Merry Bradley in 1924, they proceeded to have five children, appropriately spaced. Gamble did not want to reduce the birthrate for every kind of person; rather, there were some kinds of people (such as himself) who should have lots of children and some (the "unfit") who should have only a few or none at all. The official biography of Gamble, vetted thoroughly by the Gamble family and edited by family friend Emily Flint, has no reservations about discussing his eugenic views: "Gamble was not disturbed by questions about practicing what he preached [concerning population control]. In his view, he did practice what he preached, as all of his children were planned and wanted. People of good stock should have more children."[94] The issue appeared to be a bit of a joke among family friends, as some comments by Stuart Mudd indicate: "Since it was clear that the quality of the germ-pool in the Gamble family was well above average, Clarence and Sarah did their personal bit in reference to the differential birth rate, and the happy consequences will be apparent to anyone knowing the Gamble children and grandchildren."[95]

Gamble's promotion of positive eugenics did not stop at multiplying his own progeny. Even though neither his wife Sarah nor his parents had been college graduates, Gamble was convinced that a person with four years of college was likely to be a "fit" parent. (Of course, this was in an age when far fewer people attended school at the university level than at the present time.) In 1934, as president of the Pennsylvania birth-control affiliate, Gamble gave monetary awards through the Federation to the Bryn Mawr College class with the highest birthrate. (The class of 1914 won.)[96] In the 1940s he continued his project of promoting the birthrates of the college-educated. Still concerned about the lower birthrate among the upper and well-educated classes, he published an article in 1946 in the Harvard alumni newsletter entitled "Harvard — A Dying Race," and in 1947 he spoke to Harvard's president about a project that would mitigate "the genetic tragedy of declining American intelligence."[97] The project Gamble pitched was the founding of a Eugenics Fund, which would give professors tax-exempt "baby bonuses." Harvard, and later Princeton, evinced little interest.[98]

Gamble was able, however, to pursue his promotion of positive eugenics through another institution, the Population Reference Bureau, founded by eugenicist and anti-immigration activist Guy Irving Burch (who, as was noted in chapter one, was also a lobbyist for Sanger in the National Committee for Federal Legislation of Birth Control). Gamble became the PRB's director of college projects, a post he held from 1945 to 1956. Concerned with the effect of low birthrates among college graduates on the future of the nation's intelligence, he began to promote larger families among the students at Harvard, Princeton, and Yale, under PRB auspices.[99] Gamble's idea was too inflammatory for the AES, which was hesitant to make any concrete positive proposals, but Burch was willing to fund Gamble's "stork derby." The project was described as follows: "Fundamental objective: To initiate discussion of differential birth rates. Possible secondary result: Slight increase in birthrate of college graduates."[100] This project did not sit well with the more cautious eugenicist Robert C. Cook, who took over PRB in 1951. Gamble was removed soon thereafter.[101]

As the Williams biography points out, positive eugenics was not Gamble's only eugenic concern. "He was interested in the management of reproduction at both ends of the survival-of-the-fittest ladder.... For some years, he had sought to suppress the hereditary forms of mental retardation and mental illness by publicizing state laws providing for the sterilization of these classes of institutionalized patients."[102] In an interview with Christopher Tietze, James Reed recalled, "I remember you wrote [Gamble] a letter one time, and you explained to him why sterilization was not a good eugenic tool. That in other words, you could never sterilize enough people to make any difference, even if you accepted his premises."[103] Gamble was evidently not persuaded, because eugenic sterilization remained a central preoccupation.[104]

He was actively involved in Birthright, the sterilization organization that Dickinson helped to found. Dickinson convinced Gamble that Birthright was the most effective eugenic organization, and so the latter supported the organization generously with his money, with the proviso that it start up a research division that Gamble would head up.[105] He also served as Birthright's field director until 1947, when he was terminated by the unstable founder of the organization, Marian Olden,[106] but not before he had started up several state and local organizations. As he later would do with birth control, Gamble encouraged the formation of local sterilization clinics, establishing more than twenty throughout the Midwest and the South. He also wrote several articles on eugenic sterilization for medical journals and also for more popular publications, including *Eugenical News*. In them he compared sterilization to smallpox vaccines: the "feeble-minded" children who would never be born due to sterilization were analogous to the smallpox epidemics which would never occur due to vaccinations.[107] In another article, he argued that the sterilization of 5,112 institutionalized California children had saved the state over $21 million in comparison to what the cost of segregating them by sex would have been.[108]

Gamble repeatedly targeted poor populations for fieldwork, both in America and abroad. For example, he sponsored a test and distribution of contraceptive jelly in Logan County, West Virginia, an impoverished Appalachian area. North Carolina received special attention from Gamble. He funded the state health department from 1936 to 1941 to distribute contraceptives through the county health care system, relying mostly on foam powder.[109] Among the objectives of the birth-control nurse (who was paid by Gamble) were, "To curb the high birth rate among dependent families and ... to endeavor to increase the birthrate among the physically fit, and the financially and intellectually competent."[110] The state continued that work afterward with public funding, a situation that was always Gamble's ideal: he would provide start-up money, and then local funds or, ideally, the government would take over. In this way, he initiated contraceptive services within the public health systems of South Carolina, Alabama, Florida, Georgia, Mississippi, and Virginia.[111]

North Carolina was also the target for Gamble's funding and promotion of intelligence testing and eugenic sterilization: in 1945 he funded IQ tests for schoolchildren in Orange County, and that same year he paid the salary of a sociologist who provided sterilization screening services to the North Carolina Eugenic Board. Yet in 1947, he complained about the slow pace of the sterilizations.

> To date less [sic] than 2,000 insane and mentally defective North Carolinians have been sterilized under the existing law — a figure that represents less than one out of every 41 of the State's estimated mentally unfit. This means that for every one man or woman who has been sterilized, there are 40 others who can continue to pour defective genes into the State's blood stream to pollute and degrade future generations.[112]

To help remedy the "dysgenic" situation, Gamble had one of his contraceptive fieldworkers, Elsie Wulkop, found the Human Betterment League of North Carolina, a branch of Birthright. He also promoted the use of sterilization on welfare recipients as well as on the institutionalized. One historian noted, "By helping to refocus eugenic sterilization from the state's institutions to the welfare rolls of each county, in three years Gamble more than doubled the number of eugenic sterilizations."[113]

Gamble's preoccupation with the fertility of the poor was not unique among Planned Parenthood workers. For example, Frances Hand Ferguson, who (as we have seen) served in various administrative positions within PPFA, argued for something very much like Gamble's hit-and-run style of contraceptive distribution, despite her professed disagreement with him and his methods. Of the medical profession, she said:

They've held us back.... And I think they still are. They talk about total medical care, and it's a great concept, but for instance, pap smears—well, that's marvelous for every person that comes in to a clinic, but when you think that cancer among the young people is, I don't know what percentage, one tenth of one percent, or something, to spend the money and effort on all those pap smears on young people—it seems to me that's over-gilding the lily. Take that money and use it to reach other people, more people in the Appalachians, or offer more birth control methods.[114]

Besides the fact that Ferguson dangerously underestimates the incidence of cervical cancer among sexually active teenagers, her statement indicates the fixation of control activists with poor Americans, whose greatest need, according to Planned Parenthood, is not preventive health care or improved education but birth control, plain and simple.

Gamble's (and later Sanger's) main obsession was to find what was called a "simple method" that would be able to be used by anyone, at the cheapest possible cost. In the attempt to accomplish this end, he tested foams, jellies, powders, and even salt solutions, all in the hopes of finding a universally available and affordable contraceptive, one that could be used effectively in international population work. He began testing contraceptive methods in 1934, through a research program of the National Committee on Maternal Health, which he partially funded.[115]

One of his fieldworkers, Edna Rankin McKinnon, recalled his motives for rejecting the accepted (and most effective) method at the time, which consisted of a diaphragm coated with spermicidal jelly.

He felt right from the start that the diaphragm and jelly method was clumsy, expensive and would not reach the masses. He was in everybody's hair all the time trying to get these simple methods. He would carry on research projects wherever he could get a doctor that would even listen to him. He did it in Berea, and he did it in the Kentucky Mountains. I remember in Nashville, Tennessee he had a woman doctor doing tests on the cauterization of the entrances into the uterus. You could never know where he was having some little project done.[116]

In such a situation, the safety, comfort, and ethical acceptability of the methods under study often become less important than the overarching demographic question: will its use reduce birthrates? Gamble's unsupervised testing on human subjects—invariably women, who very likely were not told the health risks and failure rates of the contraception, partly because that information would not have even been known yet—betrayed a cavalier disregard for the health and dignity of the women involved.[117]

This attitude got Gamble in trouble with the Indian affiliate of IPPF, headed by a formidable Brahmin named Lady Rama Rau. McKinnon described the tense situation as a case of unreasonable demands on the part of the Indians.

> Then he [Gamble] set up little investigatory projects to test out the salt and sponge foaming powder and sponge and salt. Each missionary doctor he would set up with a self-help project, that wasn't very costly. We discovered that in India the Planned Parenthood Federation felt that only the best method was good enough for the Indians. They were doing the diaphragm method only, which we had learned was too expensive and clumsy — impossible to do on a mass scale. At that point Lady Rama Rau began to be very angry at Clarence Gambell [sic], because she claimed that he was using her people in an experimental fashion. Actually he had done identical experiments among the American people for many years; nevertheless she was angry that he was trying out simple methods in India.[118]

It occurred to neither McKinnon nor Gamble that perhaps the point was that *all* women, Indian or not, deserved to be treated as persons with dignity and not as means to the end of reducing the fertility of their nation or income class. I have not seen any evidence that, in Gamble's tests on either Americans or Asians, the women were informed that they were using an experimental contraceptive that might not be effective or safe. One fieldworker herself became pregnant (twice) using the very contraceptive jelly whose benefits she was touting to the poor women in North Carolina.[119]

Many people within Planned Parenthood itself had objections to Gamble's promotion of the salt-solution method, the use of a saltwater solution as a kind of spermicide. Dr. Helena Wright, the chairwoman of the IPPF medical advisory committee, stated in 1952 that she believed the salt solution recommended by Gamble was— at 20 percent salt, eight times saltier than sea water — likely to dry out vaginal membranes and cause irritation. There is no record of Gamble's response to this criticism.[120] PPFA decided not to include the method in their manual of contraceptive practices, even though the medical director at that time, Mary Steichen Calderone, approved of simple methods. This position angered Gamble, but Calderone argued that the salt method would only be appropriate for use in developing countries.

> [Simple methods] might work for outside the country, but for most people in this country we should begin to develop a *medical* attitude toward birth control as a *medical* technique rather than a homemade method.[121]

In other words, substandard methods might be good enough for other countries, but Americans would demand — and would receive — only the best.[122]

This obsession with lowering the fertility of the poor, even if it required substandard methods, was clearly the primary concern of Gamble and probably also of many of his fellow birth controllers. Even historian James Reed, who downplays the involvement of birth controllers in eugenics, acknowledges that "Dr. Gamble's principal concern was differential fertility among classes and the high cost of social programs for the poor."[123] Reed contrasts this concern with Sanger's supposed pure feminism, but Reed's position is untenable, considering that even though Gamble alienated just about everyone else in the control movement, Sanger still repeatedly defended him — not an easy thing to do unless one had substantial agreements with Gamble and his methods. The contrast, therefore, between Gamble and Sanger is less than might be supposed.

In fact, Sanger gave continued, unqualified support to Gamble, arguing that he was "gifted with a pioneer spirit" and his work was "most essential to the progress and expansion of the IPPF's program."[124] She sympathized with those who bore the brunt of Gamble's continuing stream of outrageous ideas, but in the end she admired his independence and single-mindedness, in part because he was one of the few American birth controllers who was as internationally minded as she was. In addition, despite encouraging the diaphragm and jelly method in her own clinic, she came to believe with Gamble that the future of population control lay in the "simple methods," and for this reason she worked actively with Katherine Dexter McCormick to fund and encourage the research by Gregory Pincus and John Rock on hormonal contraceptions — what would become the birth-control pill. For all these reasons, she remained a fan of Gamble. "You have been a wonderful supporter in the Planned Parenthood cause, very independent, never a follower, always a lone wolf — but far too modest to get correct acknowledgment for the fine work you have had done. However, thats [*sic*] been your way and my heartfelt thanks for it, also for getting your family's interest into the Cause is [*sic*] to pass the torch along after us."[125] Sanger was so supportive of Gamble's efforts that she hoped he would take over her position as president of IPPF in 1953,[126] but the opposition to him within the organization was sufficient to preclude that option. Anyway, by the mid–1950s, Gamble had had enough with the conservatism of IPPF. He set out to found his own organization, which he could run however he pleased.

The Pathfinder Fund was founded in 1957, its board of directors consisting of various Gambles and their spouses. As a tax-exempt foundation, it allowed Gamble to continue to fund the activities of his various fieldworkers.[127] As Emily Mudd remembered it, it was a matter of Gamble having complete control over how his money was used.

> Well, he couldn't tolerate the misuse of funds. Granted that he felt he could get more out of his money than somebody else could.... I think he felt that he knew how to do things. He knew how to achieve the goals that he felt were important better than the others did, and he did not believe in working through committees.[128]

Dr. Elton Kessel was the first paid executive of Pathfinder, brought into the organization in April 1966, as Gamble realized he was becoming ill and unable to continue his work indefinitely.[129] He died a few months later of leukemia and complications. Among his last, dying words were, ironically enough, "survival of the fittest."[130]

Kessel was Pathfinder's contact with the federal government's Agency for International Development (USAID) and its newly established population point man, the eccentric and often wildly overzealous Reimert Ravenholt, notorious for "dumping" masses of defective contraceptives on developing countries in the belief that some birth control—even if ineffective or downright dangerous—was better than none at all. In this respect, Ravenholt echoed Gamble's own views regarding simple methods.[131] (Ravenholt's career will be addressed in more detail in the fifth chapter.)

Emily Mudd recalled that USAID could only have stepped in to fund Pathfinder after Gamble's departure: "Dr. Gamble, I guess, never would have asked the government for funding, he wouldn't have done that because he couldn't have controlled it and he didn't want to have to work within the restrictions that any government source would put."[132] Nevertheless, USAID soon began supporting the Fund to upwards of 90 percent of their income, a situation continuing to this day. A letter from Ravenholt to Stuart Mudd explained that the two organizations had compatible goals and harmonious methods.[133] Ravenholt believed, at least according to Mudd's account, that Pathfinder could go places and do things that USAID could not.[134]

USAID funding seemed to elevate Pathfinder to a new level of respectability. At the present time, what was once the somewhat-disreputable Gamble organization has become mainstream enough to have received a prestigious population-control award from the United Nations Population Fund (UNFPA) in 1996.[135]

Indeed, despite the problems PPFA and IPPF had with Gamble, their views were not, in the end, so divergent. In an interview, Planned Parenthood activist Frances Hand Ferguson observed that another long-standing Planned Parenthood activist, Lorraine Campbell, having had to deal with Gamble eccentricities for many years, would "have had a lot to say over Clarence Gamble, I'm sure." The interviewer, James Reed, responded, "She doesn't have that much to say about Clarence Gamble because his son, Richard, is still a supporter of the movement in Massachusetts."[136] Richard has indeed remained a force within that state's Planned Parenthood affiliate. In 1976, he married Nicki Nichols, whom he had, two years before, helped to hire as executive director of the Planned Parenthood League of Massachusetts. (Until his marriage to Nichols, he had served on the PPLM board of directors.)[137] Until her retirement in the fall of 1998, Nicki Gamble was PPLM's executive director, and she continued on as president and as a chief media spokeswoman. Despite the fact that, according to Richard's sister Judy, Clarence thought that "conspicuous consumption was a very bad thing,"[138] Richard and Nicki Gamble built in Nantucket "an enormous mansion, surrounded by water and dunes and decorated in zenith style. If the house cost less than $5 million — and the Gambles aren't saying — everyone would be shocked."[139] It seems that, despite PPLM's desire "to change its image as an organization run by privileged white ladies,"[140] it has not yet shaken its old habits: the rich still distribute contraceptives to the poor.

With Richard Gamble still having such a prominent role within the state and hosting Planned Parenthood fund-raisers at his Nantucket mansion, one cannot help but wonder about the repercussions of having the son of eugenicist Clarence Gamble continue the Gamble influence within the birth-control movement. It was Richard who, during a population-control trip to India with his father, reportedly told the native doctors that the rice-jelly method "must be better than foolproof, it must be coolie-proof" and that he could see no reason why the Indian women would object to the messiness of the rice jelly, since "they eat it with their fingers!" As a result, although the Indians "were prepared to believe Dr. Gamble had his heart in the right place even if he went about things in the wrong way, they were not prepared to accept Richard. He was considered brash and offensive."[141] The case of Clarence Gamble and his family suggests that feminists should be more careful who their bedfellows are.

V. Sanger's Friend Dorothy Brush

Another high-ranking Planned Parenthood activist, Dorothy Brush, was deeply committed to the twin dogmas of eugenics and population control. Unfortunately, historical scholarship on Sanger, while pointing out Brush's importance as a personal friend and confidante of Sanger, has neglected to examine Brush's deep involvement with organized eugenics, a scholarly lacuna that this section will try to fill. In so doing, I hope to show how Sanger's eugenic ideology had an impact even in her personal life.

Dorothy Brush followed Sanger's activist program enthusiastically and viewed Sanger herself almost worshipfully, even writing a melodramatic play called "Margaret." She met Sanger soon after the death of her first husband, when Brush moved from her native Cleveland to New York in the hopes of finding projects to occupy her time. What she found was Margaret Sanger, whom she interviewed for a woman's magazine. Soon she was traveling with Sanger through the Orient in 1937 and became a reliable financial and personal supporter.[142]

The eugenic Brush Foundation, founded by Dorothy's family, provided the start-up money for IPPF.[143] Writing about the Brush Foundation, Dorothy noted that, while many foundations were shortsightedly focused on easing social ills, her family's fund sought "to check misery at its source by breeding out the unfit and limiting the numbers of those born into the world"—a statement which clearly reveals the marriage of eugenic and population concerns.[144] Dorothy was accurately reflecting the two core beliefs of the Brush Foundation, on whose board of managers she served for her whole life.

The Brush Foundation was initiated in the 1920s by Charles Francis Brush of Cleveland, a scientist who invented and sold electronic equipment, later merging his company with two others to form the General Electric Company in 1891. The foundation was dedicated to the memory of Brush's son Charles Francis Brush, Jr., who was also Dorothy Brush's first husband. The intent of the foundation was to "finance efforts contributing toward betterment of human Stock and toward regulation of the increase of population...."[145] Words such as "stock" and "betterment" were standard eugenic catchwords, and the interest in "the increase of population" makes clear that it is a natural extension for eugenics to focus on population growth as an area for inquiry and "regulation." Already in the late 1920s, then, the institutional movement of eugenicists toward the population field had begun.

To these ends, the foundation made its first grant in 1929 to fund a birth-control clinic in Cleveland, the home of the foundation. Another of the Brush Foundation's projects was the funding of a "Symposium on Race Betterment," in Dayton, Ohio, on October 10, 1929. This gathering was "the first of its kind ever held in Ohio," one of its aims being the "study of the proposal to restrict parentage to include only those people who show no serious heredity taints such as feeble-mindedness, and who have no social diseases...."[146] According to the eugenicists gathered in Cleveland, the rationale for restriction was the prevention of "an increased tax burden."[147] The elimination of the welfare burden through limiting the children of the "unfit" could be done by one of two methods, and "mercy," according to the conference proceedings, would decide which one should prevail: either the segregation and denial of marriage for the "unfit" or else merely their sterilization.[148]

Regarding the latter option, the drastic California law (under which over 20,000 people were sterilized by the end of 1963) is cited approvingly as a model law, and the symposium report notes, "The Brush Foundation of Cleveland is actively engaged in such a campaign of education [for sterilization laws], and should receive the support of every organized agency engaged in social work."[149] A significant benefit of sterilization, according to the Brush Foundation, is that it would allow the release of segregated feebleminded people, so that they could engage in menial work serving the fit. "Society needs the services of its simple minded ditch-diggers and scrubwomen, and can ill afford to adopt a policy that would permanently deprive them of liberty."[150] What the "simple minded" could afford personally is not addressed.

Dorothy Brush did not restrict her eugenic activism to the family foundation. She served on the AES board of directors.[151] She was also involved in the Human Betterment Association of America (as Birthright was later called). In this, she was not alone among Sanger's followers. In the 1960s, other PPFA types involved in the HBAA (later the Association for Voluntary Sterilization and now Engender Health) included Guttmacher as a member of the medical committee, Frances Ferguson as a member of the executive committee, population controller Hugh Moore as president, Sanger biographer Lawrence Lader as a board member, and PPFA lawyer Harriet Pilpel as the legal counsel.[152]

Yet the Brush Foundation remained the most important vehicle for Brush's eugenic advocacy, and it was actively involved in Margaret Sanger's efforts. For example, in 1928, Sanger applied to the Brush Foundation on behalf of the American Birth Control League, hoping for financial assistance.[153] In 1930, the foundation voluntarily wrote to Sanger, wanting the published proceedings of the Seventh International Birth Control Conference in Zurich and saying that the foundation was "very much interested" in the topic.[154]

Financial support was crucial when IPPF was starting out. As Gamble wrote to Dorothy Brush in 1957, "The quotations from the report of the Brush Foundation show what large financing they have put into birth control. Where would the IPPF have been without them?"[155] The foundation's history notes, "For several years beginning in 1949, the Brush Foundation provided substantially all of the financial support for the International Planned Parenthood Foundation."[156] In fact, before IPPF became a tax-deductible organization, the Brush Foundation received contributions on behalf of IPPF, thereby enabling the latter's donors to receive tax deductions.

Several of the men involved with the Brush Foundation were involved with eugenic population control in other capacities. The Brush's treasurer, Jerome C. Fisher, was IPPF's co-treasurer until his death in 1954, when he was succeeded by the next Brush treasurer, Rufus S. Day, Jr. P. K. Whelpton served on the Brush board, probably because he was a respected demographer who was also a eugenicist and who had worked with foundations before.

All of this activity in population control did not cause the foundation to forget its original commitment to eugenics because, of course, the two are intrinsically related. From the foundation's beginning until 1980, it was estimated that it had given over $860,000 to family planning (mostly to PPFA and IPPF and their affiliates), while over $1,081,000 had been devoted to scientific projects, including eugenic research into "genetic disease" and child development. Among other eugenic organizations the foundation supported were the Association for Voluntary Sterilization, Gamble's Pathfinder International, and the Human Betterment Association. In even more recent times, the foundation has given to cytogenetic research projects, "in keeping with the instructions in Mr. Brush's Deed of Gift to further scientific research in the field of eugenics." This research included the practical eugenic application of amniocentesis testing, which allows the fetus's genetic makeup to be tested so that any disabled fetus can be aborted.[157] (This practice of contemporary eugenics, sometimes called "search-and-destroy" abortions, was examined at the end of the previous chapter.) Perhaps the Brush Foundation's original commitment to both population control and eugenics was not forgotten because Dorothy Brush herself never forgot it. Population control after all flows naturally from a eugenic ideology of control.

In 1957, she wrote to fellow birth controller Anne Kennedy about her desire to further her writing career, noting that she was already writing book reviews for the *Eugenics Quarterly*.[158] Writing under the title of "Chairman, Brush Foundation for Race Betterment," she reviewed the published proceedings of the Fifth International Planned Parenthood Federation Conference in Tokyo in 1955. She explained that its seven chapters deal with aspects of birth control related to, among other things, eugenics.[159] The eugenic topics included "Genetic Aspects of Population Replacement" by Frederick Osborn and C. P. Blacker's speech on the history of the "Family Planning and Eugenics Movement in the Mid-Twentieth Century."[160]

Reflecting Dorothy Brush's interests in eugenics, the current projects of the Brush Foundation epitomize the cooptation of feminist language for the furtherance of eugenic/population-control activities. Birth controllers have often fretted over increased funding for women's education and health care, viewing these programs as competing with their own (in addition to irresponsibly encouraging poor women to breed more).[161] The Brush Foundation shows itself to still have a narrow view of women's health and rights, dictated more by demography than by feminism. The foundation has funded abortion-rights projects since 1974, claiming a concern for women's rights and freedom, but it seems evident, in its funding of such projects as a Planned Parenthood initiative targeting Native Americans, that its concern is less feminist than demographic and eugenic. Its current international grants are reserved for population-control projects in developing countries (including those of Pathfinder International), and many of its domestic grants also target low-income women.[162] Women, especially those in the organizations which are being funded by the foundation, must ask themselves if cooperating with control institutions such as the Brush Foundation is not a betrayal of the basic human rights of poor women.[163]

Conclusion

This chapter has presented brief biographies of five people with whom Sanger worked very closely. All of them were explicit eugenicists. By this I mean that each had some leadership role within official, self-consciously eugenic institutions, whether with the American Eugenics Society, the pro-sterilization groups, or the eugenically oriented Brush Foundation. All of them, with the exception of Dorothy Brush, are acknowledged as eugenicists in many standard works of eugenic historiography.[164] Yet one would never know that from reading much of the feminist historiography concerning Sanger. In evading the question of Sanger's eugenic involvement—failing to mention something as basic as her AES membership—this scholarship makes at most passing mention of the deep eugenic commitments of many of her coworkers.[165] Other activists could have been mentioned here: both doctors of Sanger's clinic, Dorothy Bocker and Hannah

Stone, were supporters of eugenics, for instance, a fact rarely mentioned in much Sanger scholarship.[166]

Despite this academic silence, we have seen that the historical record is quite clear that Sanger's involvement with eugenics included constant collaboration with professional eugenicists. This involvement was not simply pragmatic but also principled, as her own private statements show. Frederick Osborn in America and C. P. Blacker in England were the leading eugenicists in their respective countries, while the latter was also an important leader within the International Planned Parenthood Federation. Robert Latou Dickinson and Clarence Gamble devoted themselves full-time to birth-control promotion, and they were motivated to a great extent by their eugenic beliefs. Dorothy Brush found in Sanger's activity a cause that reinforced her own eugenic commitments, and she became a close personal friend and confidante of Sanger. The fact that Sanger both recruited and naturally attracted other confirmed eugenicists indicates the high degree of cross-fertilization between the birth-control and the eugenics movements. The former was the activist arm and the latter the research arm of the control movement, and while the two sides often bickered with each other and sometimes distrusted the other's approach, there existed a fundamental philosophical harmony between the two.

CHAPTER FOUR

Quality, Not Quantity: Population Control and Eugenics

"The most penetrating thinkers ... are coming to see that a qualitative factor as opposed to a quantitative one is of primary importance in dealing with the great masses of humanity."— Margaret Sanger, Pivot of Civilization, *1922*[1]

"We get whatever we reward for. If we reward the lazy, their tribe will increase."— Garrett Hardin, The Ostrich Factor, *1999*[2]

Eugenics has not really died out; it has just taken on new projects. Since explicit eugenics became more unpopular after World War II, its proponents drifted into new areas in which they could translate camouflaged eugenic doctrines into praxis. Speaking generally, two of these main areas can be identified: the "new eugenics" and population control. The relation of the "new eugenics" to Sanger's movement is complex. It is carried on by scientists who generally dislike the messy arena of political involvement and prefer to address eugenic/genetic questions "scientifically." Despite this difference from Sanger and her followers, however, the common ethical justifications for contemporary eugenic projects repeated by even the larger public reflect the fact that Sanger and Planned Parenthood have effectively inured the American conscience with the control ideology. We have seen Sanger's connection to eugenics and her close working relationships with other eugenicists; now we must explore the other area in which they all were active, population control, in order to present further historical evidence of one of this book's central theses: population control is grounded in eugenic ideology. That is, the perceived opposition between quantity and genetic quality characteristic of eugenic ideology underlies the population-control movement.[3] If this is not understood, Sanger's world-historical legacy, as the one who most effectively implemented the eugenic ideology, simply cannot be recognized.

All the main players in the formative early period of demography and population activism had at least a minor and often a major role to play in the eugenics movement as well, and frequently they were drawn to population control because of their eugenic commitments. If this fact were of merely historical interest, then a chapter devoted to the eugenic/population control link could be written almost as an afterthought, but the contemporary situation demands otherwise: the historical (and ideological) relation of population control to eugenics firmly established the priorities and approach of what is today a very powerful movement, a billion-dollar industry that receives a significant portion of our foreign aid.

For an example of the eugenic mindset explicitly driving population-control ideology, one needs only to look at Garrett Hardin (who died in 2003 with his wife in a double suicide), an influential early population-control theorizer and friend of the popularizer Paul Ehrlich. Demonstrating a typical eugenic distrust of the fertility of the poor and an animus against social-welfare programs, Hardin warns in a recent book, "*We get whatever we reward for....* If we reward the lazy, their tribe will increase." Instead of providing altruistic support for the "unfit," we should let nature take its course in eliminating them through starvation and disease, because, he claims, evolution shows us that "nature invests in success." This approach, he insists, is the solution to the population problem. Echoing Sanger and other eugenicists, he decries the fact that propaganda by such population-control groups as Zero Population Growth (ZPG) reaches only academics and well-educated people, thereby decreasing "the relative number of educated people compared with the uneducated. I don't know of anyone who regards that as a desirable result."[4] Aside from the fact that Hardin seems to think that education is genetically inherited, the most revealing aspect of his statement is that he appears to have surrounded himself with eugenicists.[5]

Indeed, the inbred nature of the population-control movement is such that its ideology has proved remarkably resistant to modification, with the result that eugenic attitudes have continued to dominate its thinking, either overtly, as in the case of China, or covertly, as in the paternalistic thinking of bureaucrats who would tell the women of the Southern

Hemisphere how many children they should have. This chapter will examine the establishment and continuation of eugenic beliefs within the population-control movement by beginning with Malthus. I will then look at the ideological similarities between eugenics and population control on the subject of coercion, before mapping the mutation of eugenics into population control. Lastly, the intriguing case of the eugenic Council on Population Policy will be examined. I will continue the story in the next chapter by examining how wealthy eugenic donors have shaped the philosophy of prominent contemporary population-control organizations such as the Population Council, before looking at the often misogynistic policies that the United States government, especially the State Department, has enforced through its influence over poorer countries.

This chapter will not directly address the scientific evidence for or against the existence of a population problem; it is intended as a historical analysis, not as an exercise in demography, economics, or biology. However, I do point out how biased the "science" that underlies our current analyses of the population "problem" has been: from the beginning, it was driven by the eugenic prejudices of certain wealthy donors and foundations, and this simple historical fact renders suspect the evidence accumulated by the activist scientists who were trained in the programs of the Population Council, the Milbank Memorial Fund, and other donors. My point, thus, is that science is always at risk of being distorted by ideology, so that the biases of the scientists can infect the objectivity of their conclusions.

Regardless, whatever the actual scientific value of demographic predictions concerning population growth, there are ethical realities that must be recognized (else might makes right). Nothing, not even apocalyptic warnings about "overpopulation"—which, in any case, have invariably turned out to be incorrect—should compel us to disregard the rights and dignity of any human person. Nothing can justify the forcible sterilization of a woman; we need to find better and more critically conscious ways to deal with our problems, ways that are not built on the demonization of female fertility.

Malthus and His Followers

The father of population control was a British minister named Thomas R. Malthus.[6] Born in 1766, he watched with alarm the events occurring across the Channel in France and sought to disprove the radical political theory associated with the French Revolution, namely, that human reason could directly transform the political landscape by instituting Enlightenment policies and structures. Against this principle, Malthus wrote *An Essay on the Principle of Population* (appearing in an early form in 1797), which insisted that "vice and misery" would always be present in society; they could not be eliminated through reason, because they served the purpose of checking population so that it would not outstrip food production.[7] It was a biological inevitability, he asserted, that population would always increase geometrically, that is, doubling itself every twenty-five years or so, while food production would increase only arithmetically during the same time.[8]

In order to prevent this biological disaster, he argued, two types of checks operate naturally. The first, the "preventive" check, arises from the ability to calculate bad future consequences: a person can foresee that a large family will be difficult to support, so he or she chooses either moral restraint — manifested in the postponement of marriage and moderation within marriage — or else vice — seen in the recourse to prostitutes or to contraception.[9] Unlike his followers, the pro-contraception Neo-Malthusians, Malthus himself always viewed self-restraint, not birth control, as the answer to the population problem.[10]

The second type of check, called a "positive" check, affects the poor most often, in that it consists of "every cause, whether arising from vice or misery, which in any degree contributes to shorten the natural duration of human life." Among these causes he enumerates poverty, crowds, diseases, war, pestilence, and famine.[11] When preventive checks do not function, when virtuous restraint is inoperative, then positive checks arise naturally to keep population down. The final check that is activated when all the others fail is famine.

Those who suffer most from the positive checks are also those who are least likely to exercise a preventive check on their own reproduction. Malthus states that "there are few states in which there is not a constant effort in the population to increase beyond the means of subsistence. This constant effort as constantly tends to subject the lower classes of society to distress, and to prevent any great permanent amelioration of their condition."[12] In this statement can be found the kernel of Malthus's political economics, as opposed to that of the radical French thinkers: as long as population increases, which it inevitably must, and when virtue fails, as is likely, natural checks such as war and famine will arise to decimate the population and thereby destroy order in the society. Any society which tries to build its social-political institutions on reason alone, in the hopes of ameliorating the distress of its lower classes, will invariably fail if it does not take into account the pressures of population and seek to ease them through education and the encouragement of moral restraint.

Malthus was trained in the English utilitarianism prevalent in his day, and this philosophy fundamentally shapes his ideology. The utilitarianism he learned was developed by William Paley, who taught that pleasure and pain were the rewards and punishments that followed respectively from either good or evil actions. Thus, if the sum total of pleasure in the community is maximized and that of pain is minimized, then the community and the individuals within it would be acting morally. Malthus extended this theory to population by arguing that continence, as the solution to population growth, had to be moral because it maximized happiness and minimized misery.[13] An unfortunate by-product of this way of thinking is that the suffering of the poor can often be viewed as the result of immoral activity, instead of being seen as the result of injustice. Utilitarianism also legitimates allowing the suffering of many if it seems to benefit the community as a whole, and, not surprisingly, the ones whose suffering is allowed to occur are invariably the powerless, who cannot protest easily. Thus, Malthus critiqued the Poor Laws in England by noting that, "if the poor laws had never existed in this country, though there might have been a few more instances of very severe distress, the aggregate mass of happiness among the common people would have been much greater than it is at present," because, he believed, the lack of the financial assistance provided by the welfare laws would have discouraged the poor from having more children and thereby perpetuating their misery.[14]

In an early version of the *Essay,* Malthus spelled out explicitly the problem with welfare programs.

> A man who is born into a world already possessed, if he cannot get subsistence from his parents on whom he has a just demand, and if the society do not want his labour, has no claim of *right* to the smallest portion of food, and, in fact, has no business to be where he is. At nature's mighty feast there is no vacant cover for him. She tells him to be gone, and will quickly execute her own orders, if he do not work upon the compassion of some of her guests.... The guests learn too late their error, in counteracting those strict orders to all intruders, issued by the great mistress of the feast, who, wishing that all her guests should have plenty, and knowing that she could not provide for unlimited numbers, humanely refused to admit fresh comers when her table was already full.[15]

Malthus's problematic moral vision, with its exclusionary and elitist aspects (as well as its extreme concept of private property), was proffered as a way of dealing with the supposedly cruel reality of population growth, which he believed would always exceed the amount of food grown. Yet this "law" was not true even during Malthus's own lifetime.[16] For example, the nineteenth century saw a greater-than-arithmetic increase in American production of wheat, while our own century has witnessed a massive increase in food productivity. Soybean growth, for example, has gone from 14 million bushels in 1930 to more than 1.5 billion bushels in 1973.[17] The increase in productivity continues to this day. These immense advances are in large part due to the development of agricultural technologies.[18] The wildcard of human insight and creativity has simply not been attended to by population controllers.

The specter of famine has been invoked more than once by twentieth-century population-control hysterics such as William Vogt and Paul Ehrlich; the latter predicted that Americans would be starving in the streets by the 1970s. He acknowledged his dishonesty in 1990: "Everyone wants to know what's going to happen. And you never know what's going to happen. So, the question is, Do you say, 'I don't know,' in which case they all go back to bed — or do you say, 'Hell, in ten years you're likely to be going without food and water' and [get] their attention?"[19] Among those who were convinced by these kinds of Neo-Malthusian arguments was Margaret Sanger.

Sanger on Population Control

As the first chapter showed, Margaret Sanger was a longtime advocate of population control, well before the subject had received much attention from scientists or wealthy philanthropists in the United States. Already in her 1917 book, *The Case for Birth Control*, a whole chapter is devoted to the topic of a supposedly excessive birthrate, and this at a time when the chief demographic concern was "race suicide," a phrase popularized by Teddy Roosevelt to indicate a too-low rate of reproduction.[20] Until well after World War II, Americans were more concerned about too few people than too many, based on evidence that the First World's population was decreasing, jeopardizing geopolitical power and economic stability.

Sanger was one of the first activists who tried to invert that concern. She was tutored to fear population growth by the English Neo-Malthusians, including Alice Drysdale and Havelock Ellis. Later Sanger would reflect upon this time with nostalgia: "I learned that Britain had a whole century behind her in Malthusian and Neo-Malthusian agitation. I learned of the Rev. Robert Malthus and his controversial theories. Many of Malthus's critics offer glib *solutions*, but they do not understand the population *problem*. Malthus did...."[21]

The population problem for Neo-Malthusians has as much to do with quality as with quantity: the solution to the problem of too many people was fewer and better people. The Neo-Malthusians were already thinking in terms of quality over quantity around the turn of the century; an early broadsheet for the Malthusian League in Britain included the proposition "That Quality is better than mere Quantity in children."[22] The Neo-Malthusian C. V. Drysdale expanded on the theme in 1914 when he explained to the Royal Colonial Institute that the British were able to colonize so efficiently not because of their numbers but rather because of their racial superiority; a few Brits could conquer the world much more efficiently than many darker types, according to Drysdale. Thus, what was important for England was to maintain and improve its quality, not increase its quantity.[23]

Sanger far extended the reach of these Neo-Malthusian ideas, trailblazing their institutional dissemination in the United States. One of Sanger's organizational and publicity techniques centered around planning conferences at which various experts could gather and express their support for her work, and she consistently included the population angle in the programs of these meetings. In 1922, the American Birth Control League participated in the Fifth International Neo-Malthusian and Birth Control Congress in London. (Among the topics covered was the eugenic aspect of birth control.) Various diversions were planned for the participants, including an "automobile excursion to the Rookery, Dorking, the home of the Rev. T. R. Malthus," plus an "outdoor Propaganda Meeting in a poor neighborhood; preceded by a visit to the Malthusian League's Welfare Centre in which Birth Control information is given to poor mothers...."[24]

Another Sanger conference that prominently featured population questions, the Sixth International Neo-Malthusian and Birth Control Conference, was held in 1925 in New York. Various Neo-Malthusians from all over the world attended, and the conference was a huge success in terms of publicity for her cause.[25] Eugenicist Raymond Pearl telegraphed his greetings, proclaiming that "Birth Control seems to offer the only method at once humane and intelligent of meeting the menace of population growth without fundamentally altering our civilization and standards of living."[26]

Sanger edited the four volumes of papers that came out of the conference, papers which tended, quite correctly, to emphasize the eugenic nature of population control. One thick volume was dedicated to "Medical and Eugenic Aspects of Birth Control," and its table of contents reads like a Who's Who of prominent eugenicists, including C. C. Little, H. H. Laughlin, Havelock Ellis, and Georges de Lapouge.[27]

Sanger's mentor Ellis devoted his essay, "The Evolutionary Meaning of Birth Control," to an explication of Malthusian population theory married to a eugenic understanding of birth control. According to Ellis, population *will* be controlled, whether by the forces of famine and disease or by cruel and primitive practices such as infanticide. Birth control enables population to be controlled "rationally"—that is, eugenically—so that the unfit are the first to have their procreation restricted. As he concluded, "The only method which comes before us today as a reasonably practical instrument, whatever its defects, for effecting the limitation of the family and eugenically moulding the future race, is the method of contraception...."[28]

Some of the conference participants evinced a eugenic racism combined with an obsession with population control: they feared that other races would submerge the white race in a sea of color. Such was the case with Dr. S. Adolphus Knopf, who said ominously, "We can only hope that the alarming increase of the yellow and black races may be checked in time to prevent a catastrophe to our present civilization."[29] Echoing Knopf's concern, although without his blatant racism, was the conference's "Resolutions Committee," a group of six including both Sanger and C. V. Drysdale. They concluded that "the present situation as regards Birth Control is highly disgenic [*sic*]." This was due to the fact that the "educated and privileged classes" had access to contraception, but the "poor and ignorant" did not, "thus causing an unfavorable differential birth rate."[30] That the old eugenic obsession about the differential birthrate is cited is significant, in that it makes clear that Sanger and other Neo-Malthusians were primarily concerned about the overpopulation of the *poor* and the otherwise unfit, as opposed to a simple excess of people in general. Population control, in other words, was about decreasing quantity (among the "unfit") in order to increase quality.

Continuing the momentum of the 1926 conference, Sanger plunged immediately into organizing an international conference to be held in 1927 in Geneva, Switzerland. Helping her was Edith How-Martyn in England, who later ran the Sanger-sponsored Birth Control International Information Centre in London, putting out pamphlets that fretted over the fact that birth control "is practised least in what are economically, and some would say genetically, the lowest social grades."[31] The chairman of the conference was the Englishman Sir Bernard Mallet, who also served as the president of the English Eugenics Society. The Preliminary Advisory Council of twenty-eight scientists was heavily loaded with eugenicists, including Prof. Eugen Fischer of Germany, who was later involved with the Nazi eugenic project; future Nazi Erwin Baur also participated.[32]

In organizing the conference, Sanger worked closely with Raymond

Pearl, who had hoped to establish an international scientific population organization at the conference. Accordingly, the International Union for the Scientific Investigation of Population Problems (IUSIPP, later the International Union for the Scientific Study of Population, or IUSSP) was formed at the close of the conference, with the financial assistance of various Rockefeller foundations.[33] The IUSSP was also funded by the Milbank Memorial Fund, which "became the major source of financial sustenance for the infant organization in its first perilous years of life."[34] By the 1970s, the IUSSP was financially propped up by the Population Council, the UN World Population Fund, and UNESCO, while working informally with the International Planned Parenthood Federation.[35]

All of the money and networking paid off: demographer and eugenicist Frank Lorimer has noted the importance of both the Geneva conference and the founding of the IUSSP as pioneering endeavors of the population-control movement, since before 1927 there was little coordination of the eugenic, Neo-Malthusian, sociological, and demographic interests of population controllers.[36] The IUSSP is supposedly a purely scientific organization, with no ambitions to dabble in political matters or social policy questions, but Lorimer, a former president and executive director, acknowledged that the IUSSP has been "highly effective" in promoting support for population control throughout the world, "especially in regions now bound in poverty."[37] It held its 1935 conference in Berlin and, while Pearl was hesitant about the political atmosphere of Berlin at that time, other Americans, such as eugenicist Clarence G. Campbell, embraced the Nazi agenda, at one point offering a toast "to that great leader, Adolf Hitler!"[38]

The American affiliate of the International Union was the Population Association of America (PAA), founded in 1931 with eugenicist Henry Pratt Fairchild as its first president.[39] The organizational meeting in December 1930 was attended by thirteen people, including Sanger (who had found money for the venture from the Milbank Memorial Fund), Harry Laughlin, and P. K. Whelpton, as well as personnel from various foundations. A list of people interested in population questions was drawn up, and those on the list were invited for a conference the following May. Historian Dennis Hodgson has observed that "a full range of eugenicists was invited, from the unrestrained to the temperate," including Guy Irving Burch, Charles Davenport, Clarence Gamble, Frederick Osborn, Raymond Pearl, and Leon Whitney.[40] The mission statement of the PAA stressed that its interest in population included "both its quantitative and its qualitative aspects," and when the mission statement was revised in 1974, this language was retained.[41]

Indeed, the entire population-control movement, based supposedly on an objective scientific consensus about the dangers of population growth, was controlled by the agenda of a handful of eugenicists (perhaps the majority of which were not formally trained scientists). The reminiscences of demographer and eugenicist Frank Notestein (a great admirer of Frederick Osborn) concerning the founding of the PAA are telling. Initially the IUSSP had a branch in the United States, the American National Committee, which preceded and was ostensibly "independent" of the PAA, but then "decided" to merge with the latter. Notestein's report of this process indicates the artificial nature of such inter-organizational diplomacy.

> I still remember when about a dozen of us would meet in [Louis] Dublin's office at the Metropolitan [Life Insurance Company] as the members of the American National Committee of the International Union for the Scientific Study of Population Problems and draw up a memorandum to the new Population Association of America. We would then adjourn our meeting and quickly travel to the Town Hall Club, where the same group would assemble as the College of Fellows of the new Population Association of America of which we were the crème de la crème. As such we received the memorandum from the American National Committee, pondered its merit, and passed on the results of our superior wisdom together with notice of the action taken to the body of the Association. The College then hastily adjourned to reconstitute itself as the Association and receive with gratitude the result of the College's mature wisdom.[42]

This example demonstrates the inbred nature of the population-control movement, the concrete impact of which is that no one challenges the received wisdom: multiple groups without multiple viewpoints. The plethora of organization names gives the impression that there is some broad-based scientific consensus that an overpopulation problem exists. But in reality, the population-control movement was initiated by a few dozen eugenicists with often dubious scientific credentials. This clubby milieu, in which a well-heeled set of ideologically motivated activists makes pronouncements patined with scientific "authority," still holds sway in the population-control movement.

Not surprisingly, the Rockefellers also funded the PAA in addition to the IUSSP, given the overlap in personnel of those two groups. Rockefeller staffer Arthur W. Packard noted in an internal memo that the PAA's interest in researching the effects of birth control on the quantity and quality of the population made it a viable candidate for Rockefeller funding; other documents show that Rockefeller staffers were very interested in the PAA's research on "how Relief can be administered without encouraging more children, especially among lower intelligence-ability groups."[43]

Notestein has acknowledged that the attention paid to population issues in the 1930s had a lot to do with "the depression, with its unemployment."[44] He clearly presents the eugenic "solution" to poverty: "I can't see a time ever when birth control shouldn't be foisted on some parts of our population," that segment being, of course, the lower class,[45] and when he was the president of the Rockefeller-funded Population Council, he gave a talk in Karachi that promoted the eugenic notion that economic growth "requires also qualitative changes in the people."[46] In this, he was simply reflecting the biases of the Council's founder, John D. Rockefeller 3rd, who encouraged the Rockefeller Foundation to get involved in population control, especially in one area that "intrigues me very much — the quality of the population. Obviously it is a tough one and a long-range one but pretty important to generations to come."[47]

Sanger's own commitment to eugenic population-control activities never wavered. Toward the end of her life, in 1950, she stated, "The basic truth that we insist upon ... is that there is a population problem and we know that this problem involves the whole human race, both living and potential." To further her point, she gave the example of Great Britain, a small yet thriving nation in the time of Shakespeare. "What is England producing today with her hungry fifty million human beings struggling for survival? She had then a race of quality, now it's merely quantity."[48] Throughout her life Sanger was obsessed with achieving a race of quality, not quantity.

The Coercive Ideology of Eugenic Population Control

General ignorance about the history of the population-control movement makes it impossible to adequately assess the depth of Sanger's own, eugenically motivated, commitment to population control. As with her importance for eugenics in general, recognition of her pivotal role in the institution of population control requires an understanding of the larger historical context. Otherwise, historical naivete will simply cause one to fail to take Sanger seriously, both in what she said, as well as in what she did. Sanger was, in fact, not the only eugenicist who was obsessed with population control. Indeed, one of the most basic historical facts of the population-control movement is that it was initiated by explicitly eugenic ideologues. So, an examination of the historical context clarifies the eugenic legacy Sanger bequeathed to us, a legacy transmitted by means of the institutions she established, which are committed to the control of female fertility. Let us now turn to an examination of this larger histori-cal context, which clarifies Sanger's role and importance and which enables us to better understand our present.

The historical record of the population-control movement is quite clear: eugenicists set the agenda. For example, in 1972 demographer Michael Teitelbaum claimed, "Population policies have genetic implica-tions. Indeed, the issue of genetic 'quality' has been one of the primary concerns of many persons interested in population matters, especially dur-ing the first half of this century."[49] This section will focus on the eugenic ideology that explains such a statement while the remainder of the chap-ter will further describe the personnel that did double duty for ostensibly distinct eugenics and population-control organizations and how Sanger and Planned Parenthood fit into the picture.[50]

Ideological similarity between population control and eugenics is not hard to discern. Both movements demand the sacrifice of individual desires and rights (especially in the area of reproduction) for the "greater" soci-etal good, whether that good be genetic or demographic. For example, one of the most prominent population-control propagandizers, Garrett Hardin, in complaining that "in every nation women want more children than the community needs," has argued that since parenthood is not a right but a privilege, women should be forcibly sterilized after having a certain number of children. In case there was doubt in anyone's mind that population-control policies are not in harmony with women's rights, Hardin emphasizes, "The Women's Liberation Movement may not like it, but control must be exerted through females.... Biology makes women responsible."[51] Oddly enough for a biologist, Hardin seems to have for-gotten that men play a role in conception also. He reveals also that qual-ity, not just quantity, is of concern to him, when he reiterates old eugenic themes about a person's genes belonging not to one's self but rather to society: "'My' child's germ plasm is not *mine*; it is really only part of the community's store." Thus, society as a whole has the right, according to Hardin, to take control of "its" germ plasm by refusing to allow some of it to be perpetuated.[52]

As we will see, sometimes this coercion occurs through outright force, while other times it happens through providing monetary incentives for the abjectly poor to be sterilized or to receive one of the long-lasting chem-ical contraceptives; Hardin himself promotes anti-child tax measures, arguing that "coercion is a dirty word to most liberals now, but it need not forever be so." He advocates repeating the word "coercion" over and over again "without apology or embarrassment," until the horror it induces melts away by sheer dint of repetition (a favorite method of propagandists).[53] His most recent book, funded in part by the eugenic Pioneer Fund, advocates "mutual coercion mutually agreed upon,"[54] an impressively Orwellian turn of phrase. What Hardin's formula boils down to is the control of the marginalized by the elite.

Others, such as Bernard Berelson, president emeritus and senior fellow of the Population Council at his death in 1979, have advocated that incentives be used initially and that coercion be used only as a last resort; in other words, population-control programs should "employ less severe measures where possible and only ascend to harsher measures if the problem at hand, as a matter of (established) fact, is clearly grave enough to warrant it."[55] Such a formulation leaves an enormous loophole for all sorts of oppressive actions in the name of "grave" circumstances. Indeed, Berelson earlier had proposed adding contraceptives to urban water supplies.[56] He also supported the use of coercive incentives, perversely claiming that they actually *increase* human freedom (since the targeted person now has the option to receive an incentive that was not previously available), while neglecting to observe that a starving person may feel she has no choice but to trade in her fertility for food.[57]

Similarly, a 1991 paper cowritten by a Planned Parenthood operative acknowledges, "By their nature, incentives and disincentives are aimed primarily at the poor, since it is mainly the poor who will be susceptible to them." Yet this same paper also cheerfully embraced incentives, perhaps *because* the poor would thereby reduce their fertility.[58] Today, UNFPA, IPPF, and other population-control groups oppose incentives, yet these same groups continue to cooperate and even defend governments who use these schemes, while the World Bank and USAID have more or less supported incentive programs.[59] As Hardin's rhetoric reminds us, the persons who are so abused are almost always women.

Another typical perspective on this issue has been given by Christopher Tietze, an employee of the Population Council. Tietze chose the path of equivocation: in one interview, he echoed Sanger's strategy of redefining freedom by simultaneously insisting he supported both freedom and also coercion, without seeing any conflict between the two positions.

> I believe the voluntary system must survive. This is the only way we can maintain a free society. However, I do not think it wrong at all to have incentives. I think the bigger the incentives the better. If a country's having trouble in having a voluntary acceptance of whatever its population policy is, then they should encourage people to accept it by offering them candy, or whatever it is that one offers adults in order to make them conform to patterns that are considered acceptable by the government.[60]

Given all of these attitudes, held by some of the most influential actors within the population-control lobby in the 1960s, 1970s, and 1980s, it should come as no surprise that UNFPA, the Population Council, and IPPF all agreed in a background document for the International Conference on Family Planning in the 1980s that

> when the provision of contraceptive information and services does not bring down the fertility level quickly enough to help speed up development, governments may decide to limit the freedom of choice of the present generation so that future generations may have a better chance to enjoy their basic rights.[61]

The official eugenic groups welcomed the channeling of eugenics into population control, because they understood that once consciences are dulled enough to make coercion acceptable in an "emergency" situation like a "population explosion," the practice of force can be more easily applied in other "urgent" situations. As eugenicist Carl Bajema said in 1971, "[I]t is but a short step to compulsory control of genetic quality once compulsory programs aimed at controlling population size have been adopted."[62] The marriage between population control and genetic control was so close that some eugenicists in the 1970s harbored hopes that the more popular movement of population control would lend some respectability — as well as legal momentum — to their somewhat publicly discredited movement.

Already in the 1950s, many who embraced the control ideology called for eugenic measures masquerading as domestic population policy. For example, one conference of notable demographers, including the former president of PPFA, Frances Ferguson, chastised the United States for being "a backward country" in its own domestic population policy.[63] This "backwardness" was due to America's blindness about the genetic implications of its social welfare system. Echoing classic eugenic language, the proceedings read:

> A disproportionate number of children tends, in each generation, to be born to a group of parents who are socially handicapped either through ill health, poverty, incompetence, low mental ability or emotional disturbance. The children in these disadvantaged families contribute more than their proportion of juvenile delinquency, and have a retarding effect on education. They tend to lower in each generation the quality of the people.[64]

Instead of running from eugenics, the population controllers urged the government to establish a domestic population policy that would "encourage genetic improvement from one generation to another."[65]

Still today, prominent eugenic scientists publicly acknowledge that population control and eugenics go hand in hand; Philippe Rushton goes so far as to say: "People often describe the world population as out of control. That very soon touches the nerve of race differences in reproduction. Population policy touches on who's going to reproduce. It touches on eugenics."[66] With that sort of controlling racism in the background, it is no accident that the alarm about over-population was first sounded over the reproductive rates of the less-developed countries, not over the rate of growth of, say, the Netherlands—which has a higher population density than India.[67]

The Eugenicists Become Demographers

How did this confluence of ideology come about? Feminist historian Linda Gordon has noted that eugenicists made an easy transition into population control when outright eugenics became too unpalatable for the American public to stomach: "The eugenics people slid into the population control movement gracefully, naturally, imperceptibly … there was nothing to separate the two movements because there was no tension between their two sorts of goals."[68] At this point, it is illuminating to examine in detail a precise juncture in the relationship of population control to eugenics: in what ways was the historical development of demography tied to eugenics? In order to answer this question, let us analyze some of the institutions connected with these fields.

The first research institution in population, the Scripps Foundation for Research in Population Problems, was established in 1922, at Miami University in Ohio, and eugenicist and sociologist Warren S. Thompson was tapped to lead it. According to Frank Notestein, the Scripps Foundation arose because Edward Scripps, who made his money from the newspaper chain, was "concerned" about the population of Asia and came across Thompson's dissertation, which addressed Malthusian theory.[69]

Continuing the work begun in his dissertation, Thompson published articles about upper-class "race suicide" and expanded his research with P. K. Whelpton, who joined him in 1924.[70] He also worked with Osborn on population issues before joining the AES Board in 1935. Osborn noted, "Supported with foundation funds, [Thompson and Whelpton] applied themselves to the broader political and social implications of growth and change in world populations, and to the study of the differential growth and replacement of socioeconomic groups in the United States."[71] Whelpton also pursued a study motivated by positive eugenics, funded by the

Population Council, which was intended to determine the rates of reproduction of college graduates—that is, the "fit."[72] He continued his
involvement with eugenic birth control by holding a position on the board
of the eugenic Brush Foundation, which was described in the last chapter, and worked as the director of the Population Division of the United
Nations, succeeding Frank Notestein.[73]

The Milbank Memorial Fund (MMF) followed Scripps's lead in 1928,
setting up a Research Division of demographers who would be funded to
do scientific studies that would examine population questions.[74] As
Dorothy G. Wiehl, one of the first demographers who worked there,
remembered it, the link between demography and eugenics was at the
forefront of the scientists' minds.

> In the mid–1920s, the interest in population centered more in the eugenic
> implications of differential birth rates and the rapid decrease in mortality
> of infants and children.... The question asked by many was: "Are the unfit
> being kept alive?" Again, in [the report on] Health and Environment ...
> [MMF staff demographer Edgar] Sydenstricker referred to a then current
> argument as to whether "the increase in death rate of persons over 50 years
> of age is due wholly or in part to a deterioration of vitality," which, he said,
> raised the question "Are the American people breeding a stock with a lower
> inherited capacity to survive?" It was in this climate of opinion and spec-
> ulative philosophizing that the Fund began its studies of differential fer-
> tility and became involved in studying the effectiveness of birth control
> methods.[75]

In other words, it was within a *eugenic* climate that workers at Milbank
decided to study the relative fertility of the rich and the poor, as well as
the efficacy of different forms of contraception.

Another Milbank demographer, Frank Notestein, was hired by the
fund's Research Division in 1928, and his first assignment was to determine the relationship of social class to fertility in the 1910 census—in other
words, yet again the concern was differential fertility. The motivation for
the study, according to the advisory committee for the division (a committee which included eugenicist Raymond Pearl), was the "intelligent"
guidance of public health services and "social amelioration" for the poor.
This amelioration would include reducing their reproduction, if necessary,
so that, "if public health activities, as well as other efforts toward the social
amelioration are to be guided intelligently, it is highly desirable to have
some knowledge of the changes in the rate at which various groups reproduce themselves, of the changes in the extent to which specific social groups
are recruited from the other social classes, and of the general constitu-
tional or physical characteristics of these groups or classes."[76]

Likewise, demographer Clyde V. Kiser first came on board with the Milbank Memorial Fund as a "Milbank Fellow" in 1931 with the task of analyzing differential fertility in 1900 and "the trends in fertility differentials among native white women in the east North Central States"; he later was on the staff of the Population Council.[77] In addition, Kiser served on the board of directors of the American Eugenics Society through the 1970s.[78] At about the time Kiser was hired at Milbank, the fund began its research in contraception. Kiser remembered, "Mr. [John A.] Kingsbury, Secretary of the Fund, and Mr. Thomas Cocran, a member of the Board, were devotees of Margaret Sanger. Probably Mr. Kingsbury regarded birth control as something desirable from the standpoint of social welfare [a catchphrase for eugenics]."[79] At the June 16, 1931, meeting of the Fund's board of directors, it was decided that contributions to the birth-control movement would be made through the Research Division.[80]

As a result, the MMF became the first foundation to fund comparative contraception studies. A study of this sort was originally to be directed by the eugenicist demographer Raymond Pearl, using the records from Sanger's Clinical Research Bureau; Dr. Dorothy Bocker, the first doctor who directed Sanger's clinic, had recorded information about her patients that claimed to validate eugenic family trees, as well as show the cost to the community of uncontrolled reproduction. This eugenic interest is not surprising, given that Bocker believed strongly in sterilization for the "unfit," in order to stop the multiplication of the feebleminded.[81] According to Dr. Bocker's statistics, fully 31 percent of the clinic visitors were prescribed contraception on the basis of their "dysgenic" ancestry.[82]

Pearl is a perfect example of the intermarriage between eugenics and demography. He has often been cited as an opponent of eugenics, because he denounced popular eugenics as unscientific in a 1927 article in the *American Mercury*. Yet, as scholars such as Allen and Barkan note, Pearl was concerned only with unscientific claims by eugenicists that he believed were not in accord with scientific rationalism, rather than any opposition to the fundamental injustice inherent within eugenics.[83] Thus, despite his apparent disagreement with many eugenicists, he continued to approve of eugenics to such a degree that he was one of only 73 participants in the AES's Third International Congress of Eugenics in 1932.[84] He was described by Frank Notestein as "full of Galtonian eugenics, skeptical of reformers, doubtful of the long-run success of efforts to control tuberculosis because it would just breed weaklings, and convinced that the advocates of birth control took much too narrow a view of the determinants of growth, which was controlled by basic biological systems."[85] Despite this disagreement with birth-control workers, he still worked closely with Sanger through the 1920s. To his credit, he later disavowed any notion that the misuse of or the refusal to use contraception was due to genetic inferiority.[86]

In 1934 Pearl was still advocating some racist and eugenic doctrines such as the lesser intelligence of the black person based on old and inaccurate measurements that purported to show a smaller skull capacity and brain weight on the part of blacks. His racism extended to Jews as well, as made clear in his approval of Harvard's policy of excluding Jewish students. Pearl framed the issue this way: "The real question seems to me to come to this. Whose world is this to be, ours or the Jews?"[87] In a letter to his good friend, mentor, and persistent eugenicist Edward East, Pearl objects to East's having referred to Pearl a young Jewish scientist who wished to obtain some bibliographic information on population questions: "By the way, who is this Jew of yours…? I like his nerve and think he ought to go far, but just how did he ever get the notion that I have no other amusements in life except making bibliographies for lazy Jews?"[88] The young Jew in question? None other than Gregory Pincus, who was later instrumental in developing the birth-control pill.

As a eugenic demographer, Pearl was a forerunner of the type of population professional that would later be pervasive both within the family-planning movement and the huge population-control enterprise. In an interview, Mrs. Alan F. Guttmacher reflected on Pearl's birth-control activities in Baltimore, which centered around "statistical purposes, really," that is, using the clinic "for statistical and demographical use, and I believe they used patients more, you know, to see how things were working out for statistical purposes."[89]

Milbank's population-control activities did not end with Pearl's statistical studies. In 1936, Osborn convinced Milbank to set up a population-research office at Princeton (Osborn's alma mater) under Notestein, called the Office of Population Research.[90] Soon after the Rockefeller-funded Population Council was established in 1952, Notestein would succeed Osborn as its president in 1959 (although the latter remained involved in the organization).[91] Milbank's tie to Osborn, who served on the Fund's advisory board, continued in the period from 1959 to 1965, during which the Fund gave $28,000 to the American Eugenics Society,[92] and other grants were made at least through 1970.[93] The initial purpose of this money was "to develop and carry out plans for establishing [the AES] on a more permanent financial base without a break in the continuity of the work it is now doing."[94] The professional success of Notestein was good news for Sanger's groups. As Frederick Osborn had noted in a letter to a Birth Control Federation of America official almost twenty years earlier, while many population scholars were leery of being publicly involved with Sanger,

"Notestein doesn't feel the same way. He doesn't like to make outside affiliations, but his interest in the Birth Control Federation and in the Birth Control movement is very strong.... It seems to me a very fortunate break for you, as Notestein is, on the whole, probably the most impressive and competent figure in the population group today."[95]

Another well-respected demographic pioneer who was connected to the AES was Frank Lorimer. Described by Notestein as a "refugee from the clergy to John Dewey's philosophy," Lorimer served as executive director of the IUSSP in the late forties and later its president.[96] His friendship with Notestein would enable the IUSSP to play an important role within the UN's Population Division, and Lorimer also worked extensively with Osborn on eugenic and population-control problems, believing that "concern about the possible erosion of the human genetic pool and about the social implications of differential reproduction is no less imperative than concern about the erosion of the environment."[97] He lauded Osborn's importance to demography in an essay on the historical development of the discipline, in which he described the book that the two had co-authored on population genetics.[98]

Lorimer explained the overlap between such fields as demography and eugenics as a result of the relatively narrow field of inquiry to which strict demography is confined. After all, he pointed out, if the demographer stuck merely to statistics, it would be about as exciting a job as that of the chemist who analyzes the chemical structures of things. Demography is exciting for its practitioners— and, one might add, both powerful and dangerous— when it analyzes the eugenic and social implications of its statistical research. As he remarked, "The demographer is *inevitably* involved in investigating the biological and social correlates of demographic processes. Significant demography is *necessarily* interdisciplinary."[99] Accordingly, he prepared a paper on "the fertility of socially handicapped persons" for an American Eugenics Society meeting attended by such notable eugenic population controllers as Alan Guttmacher, Dudley Kirk, Clyde Kiser, Frederick Osborn, and Christopher Tietze.[100]

As we have seen, in addition to those who participated at the AES meeting, other eugenic demographers included Thompson, Sydenstricker, Pearl, and Notestein. Other pioneers in the development of demography, according to demographers themselves, include the original eugenicist Francis Galton and his disciple, Karl Pearson.[101]

Demography generates an indispensable aura of scientific legitimacy for the population-control movement. But we have seen how in fact the establishment of this new "science" was largely carried out under eugenic auspices by eugenic individuals. Population control was, as a matter of historical record, a eugenic initiative from the beginning. Indeed, the American Eugenics Society board and officers during the 1950s reads like a veritable Who's Who of the population-control movement. At this time, Alan Guttmacher was its vice president (and also served on its Medical Genetics Committee). The AES board included Dorothy Brush (a board member of the Brush Foundation), Robert C. Cook (the director of the Population Research Bureau), Frances Ferguson (one-time PPFA president), Dudley Kirk (Demographic Director, Population Council, and later president of the American Eugenics Society in the 1970s), Clyde V. Kiser (Milbank Memorial Fund), Frank Lorimer (Professor of Population Studies, American University), Emily H. Mudd (involved with PPFA and genetic counseling in Pennsylvania), and Warren S. Thompson (Scripps Foundation for Population Research, Miami University). Lorimer also served on the editorial board of the *Eugenics Quarterly* and on the committee for Research in Intelligence and Personality.[102]

With such decisive involvement of eugenic operatives in the development of demography, it is little wonder that feminists and other astute observers recognize destructive elitism and misogyny within the population-control movement.

The Council on Population Policy

Again, it is one of the central contentions of this book that — by virtue of a shared eugenic ideology of control — professional eugenicists, birth-control advocates, and population controllers constitute a single control movement with a near identity of interest, even if they have not always gotten along. The widespread overlap among organizations committed to eugenic goals as traced in previous chapters is mirrored in the "incestuous" structure of the population controllers, as one activist put it in Bachrach and Bergman's illuminating study of the make-up of the movement. Population controllers have given other colorful descriptions of their movement: "a Mafia-like structure," "a tight little community," and "an interlocking directorate."[103] All of the participants know all the others; they are involved in the same organizations, such as Planned Parenthood or the Population Council, while they simultaneously do research at the same population centers in universities and set the same kinds of government policy in family-planning funding. As one foundation staff member said, "The determination of priorities is made by members of the professional community in intimate dialogue with one another...."[104]

Sanger herself constantly sought to bring together the experts on birth control, population, and eugenics, even if she always wanted to retain control of the resulting coalitions. In the early 1920s, she pushed for a merger with the Eugenics Research Association, but the ERA eventually refused. When the idea of a joint publication combining the AES's *Eugenics* and Sanger's *Birth Control Review* surfaced in 1928, Leon Whitney (then the executive secretary of the AES) strongly pushed for its approval, but other eugenicists, mindful of Sanger's public repudiation of positive eugenics, shot down the idea.[105] In protesting the alliance, Charles Benedict Davenport, a committed positive eugenicist and a would-be sober scientist, recognized with clarity Sanger's philosophy: "...she thinks that birth control is the same as eugenics, and eugenics is birth control, and she would, naturally, seize with avidity a proposal that we should blend birth control and eugenics in some way, such as the proposed [joint] magazine."[106]

The idea never did fully die, and eventually other eugenicists came around to see benefits in greater organizational cohesiveness, especially when the Great Depression crippled the eugenics movement financially. A notable attempt at organizational unity was a proposed merger between the American Eugenics Society and the American Birth Control League in 1933 that would eventually become an umbrella group called the Council on Population Policy.[107] By this time Sanger had long ceased to run the ABCL, but her participation in the formation of the Council was eagerly solicited by eugenicist and population-control advocate Henry Pratt Fairchild and other allies and, on her part, gladly offered. The history of this project will illuminate the ease with which the members of the control movement traveled between eugenics, birth-control advocacy, and population control.

Fairchild first proposed a merger between the AES, the ABCL, and the Population Association of America in 1931.[108] The issue was investigated seriously in 1933, when a series of interviews was conducted with various important eugenicists by the ABCL staff prior to its March 2 board of directors meeting. The purpose was to ascertain whether the proposed merger would be helpful to the joint cause, and most people believed that it would. Even though Sanger was not any longer connected to the ABCL and had a fairly hostile relationship with its leader, Eleanor Jones, she was also interviewed and was eager to be involved on the new organization's board.[109] Nearly all those interviewed agreed, initially, that a name like Eugenic Birth Control would be unobjectionable. At this point in the AES's history, the group had been functionally inactive for about two years due to the shakeup after Frederick Osborn's entrance, and so a merger with a stronger group seemed practical. According to one interviewee, given that the "congruity of interests" between the two groups "is obvious," potential donors would find the resulting merged group very attractive in the breadth of its involvement in eugenic projects.[110]

After the various responses to the interviews were presented to the ABCL board, it appointed a committee to continue to examine the question and named Fairchild its chairman.[111] Among the possible objectives of the new organization would be "race improvement by birth selection" and "immigrant regulation."[112] As the logical next step, leading eugenicist Frederick Osborn was interviewed. Leery as always of the unscientific nature of the birth-control movement's popularizing activities, he suggested that the time was not ripe for the merger but allowed that it might be so in the future.[113] Undaunted, the "Committee to Inquire into the Desirability of Consolidating the American Birth Control League with the American Eugenics Society" held a meeting at the ABCL office on June 7.

Instead of naming the proposed federation something along the lines of Eugenic Birth Control, as had been earlier suggested, ABCL leader Eleanor Jones recommended that the name refer to population problems— and the motion carried unanimously. In making this recommendation, Jones was not retreating from the earlier commitment to eugenic birth control voiced by the committee, but rather solidifying it. As Dr. Clarence Cook Little suggested, the activities of the new group were to center around "population problems, eugenics and birth control." In the terms of this book, all these issues were different aspects of the same fundamental ideology of control.[114] Thus, it is evident that already in 1933, at the very beginning of the modern practice of demography as a science, population control was embraced by the leading eugenicists and birth controllers as an essential part of their agenda.

By the end of 1933, it was clear that the mistrust of Sanger's powerful will to control organizations and the old distaste for birth-control activism by the eugenic old guard would shipwreck anything so significant as a merger between the major players. But it seemed as if they could stomach a federation. Accordingly, the new federation was established and named the Council on Population Policy and appears to have lasted through about 1935. Before its eventual disintegration, Osborn had come around and agreed to serve as chairman of the group; eugenicists Dickinson, Fairchild, and Ellsworth Huntington were major players. Ironically enough, Sanger was appointed head of the "Committee on Co-Ordination," although cooperation with others was not her forte.[115] It is not clear why the federation disappeared so quickly; probably the mix of several strong and egoistic personalities brought about its demise.[116] Among the groups invited to participate in the new federation were all the major players in the control movement: Sanger's National Committee for Federal

Legislation on Birth Control, the Population Association of America, the ABCL, the AES, the Eugenics Research Association, the American Genetic Association, and Robert Latou Dickinson's National Committee on Maternal Health. In addition, private foundations were represented, including the Brush, Scripps, and the Milbank Memorial Fund foundations.[117]

It did succeed, briefly, in bringing together the leaders of the various important organizations and thus provides a fascinating microcosmic glimpse of the control movement as brought together to further its ideology. The Council on Population Policy typifies the historical course of the control movement: united by a commitment to eugenics, population control, and birth control, yet so often divided simply by egos. Their shared ideology, however, remained dangerous: by 1934 it was agreed upon by all those involved with the Council on Population Policy that they shared "a conviction that the quantitative and qualitative aspects of population improvement could no longer be regarded as separate interests."[118]

CHAPTER FIVE

Money Means Power:
The Rich Have
Their Say

"The genetic changes going on in the replacement of the population may be more important than changes taking place in their number.... Large sums will be needed for research in the broad field of human quality."— The Population Council, Annual Report, 1956

"My conviction is that if you are really serious about the costs of population, you should not promote the less effective methods.... There are times when somebody has to decide for people."— National-level administrator of population programs in the Philippines, 1980s

Demography never got off the ground as a scientific discipline until it garnered the support of a few rich men. Big foundations instituted by the wealthy have played a major role in the popularization of population and birth control, and their influence continues today: population control is an object lesson in how the agenda-shaping power of the wealthy, acting through foundations that sponsor biased research, can make a pet issue a worldwide concern.[1] As Osborn said, "In the United States early work in population had little support except from American foundations."[2] In other words, population control was always an elitist preoccupation, a "rich man's club," as some of the leading population-control participants themselves have said, a club run by people with names such as Ford, Rockefeller, Scripps, Mellon, and Carnegie.[3] Indeed, the first Ford Foundation

donations to the population-control cause in 1952 were initiated because —
as Bernard Berelson, former president of the Population Council,
recalled — the vice president of the foundation

> was looking for a subject matter that would attract the Board's support in
> the behavioral sciences, and he knew that two Board members were inter-
> ested in population and they, so to speak, were interested in population
> because their wives were Planned Parenthood nuts and were always bug-
> ging them, "Well, what are you doing about population?" And it had a con-
> creteness to it, and Rowant said, "Let's do that. Let's have a study. Let's
> see what we can do about population."[4]

This chapter will show that the research into population issues is often
dominated by the population-control agenda; examine the history of funding for population-control groups by wealthy individuals and their foundations; look at one current example of such activism by analyzing Ted
Turner's actions and motivations; and conclude with a summary of the
shared ideology of control underlying both eugenics and population control.

Science vs. Ideology

From the beginning, demographic research was conducted by individuals (some with scientific training, others merely enthusiastic, leisured
amateurs) with a marked background in eugenic activism. These individuals were funded and directed by foundations, which were themselves
run by prominent, wealthy, and committed eugenicists. Examples of foundation involvement in initiating and keeping afloat studies in population
are numerous, and the previous chapter detailed some of the early studies in differential fertility. The Milbank Memorial Fund and the various
Rockefeller foundations were among the earliest contributors: both Milbank and the Rockefellers funded Raymond Pearl's International Union
for the Scientific Study of Population for $60,000 over three of its earliest
years of existence.[5]

The eugenic bias motivating foundation-sponsored research demonstrates why this funding is so problematic: the bias inevitably becomes
projected onto the research that is chosen for funding. Unfortunately, the
problem is not of mere historical interest. For example, in sociologist Donald Warwick's case, his research project, bankrolled by the United Nations
Fund for Population Activities (UNFPA) in the 1970s, was designed to
explore the multicultural ethics of population control but was quashed

due to the Fund's insistence that the results be in line with its own pro–population control values. The matter became especially sticky when the project in question tried to analyze the motivations of UNFPA-donor agencies (such as the United States Agency for International Development [USAID] and the International Planned Parenthood Federation [IPPF]). As a result of the furor over Warwick's research, then-executive director Rafael Salas refused to allow any more UNFPA funding of studies of the Fund's own donors.[6] As Warwick summarized his relationship with UNFPA, "[I]t is difficult to carry out serious research when agreements with the funding source are subject to change for political reasons."[7]

Warwick's conclusion, that "of all the spheres of national development, population has been the most donor driven," is borne out by even a cursory examination of the population programs in less-developed countries.[8] A certain type of what we would now call non-governmental organizations (NGOs), namely, well-funded population organizations based in the United States and Europe, have been able to dictate the development of population-control activities in Third World countries. Their leaders, typified by the aggressive Clarence Gamble, have been involved in the establishment of international population programs aimed at developing countries from beginning to end—from the initial diagnosis of a population problem, to the proffering of "technical assistance" to solve that problem, to the funding and staffing of family-planning clinics and population offices. The imperialistic danger of such an approach becomes even clearer when one is critically conscious of eugenic motivations for this push for population control. Indeed, despite the lip service given to recognizing the values of local cultures, the paradigm of population controllers for dealing with cultural differences—especially in the formative years of the 1960s—remains that of the "cultural obstacle." In this view, a particular culture's values are seen only as a barrier to the absolute value of birth control, a barrier which must somehow be surmounted instead of respected.[9] "A handful of politicians, a band of population control zealots, a few demographers, and a small number of foundation executives made the difference" in promoting population control within developing countries, admitted Peter Donaldson, then president of the Population Reference Bureau (eugenicist Guy Irving Burch's group), in explaining why almost all of the impetus for population control came from First World countries.[10]

The UNFPA is not the only source of population funding that demands certain predetermined results from "objective" scientific research. Former USAID population-division director Reimert Ravenholt reportedly once slugged the leader of the Office of Population's research division when a study "didn't turn out the way he thought it should."[11] In another instance, in 1984, a letter from the Andrew W. Mellon Foundation to the American Association for the Advancement of Science (AAAS) scolded the latter — actually a pro–population control group — for the appearance of "diffidence" regarding "the malign consequences of rapid population increase." The AAAS project was to determine the relationship between population, resources, and the environment, and the proposal was apparently not titled in such a way as to make absolutely clear that the results would reinforce the status quo of population research.

> Should such diffidence [regarding population control] exist, I would suppose that it might cripple the program and that therefore the exercise might as well be halted forthwith.... [T]he crucial element in any responsible approach to the overall problem will be restraint of population increase. Although it may be unscientific to make the statement that boldly, I do so because I think that outcome so highly probable that if your group finds it unpalatable perhaps the exercise should be abandoned.[12]

In other words, Mellon, one of the most generous funding sources for population research, was not willing to give money to a project with any whiff of dissent from the pro–population control party line. What did the AAAS do? What perhaps the majority of academicians and scholarly organizations would do in the face of denial of funding — it tailored its research project to fit Mellon's preferences. To whom would an economist or biologist turn for funding if he or she wished to explore the possible *benefits* of population growth in developing countries? There is indeed an almost unanimous "scientific" chorus regarding population control — but this unanimity is due in large part to the almost unanimous value system held by the major donors to population research.

With this in mind, we can turn to an examination of the research promoted by the population-control lobby. A major effort has been directed to producing "scientific" evidence showing that target populations in developing countries have the same belief system as the population controllers. One of the most common types of demographic study done from the 1950s through the 1970s was the KAP survey, the aim of which was to study the knowledge of, attitude toward, and practice of birth control in certain populations. It has been noted that, "while it may have begun as an instrument of scientific understanding, [the KAP study] gradually became an effective tool of political persuasion."[13] J. Mayone Stycos, a demographer who specialized in Latin America, openly acknowledged that the KAP survey was a tool that could be used in a way "similar to any *market research project*: to demonstrate the existence of a demand for goods and services, in this case birth control...."[14] In other words, demographers doing KAP surveys were ultimately salespeople, whose product was population control through contraception. When the political efficacy of the KAP survey was demonstrated, wealthy foundations jumped and enthusiastically funded the surveys.[15] Yet KAP studies were fundamentally flawed in many ways, including the fact that, by only interviewing women, the surveys viewed reproduction in an individualistic (and, thus, late Western) manner that did not take account of the non-atomized nature of the social and familial structure of traditional societies, in which, for example, the wishes of parents, parents-in-law, husband, siblings, and the community matter deeply to a woman of childbearing age.[16] In addition, the questionnaires utilized leading questions ("Would you approve of a simple, harmless method that would keep you from getting pregnant too often?"), often with built-in assumptions, such as the number of children to be desired, that do not fit in well with the worldview of many Third World women.[17] Given the loaded nature of the questions and the overall weakness of the research design, it is no surprise that the questioners elicited exactly the kind of results they wanted. One Indian villager explained, "It is sometimes better to lie. It stops you from hurting people, does you no harm, and might even help them."[18]

In addition to targeting the fertile bodies of the impoverished, population-control science has also targeted the fertile minds of Western youth, thereby reproducing the biases of the past through the mechanisms of academia and the public education system. One professor in political geography at Claremont College reported success in indoctrinating some two hundred "girls" attending a required course. Among the "scientific" materials he passed out was Hugh Moore's *The Population Bomb*.[19] The Population Council has not flinched from promoting "education" in matters of population quality as well as quantity, a fact indicated by its co-sponsorship of a conference in 1961, with the American Eugenics Society, on the teaching of "genetics" (from a definite eugenic perspective).[20]

All these activists form what Bachrach and Bergman call the "Population Coalition," that is, a coalition of scientists, academics, foundations, and activists, or what I have called the control movement. Within this movement, Bachrach and Bergman have identified two forms of "non-decision-making" that facilitate the perpetuation of existing attitudes toward population control, either through "strengthening and sustaining the mobilization of bias" in a way "that reinforces the established way of looking at things" or else through the active discrediting of "emerging hostile positions"— viewpoints that would contradict the established position that population growth is always detrimental. That is, population control is made into a matter of common sense. Some members of the control movement have attempted to break out from the mainstream and propose new ideas, but even they remain stuck in the old framework. For example, an influential and ground-breaking article by demographer Kingsley Davis in 1967 proposed taking seriously the pronatalist cultural "barriers" to population control and reformulating approaches accordingly.[21] Yet, as Bachrach and Bergman point out, Davis takes an aggressive position regarding those cultures, to the extent that he redefines "voluntarism" much as we saw Tietze doing before: Davis advocates reforming *cultures* to reflect Western antinatalism, instead of reforming population control; as a result, he advocates both cultural imperialism and the subjection of women to a societal pressure artificially generated by population-control agitprop.[22] The rejection by Davis of anything like real freedom is expressed elsewhere in a statement he made for an IPPF newsletter in 1982, where he asked: "Why does the family planning movement ... have as its slogan, 'every woman has the right to have as many children as she wants'? We would not justify traffic control by saying that 'every driver has the right to drive as he pleases.'"[23]

The ideology in which Davis and the other members of the control movement are stuck has been perpetuated by the biases of large foundations up to the present time. Steven W. Sinding, director of population sciences at the Rockefeller Foundation and former head of the Office of Population within USAID, believes that foundations were responsible for bringing the ideology of the population coalition back into public consciousness in the 1980s.[24] As one commentator summarized the situation, "Rapid growth of the world's population is becoming a major topic of public discussion in the United States after a decade of neglect, thanks in large measure to several major American philanthropies and the charities they support."[25] In other words, just as population control was a "rich man's club" from the beginning, placed on the American agenda by the ceaseless flow of dollars into scientific and public-affairs organizations, so too today is any flagging interest in the topic propped up by the funding of the world's wealthiest people. Let us now analyze the history of this sort of activism, in order to better understand the current situation.

Control of Population: 1950s to the Present

The Population Council

The Rockefeller family and its foundations have been the most involved in the whole range of eugenic activities, from funding Sanger's groups to bankrolling German eugenic studies of race, from founding and paying for the activities of the Population Council in 1952 to eventually absorbing Robert Latou Dickinson's and Clarence Gamble's National Committee on Maternal Health in 1967. In 1934, the Rockefeller Foundation gave its first population grant to the Social Science Research Council for a study of population distribution.[26] The Rockefeller Foundation's Warren Weaver, head of the Natural Science Division and no stranger to population research, stated in the division's 1934 progress report, "The challenge … is obvious…. Can we develop so sound and extensive a genetics that we can hope to breed, in the future, superior men?"[27] From 1937 to 1943, the Foundation also gave over $76,000 to Dickinson's and Gamble's National Committee on Maternal Health for the study of fertility, and it supported Pearl's IUSSP "in its critical early years."[28]

Yet it was John D. Rockefeller 3rd, not the Rockefeller Foundation itself, who was responsible for the Population Council, perhaps the most permanently successful of all the Rockefeller population enterprises. At Princeton, he studied Malthus and other eugenicists.[29] By 1934, while he was working in the Rockefeller offices, he wrote a letter to his father, prompted by the termination of the Rockefeller-funded Bureau of Social Hygiene. The letter states an important conclusion to which the younger Rockefeller had come.

> In concluding, may I add one further statement in regard to my interest in birth control. I have come pretty definitely to the conclusion that it is the field in which I will be interested, for the present at least, to concentrate my own giving, as I feel it is so fundamental and underlying. While I would not, of course, expect to contribute in the amounts that I have suggested for your consideration, … I would be more than glad to supplement your gifts or make independent ones of my own; or I could confine my financial efforts to individuals, organizations and projects to which you were not giving.[30]

Rockefeller 3rd's desire to concentrate his energies and his money on birth control and eugenics would play itself out in the next four decades in extensive monetary support and lobbying activities for eugenics, population control, birth control, and abortion rights. He, as well as his staff, viewed these issues as various aspects of a whole, not unlike Margaret Sanger, whose control ideology he shared. His interest in the population side of the question began to flower in the 1940s, when he spent much time in the Far East and became concerned with its population growth, so he invited Frank Notestein, Irene Taeuber, and other demographers to take a cruise through the region at the Rockefeller Foundation's expense for the purpose of writing up a report on its demographic state.[31] Yet the Foundation was not yet inclined to fund population control to any great degree in the later 1940s and early 1950s, so he decided to set out on his own.

The decision to begin the Population Council occurred, significantly, in the men's room of an upper floor of Rockefeller Center, when Lewis Strauss, a former banker and recent hire at the Rockefeller Brothers Fund, told Rockefeller that the National Academy of Sciences under Detlev Bronk would be "happy" to sponsor an initial meeting of demographers and others involved in the birth-control movement.[32] Accordingly, an exclusive, invitation-only Conference on Population Problems was held in Williamsburg, Virginia, in the summer of 1952. As Rockefeller was mulling over becoming president of the Population Council, some staff members of the Rockefeller Foundation pondered the advisability of his taking the job and concluded that "one of the things that he most needs is some activity which will occupy his full time five days a week."[33] Thus the Population Council was nurtured by the Rockefeller funding machine partly because the otherwise unemployed heir needed to avoid restless ennui.

The participants at the conference were hand-picked representatives of the pro–population control position; indeed, at the suggestion that the organization coming out of the conference might want to include people who opposed this position, Kingsley Davis responded, "If the committee were required to have representation of diametrically opposed points of view, it would be hamstrung. To get this thing really moving, we have to assume the committee will have in mind people with similar points of view."[34]

The reluctance to include other opinions within the Population Council shows how false the official story regarding its formation is. For example, one population-control advocate states that the Council was founded after a National Academy of Sciences meeting in 1952, held at Rockefeller's urging, that recommended an organization devoted to the scientific study of population.[35] This sort of spin implies that purely scientific motives impelled the Council's formation. Yet there was no real debate at the Williamsburg meeting about the need for population control; all those who attended the meeting were only invited to begin with because they had the "right" opinions.[36]

One of the shared opinions was a predisposition to support eugenics. Linda Gordon has noted that at least six of the ten men on the Population Council's demographic and medical advisory boards were involved with eugenics.[37] In accordance with this bias, an early draft of the Council's charter asserted that population control was only for certain kinds of people, not for the eugenically fit, and the Council also hoped from the beginning to encourage research that would enable "parents who are above the average in intelligence, quality of personality and affection" to "have larger than average families."[38] Thus, the Council's concern was not for over-population in general but rather for the reproduction of certain kinds of people. The final draft changed the explicitly positive-eugenic statement to a call for research "in both the quantitative and qualitative aspects of population in the United States," rhetoric that readers of this book will easily decode.[39] The Council's charter accurately reflects the eugenic concerns of those who came to the 1952 conference, at which a long discussion concerning genetic mutation and the supposed decline in the quality of the gene pool took place, with one participant complaining that "modern civilization had reduced the operation of natural selection by saving more 'weak' lives and enabling them to reproduce."[40] Detlev Bronk summarized the discussion by saying that the question of genetic quality "is certainly related in a very important way to any control measures for the population and to the more effective utilization of resources by our populations, provided we do not permit a continual deterioration of the race."[41] Rockefeller himself confessed that the study of population quality "intrigues me very much."[42]

Despite such eruptions of ideology, the Population Council strove to be an unimpeachably scholarly voice within the population-control movement, its members tending to regard the more activist tendencies of Planned Parenthood as somewhat distasteful. It was able to quickly draw in huge sums of money, including a $600,000 grant in 1954 from the Ford Foundation, followed by $1 million in 1957 and $1.4 million in 1959, and $1.2 million from its main benefactor, John D. Rockefeller 3rd, as well as significant contributions from Mrs. Alan M. Scaife and Cordelia Scaife May from the Mellon family.[43] Yet despite the desire to be scholarly, "[f]rom the outset, ... the council was policy oriented," perhaps because it drew its staff from the pool of ideologically driven demographers who came out of the earliest eugenic population-control organizations in the 1930s and 1940s.[44] Accordingly, the man first tapped to administratively direct the council as executive vice president (and who, starting in 1957, served as president) was not, as one might expect, a scientist or a professor but a retired businessman from a wealthy family, none other than eugenicist Frederick Osborn. Rockefeller 3rd had praised Osborn in 1939 for "doing a grand job in a very important field."[45] The field? Eugenics. From early on he had relied on Osborn to keep him personally up-to-date on the goings-on of the American Eugenics Society and events in the eugenic and population fields in general, and this reliance would now be formalized by giving Osborn the chief administrative position in the Population Council.[46] Perhaps he was also chosen because his experience in propaganda as the head of the U.S. Army and Air Force Information and Education Division during World War II would place him in good stead within the fledgling population-control movement. In any case, Notestein has noted that Osborn, along with Dudley Kirk, set "the tone and pattern of [the Council's] work."[47] Rockefeller reminisced later that Osborn was "for many years ... interested in demography but particularly in the question of eugenics, which, according to my understanding, is quality in population, quality in people, rather than so much concern about numbers, although obviously the two are related."[48]

Among the patterns set by Osborn for the Population Council was the close interaction between it and the AES, since, as the Council's annual report in 1956 noted, it had a role to play in the promotion of eugenics:

> In the United States and among European peoples generally, where growth in numbers is at a rate which does not immediately endanger the level of living, the genetic changes going on in the replacement of the population may be more important than changes taking place in their number.... Large sums will be needed for research in the broad field of human quality.[49]

Among the grants that the Population Council made were those devoted to twin studies, in which twins raised in different homes were tracked. This particular kind of genetic research was a favorite of eugenicists, because, it was believed, many traits could be proven to be genetic if they were found in both twins. These sorts of studies were common in Nazi Germany in the 1930s, and the Rockefeller Foundation had funded many of them. In the 1940s and 1950s, the Population Council under Osborn took over the responsibility of funding most of the twin studies conducted in America. At his presentation before the Council's board of trustees, Osborn opined that twin studies would "seem to be a proper function of the Council and might have far-reaching results in its work."[50] For one proposed large-scale study, the Council was to work with Alan Guttmacher and other eugenicists.[51] This study was meant to focus on intelligence, since it was believed that twin studies were the best mechanism for determining the thorny question of the heritability of IQ. It was hoped that the study would be "big," carried out under private auspices.[52] It foundered due partly to difficulties in finding a competent scientist who would be willing to direct it.

The connection between the Population Council and the AES remained strong even after Osborn left the presidency of the former in 1959 (while remaining in charge of the latter), in part because he remained a trustee of the Council for many more years. In 1966, Osborn wrote to Richard C. Lewontin congratulating him on his election to the board of directors of the AES for 1968 and then noting that the organization wished to invite representatives from various population groups, such as the Ford Foundation and the Population Council, "so as to get them acquainted with what is going on in this field [human population genetics]."[53] Such lobbying for eugenics had already proven effective: Population Council annual reports in the 1950s noted grants for $12,000 to the AES for the publication expenses of the *Eugenics Quarterly* and for $4,000 to the Population Reference Bureau for "a survey of the number of children of graduates of American colleges and universities, under the direction of Mr. Robert Cook and Professor P. K. Whelpton."[54]

In addition, a series of fellowships in medical genetics were sponsored by the Population Council, to be disbursed through the AES, in the 1950s and 1960s.[55] The AES Annual Report noted:

> The officers of the Society have been asked for the past several years to make recommendations to the Population Council for the award of fellowships for study in medical genetics.... As a result of these successful recommendations the arrangement with the Population Council has been formalized, and for 1958 and 1959 the Society has been asked to make recommendations to the Population Council for medical-genetic fellowships up to an amount of $5,000 for the last six months of 1958 and of $10,000 for 1959.[56]

One demographer who took advantage of the Population Council eugenic fellowships was Carl Jay Bajema, whose main research interest was the relation of natural selection to human intelligence. Not one to slight the practical implications of his research, he also was a member of the Population Association of America and the vice president of the Planned Parenthood Association of Kent County, Michigan.[57] The Population Council (PC) also provided funds for Bajema to make a European study tour in 1971 and to present a paper on the relationship between natural selection and intelligence at a genetics conference. While in Europe, Bajema researched Osborn's "eugenic hypothesis," gathering enough information to publish papers on eugenics and to help the latter revise *The Future of Human Heredity: An Introduction to Eugenics in Modern Society.*[58]

Another joint PC/AES project was a conference in 1970 on "Differential Reproduction in Individuals with Mental and Physical Disorders." The prologue of the printed proceedings, entitled "A Foundation for Informed Eugenics," lamented, "Who's minding the quality of the human gene pool? Hardly anyone, it seems...."[59] However, the authors pointed out that the public acceptance and political momentum provided by the population-control movement would allow for the scientific selection and engineering of "desirable" traits. "Once the range of family sizes has been reduced to zero to three, an opportunity for selection will still exist that could be cautiously pursued by an enlightened society."[60] In other words, the control ethic popularized by population control could be extended from quantity to quality, completing the eugenic circle.

Interestingly enough, one of the participants of the 1970 PC/AES gathering was Harriet Pilpel, lawyer for both the Association for Voluntary Sterilization (formerly the notorious eugenic group Birthright, Inc.) and also for the Planned Parenthood Federation of America (PPFA), and she remained in that latter capacity until her death in the early 1980s. At the gathering in question, she presented a paper on "Family Planning and the Law," which was a response to the previous lecture regarding the sterilization of the mentally disabled.[61] This was familiar ground for Pilpel, who had for a long time provided legal guidance for the AVS; at their 1973 conference, she would present model legislation that would allow the parents or guardian of a legally incompetent person to apply to a board (suspiciously resembling the Eugenics Boards established by the older eugenic sterilization laws) for their child or ward to be sterilized.[62]

Pilpel is one person among many who was involved both in population control and in eugenics. Dudley Kirk, the head of the AES, came on board the Population Council as Demographic Director in 1954. Christopher Tietze was also under the Council's umbrella: a biostatistician from Germany who had dabbled in eugenics, he worked for Clarence Gamble at the National Committee on Maternal Health before the NCMH was absorbed by the Population Council. He did many statistical studies on the safety and effectiveness of various contraceptives, including work in Puerto Rico and the coordination of many studies on the intrauterine device. As early as 1946, he proposed that the Rockefeller Foundation consider funding "an intensive experiment ... to develop public health methods for controlling the growth of population in Puerto Rico.... For the greatest success and local acceptance, the project should appear, as far as possible, to be Puerto Rican in origin and operation."[63]

At the NCMH, Tietze was essentially on the Population Council (and thus the Rockefellers') payroll. The Council to this day funds projects much like Tietze's. Its continuing power indicates the staying power of the Rockefellers' funding of population control. The Population Council has focused on contraceptive research, developing and promoting the IUD, the simple contraceptive so favored by Alan Guttmacher and others due to the low amount of "motivation" necessary for its continued use. As

Tietze put it, the IUD was considered to be the best bet in the poorer parts of the world: "[I]t was anticipated that the continuation rate with the IUD would be much better than with the pill certainly in the developing areas of the world. I think that has proved now to be the case."[64]

A more recent example of Population Council interest in contraceptive research is the foundation's sponsorship of research into Norplant, the long-lasting hormonal contraceptive which has disturbed many feminists, while the group also holds the patent rights for both Depo-Provera and the abortion pill RU-486, called by one feminist "pesticidal, or more specifically femicidal weapons."[65] We will examine Norplant in more detail in chapter seven; for now, it is sufficient to summarize the drug's dubious history. The Population Council began to research Norplant in 1966, beginning its clinical trials in Chile (a convenient foreign testing site) in 1974.[66] IPPF has been heavily involved, first in testing the hormone-delivery system abroad, then reviewing the drug favorably in 1985, and finally promoting it one year later in countries ill-equipped to deal with side effects and efficient removal.[67] The drug was not approved in the United States until 1990 due to its persistent and often serious side effects.

Norplant entails the implanting of six rods, each containing 36 mg of progestin, under a woman's skin (usually in the upper arm). The rods are effective for five years; after that time, they must be removed by a doctor. The fact that the mechanism cannot be removed by the woman herself forces her to rely on the local family-planning personnel for removal, and there have been several documented cases where removal has been refused, due to the population-control objectives of the workers: better an unhappy but infertile woman than a content but fertile woman, in their calculus.[68] As one "national-level administrator" of the population program in the Philippines put it, "My conviction is that if you are really serious about the costs of population, you should not promote the less effective methods.... There are times when somebody has to decide for people. If you are going to allow every individual to put up reasons for a decision you are going to take, nothing will be accomplished."[69] The dangerous promotion of Norplant overseas is an instance of this sort of attitude: while the Population Council has stressed that careful counseling must accompany Norplant insertion, it has irresponsibly promoted the drug in countries, such as Indonesia, whose population-control policies are anything but careful. The UNFPA has even decided that China, of all places, should produce and utilize Norplant, and the group is taking steps to assist that activity.[70]

The man behind the Norplant research, Dr. Sheldon Segal, was also involved with eugenics; at one population-control conference, he complained that the pill might negatively "influence the genetic characteristics of future generations."[71] Segal was also involved with the eugenic Human Betterment Association.[72] More recently, Segal has loudly protested certain coercive strategies for using Norplant against the poor, yet why did he develop a contraceptive that is effective for five years and impossible for a woman to remove, even should she change her mind?[73] The capacity to coerce is intrinsic to its design. As the seventh chapter will show, such non-user-controlled contraceptive methods were developed with an eye to providing the "insufficiently motivated" woman in the inner city and in the Third World with birth control that could not be removed without the tacit consent of a doctor.

The Rockefellers were not the only source of support for the fledgling population-control movement. Let us now examine the role played by another wealthy man in promoting a similarly oppressive approach to controlling the fertility of the world's poor, especially that of women of color.

Hugh Moore and Planned Parenthood-World Population

Hugh Moore, who made his fortune through the invention of the disposable paper Dixie cup, was known to the more scholarly demographers as a loose cannon. He said that William Vogt's *Road to Survival* served the purpose of "really waking me up" to the dangers of over-population, including, so Moore thought, war and "the spread of tyranny and communism." Later he would state that it was "his primary interest in peace which had induced his interest in population problems."[74] He paid for a research assistant for Vogt while the latter was at PPFA; he served as vice chairman of PPFA; and later he became very involved in the International Planned Parenthood Federation.[75] Moore also provided the help of a part-time administrative assistant, Thomas O. Griessemer (who later became secretary of IPPF's Western Hemisphere Region), at no cost to IPPF, before Moore branched out to form the Population Action Committee (PAC) in 1953, the World Population Emergency Campaign (WPEC) in 1960, and the Population Crisis Committee (now Population Action International) in 1965. The WPEC was intended to give IPPF hundreds of thousands of dollars in big-business support, and it accomplished its goal by the time it merged with PPFA in 1961 to form the short-lived entity Planned Parenthood-World Population.[76] Moore also refinanced eugenicist Guy Irving Burch's Population Reference Bureau, which was about to go bankrupt, in 1966, raising enough to fund a $400,000 budget for it.[77] Not one to focus his energies too narrowly, Moore also served as the president of the Association for Voluntary Sterilization beginning in 1965, leaving it financially secure enough at his death in 1972 that it has been able to prosper since, although it has also received considerable sums from the United States Agency for International Development (USAID).[78]

Moore's personality was described by Frances Hand Ferguson as reckless and determined, more than a little like Clarence Gamble's: "[T]hose men do what they want, and they just push people aside who get in their way."[79] One of the things that he did over the objections of many of the more cautious population controllers was to publish a pamphlet in 1954 entitled *The Population Bomb*. Using scare tactics and a dubious smattering of statistics, the pamphlet was so popular that his organizations were able to distribute over 1.5 million copies of it by 1967.[80] At least one leader within PPFA thought it was "a great little pamphlet," despite its hyperbole.[81] He later published a follow-up piece, *The Population Bomb: Is Voluntary Human Sterilization the Answer?* to which both Alan Guttmacher and the Human Betterment Association's H. Curtis Wood contributed. This brochure complained, "Many cultures have not yet caught up with the new facts of life. A recent survey around Calcutta revealed that 95 per cent of the people were uninterested in the use of contraceptives."[82] The pamphlet's disregard of native cultures and the promotion of sterilization as the once-and-for-all solution to population growth exemplified Moore's insensitivity towards non-Western cultures and his obsession with demographic control, leading to a willingness to run roughshod over those who did not agree with his apocalyptic forecasts.

The same extremism showed up in his ad campaigns, run in major newspapers such as the *New York Times* and the *Washington Post*. His headlines blared, "Have You Ever Been Mugged? Well, You May Be!" and tried to inflame nativism in the public by asking "How Many People Do *You* Want in Your Country?"[83] One ad complained, "Without population control, the Food for Peace program will be a mere stopgap, saving the lives of those who would produce still more hungry people."[84]

Despite Moore's extremism, the merger between PPFA and the WPEC was fortunate from PPFA's perspective, because, as Ferguson points out, Moore had not been previously interested in birth control in the United States: "As we saw it, he wasn't interested in the Americans. He was interested only in over-population, and the personal angle [regarding birth control] was absolutely out from his point of view, the *Bomb* brings that out all the time — too many people." In this regard, Moore was like many of the other, newly converted control activists: he was wealthy, male, and uninterested in the program of female self-determination and sexual freedom that was so compelling to Sanger and her followers (this phenomenon of the new male activist will be examined in more detail in the seventh chapter). Of the trio of birth control, eugenics, and population control, the first was primarily of interest in order to serve the other two. Thus Moore fell behind Sanger's ideological supplementation of Neo-Malthusianism, which joined racial progress to the sexual "liberation" of women. Ferguson acknowledged, "Hugh Moore thought very little of women. Talk about a double-standard, to him women were really low.... I used to say he always thought women were lower than gorillas or ... monkeys. He had really not much use for women as a whole at all."[85]

In 1954 Moore wrote John D. Rockefeller 3rd that "we are not primarily interested in the sociological or humanitarian aspects of birth control. We are interested in the use which the Communists make of hungry people in their drive to conquer the earth."[86] In the end, Moore looked upon "hungry people" not primarily as people at all but as means to an end, as a potential buffer against communism. In this way, Moore played a huge role in solidifying the takeover of the leadership of PPFA, transforming its power base from ladies-who-lunch to wealthy businessmen who brought an agenda that heightened the eugenic and materially misogynistic programs of Planned Parenthood.[87]

Government Weighs In

Despite being pushed by businessmen like Rockefeller and Moore, the United States government entered the population field somewhat later than did those of the Scandinavian countries, but it made up for its tardiness by its zeal and the extent of its funding. The Scandinavian projects were organized for the eugenic purpose of promoting the quality of the population over its quantity. For example, the Swedish Population Commission, according to Alva Myrdal in 1939, adopted population measures that would safeguard "the quality of its population," since "Sweden wishes to maintain a constant population and believes that quantity should not be secured by sacrificing quality."[88] Nevertheless, the quantity of those in the developing world came to be a concern: by 1958, the Swedish government was giving population-control assistance directly to Ceylon.[89]

In America, as early as 1929, Sanger was calling for a federal commission to study population, "both in its qualitative and quantitative aspects" for the purpose of protecting "the purity of our national bloodstream" and preventing the overcrowding of "public institutions with public wards at enormous economic loss."[90] Fortunately, her call went unheeded by President Hoover. Three decades later, however, the United

States government embarked on its adventure in population control (though with a less explicitly eugenic rationale than that advanced by Sanger), with the 1959 report of a federal commission, the Committee to Study the United States Military Assistance Program, headed by General William H. Draper, a former investment banker. Close friend Hugh Moore pressured Draper into making the committee's report the unlikely means for providing population control with a national forum. The final document reflects Moore's preoccupation with over-population as a potential tool in the hands of communist radicals, as it might provide "opportunities for communist political and economic domination" in poorer parts of the world.[91] After a firestorm of controversy, the report's recommendations were rejected, but Moore had accomplished two things: he had managed to get the issue raised at a high level in government, and he had converted General Draper to the side of population control.

Draper's influence cannot be overestimated. Even if his recommendations were not put immediately into play, his access to the upper echelons of the federal government initiated the population-control funding process. The control movement needed someone about whom it could be said, "There is nobody [the] State [Department] would listen to more than Draper."[92] Even so, it was acknowledged that while Draper was the key to securing government support, the role of designing and implementing solutions fell upon groups like Pathfinder Fund and Sanger's organizations. Planned Parenthood, after all, was crucial to keeping the population issue alive and in the public eye long enough to gain an ally like Draper (who later became the leader of Moore's Population Crisis Committee): PPFA and IPPF created the conditions that made an aggressive, government-funded, global population-control policy possible at all. As Linda Gordon has observed, the other population-control groups "were all descended, in a direct line" from PPFA.[93]

The turning point for the commitment of the federal government to the promotion of population and birth control came with the Johnson administration. It has been noted that, during the late 1960s, "a loose social relationship existed" between government officials in key places within the administration and the control-movement representatives who came to lobby them. This relationship arose from their "attending the same schools, belonging to the same clubs, and sharing similar general views of the world and their place in it."[94] Relying upon the good-old-boy network in which PPFA's and the Population Council's male leaders thrived, they lobbied aides and agencies formally and informally, relying on dinner parties, contacts, and prestige, all the while moving comfortably in a world fundamentally inaccessible to anyone who might object to population control — especially the poor women who were its targets. As a result, federal funding for birth control, in the name of population control and the War on Poverty, began during Johnson's administration and continued and deepened under Nixon's. LBJ in fact used the prestige of the presidential office to enunciate straightforward Neo-Malthusian sentiment in his 1967 State of the Union address: "Next to the pursuit of peace, the really great challenge to the human family is the race between food supply and population increase. That race tonight is being lost. The time for rhetoric has clearly passed. The time for concerted action is here, and we must get on with the job."[95] And Nixon sent to Congress the first presidential Message on Population in 1969.[96]

The first cabinet members to support domestic birth-control funding in the Johnson administration were Willard Wirtz, the secretary of labor, and Stewart Udall, secretary of the interior, who was also in charge of the federal health programs for Native Americans and the American territories in the Pacific.[97] The Native American population was quickly subjected to a sterilization campaign that must be described, given the breathtaking percentage of Native American women of childbearing age involved, as effectively genocidal. These sterilizations were frequently performed without adequate informed consent, in federally funded Indian Health Service (IHS) hospitals. The large number of sterilizations began in earnest in 1966 when Medicaid came into existence and funded the operation for low-income people, and in 1976 the General Accounting Office, in an audit examining one-third of the IHS districts, revealed that 3,406 Native American women, who were given consent forms "not in … compliance with regulations," were sterilized from 1973 to 1976.[98] Based on these figures and her own research, Native American physician Constance Redbird Uri estimated that up to one-quarter of Indian women of childbearing age had been sterilized by 1977; in one hospital in Oklahoma, one-fourth of the women admitted (for any reason) left sterilized.[99] She reported that a doctor told her that he had performed a hysterectomy on one Native American woman, instead of a much simpler and safer operation that would have preserved the woman's fertility, because, he claimed, "the Indian woman's tissue is different." She also gathered evidence that all the pureblood women of the Kaw tribe in Oklahoma were sterilized in the 1970s— a truly genocidal process.[100] This campaign of coerced sterilization begun in the mid–1960s had predecessors: for example, in the 1930s the Abenaki Native American tribe in Vermont was especially targeted for sterilization.[101]

Unfortunately, and amazingly, problems with the Indian Health Service seem to persist: its clinics gave up to 200 Native American women the hormonal shot Depo-Provera in 1987, despite the fact that the FDA had not yet approved it for use.[102] More recently, in South Dakota, IHS was again accused of not following informed-consent procedures, this time for Norplant, and apparently promoted the long-acting hormonal contraceptive to Native American women who should not use it due to contraindicating, preexisting medical conditions.[103] The Native American Women's Health Education Resource Center reports that one woman was recently told by her doctors that they would remove the implant only if she would agree to a tubal ligation.[104] The genocidal dreams of bureaucrats still cast their shadow on American soil.

Native Americans are not the only group targeted by the federal population-control activists, first supported by the Johnson administration, because getting contraception to *all* the poor was always the focus of the federally funded family-planning programs, both domestic and international. By late 1965, the Office of Economic Opportunity was funding over a dozen projects in the U.S. targeting low-income women, most of them developed by Planned Parenthood affiliates.[105]

Likewise, in the federal government's population-control activities abroad, USAID depended on private groups such as the Population Council, PPFA, and IPPF to carry out its projects.[106] In 1965 Draper had received from the State Department's deputy assistant for Latin America, William Rogers, a "forthright" expression of "interest and promised cooperation of the State Department and AID in all appropriate ways for the efforts" of IPPF and Draper in Mexico and Brazil. This support cashed out as a $100,000 grant to the fledgling Sociedade Civil Bem-Estar Familiar no Brasil (or BEMFAM), the new IPPF affiliate in Brazil.[107] BEMFAM has often been touted by IPPF as a textbook example of a grassroots, women-organized national group that sprang up out of native desires for family planning. Actually, the organization was founded in the same way as were other population-control groups initiated in the post–World War II period: by a few, fairly privileged men, obsessed with demographic targets, who were richly funded by private foundations and then USAID. According to a Population Council contact, the organization consisted of two men: Dr. Glycon de Paiva, a "prominent engineer and businessman," and Dr. Paulo C. A. Antunes, "a leading physician." They developed a budget that they expected would be funded by USAID, IPPF, the Ford Foundation, and the Population Council — all non-native funding sources.[108] Furthermore, in their statements about the aims of the new group, the two men did not even bother to mention any desire to empower women; rather, BEMFAM's sole purpose was "to deal with the population problem in Brazil."[109]

Beginning in 1966, population-control discourse in America was significantly radicalized when Dr. Reimert ("Ray") T. Ravenholt, an epidemiologist, was appointed to head USAID's Population Branch, holding the position until 1979. Ravenholt assimilated his view of population growth to his training in epidemiology: overpopulation was a disease that had to be eradicated, and the best form of medicine, in Ravenholt's eyes, was the birth-control pill. Oral contraceptives, he told a meeting connected with the 1974 UN-sponsored World Population Conference in Bucharest, "should be as available as aspirin."[110] USAID's international assistance up to then had been confined to technical assistance, but Ravenholt began to argue that the U.S. would most efficiently assist developing countries by flooding them with huge amounts of oral contraceptives.[111] One observer called Ravenholt's "inundation" method of contraceptive distribution "the most massive medical experiment in the history of the world," with no concomitant safety controls: Ravenholt would choose pills of varying types and brands each year, basing his choice solely on which pharmaceutical company offered the lowest bid, without taking into account possible side effects.[112] This kind of scorched-earth approach to population control shifted the whole movement to extremity: almost anyone would look moderate in comparison to Ravenholt, and incremental strategies began to appear excessively cautious.

Due partly to Draper's lobbying and Ravenholt's doggedness, USAID began to give direct monetary grants to groups such as IPPF and Gamble's Pathfinder Fund. To prod USAID into concentrating more heavily on the population-control front, in 1967 Congress passed Title X language for the Foreign Assistance Act earmarking a huge increase in population-control funding (including, for the first time, direct funding of contraceptives) to governments, UN agencies, and all manner of nonprofit population-control groups.[113] Suddenly, Ravenholt's Population Branch office (which in 1969 became the Office of Population with a $50 million budget) was in charge of huge amounts of money, and private population-control groups such as PPFA filled the absolutely indispensable role of providing the institutional infrastructure that would spend the largesse.[114] As both Sanger and Gamble had foreseen, once government got involved, Planned Parenthood and Gamble's Pathfinder Fund would be able to spend great sums of money carrying out their original eugenic and population-control mandates, and with people like Gamble and PPFA's Alan Guttmacher directing the organizational bureaucracy, the continued influence of eugenics was inevitable.

USAID was not the only governmental body on the world scene interested in international population control, but the United States' international position made its policy on population control incredibly influential.

Even before the U.S. government became committed to the project, Americans were motive forces. Draper was one of the many well-connected American population-controllers who molded the United Nations' attitude about population. The Population Division of the UN's Secretariat was founded in 1946, with Frank Notestein as the first Consultant Director, followed by Frank Lorimer. The latter was in charge of planning for the 1954 World Population Conference, which was to include a session on "social and biological aspects of demographic changes."[115] Despite this inside track, the population establishment wanted a greater UN commitment to population control. In a private meeting with the UN's Undersecretary Philippe de Seynes in 1967, Draper, John D. Rockefeller 3rd, and various officials of IPPF and the Population Council decided that the UN needed to commit more of its immense resources to the support of population control. As a result, the United Nations Fund for Population Activities (UNFPA, now known as the United Nations Population Fund) was organized.[116] Among others, eugenic demographers Philip Hauser and Ansley J. Coale were involved at the beginning.

Notestein observed that the UN managed quietly to build up support for population control among important bureaucrats, while avoiding the overt "ideologic battles" that might have occurred had other member nations been more aware of what was in the works.[117] Eventually, however, the fact that UNFPA was initiated by the private urging of a few well-connected wealthy people, instead of being officially authorized by the General Assembly, created quite a bit of controversy. (The formation of the agency was later approved after the fact by the Assembly.) UNFPA, like USAID, found it most convenient to utilize pre-existing population-control organizations, thereby solidifying the wealth and influence of such groups as PPFA, IPPF, the Population Council, and the Pathfinder Fund.[118] Now the International Planned Parenthood Federation, which only twelve years before this had been designated by one insider as existing "only on paper without the means or the leadership to provide effective service or function in any formal way as a coordinating agency," was suddenly funded to such a degree that it could participate in high-level talks with UN officials.[119]

The important role played by groups such as IPPF and the Pathfinder Fund in U.S. and UN population-control activities perhaps inevitably led to real human-rights problems out in the field, given that the organizations were based on a eugenic ideology that ignored human costs in the pursuit of demographic reduction, and the situation was exacerbated by Ravenholt's cavalier attitude. Coercive policies soon began to be mandated by USAID. By 1968, the Food for Peace Act made its aid contingent on the establishment of "voluntary family planning programs" in developing countries.[120] Such policies indicate how coercive the American foreign aid was, since it necessitated the promotion of "voluntary" contraceptive use in exchange for food. Indeed, despite the fiction perpetuated by USAID that America would only get involved in population control when countries asked for help, it was clear that "the stimulus came almost entirely" from forces outside the developing world.[121] Ravenholt himself acknowledged that objections to population control by indigent peoples and governments necessitated that USAID bypass working with governments and instead utilize groups such as UNFPA and IPPF as private agents within the country.[122] In other words, whether wanted or not, USAID would find a way to get into a developing country and control its population. PPFA operated on the same principle, as former president Frances Hand Ferguson revealed: "We, supposedly, don't go to work in a country until a group of leaders in that country come to us and say, 'Please, we need help to form a Planned Parenthood unit within our country.' What we do is send out field workers, and help them get started."[123]

Other abuses from USAID-funded programs arose from Ravenholt's eager push for sterilization. In 1977, he said that USAID had as a goal the sterilization of one-quarter of the fertile women in the world, or about 100,000,000 women.[124] A grotesque vision of such enormity naturally led to tolerance for the brutal Indian population-control sterilization camps. As early as 1964, family planners in India were recommending pay raises to "industrial workers" if they would get sterilized.[125] In the mid–1960s, India began mandating family-planning workers to meet target numbers of birth-control "acceptors," as well as offering monetary incentives to help impoverished people to "choose" to utilize contraceptives.[126] Then, in the early 1970s, vasectomy camps were set up in Kerala and Gujarat, in which hundreds of thousands of men received $6, a bag of supplies, and a new sari for the wife in exchange for sterilization.[127] USAID money was used to finance the incentives.[128]

In 1975, the situation worsened when Prime Minister Indira Gandhi declared Emergency Rule, and forced sterilizations became routine. Among the pressures put on local officials was the suspension of their salaries unless sterilization quotas were met. In the last six months of 1976, 6.5 million people were sterilized, including many men (often elderly) forcibly given vasectomies. Among the Americans who voiced their support for the program were World Bank president Robert McNamara and Paul Ehrlich, author of *The Population Bomb*, the latter saying, "We should have volunteered logistical support in the form of helicopters, vehicles and surgical instruments.... Coercion? Perhaps, but coercion in a good cause."

UNFPA, foreshadowing their ethical insouciance and public-relations mendacity concerning the human-rights violations in the Chinese program, insisted that few abuses occurred.[129]

Other observers disagreed. Leona Baumgartner, a population-control advocate who served as an assistant administrator with USAID from 1962 to 1965, complained, "I think if we hadn't pushed as hard, there would have been better success.... Take India ... [Ravenholt] pushed for sterilization ... all those camps all over.... My God, they were horrible. I think he pushed too fast, too hard."[130] The men targeted for sterilization were mostly Muslim, a religious minority in India; some poor Muslim villages were threatened with police-initiated arson and extermination if the men would not submit to sterilization.[131]

India during the Emergency had one of the few sterilization campaigns that targeted men. By 1977–78, however, the proportion had radically shifted and female sterilization made up 80 percent of all Indian sterilizations, perhaps as a negative response to the vasectomy campaigns, and the percentage was up to 97 percent by 1994.[132] Even into the 1990s, many Indians complained that the national family-planning program conducted sterilizations in unsanitary conditions, while the continuation of targets led to doctors performing as many sterilizations as possible in mass sterilization camps.[133] One observer complained, "I call it downright body snatching. Family planning has degenerated into quotas, and human beings have become targets."[134] In response to the criticisms, in 1997 the Ministry of Family Welfare (in charge of the population program) eliminated the use of targets, but some family planners have admitted that "the paradigm shift does not seem to have percolated down" to the lower level. Indeed, the new paradigm has caused much discontent within the Indian population-control bureaucracy, since many officials view the absence of incentives as indicating a "lack of political will" in addressing overpopulation and as causing a "lack of accountability" among local population controllers.[135] At present, the Indian government has allowed individual states to set their own goals and methods, and some provinces, such as Gujarat, have made moves to institute two-children policies. The Union Minister for Health and Family Welfare, Dr. C. P. Thakur, said that his ministry was not in favor of coercion, but refused to commit to stopping abuses perpetuated by other levels of government: the states, he said, "are free to do what they want in this regard."[136]

The continuation of abuses in India up to the present day should serve as a reminder that the lip service paid to human rights by population controllers is often more a rhetorical flourish than indicative of real commitment to promoting women's health and rights.

Powerful, demographically obsessed, forces—including the super-wealthy—continue to target the fertility of the poor.

Ted Turner vs. the "Dumbs"

Media mogul and Cable News Network founder Ted Turner has funded population-control activities to the tune of over $1 billion. He created the United Nations Foundation in January 1998 with a $1 billion grant for the sole purpose of supporting UN projects and assisting with its public image, damaged in part by the UN's continued support of totalitarian population-control programs in developing countries. Turner's foundation heavily funds population-control activities in Third World countries, including a project to indoctrinate journalists in control-movement values by sending them on one- or two-week trips to family-planning clinics in developing countries.[137] The foundation has targeted the business community as a "natural ally." United Nations Foundation president and population controller Timothy E. Wirth says, "For American trade and American business around the world, stability is absolutely imperative for the conduct of business," and this stability is secured, both Wirth and Turner assert, through population control.[138]

An only slightly refurbished version of the old control ideology seems to underlie Turner's rhetoric and actions. For example, among the 1996 beneficiaries of Turner's other population-control fund, the Turner Foundation, were China's notorious State Family Planning Commission, responsible for so much coercion and human-rights abuse, and Population Communications International, Inc., which aims to change "cultural norms regarding family size, status of women and use of family planning services through media blitzes that include serial dramas on radio and television as well as news and informational programs."[139] Turner does not seem to care about the fact that the targets of these "media blitzes" might resent their evening news being used as a propaganda tool, nor that this project expresses a patronizing and neo-colonial attitude toward other cultures that deems it necessary to challenge well-established "cultural norms" through the agency of 30-second sound bites.

Feminist Betsy Hartmann, among others, protests that Turner has promoted an "alarmist" view of population that could conflict with the fight for women's rights.[140] Hartmann's judgment is given credence by Turner's own words. At a fund-raising dinner for the radical population-control group Zero Population Growth (ZPG) in 1996, attended by "some of the most influential people in entertainment, business and government," Turner declared:

> I really believe that there are huge forces arrayed against us. The forces of
> ignorance, lack of education and prejudice and hatred and fear. The forces
> of darkness in general. And then on our side we have the forces of light.
> The force of education, the force of understanding, the force of intelligence,
> the force of courage. How can we not win? We're smarter than they are.
> In the end, I'll put my money on the smart people against the dummies.
> If the smarts can't beat the dumbs, we're really not that smart, are we? And
> we have a lot more fun than they do, because we're right and they're
> wrong![141]

Perhaps Turner is simply "having fun" in being so ironic: the "huge
forces" arrayed against the global elite are largely constituted by the poor
and powerless Third World women who struggle, often in vain, against
coercive family planning. But maybe Turner is right to suggest that a
"smart" would rather oppress than be oppressed.

For Turner, money makes might, and might makes right. Often hailed
as being "forthright," the more appropriate adjective for Turner would
probably be "simplistic"; his logic does not get any more complex than the
following brainteaser: "We have two courses of action. We can be a bunch
of dumbasses and go to extinction like the dodo. Or we can be real smart
and intelligent, and progress to a brave new world."[142] Turner unwittingly
evokes the true, nightmarish reality behind his control ideology, the nature
of which Aldous Huxley portrays in *Brave New World*.

If this description of Turner's control ideology seems excessive, one
only has to reflect on what he considers the solution to over-population,
which is nothing less than the Chinese one-child policy on a worldwide
scale for the next century.[143] Significantly, he believes (as does the Chinese
government) that women are ultimately responsible for any progress or
lack thereof in the field of population control.

> The simplest answer is that the world population should be about two bil-
> lion, and we've got six billion right now. I haven't done the actuarial tables,
> but if every woman in the world voluntarily stepped up and said, "I'll only
> have one child," and if we did that for the next 80 to 100 years, that would
> reduce the kind of suffering we're having.[144]

Upon reading this statement, one might be surprised to learn that Turner
himself has five children by three wives.

Turner's preoccupation with the reproduction of those who fall outside the super-wealthy class probably has something to do with his desire
to own huge tracts of land as personal playgrounds for himself and a few
select friends. At last count, Turner owned almost 1.5 percent of New Mexico,[145] in addition to 11,000 acres in Argentina, at least 150,000 acres in

Montana, and 25,000 in the Southeast.[146] He is the largest private landowner in America.[147] As Turner said regarding his seemingly insatiable lust for land, "You ever make puzzles when you were a kid? First, you put the corners in. Then you try to get the border done. And then you try to fill it in. So I've got property on both coasts and in Montana, which is a Canadian border, and in New Mexico, which is a Mexican border. Now, I am trying to fill in."[148] And the more people there are, the more they would presumably take up land on which Turner and his celebrity friends could frolic without having ordinary people cluttering up the view.[149]

Turner's latest gambit has been to pressure two of the richest men in America, Bill Gates and Warren Buffett, to give away large sums of their wealth to population control. The former has given millions to population causes, including $1.7 million to the United Nations Population Fund.[150] Buffett, for his part, has reportedly given the Population Council $2 million for research on RU-486, the abortion pill, despite his legendary stinginess.[151] And both Gates and Buffett share Turner's interest in the Chinese program: the two visited a government population-control clinic in China in 1995.[152]

Controlling Population

Donald Warwick observed the gap between rhetoric and reality in the population-control movement as early as the 1970s: "[Government officials] insisted ever more loudly that the purpose of family planning programs was individual and family welfare rather than population control. At the same time, program administrators went on acting as they had all along, and they sometimes moved even closer to outright control."[153]

A 1969 internal memo by Frederick S. Jaffe, then vice president of Planned Parenthood-World Population, to Bernard Berelson at the Population Council is illustrative of this desire to achieve outright control. Jaffe laid out several possible measures that would reduce American fertility. Some of these measures would affect everyone equally—from encouraging the postponement or avoidance of marriage to putting fertility control agents in the water supply. Others would target those who might have insufficient motivation to prevent "unwanted pregnancies" on their own. These measures would include cash payments for sterilization, contraception, and abortion. Other measures would have an impact based on socioeconomic status. For families with more than a certain number of children, Jaffe encourages tax penalties (including a substantial marriage penalty and a child tax); the elimination of maternity leave or benefits; the end of welfare benefits after two children; a work requirement for women (with few child-care facilities); and the elimination of government-subsidized medical care, scholarships, housing, and so forth. Finally, Jaffe's proposed social controls would include compulsory abortion for out-of-wedlock pregnancies; forced sterilization after the second child; and refusal of permission to bear children for all but a select group of adults, among other policies.[154] Do these proposals become any less shocking, and any less indicative of a very dangerous mindset, when it is known that, after the memo was leaked, Jaffe weakly protested that the measures in the memo were meant as a kind of thought-experiment? (One is reminded of Sanger's complaint that the only thing wrong with eugenic sterilization is its impracticality.)

And not all of the shocking proposals have been confined to personal correspondence. For example, Germaine Greer quotes demographer Kingsley Davis's testimony before the House Select Committee on Population in 1978: "If you want to adopt very extreme means of controlling fertility I can immediately think of some, such as breaking down the family system, for example, by not giving children the family name of the parents; in fact not letting them know who the parents are and vice versa. Soon the motivation for having children would be seriously reduced."[155] More recently, King and Elliott have argued that the "high status of 'the child' in Western liberalism," as well as "the cultural attitudes of the [global] South that favor high fertility," need to be broken down, while they praise China's "courage" and "cultural independence" for instituting the repressive one-child policy.[156]

Willingness to directly pressure women into sterility persists to this day. As Professor John Caldwell reported to the Ford Foundation in the early 1990s, social scientists "literally talked down the birthrate" in developing countries.[157] For example, in Indonesia the United Nations Population Fund has created youth clubs, such as the "Family Planning Girl Scouts," to brainwash young girls into accepting the developed world's vision of family life. Bribed with various incentives, the girls have the dubious privilege of helping to insert Norplant contraceptive capsules into the arms of other women — a paradigm illustration of females being themselves coopted into becoming tools of anti-woman ideology.[158]

The 1994 International Conference on Population and Development (ICPD) in Cairo claimed to have changed all that — to have reached a new "consensus" on population control that moved away from an obsession with demographics and toward a promotion of women's rights. For example, "Principle 8" of the Programme of Action explicitly states that "reproductive health-care programmes should provide the widest range of services without any form of coercion." "Principle 4" advocates "gender equality and equity and the empowerment of women."[159] Yet the ultimate goal of the ICPD's Programme of Action remains a decrease in population: the putative support of women's health and rights is only a means to this end. When the right of women to refuse birth control interferes with the overriding demographic aims, then the former is sacrificed to the latter.[160]

Such deft linguistic moves have been made by population controllers before. For example, at the 1974 World Population Conference in Bucharest, the Population Council reacted adeptly when Third World countries insisted that complex economic and social problems not be blamed in an overly simplistic way on population growth. The Indian government's delegation, for example, had argued that economic "development is the best contraceptive." John D. Rockefeller 3rd startled the delegates by seconding this sentiment: "I believe that the place for population planning is within the context of modern economic and social development...."[161] Charles and Bernadine Zukowski, from the Pathfinder Fund, complained in a letter to Richard Gamble, "The U.S. was the constant target for disparaging comment...," precisely because it was seen as offering birth control and little else.[162]

But out of Bucharest came not so much a change in the way population controllers concretely conduct themselves but simply a change in rhetoric. It became imperative to stress the importance of women's rights and of economic development, but little changed in the field. Even Rockefeller himself, after the conference, reassured a wealthy donor that despite the revisionist rhetoric of Bucharest that he himself had mouthed, in fact, nothing had really changed: Cordelia Scaife May, an heir of the enormous Scaife-Mellon fortune, refused to believe that improvements in development would change anything; rather, demographic reduction was "the *sine qua non* for further development in the world."[163] Significantly, despite the Council's language, Sheldon Segal and other Council staffers argued that there was "no difference" between her view and that of the Council (albeit without convincing her).[164]

Bucharest or Cairo: in the end, "development" means "contraception" for the population-control movement.[165] The 1997 UNFPA document *Coming Up Short: Struggling to Implement the Cairo Programme of Action* laments that "over the next 30 years, 97 per cent of population growth is projected to be in developing countries." Faced with having so many people of color on this planet, the UNFPA points out that "just to maintain *current* rates of contraceptive use, about 100 million more couples" would have to contracept. To increase rates of use, 175 million more couples would have to use birth control. The fact that birth-control use is singled out by UNFPA as opposed to, for example, female education (given lip service in the Cairo document) is indicative of UNFPA's real concern.[166] UNFPA's vaunted commitment to non-coercive population control would be more convincing if it did not support openly coercive governmental programs. UNFPA's continuing acceptance of China's brutal population policy alone is sufficient to expose the language of the Cairo document to be mere rhetoric, signifying nothing that could reassure women and families in the developing world.

This chapter has examined the history of population-control activism since the mid-twentieth century in light of the powerful donors who set its agenda. This story will be taken up in the seventh chapter, which will analyze in more detail how Planned Parenthood opened its doors to the influence of wealthy businessmen. First, however, let us see how the commitment of the population-control movement to the control of female fertility has had tragic consequences for the marginalized women and girls who have been forcibly sterilized by the hundreds of thousands (if not millions) in the last century.

CHAPTER SIX

"Sterilize All the Unfit!"

"[A]sk the government to first take off the burdens of the insane and feebleminded from your backs. Sterilization for these is the remedy."— Margaret Sanger, 1926[1]

"No ovary is good enough to leave in and no testicle is bad enough to take out."— Anonymous doctor, 1969[2]

The front-page story of the August 29, 1997, *Washington Post* announced "Sweden Sterilized Thousands of 'Useless' Citizens for Decades."[3] The article goes on to relate the Swedes' shock at their eugenic law that sterilized 62,000 persons between 1934 and 1974. The victims included a woman whose poor vision prevented her from reading the blackboard and caused her to be labeled mentally retarded. According to Maija Runcis, a historian who investigated the eugenic sterilization program, many Swedes have reacted with horrified disbelief: "Everything was so good, so equal. Nobody had seen the back yard." The country's social-welfare tradition and liberal attitudes were thought to be proof against such horrors, yet the Scandinavian example again demonstrates that eugenic bigotry is at least as at home on the left as on the right. The Swedish minister of health and social affairs, Margot Wallstrom, in response to a question about how the Swedish government could have allowed the eugenics program to continue, responded with bewilderment: "It's impossible for me to say. I belong to another political generation. I can hardly explain this."[4]

An explanation, however, is not so hard to find; it lies in the commitment of an efficient bureaucracy to an ethic of societal control, which compromises progressive ideals. Sweden was not the only Scandinavian

179

country to embrace eugenic ideology. In fact, Sweden, Denmark, Norway, and Finland all had eugenic programs of some sort, programs which were considered complementary to the welfare state.[5]

Although we have reflected even less on our guilt than have the Swedes, America led the way in legalizing and promoting coerced eugenic sterilizations. Although this trend has ostensibly disappeared, partly due to the agitation of feminists in the 1970s, I will show that it continues, although the eugenic rationale has mutated into one of population control and welfare cost-cutting. This chapter will give a brief historical analysis of eugenic sterilization, detail Sanger's support for the procedure, and then show that the historical roots of today's international family-planning and population-control organizations show an acceptance of and even active advocacy for coerced sterilization. Lastly, I will argue that, while this practice no longer has the same legal and cultural approval within our country it once enjoyed, it continues surreptitiously today both here and outside our borders by means of America's great influence in the international family-planning and population-control movement. The consequences to women should not be overlooked: women are overwhelmingly the targets of choice for sterilization drives and propaganda.[6]

Before exploring these topics, a preliminary question should be addressed: is it appropriate to conflate eugenic sterilization and sterilization for population-control purposes? This chapter will address this concern in two ways, first, by showing how deep was (and is) the involvement of population-control activists in eugenic-sterilization organizations and, second, by showing how both population control and eugenics represent a shared ethic of control targeting the female body in the interests of a putatively greater societal good.

A Brief History of Eugenic Sterilization

Sterilization was considered one of the two most effective weapons in the negative eugenics arsenal, the other being "segregation" in mental institutions. Segregation's purpose, according to the eugenicist, was to protect society from the "genetic menace" of the mentally disabled.[7] Yet no eugenicist thought it possible to segregate all the "unfit": their proportion of the population was commonly estimated to be 15 percent. Hence the need for sterilization. Segregation was also considered too expensive. Philip Reilly notes that the lack of funding for institutions furthered the frequency of eugenic sterilization during the Depression. Often sterilization was the condition for an inmate's return to society, introducing a definite element of coercion into the inmates' "voluntary consent" to the operation: how free is one if given the "choice" of either gaining freedom through the permanent loss of one's fertility or else continued institutionalization?[8] It is also by no means clear that the (usually) young women who "chose" the operation were fully informed as to its permanent effects. The economic calculation continued beyond the Depression, for even in 1949, eugenicist and birth-control activist Clarence Gamble stressed "the high cost of segregation used as an alternative method [to sterilization] of protection from parenthood."[9] A pamphlet for Birthright, Inc., a group that advocated "sterilization for human betterment,"exclaimed, "CHARITY IS NOT ENOUGH.... After the bills are paid, nothing will have been solved permanently; 90 per cent of the feebleminded will remain in the community to reproduce and most of their children will inherit this handicap."[10]

Women were consistently the primary targets for eugenic sterilization. The data gathered by the Human Betterment Foundation (a eugenics group founded by California businessman Eugene S. Gosney) beginning in 1927 show a severe gender imbalance: no fewer than two-thirds of those sterilized were women, in spite of the fact that men outnumbered women in state institutions for the mentally retarded. Institutions reported that some women were admitted for the sole purpose of sterilizing and then releasing them.[11] That such an imbalance occurred, despite the much greater danger of the operation for women, indicates that the male-dominated medical profession placed the responsibility for perpetuating "dysgenic" traits on women more than men.[12]

In spite of America's pioneering involvement in coercive eugenic sterilization, what comes to mind for most Americans when eugenics is mentioned is Nazi Germany. It is estimated that approximately 320,000 Germans were sterilized from 1934 to 1940; concentration camps replaced the surgeon's knife after 1940.[13] The exact number, however, cannot be known, although estimates range up to 3.5 million.[14] And as many as 2 million Eastern European women in concentration camps were sterilized.[15]

It is necessary always to remember the unique character of the Nazi regime — above all its genocidal anti–Semitism. But bearing witness to the victims of Nazi evil must include our never overlooking evils for which we ourselves bear responsibility: in this case, we must recognize that the Nazi regime had no monopoly on the implementation of eugenic ideology. Pretending otherwise allows too many of us to overlook America's own eugenic past and the very real crimes committed here and abroad by American activists with American money — and too often through governmental power. It is easy to rationalize that because America is not overtly genocidal or anti–Semitic, therefore the country has not been guilty of great moral evil. Unfortunately, the historical record points to a different conclusion. The American involvement in forced sterilization actually predated the Nazis'. Though not untouched by anti–Semitism, it was more universally characterized by the generalized elitist bigotry of a eugenics mindset that condemned the "unfit" of any race, whether epileptic, mentally disabled, or simply poor, to permanent sterility. The eugenicists in Scandinavia depended on America's legal and cultural precedent of eugenic sterilization.

The Nazis also turned to the expertise of American eugenicists: the template for the Nazi sterilization law was the model law proposed by the American Eugenics Record Office and written by Harry H. Laughlin.[16] This law did not target certain races but rather specific, seemingly genetic, disorders. (None of the 27 state laws that by 1932 allowed eugenic sterilization list Jewish ethnicity as an indication for sterilization.) The Nazi law followed suit, in that it gave nine supposedly genetic conditions which indicated compulsory sterilization, without mentioning race: feeble-mindedness, schizophrenia, manic-depressive insanity, hereditary epilepsy, Huntington's chorea, blindness, deafness, severe physical deformity, and severe habitual drunkenness.[17] Laughlin, who was published frequently in Margaret Sanger's *Birth Control Review*, remained a great admirer of the German eugenics program, and the admiration was mutual: in 1936, two years after the passage of the Nazi sterilization law, Laughlin and other Americans were given honorary doctorates from the University of Heidelberg.[18] Thus, the original Nazi involvement in sterilization was broader than anti–Semitism, involving a bigotry that targeted many of the disabled, and America participated and even led the way in this scapegoating victimization in the name of societal improvement and control.

In no way do I intend to minimize Nazi or American anti–Semitism. Rather, my aim is to point out that the ethos of social control over life and reproduction that characterizes the eugenics movement as a whole abets racism. There are many American intellectuals who were motivated to pursue eugenic projects by anti–Semitic hatred, yet we should not forget that there were others who did not seem to be preoccupied by the question of race — Margaret Sanger among them, as has been shown — but who were nonetheless wholehearted advocates of denying women the freedom to be parents when it would serve eugenic purposes. This more generalized eugenic elitist bigotry has shown itself quite capable of profound violations of human dignity. Long after the Allies ended the nightmare of the Nazi regime certain powerful Americans pursued eugenic projects. Still today there are many such who manifest a predilection to eugenic biases in their desire to maintain technological control over the reproductive power of women and girls here and in the Third World. As in the past, females are indeed the primary targets of such exercises in social engineering. When one group is designated inferior and stripped of its rights, all marginalized persons—and always women and girls—are thereby endangered: this is the vital lesson that the history of eugenics can teach feminism.[19]

What, then, was the extent of America's participation in the experiment of coercive sterilization? The peak of America's intellectual and legal approval of forced sterilization was the 1927 Supreme Court *Buck v. Bell* decision, which, by a vote of 8-1, allowed the state of Virginia to sterilize an institutionalized, allegedly "feebleminded," single mother and maintained the constitutionality of its sterilization law. Justice Oliver Wendell Holmes wrote in the decision, "It is better for all the world if, instead of waiting to execute degenerate offspring for crime or to let them starve for their imbecility, society can prevent those who are manifestly unfit from continuing their kind.... Three generations of imbeciles is enough."[20] A friend of Holmes, British eugenic socialist and jurist Professor Harold Laski, wrote him jovially after the decision, "My love to you both. Get that stomach better, please. Sterilise all the unfit, among whom I include all fundamentalists."[21]

The *Buck* decision, now recognizable as a barbaric assault on the dignity of a whole class of persons, was quite in accordance with the intellectual currents of the time.[22] The Virginia law remained in place from 1924 to 1972, during which time at least 7,500 people in that state were sterilized. Carrie Buck and her sister Doris were still alive in 1980 when journalists tracked them down. Doris was also sterilized under the Virginia law, although she was never told the truth about her operation or its effects.[23] Neither was "feebleminded"; Carrie was committed to the institution to hide the fact that she had become pregnant because of incest.[24] The governors of five states, including Virginia, have apologized to the victims of their sterilization laws.[25]

It is testimony to the strange eugenic collusion between right and left that the *Buck* decision, defended by the socialist Laski, was actually cited during the Nuremberg trials as part of SS officer Otto Hofmann's defense. A document entered in Hofmann's defense by the Information Service of the Racial-Political Office of the Reich Administration detailed the "Race Protection Laws of Other Countries" in an effort to show that Hofmann's activities had precedent in other nations, such as the enlightened United States of America.[26]

One would think that the evident horrors of Nazi savagery would have turned American proponents away from sterilization (an integral element of that savagery), yet the post-war years were marked mostly by rationalizing, not repentance. Reilly remarks, "Revulsion over Germany's racist politics did little to curtail American programs before or after World War II. Indeed, American advocates pointed to Germany to illustrate how an enlightened sterilization program might quickly reach its goals."[27] By 1943 over half of our states had then or had had at one time eugenic sterilization laws. Incredibly, such laws are still on the books in some states today.

The number of sterilizations performed under these laws, from 1907 to 1964, has been estimated at over 63,500 — more than in Sweden — for more than thirty-four indications.[28] The target was usually the mentally retarded.[29] In response, the American Academy of Pediatrics has come out in opposition to sterilization for the mentally handicapped when performed for mere convenience, as has the American College of Obstetrics and Gynecology (although it ominously allows sterilization for incompetent persons without consent when the "best interests" of the patient demand it, a term not well-defined).[30]

In spite of the shift in attitude against sterilization of the mentally disabled, it is not clear how much protection they actually have. Although state-court rulings indicate that a hearing and due process, in addition to parental consent, are now legally necessary to perform a sterilization on the mentally disabled, even those precautions do not guarantee that a woman's or girl's dignity would be respected today.[31] Various studies of the parents of the mentally disabled indicate that they often balance their children's right to be free from unnecessary invasive surgery with a desire to reduce the difficulty of caring for their mentally disabled children. One study showed that 14 percent of such parents considered sterilization appropriate when done for the purpose of managing their daughters' menstruation.[32] In addition, families sometimes betray certain eugenic preconceptions in their fears that the children of their disabled children would also be mentally disabled and thus a "burden" to society. Such anxiety can lead to physicians proceeding with a sterilization for the sake of the family, not of the person being sterilized.[33] In addition, the professionals, such as judges and social-service professionals, who work with the disabled and who must make judgments about their sterilization at judicial hearings, are often not prepared with any measure of expertise, some even using derogatory terms for the mentally retarded.[34] In one study, only half of surveyed professionals who dealt with the disabled (including judges, lawyers, doctors, nurse practitioners, family-planning professionals, social workers, developmental-disabilities workers, and educators) were found to have an unbiased attitude toward people with disabilities.[35]

But sterilization abuse is not just driven by bigotry against the disabled — the poor have also come under attack. By 1969, federally supported family-planning clinics could provide sterilization to their primarily poor clientele. In the early 1970s, it came to light that many people were sterilized unknowingly or forcibly under Medicaid laws. The most infamous case was that of the African-American Relf sisters from Montgomery, Alabama. In June 1973, Mary Alice and Minnie Relf were sterilized, without their knowledge, at the tender ages of twelve and fourteen, respectively; their sixteen-year-old sister had the presence of mind to lock herself in her room and refuse to come out when the family-planning nurse came calling for her.[36] Their mother, who was illiterate, put her X on the consent form when the family-planning nurse told her that her daughters needed some shots. The reason? Boys were "hanging around" the girls, who were considered to be without the "mental talents" to use contraception.[37] Eleven other teenagers in Montgomery had been sterilized, while officials in North Carolina — where Clarence Gamble had established his pet eugenics programs— told Nial Ruth Cox that she would have to be sterilized (at age eighteen) if she wished to continue to receive welfare payments.[38] In South Carolina, three physicians entered into a pact to deliver the third child of any welfare mother only on the condition that she be sterilized post-partum. One nurse defended the procedure by claiming, "This is not a civil rights thing, or a racial thing, it is just welfare."[39] In other words, the doctors were equal-opportunity sterilizers, but only the poor need apply. After all, the good doctor, Clovis Pierce, was "tired of people running around and having babies and paying for them with my taxes," although Dr. Pierce evidently did not have to debate with his conscience for long over accepting around $60,000 of tax-generated government funds for the sterilizations.[40]

Other victims have included Mexican Americans sterilized at Los Angeles County Hospital without their consent or even knowledge, as well as 3,406 Native American women sterilized by the Indian Health Service between 1973 and 1976, without being informed of the permanence of the operation.[41] According to Dr. Connie Uri in her testimony before a Senate committee, by 1976 almost 25 percent of all fertile Native American females had been sterilized.[42] This fact indicates that targeting the poor has genocidal effects, whether or not racism is one of the explicit motivations.

In his 1974 ruling on the Relf case, Federal District Judge Gerhard Gesell said, "…[T]here is uncontroverted evidence in the record that minors and other incompetents have been sterilized with federal funds and that an indefinite number of poor people have been improperly coerced into accepting a sterilization operation under the threat that various federally supported welfare benefits would be withdrawn unless they submitted to irreversible sterilization." He estimated that from 100,000 to 150,000 low-income women had been sterilized in recent years.[43] Obviously, doctors were motivated by a desire to see fewer poor women reproduce, as well as by simple racism. Many doctors have also taken seriously the hysteria over overpopulation, seeing a possibility to "solve" the problem through permanent infertility.[44]

The feminist outcry against sterilization abuses led to a series of stricter regulations regarding sterilizing Medicaid recipients. Feminists were particularly active in New York City, although Planned Parenthood and the Association for Voluntary Sterilization (the eugenic and population-control group formerly named Birthright) both lobbied *against* proposed New York legislation that would have ensured more protective sterilization regulations in all city health facilities.[45] The Committee to End Sterilization Abuse (CESA) was formed in 1974 as a pioneering feminist group that took a strong stand both for women's rights and against the abuse of the poor.[46] As feminist Thomas M. Shapiro has argued, aside from gender, welfare status provides "the most powerful positive predictor of the likelihood of one's being sterilized."[47]

As a result of feminist activism against this violent bigotry against the poor and the disabled, new regulations against sterilization abuse were passed at both the local and federal levels: in 1974, the federal Department of Health, Education, and Welfare instituted new guidelines, and Judge Gesell also disallowed coercion and the federally funded sterilization of minors.[48] Yet it is not clear how well, if at all, the regulations have been enforced.[49] Two studies issued by the Health Research Group in 1979 and 1981 showed only about a 30 percent rate of complete compliance with the regulations by hospitals, although it seems as if the most blatant instances of coercion have diminished.[50]

What feminist groups like CESA realized was that, in addition to bigotry against the disabled, the poor, and minorities, sexism was also at work. Many doctors in the 1960s and 1970s viewed the healthy female reproductive system as a big mess needing a scientific hand to reorder it. As one doctor argued in 1970, "After the last planned pregnancy, the uterus becomes a useless, bleeding, symptom-producing, potentially cancer-bearing organ and therefore should be removed. If, in addition, both ovaries are removed, further benefits accrue."[51]

Another reason why female sterilization is often pushed, as opposed to the simpler male operation, has to do also with a medical misogyny that views a woman's body as a surgical training ground. One resident reported that the doctors preferred hysterectomies to tubal ligation, because "...we like to do a hysterectomy, it's more of a challenge ... you know a well-trained chimpanzee can do a tubal ligation ... and it's good experience for the junior resident ... good training."[52] The greater complexity (and thus "challenge") of female sterilization has led many doctors to encourage women, as opposed to their male partners, to be the ones sterilized. Also, some male doctors perhaps project their own discomfort regarding male impotence onto their patients, or else they reinforce their male patients' fears. Alan Guttmacher, considered in his time to be "the most influential birth-control advocate in the world," justified his reluctance to sterilize men by saying, "I never urge men to be sterilized, since sexual behavior has very little to do with what is below the waist, but rather is largely dependent on what goes on above the neck, in the brain.... I can only repeat that it is most unwise to sterilize the husband simply because it is easier."[53] Another doctor simply said at a medical conference, "No ovary is good enough to leave in and no testicle is bad enough to take out."[54]

Sanger's Support of Sterilization

Far from condemning forced sterilization, Margaret Sanger demonstrated the depth of her allegiance to the eugenic party line by advocating the sterilization of all "defectives." Sanger's view did not limit eugenic sterilization to purely voluntary operations, but rather, as can be seen in *The Pivot of Civilization*, she criticized the "long-practiced policy of *laiser-faire* [sic]" regarding what was at present "the emergency problem of segregation and sterilization."[55] This is one of the many places where Sanger's commitment to female liberation and freedom is completely compromised by her eugenic beliefs: forcible sterilization of the "unfit," she believed, was more important than the freedom to have children. She requested the federal government to "set a sensible example to the world by offering a bonus or a yearly pension to all obviously unfit parents" to be sterilized. Thus, she rehearses the eugenic cost-benefit analysis of the problem of poverty and mental disease that considers welfare costs, and thus the reproductive capacity of the poor, an unacceptable imposition on the "fit." As she told the readers of the *Birth Control Review*, "[A]sk the government to *first* take off the burdens of the insane and feebleminded from your backs. Sterilization for these is the remedy."[56]

She again encouraged government-implemented eugenic sterilization in 1932, when she gave a speech, "A Plan for Peace," which called for a federally established "Parliament of Population." Among its eugenic goals would be "to raise the level and increase the general intelligence of population." The speech, reprinted in the April 1932 *Birth Control Review*, called for "a stern and rigid policy of sterilization and segregation to that grade of population whose progeny is already tainted, or whose inheritance is such that objectionable traits may be transmitted to offspring … [and] to give certain dysgenic groups in our population their choice of segregation or sterilization."[57] Sanger's promotion of forced sterilization, coming only a year before the Nazi's infamous 1933 sterilization law, shows again the confluence between American eugenic thought and that of the Nazis.

The few reservations that Sanger did express concerning forced sterilization had only to do with its limited efficacy, not its unethical nature. In the February 1919 *Birth Control Review*, she lamented, "While I personally believe in the sterilization of the feeble-minded, the insane and the syphiletic [*sic*], I have not been able to discover that these measures are more than superficial deterrents when applied to the constantly growing stream of the unfit."[58] That is, birth control was always her preference as the most effective means of controlling the reproduction of the "unfit," but her support for forced sterilization was nevertheless constant — revealing the eugenic ends birth control was always meant to serve in her eyes.

Sanger's acceptance of eugenic sterilization was not, as has sometimes been implied, a youthful flirtation with eugenic science that was later rejected. Towards the end of her life, in 1950, she received the Lasker Award and sent her son Grant to read a speech she wrote for the occasion. After decrying that the "self supporting, creative human being" was forced into supporting "the ever increasing and numerous dependent, delinquent and unbalanced masses," she called for pensions to be given to "dysgenic" human beings who would agree to sterilization.[59] Her statement was warmly received by Clarence Gamble, who wrote her affectionately to thank her for her speech and to encourage her to make more statements regarding eugenic sterilization.[60]

Gamble was one of many Sanger coworkers who was deeply involved both in eugenics and coerced sterilization, as chapter three indicated. One needs only to recall that he worked to promote a eugenic sterilization law in North Carolina, funding a local branch of the pro-sterilization Human Betterment Association, while serving as the field coordinator for Birthright until 1947 and raising large sums for the national organization.[61]

Planned Parenthood, while refusing until quite late to endorse sterilization officially, still threw its hat into the pro-sterilization ring by defending the procedure against its "unscientific" detractors. One pamphlet, undated but probably from 1945, explains that irrational fear of eugenic ideals inspires these sterilization naysayers.

> It is in part fear of [the] abuse of eugenic principles that motivates opposition to state programs of sterilization.... Nevertheless, there are many cases in which sterilization solves a problem for the individuals concerned, as well as protecting society, and allows a relatively normal and satisfactory life to a person who would otherwise have to live in segregation or else become a burden to himself and a menace to others.... The California law has been the most carefully checked. Gosney and Popenoe report a high proportion of good results.[62]

The California law had the distinction of enabling California to sterilize more mentally disabled persons than did any other state in the union.

Today a preoccupation with abortion, combined with the fact that Planned Parenthood is perceived as a powerful and wealthy ally in that battle, has somewhat muted previously strong feminist criticism of the birth-control and population-control movements. Especially in the 1970s, feminist organizations and individuals condemned the practice of eugenic sterilization and the organizations, including Planned Parenthood, that promoted it.[63] Unfortunately, today, mainstream feminism tends to turn a blind eye to this issue. I would argue that women can overlook history only to their peril. There is a definite genealogy behind the present atmosphere in which the victimization of individuals, the violation of human dignity, is accepted when done for the greater social "good": women and girls always end up bearing the brunt of such scapegoating; they always end up at the other end of the knife.

A "Birthright" to Sterility

Let us now examine some of the organizations that enabled the bigotries detailed above to be so easily (and often legally) acted upon and perpetuated. This section will examine the history of what is now called Engender Health, a group that has gone through many name changes but, as its opposition to the sterilization regulations of the 1970s shows, with seemingly little change in attitude. This history demonstrates again the deep involvement of birth-control activists in eugenic sterilization.

The organizational leader of eugenic sterilization was euphemistically called "Birthright," after a statement by Franklin Delano Roosevelt, which stressed the "birthright" of every child to health and happiness. Birthright's strategy to accomplish this goal necessitated sterilization for all those "unfit" who could not, by a genetic and thus "scientific" necessity, be worthy parents. Marian S. Norton Olden founded the organization in 1943, and Sanger's coworker Clarence Gamble funded much of it. In 1951, the name was changed to the Human Betterment Association of America (HBAA), renamed the Association for Voluntary Sterilization (AVS) in the 1960s, later the Association for Voluntary Surgical Contraception (AVSC), and now it is primarily a population-control group named Engender Health.[64]

Birthright was undoubtedly a eugenic organization. One publication by Dr. H. Curtis Wood, Jr., former president of the Pennsylvania Planned Parenthood and later HBAA's president, argues that sterilization was important as a form "of birth control for those of low intelligence…. New and simpler contraceptives are being developed, but no matter how effective and simple these may be they will never be used by the mental defective."[65] Noting that such efforts are a medical responsibility in that they involve raising the national intelligence, he adds, "…*is it not reasonable also to place restrictions upon those who are manifestly unfit for parenthood and incapable of rearing normal children?*"[66] Despite Wood's activity in moving Birthright towards a more moderate public appearance from the hysterical rhetoric that characterized Olden's activism and incorporating it into Planned Parenthood's scope of activities, the reference to "restrictions" to be placed on the "unfit" woman's fertility makes clear the commitment to coercion involved. Purely pragmatic reasons made Wood publicly emphasize voluntary sterilization over the eugenic, compulsory sterilization he desired.[67]

One of the members of the Birthright board of directors, according to this pamphlet, was Guttmacher.[68] This position testifies to his longstanding interest in eugenic sterilization. In a letter from HBAA executive director Ruth Proskauer Smith to Clarence Gamble in 1958, she notes a "very successful mailing of Dr. Guttmacher's article…. Dr. Guttmacher reports many favorable comments on his formula for socioeconomic sterilizations."[69] The article in question was entitled "Puerperal [post-delivery] Sterilization on the Private and Ward Service of a large Metropolitan Hospital," and his interest in "socio-economic" sterilization indicates that Guttmacher believed being poor was a sufficient indication for the permanent removal of fertility. Proskauer Smith, it should be noted, also was actively involved with the Planned Parenthood League of Massachusetts in the 1950s.

By 1958, H. Curtis Wood was the president of the HBAA, and Guttmacher was the chairman of the Medical and Scientific Committee; a "Dear Doctor" letter from both (undated but probably from 1958) read:

By acquainting more members of the medical profession with this program, we hope to lessen current misunderstanding and misinformation so that sterilization, when indicated for organic, genetic, socio-economic or emotional reasons, will become an increasingly useful tool in the rehabilitation of the patient as a more adequate member of the family and community.[70]

Such an understanding of "rehabilitation" echoes the eugenic belief that the primary treatment for the social and medical problems of the "unfit" should be the prevention of their future offspring.

Engender Health in its various incarnations has been the most prominent "single-issue" organization agitating for sterilization measures. Yet many in the family-planning and population-control movement supported its aims. In 1964, Guttmacher, then president of the Planned Parenthood Federation of America (PPFA), lamented the lack of official connections between PPFA and HBAA: "It is unfortunate that many have to fragment their energies because many on the PPFA Board are also on the Human Betterment Board, and vice versa.... It seems to me that the two groups should take cognizance of this in their future plans."[71] Such a close connection was indeed established when the two groups began to work together in population-control outreach to less-developed countries in the 1960s, after Hugh Moore took over the sterilization organization.[72]

Unfortunately, the present policies of PPFA, IPPF, and Engender Health do little to reassure the feminist opponents of coerced and eugenic sterilization. As the first part of this chapter has shown, abuses such as those perpetrated against the Relf sisters probably in fact still go on in this country, while documented reports of coerced sterilization continue to come from countries where IPPF, Engender Health, the United Nations Population Fund (UNFPA), and the Pathfinder Fund are active. The enthusiasm for sterilization demonstrated by many family-planning clinics today is regrettably insouciant, or perhaps collaborationist. One study mentioned a particular doctor who, according to a colleague, "did wholesale sterilization — anybody handicapped or poor — if a patient couldn't pay he'd do it for free.... His motives were all wrong. I'm not big on the master race idea — that [the] less than perfect should be eliminated." Yet the same doctor was praised by a family-planning clinic administrator, who did not seem at all troubled by the doctor's "master race" ideas when she lamented, "It was wonderful for us because we could refer to him. He would sterilize anybody, anytime, no questions asked.... Now I only know a couple of doctors who will do disabled sterilizations and they are about to retire."[73] Such an attitude regarding her "wonderful" coworker demonstrates either a culpable lack of reflection or else a covert agreement with the prevention of the "less than perfect." A similar collusive dynamic among today's population-control and family-planning organizations extends beyond the local level. The next section will examine more recent manifestations of dangerous disregard for the dignity of women and girls, specifically in the area of coerced sterilization, when the control of female fertility is deemed by the powerful to be essential to the "greater good."

Contemporary Manifestations of Control Ideology: China and Peru

The fertility of the world's poor is a source of great anxiety for elites, who consider it an irrational force to be controlled or eliminated. In the following, I will briefly examine two programs of population control that have involved coerced sterilization, both of which have ties with IPPF, Engender Health, and/or the U.S. Agency for International Development (USAID).

China

Sterilization abuse, as well as coerced abortion, in China as a result of its one-child policy has received much attention. The policy was established in 1979, an about-face following a period of official disapproval of population control, which the government had condemned as a bourgeois occlusion of the inseparability of economic, social, and political problems that scapegoated the fertility of the poor.[74] China continues to insist on the need for population control for economic growth, even though other Asian countries, such as Japan, have considerably denser populations yet still thrive economically. In all likelihood, the Chinese government has found population growth to be a convenient scapegoat for its societal problems. In 1979, anthropology student Steven Mosher traveled in rural China, at a time when few foreigners were allowed to wander outside of certain "model communes," and he broke the news of the program's abuses with his horrifying first-person report of the annual or semiannual family-planning meetings designed to force women to "think straight" (i.e., conform to the state's dictates) about birth control.[75]

Sterilization quotas were initiated in late 1982, making the operation necessary for one member of every couple under forty years of age with two or more children.[76] Why sterilization? Then-spokesman for the Family Planning Commission, Wang Liancheng, noted that "experience shows that the simple methods are best ... [f]or peasants with two children."[77]

In other words, the motivation of the peasants was not sufficient to sustain the use of temporary contraception, and permanent methods would have to be enforced for the state to meet its goals. This attitude was the practical consequence of the ideology described in the *China Daily* in 1983, which insisted that "the population problem in China today is of such a pressing nature that individual whims must be subject to the interests of society as a whole."[78]

The appearance of "targets" and "quotas," that is, the requirement that specific kinds and specific numbers of people be sterilized, combined with financial incentives for government workers, led, as it usually does, to coercion. Tyrene White notes, "Under pressure to meet specific goals in a short period of time, all semblance of restraint [in China] was lost, and direct, physical coercion became an essential tool of policy implementation in many localities."[79] Pressure was exerted on the cadres (the local officials charged with enforcing family planning and other state directives) in the form of punishment when targets were not met or unauthorized pregnancies allowed, in some cases leading to the loss of 20 percent of the cadre's yearly subsidy.[80] The peasants were "lectured, harassed, publicly humiliated, fined, deprived of contract land, denied food, water, and electricity and 'mobilized' to have abortions," reports John S. Aird, respected demographer and expert on the Chinese population program.[81]

Chinese agricultural reforms, which had begun in the early 1980s, caused a relaxation in the mid–1980s of the enforcement of the one-child policy; there was a diminution in the allegations of coercion. Peasant revolt against the rule, especially in the case of the birth of a daughter, seems also to have led to the relaxation, as did the increasing occurrence of female infanticide. By 1986, policy makers allowed that couples "in real difficulties"—a code word describing the "plight" of having only a girl—would be permitted to have a second child.[82]

Unfortunately, the improved atmosphere would not last. The results of the July 1990 census contributed to a return of the harsh policies of the early 1980s. Both the failure of the country to meet population targets, as well as the extent of the underreporting of births, led to renewed pressure on women to adjust their reproduction to the official demands of the state.[83] This pressure took various forms. In the northwestern province of Shaanxi, mandatory, semiannual gynecological exams were begun in 1990. While also for the purposes of reproductive health care, the population-control rationale was not neglected: in addition to ensuring that every woman with one child had an IUD, the exams also served the purpose of pregnancy detection. One cadre claimed that the exams were "very important" in detecting unapproved pregnancies and ensuring subsequent abortions.[84] Routine sterilization campaigns have also become a standard part of the population-control effort.[85] The evidence regarding the activities of the population program for the 1995–2000 period is no better. Chinese dissident Harry Wu has reported that one hospital, which receives money from UNICEF, performs about 300 forced abortions and 100–150 forced sterilizations per month.[86]

Other than the coercion, three particular enormities of the Chinese population-control campaign have been revealed in recent years: racial minorities have been systematically targeted; disabled children have been singled out, in a classic eugenic move, as life unworthy of life; and the lack of value placed on girls has led to the abortion and infanticide of staggering numbers of females.

The written law of China states that racial minorities of fewer than 10 million people are not to be held to the one- or two-child maximums that apply to the majority populations. Yet in practice the Chinese government has used its birth policies to slow the growth of minorities perceived to be a threat to communist-party hegemony. Harry Wu has documented the systematic genocide perpetrated on Uzbeks (in China) by means of forced sterilization and abortion, while Yemlibike Fatkulin has testified to the same atrocities committed against the Uyghur minority since 1984.[87] In the name of "improving the quality of minorities" and other eugenic cover phrases, minority women are made to wear IUDs and undergo sterilization, and those who conceive without permission are forcibly aborted. One woman was sterilized while serving prison time for studying her faith, another paralyzed after a forced abortion. Fatulin reported, "According to some Uyghur family planning workers, in order to fulfill the quota of abortions, sometimes Chinese doctors are forced to kill the newborn Uyghur babies."[88]

When the control ideology is carried out, racism gains an easy outlet. And so does eugenics. As early as 1988, provincial Chinese governments implemented regulations which sought to prevent severely mentally disabled people from reproducing.[89] In December 1993, a law entitled "On Eugenics and Health Protection" (quickly changed to the "Draft Natal and Health Care Law" to avoid criticism of the bill's overtly eugenic aims) was proposed by the Public Health Ministry for the purpose of "avoiding births of inferior quality."[90] The law affected the 10.2 million mentally disabled people in China, who were required to be sterilized, while women found to be carrying "abnormal" fetuses were made to abort them.[91] In response to the international outcry when this policy was publicized, Chinese officials rushed to defend the policy, insisting that eugenic abortion would be voluntary, although eugenic sterilization would still be "required."[92]

Those protesting included representatives of disability-rights groups, who argued that legalized eugenics "is inconsistent with the duty of civilized societies to support their most vulnerable members."[93] The bill was shelved temporarily due to international reaction but was ultimately passed in October 1994, under the name "Maternal and Infantile Health Care Law."[94] (The title is an interesting foreshadowing of the Cairo conference's dressing up of the control of the fertility of poor women as a concern for women's and children's health.)

As Gisela Bock has repeatedly argued, eugenic bigotry is not usually found without sexist bigotry. Eugenics leads to a view of women as primarily reproducers of the race, for good or for ill; when this view is combined with the desire to control population, women are seen as nothing more than "at-risk reproducers." In China this misogyny has had terrifying consequences: the mass abortion and infanticide of females. A recent census showed a ratio of 119 boys born for every 100 girls, with some provinces showing ratios as high as 140 to 100.[95] Chinese baby girls are smothered, drowned, choked, and abandoned, and the women who bear them are often beaten or divorced.[96] The female babies who survive are frequently sold.[97] Although IPPF supports the Chinese program, it has acknowledged that 500,000 to 750,000 females are aborted every year in China.[98] Greenhalgh has observed, "From the vantage point of the mid–1990s, the original one-child policy, although formally gender-neutral, appears to have been callously sexist in its willful neglect of well-known prejudices against girls and their likely life-and-death consequence...."[99]

Recent news from China has only served to underline the consistency of the atrocities of the family-planning program. In the summer of 1998, partly with funds obtained by expatriate Harry Wu, Gao Xiao Duan defected from China's Fijian province, bringing with her large amounts of documentation concerning human-rights and anti-woman abuses. From 1984 until April 1998, Gao served as the chief administrator for the Yonghe Planned Birth Office (PBO), with jurisdiction over more than 22 villages and a population of over 60,000. She defected after the stress of her "double life" as both a "planned-birth officer" and a mother proved to be too painful. As she said to a U.S. House Subcommittee, "All of those 14 years, I was a monster in the daytime," jailing women or their family members who would not comply with the birth laws, while secretly adopting an "illegal" child in addition to her first-born baby girl.[100]

She labored under a sign that read:

> No permit, No marriage.
> No permit, No pregnancy.
> No permit, No baby.[101]

Her office had two basic tasks: to track, through computerized records, pertinent information about all fertile women under her jurisdiction — information including dates of marriage, pregnancies, abortions, sterilizations, and IUD insertion — and to carry out the reward/punishment component by which compliance with the population policy is enforced.[102] Thus, in the PBO building was a jail cell, recorded on videotape, in which illegally pregnant women and their family members were held until their "cooperation" was obtained. The building also had an operating room, where the medical procedures, including forced abortions and sterilizations, took place. In the first half of 1997 alone, 101 sterilizations, 228 IUD insertions, and 60 abortions were performed (including 27 second- or third-trimester procedures, one of the latter being a forced abortion on a nine-months pregnant woman).[103]

Gao's testimony also revealed new aspects of the Chinese program. For example, it was not previously documented that sterilization was used not only for contraceptive purposes but also as a punishment for noncompliance with the family-planning policy. Her secretly made videotape also showed several women who were so harmed by forced abortions that they were sterilized in the process. Also not previously known was another tactic used by the cadre enforcers, namely, the razing of noncompliant women's houses. Knowing firsthand the naivete of the claim that, if a tactic is not ordered by Beijing, it is not being done, Gao said, "No document explicitly allows dismantling of a violator's house. But, to the best of my knowledge, this practice not only exists in our province but in rural areas in other provinces as well."[104] The truth of this statement was more recently confirmed in September 2001 interviews done by Josephine Guy of the Population Research Institute (PRI) with Chinese women in the UNFPA "model county" of Sihui, Guangdong province, in southern China. The interviewer asked a woman with a forbidden child if she could have hid from pursuing government workers; she responded, "That wouldn't work. They would tear down my house. They would wreck it." Another woman testified that three homes belonging to her mother-in-law were destroyed when the former went into hiding when pregnant in order to avoid a forced second-trimester abortion. Nine people in her extended family were arrested and fined sums about equal to three years' salary.[105]

The September 2002 population law passed by the Chinese government indicates that things will not change anytime soon. The legislation calls for "unremitting efforts" in "upholding the one-child policy," even acknowledging that "the state shall employ a series of varied measures … to place population under control."[106]

The many reports of coercion have led to some controversy here in the United States.[107] The Chinese family program is supported by the United Nations Population Fund (UNFPA), which the United States has funded generously. The allegations of coercive activity on the part of China's government led in 1985 to the first of many attempts, some successful, some not, to cut off U.S. taxpayer funding of the UNFPA, given the Fund's participation in the Chinese program. UNFPA itself showed a marked lack of concern regarding the accusations of misogynistic coercion; its executive secretary, Rafael M. Salas, and later his successors have stated that their organization believes in non-coercive population control but will not deign to define what "non-coercive" might mean in other cultures.[108] In 1983, at the height of China's deployment of coercive family-planning measures, UNFPA gave its highest award to Qian Xinzhong, the head of the Chinese program, and in 1985 Salas insisted that "China has done an outstanding job on her population problem." In 1987, UNFPA called the Chinese program "one of the most successful efforts in the world today," indicating that the UNFPA's definition of "success" is broad enough to allow for extreme human-rights abuses especially suffered by women.[109] In 1998, the UNFPA committed itself to a four-year, $20-million program in China. Previous UNFPA donations have been defended on the grounds that they have only been used for "infrastructure," such as the building of a computer database for the program, but the Gao case clearly shows how easily computer technology serves the ends of totalitarian surveillance, facilitating the smooth functioning of an oppressive population-control juggernaut.[110] The 1998 program introduced UNFPA programs into 32 Chinese counties.[111]

Much of Gao's testimony reiterated what earlier observers had already reported, although without the extensive documentation. Her statements, however, indicate that these procedures have continued, despite continual governmental protestations that they are isolated, local incidents.[112] American apologists for the Chinese regime and for UNFPA have argued that the Chinese program is not really coercive and anyway, even if it is, UNFPA deserves our support because of the overriding importance of population control. As Representative Tom Lantos (D–CA) said in 2001, around the time of the war in Afghanistan, "UNFPA deserves America's whole-hearted support.... Let us not lose sight of the valuable work it is doing around the globe, including Afghanistan. Support for the UNFPA is squarely in America's national interests—and clearly in keeping with American values."[113] In Lantos's world, the wombs of Chinese and Afghan women are a threat to American interests, and regrettable overzealousness in one part of the world is more than compensated for by the reduction of the number of the poor in other sensitive areas.

For UNFPA, the "problem" of too many people in underdeveloped countries is the only problem worth solving; the flagrant violation of women's rights and health is merely a matter of bad press. For example, former UNFPA executive director Nafis Sadik received the Chinese government's Population Prize in 2002. After acknowledging that she had "the honor of being associated with China's reproductive health and family planning programme for more than two decades," as well as opening China to UNFPA in 1979, Sadik said, "I was most impressed with the strong political will of the Chinese leaders at different levels, and the great enthusiasm and seriousness [of] the Chinese people, including the reproductive health and family planning workers."[114] Her "long association" with the People's Republic of China had been, she said, "most rewarding for me and for my former colleagues at UNFPA."[115] The UNFPA continues to argue that the Chinese program is strictly voluntary, yet the 2001 interviews conducted by Josephine Guy in Sihui county, which confirmed the use of many different forms of coercion, took place only a few miles from the UNFPA Chinese office. Perhaps we are to believe that the local UNFPA representative did not know, what every other resident knew, about the coercive nature of the county family-planning program. But, in fact, the UNFPA "office" is a desk to be found within the local Office of Family Planning. Indeed the UNFPA desk touches a desk at which work for the Chinese office is conducted, work that includes enforcement of the coercive policies described in Guy's interviews: "age requirements for pregnancy; birth permits; mandatory use of IUDs; mandatory sterilization; crippling fines for non-compliance; imprisonment [of women and their relatives] for non-compliance; destruction of homes and property for non-compliance; forced abortions and forced sterilization."

The United Nations Population Fund's endorsement of oppressive programs such as China's is not an aberration among population-control groups; indeed, it stands with the International Planned Parenthood Federation in this regard, and the latter's support of the Chinese program reveals its fundamentally anti-feminist ideology. In 1983, one of the worst years in terms of human suffering from coercive policies in China, IPPF officials stated disingenuously that China's program was successful because "the masses have an understanding of family planning," adding, astonishingly, that "it is the people's own choice." At the same time, they said that China's population policies were consistent with the goals of IPPF. In November 1983, the IPPF Members' Assembly met in Nairobi and registered its official approval of the Chinese program by inviting the Chinese Family Planning Association (FPA) to affiliate with IPPF.[116] In fact, in a communication with John Aird, IPPF claimed that the quote cited above was "lifted out of context" and that, since IPPF inquired about reports of female infanticide and coercion and received the standard governmental answers—which were apparently sufficient for the IPPF representatives, despite much evidence to the contrary unearthed by the seasoned foreign press corps stationed in Beijing—IPPF had done due diligence in pursuing the allegations. In thus explaining its collaboration with the Chinese population program, IPPF displays either outright mendacity about what it knows about the program's brutality and inhumanity, or else the breathtaking and culpable blindness of those who want to be misled because a "greater good" is at stake. In either case, IPPF makes clear that its overriding concern is demographic, which buries any pro-woman concern under the avalanche of population-control obsession.

IPPF's support has not wavered over the years, despite the overwhelming evidence of massive human-rights abuses in the name of population control. The 1996 grant to the FPA from IPPF was $1 million, to be used for the purposes of "supporting and helping to implement government policy."[117] Thus IPPF indicates its willingness to fight Third World fertility at any price, even when that fight seriously compromises women's health and freedom.

Peru

Some of the most recent reports of sterilization abuse come from Peru. Population control was established late in Peru, in July 1995, by the administration of former president Alberto Fujimori. By 1996, feminist groups were getting reports of abuses performed in public-health facilities, frequently involving obstetric and gynecological procedures.[118] By around August 1997, the Population Research Institute began hearing rumors of mass sterilizations done mostly on poor women without informed consent.[119] Among the Peruvian groups who received word of coercive abuses were the Flora Tristan Center for Peruvian Women and the National Association of Catholic Physicians, and local newspapers began to publicize individual cases, according to an important January 11, 1998, *Miami Herald* article. At the time, the response from USAID officials was to refuse to speak on the record; privately, they argued that the reports were mere "conjecture."[120] David Morrison of PRI visited Peru from January 19 to 30, 1998, and from January 17 to 25, Grover Joseph Rees, staff director and chief counsel for the U.S. House Subcommittee on International Operations and Human Rights, also traveled through Peru on a fact-finding mission. It was discovered that coerced sterilization abounded: for example, some women in the little village of La Legua in northern Peru testified that they were offered food as an incentive to be sterilized. Celia Durand, mother of three, was pressured into the operation, only to die two weeks later from complications; other women, such as Alejandra Aguirre Auccapina and Juana Rosa Ochoa Chira, died after forced sterilizations. Ethnic minorities were called "pigs" or "dogs" by the family-planning workers.[121] The pressure tactics were to be expected, given the targets that were mandated for the country as a whole, as well as for individual health-care workers. The Peruvian president's health advisor, Dr. Yong Motta, stressed the necessity of targets in an interview with Morrison: "Of course the campaign has targets…. [Success is measured] through many methods, including numbers of acceptors versus nonacceptors." Motta added that USAID "is disqualified from objecting because they have been helping in the family planning program from the first."[122]

Despite USAID's knowledge of the campaigns and its acknowledgment that "experience has shown that targets are often counterproductive," it did not terminate its funding and support of the non-governmental organizations involved nor of the Peruvian government's family-planning program, confining any reservations it might have had to conversations with the organizations involved. The Peruvian Ministry of Health's report on the sterilization campaign released in July 2002 concluded that USAID knew of and supported the campaign; in fact in 1997, USAID constituted the primary donor to the family-planning program.[123] Among the USAID-funded groups involved in Peru was PRISMA, a non-governmental organization that distributes food through a United States Food for Peace grant. PRISMA, unlike other organizations involved with Food for Peace, includes required family-planning training for the women participating in the program.[124] David Morrison reported that a PRISMA family-planning worker was observed pressuring a woman to accept sterilization in exchange for food.[125] Another NGO, Pathfinder International, though not involved directly in the sterilization drives, did provide three training sessions in tubal ligation techniques for government doctors from June 1996 (when the campaigns began) to December 1997.[126] The campaigns themselves resembled those partly funded by Engender Health in countries such as India.[127]

The other major contributor, after USAID, to Peru's family-planning program was UNFPA.[128] A 2002 congressional-committee report issued by the Peruvian government exposed the deep involvement of UNFPA in the Peruvian program. The Anticoncepcion Quirurgica Voluntaria (AQV) Commission revealed that UNFPA served as the "Technical Secretary, working in coordination with [Fujimori's] National Population Council." The report claims that UNFPA not only financed but also "induced" the program.[129]

After the outcry in the United States over the Peruvian sterilization campaigns, both the USAID Assistant Administrator for Latin America and the Caribbean, Mark Schneider, and the Peruvian Ministry of Health reassured Congress in 1998 that the human-rights abuses would be corrected. Yet another fact-finding trip to Peru in December 1999 proved that forced sterilization, Depo-Provera use, and IUD insertion continued, often leading to miscarriage, injury, or death. Health workers were routinely bribed and given demographic targets to achieve, and women were called "beasts" and "dogs."[130] During this time, USAID had some 30 workers on the ground in Peru, while its donation to the Peruvian Ministry of Health was $36 million. Some of the USAID money in 2000 was going to the Ayacucho region, where continued coercion and pressure were reported.[131] PRISMA continued to be a presence in the country through 1999, through its USAID-funded distribution of contraceptives, including Depo-Provera.[132] In 2001, Luis Solari, the health minister in the administration following Fujimori's ouster, found documents which demonstrated that Fujimori ordered the sterilizations, making even clearer how involuntary the so-called Voluntary Surgical Anti-Conception program was. Over 300,000 Peruvian women, mostly poor or minority, were sterilized in a country of only 27 million.[133] As in the U.S., the native tribes were a particular focus of attention: the control movement does not stray far from genocide.

Conclusion

This chapter has focused on sterilization because this particular surgical procedure has a long history of endorsement by both eugenicists and population-control advocates. Thus, its history provides an opportunity to examine the inter-implication of the two ideologies. This chapter has indicated that the violence of coerced sterilization is based in the control ideology at the root of both eugenics and population control, an ideology that seeks to control female fertility for some greater good.

The population-control movement's dismay at the lack of "motivation" on the part of poor women indicates why sterilization, as well as some forms of semi-permanent birth control, are so popular: as John S. Aird put it regarding the Chinese program, "Once sterilized, their compliance was assured!"[134] Unfortunately for those who wish to suppress Third World reproduction according to demographic targets usually conjured by white male elites, women persist in having their own ideas about "ideal fertility," which might be very different indeed from what the authorities have planned.[135]

Another reason for the pushing of sterilization, as well as the pill, the IUD, Depo-Provera, and Norplant, may be the technological distance that these methods place between the woman and her fertility, her bodily rhythms, her sexual activity. As Germaine Greer has pointed out, what connection is there between taking a pill every morning and a sex act that may or may not occur that evening? Such distance enables sexuality and reproduction to be alienated from women, to be analyzed, predicted, and controlled "scientifically"— usually by men. This strikes at the heart of a female's experience of being at home in her body, especially in her sexual, maternal, and familial life. The alienation of female fertility undermines the holistic understanding of their bodies that many Third World women have and enables the technological control of poor women's bodies by third parties with demonstrably anti-woman aims.

Sanger's complicity with eugenic sterilization, and the complicity of the organizations she founded, is perhaps the most terrifying testimony to the dangerous and misogynistic effects of negative eugenics. The fact that this abuse did not just occur in the past but is also quite current, both here and abroad, indicates the degree of critical consciousness necessary for feminists who wish to oppose such brutal misogynism. Feminism must be willing to stand up to the perpetuators of eugenic sterilization — including family-planning clinics and organizations— and must purge itself of any residual eugenic ideology if it is to fully defend the marginalized women for whom the women's movement is the last hope of protection.

CHAPTER SEVEN

Selling Out the Sisterhood

"Screw the patients, spend your money on politics."— Linda Beglio,
Planned Parenthood Federation of America, quoted by Alfred F. Moran,
PPFA Annual Meeting, October 31, 1981[1]

Money and Men

In his panegyric to Hugh Moore, publisher of the pamphlet *The Pop-ulation Bomb*, Lawrence Lader notes that "Money and Men" were the "Essential Partners" in promoting population control.[2] An evaluation of the history of the birth-control and population-control movement can-not overlook the fact that male eugenicists were recruited from the begin-ning by Sanger to supply her organizations with prominence and funding. In the 1940s large numbers of men began to respond. By the 1960s, Planned Parenthood was directly targeting businessmen in their promotional and fund-raising materials, in an attempt to convince them that population control was necessary for the stability of foreign markets and the growth of profits. This strategy was a thorough success: today PPFA and IPPF receive huge sums from the business community.

A great deal was sacrificed, however, in Planned Parenthood's court-ing of big business. First, the new alliance guaranteed that PPFA would not be able to overcome its eugenic beginnings; the massive involvement of wealthy businessmen in PPFA sealed its ideological fate: if a critical feminist examination of conscience could not easily happen during its early, activist period, then it certainly could not be carried out when the organization was overrun with men who would not even pay lip service to women's interests. In the second place, the eugenic ideology was given a new inflection, though one certainly in harmony with the basic attitude: the elevation of profits over people. While the professional eugenicists were mostly scientists (with the notable exception of Frederick Osborn, who was a businessman and manager by training), the new male activists were accustomed to solving problems by increasing efficiency and decreasing costs. They brought a practiced managerial eye to the "problem" of human reproduction and desired to solve it by micromanaging that most foreign and feared of human powers, female fertility. Lastly, this new perspective has led to the mutilation and death of countless women and girls, despite the frequent deployment of the rhetoric of "women's health" and "reproductive rights." As this chapter will show, the determination of the male activists to find a "perfect" contraception — that is, one that would be simple, long-acting, and, ideally, irremovable except by a medical professional — led them to experiment on poor women without concern for the often catastrophic side effects.

In some ways, these men are *not* anything new; there have always been men who have sought to control the inconvenient power of female reproduction. Pacifying that power puts the woman that much more under the man's control. Now she can be made into a plaything, a toy, who can be used and then discarded without any permanent messiness (such as a child) that might tie her to him.[3] Farida Akhter, a Bangladeshi feminist activist, has complained that men are partly interested in contraception because it makes women permanently available to them. "Reproductive rights has eventually come to mean increased availability to men through the use of modern contraceptives," she observed. "This has happened because of the birth control movement's increasing alliance with the population controllers and multinational corporations."[4]

This chapter examines the truth of Akhter's contention by looking at the propaganda aimed at male leaders in business and government by birth-control and population-control operatives, before showing how this alliance had disastrous consequences for women's health and dignity through the development and promotion of dangerous methods of birth control. As a result of this alliance, women, or at least poor women, have come to be looked upon simply as "at-risk reproducers" by population controllers, a thorough flattening of female identity that legitimates the insertion of pharmaceutical concerns and government technocrats into the intimacy of human parenting. It should be noted that the new men of population control simply followed Sanger in scapegoating female fertility as the main cause of the world's ills, requiring control, but they radicalized the misogyny involved.

A Few Good Men

A series of interviews with leading family-planning activists in the 1960s and 1970s reveals a constant theme: Planned Parenthood really became a mainstream force only when the issue of population control brought powerful and wealthy men into the organization. As James W. Reed has remarked, the accession of Cass Canfield to the presidency of PPFA in the 1950s indicated that the population explosion was now a recognized "problem," beginning to draw the male big business support that did not exist prior to that time.[5] Early on, Guy Irving Burch had recognized the importance of converting men into the population-control movement.

> While birth control is a medical problem and is also a maternal health problem, it is a great deal more than these. It is a national economic, social, and even political business of the utmost importance to men as well as to women, doctors, social workers, and scientists…. To date, the average man has paid little or no attention to the subject of birth control (outside of his personal sex life). But the long depression and the war have gotten men to think more about "customers" and "manpower" and to look more seriously upon the "decline" of the birth rate, which they attribute to birth control.[6]

In 1937, D. Kenneth Rose, a fund-raiser from the public-relations agency John Price Jones, argued that the birth-control movement needed male leadership, because of the importance of penetrating the higher echelons of government. The need was "clear when we face the fact that most pivotal groups upon which advancement of birth control is dependent are controlled by men, such as, Federal and State legislatures, hospital boards, public health boards, etc."[7] Rose argued that the merger between the American Birth Control League and Sanger's clinic should result in an organization headed by a full-time president, "a man," he emphasized, who would attract "the necessary support of [other] men…."[8] Eventually, when the Birth Control Federation of America was organized, Rose himself became that full-time president, dedicated to bringing more men into the fold.

In 1939, the Citizens' Committee for Planned Parenthood produced a brochure that openly solicited male involvement. Under the large heading, "Not for Women Alone," the pamphlet noted, "Men had but a small part in this crusade — but now that medically-guided birth control has been widely accepted they are beginning to see its other far-reaching possibilities." These "possibilities" included "More Business," according to the next page, which argued, "Today the businessman sees in medically-guided birth control an effective means for preventing human and economic waste, for expanding consumption, and for raising the quality of the American people."[9] In this eugenic view of humanity, people are seen merely as potential consumers, who are either of high quality (and thus able to spend more disposable income) or are waste products, with no value to a society that regards only the economic worth of the individual.

Thus the control movement began a conscious and concerted effort in the late thirties to attract men to the movement. The rationale was simple: men had the money and the influence. Besides, conservatives such as Burch wished to reorient the whole question away from any excessively woman-oriented approach to the question. One could speculate about an unstated misogyny that may have motivated Burch and his cohorts to bring more men into the control movement. Others were not so circumspect about their misogynist motives. A statement by Frances Hand Ferguson sheds light on the motivations of Hugh Moore, the man who almost single-handedly generated public anxiety about overpopulation. (Recall that Moore's World Population Emergency Campaign merged with PPFA in 1961.) Ferguson told an interviewer in 1974, "Hugh Moore thought very little of women. Talk about double-standard, to him women were really low."[10]

Planned Parenthood did not try to appeal to "humanitarian" and still less to feminist impulses when it reached out to businessmen like Moore. The most salient feature of its approach was its appeal to the pocketbook. Birth control, according to the Committee's shrewd strategy, should be understood as a means of increasing the general standard of living and, thus, an "effective means" for "expanding consumption" and keeping foreign markets open, as well as a way of reducing taxes due to lessened welfare costs at home. In 1947, Rose introduced a formal campaign targeting men, in the hopes of raising money for PPFA. In his speech, he noted first that many men had not become involved with PPFA because they mistakenly believed that the ideal of "planned parenthood" comprised only the regulation of births. "It has not been until this year that large numbers of men have begun to recognize that Planned Parenthood is a basic preventative measure which should be integrated in the health and welfare programs of every community." By "preventative" Rose intended primarily the prevention of certain types of people: he explained that "Lt. Gen [sic] Osborn," the eugenicist, had calculated that "morons in this country are doubling their number each year," while "the insane in our institutions alone cost the tax payers a billion dollars annually."[11] Birth control would also "prevent" the proliferation of other groups, including juvenile delinquents and the physically disabled. By supporting Planned Parenthood, he argued, men could ensure that their communities and their world would be safe from these problems. PPFA needed the support of men, Rose said, both in financial affairs as well as to provide the "type of leadership" that only men could give. He closed the talk by listing the distinguished industrialists, bankers, and lawyers—all male—who had already come on board.[12]

Sanger herself had made clear through her words and her actions that she had no reservations about urging men to become involved, even though she had problems with Rose's leadership of Planned Parenthood, especially his prudential refusal to explicitly fly the banner of "birth control," instead urging the rhetorical shift to "family planning." Sanger found this to be weak-minded and pusillanimous. (Her objections to Rose may also have been motivated by her sense that the movement was slipping away from her; in any case, her stated objections did not focus on his being a man.)

Sanger wanted men to be involved: in a letter to Edna Rankin McKinnon regarding birth-control work in Chicago, she states, "It is good that you are pushing BC [birth control] over your state and I agree that it is important to get men to to [sic] talk to men in order to raise funds. Osborn is a good name and perhaps you should plan now for next winters' [sic] speakers."[13] The "good name" belongs, of course, to Frederick Osborn, the long-time secretary of the American Eugenics Society. Later, in 1954, she pointed out to a supporter that, if the latter wanted men to get involved, she should consider holding a luncheon for men, so that Sanger could come and speak about overpopulation, a topic calculated to raise interest in men.[14] We have already seen that, after the merger that formed the Birth Control Federation of America, she argued that the new president should be a "*man* who knows eugenics, population, methods, research along biological lines."[15]

Commentators such as Linda Gordon and Angela Y. Davis have underestimated Sanger's early commitment to socialism *and* eugenics, but there is no doubt that Sanger shifted toward a eugenic determinism with regard to the poor, including working women (as we will see in the last chapter), perhaps coincident with her growing interest in gaining antinatalist corporate allies. The shift bespeaks how impoverished her sense of women's rights was from the start, compromised as it was by the elitist bigotry of her control ideology.

The crucial nature of the elements of economic power and male leadership that Sanger and Rose hoped to bring to the movement was reiterated in 1952 by PPFA national director William Vogt in a speech on goals for the decade ahead given at the annual meeting. He declares, "If we are to expand financially and functionally ... one of the most important steps would seem to be the formation of a National Business-Men's Committee." The reason is that "the Planned Parenthood story has not been adequately told in terms that appeal to the business-man nor, except in exceptional communities, have we had the business guidance that we need."[16] Expanding on this theme, Frances Ferguson indicated how important the techniques of consumerist capitalism are to manage desire in a way that makes birth control appear to be a personal necessity.

> The whole drop-out problem is a very serious one. Just to count the acceptors who come to the clinics isn't counting really the lowering of a birth rate. How many of those people continue using birth control? ... But to motivate people, mass education, and so forth, you need psychologists, you need people who've been in the advertising business, you need all types of businessmen, all kinds of people putting this puzzle together to make it effective.[17]

Ferguson's perspective, that of the control movement, values demographic reduction above all else and thereby puts women's health and dignity in a clearly subordinate position. The focus on "motivation," which often means pressuring women to accept contraceptives, indicates that Planned Parenthood was more interested in manufacturing "acceptors" than in providing health care tailored to a woman's true needs. This attitude persists today: some population-control fieldworkers have acknowledged that they do not give the women coming to their clinics full information, because "if they are told of the side effects the patients may not come back."[18] Indeed, if women's health were really of such concern to population-control organizations like Planned Parenthood, why do health workers in developing countries complain of having an excess of contraceptives and a shortage of everything else? One hospital director in the Dominican Republic sighed, "Here the only things not lacking are contraceptives ... I have sent many letters reporting a shortage of supplies, and the only thing they ever send are pills, condoms, and other contraceptives!"[19]

Vogt, for one, understood that population control, regardless of the way in which it was implemented, could excite businessmen far more than the issue of women's health.

> Business-men who have studied the relationship among population, resources, and money are almost automatically missionaries for Planned

Parenthood. These men are too few among us, and we want to help develop and broaden their interest. They may best be helped to show each other how Planned Parenthood can contribute to the survival and enhancement of living standards, markets, and world peace, on which our prosperity and social well-being depend.[20]

Two years later, Vogt could report that two "Men's Luncheons" had been held in New York, and there was hope that the businessman-to-business-man evangelization had begun.[21]

People and Profits

By the sixties, Planned Parenthood's much-hoped-for outreach to businessmen was firmly established, in part due to the relentless efforts of Hugh Moore. He believed overpopulation was the primary cause of war and instability, both of which were bad for business.[22] As a result, he campaigned explicitly for a population-control policy that would eliminate this perceived threat to the bottom line. He deployed his "management and merchandising skills" that he had used to peddle paper Dixie cups to sell a new product to America: population control.[23] His organization became nothing less than corporate America's voice in the population lobby.[24]

Moore "added a new kind of respectability" to population control when he organized the World Population Emergency Campaign, con-sciously drawing upon the connections and money of various financial and industrial leaders: Eugene Black, head of the World Bank (and also a trustee of the Population Council); Will Clayton, cotton magnate and former undersecretary of State; General William H. Draper, Jr., who had numer-ous industrial and military connections; Marriner S. Eccles of the Federal Reserve Board; Rockefeller Prentice, cousin of John D. Rockefeller 3rd and wealthy in his own right; Lammot duPont Copeland of the DuPont chem-ical company (also a PPFA worker); Thomas S. Lamont of Morgan Guar-anty Trust Company; Fowler McCormick, chairman of International Harvester; and others.[25] (It has been noted that African Americans and the poor, to whom Moore directed his gospel of population control, were absent from his prestigious board.)[26] Regarding all these men with their money, wealthy New York Planned Parenthood supporter Mary Lasker said, "The success of it as of this year, ... in 1963, has come about largely through men who said that they were motivated by the fact that develop-ing nations couldn't develop if their population got ahead of their ability to produce goods and food. They publicized this fact, so a lot of people talked seriously about this, who would never talk seriously about it as a personal or human or economic matter in the United States."[27]

By 1964, PPFA had instituted its Commerce and Industry Committee, designed "to bring American business to an awareness of their stake in the U.S. and world population problems...."[28] Male leaders in business, economics, and government were frequently quoted in PPFA literature, which sometimes involved the reprinting of whole speeches. For example, a pamphlet entitled "Citizen Responsibility in the Population Crisis" reprinted a speech by Marriner S. Eccles, in which he urged the business community "in its own enlightened self-interest, strongly [to] support this cause both morally and financially. The prevailing notions that surging populations guarantee increasing profits is a fallacy.... Capitalism wherever it may be cannot expect to survive as an island of abundance in a sea of poverty."[29] The phrase "enlightened self-interest" was aptly chosen, for Planned Parenthood appealed to this motivation constantly. A fund-raising letter for PPFA-World Population Emergency Campaign from Cass Canfield opined, "Unless this problem of human births is dealt with, much of the world will be so crowded and so inadequate in resources, that free societies will be unable to endure."[30]

A prime example of the self-interest lobbying approach by PPFA is a curious packet of index cards, printed probably in 1966 or 1967, bearing the title, in bright red, "People and Profits: The American Businessman's Stake in Family Planning." The cards were evidently used as part of a visual presentation to be made by Planned Parenthood workers to businessmen in order to solicit donations more successfully. The cards, with their slogans and graphs, provide a glimpse of the inside workings of Planned Parenthood's strategy.

The first card features the heading, "Planned Parenthood — A Boon to Business" and goes on to give a summary of the whole presentation.

* More babies no longer mean more profits.
* The population explosion is a major roadblock to economic progress.
* Family planning holds the key.
* To meet the problem, Planned Parenthood needs an additional $20 million by 1970.[31]

The message in a nutshell: population growth is bad for business, but donating to Planned Parenthood is good for the bottom line.

PPFA claimed over and over again that investing in birth control and population control was cost-effective. After quoting Joseph Kershaw, from the Office of Economic Opportunity, to the effect that birth control "is probably the single most cost-effective anti-poverty measure," it goes on to claim that "$10 million invested in Planned Parenthood will save $10 Billion." In other words, an ounce of birth-control prevention is worth a pound of welfare cure. PPFA insisted, with a straight face but without evidence to back up its assertion, that "the cost-benefits ratio of family planning in America is about 100-to-1."[32]

The introduction of cost-benefits language into the family-planning discussion is jarring but, unfortunately, all too common, both then and now. The argument turned on the reproduction of the poor, presumably welfare-dependent, mother. Conjuring the old eugenics bugaboo of "pauperism," PPFA paints a picture of inevitable poverty, whether due to genetics or to the environment of the mother or to both. When poor mothers have children, "welfare costs skyrocket as poverty conditions are perpetuated."[33] The key factor behind the increasing costs is a dearth of birth control, which then perpetuates poverty.[34] In light of the danger that the poor posed to the American way of life, they needed to be more effectively contracepted within America, "to relieve poverty, reduce welfare dependency, diminish infant mortality and bring millions more into the mainstream of the 'affluent society.'" The obvious conclusion? "Planned Parenthood is the only organization through which American businessmen can help to meet today's population crisis at home and abroad."[35]

Business's international concerns were protected by Planned Parenthood as well, in that population control would prevent the unrest supposedly generated by population pressures. The cards noted that the "prosperity and stability" of Latin America was "A Vital Stake for U.S. Business."[36] Planned Parenthood hoped to solicit $10 million to be disbursed internationally by 1970. A list of the "enormous cost benefits" of the international population-control work comprised the following: "*Individual incomes raised *Military budgets reduced *Tax rates lowered *More capital investment in industry and agriculture."[37] After all, as one heading stressed, "$20 Million Invested in Planned Parenthood Can Turn the Tide."[38] Presumably a tide of people is meant. Against the uncertainty posed by human reproduction not controlled by an elite, PPFA offered the security of global consumerism and happy natives.

> *Planned Parenthood represents the most effective form of safeguard for U.S. investments abroad.* By averting unrest and social upheaval stemming from overpopulation, poverty and famine, family planning can provide a foundation for peaceful progress. *The developing nations will become more affluent, their people will become better customers for American products,* when competent family planning services are made available for all.[39]

Birth control was to become the new opiate for the masses.

"Something Like a War"

By the early 1970s, the profile of the average population-control supporter could be described by population-control advocate Phyllis Piotrow as "male, active in the business world, and more concerned with economics than biology...."[40] Zero Population Growth's membership was always predominantly "highly educated white males with a median age under thirty."[41] From the early years wealth was not alien to Margaret Sanger's movement: her Committee of One Hundred wealthy women in 1916 testifies to that. Yet the wealth was usually connected to society ladies. The new face of population control represented the peaking interest of men in the effect of population on *their* interests, namely, on economics and politics, arenas from which women were still by and large shut out.

With the big-business support came a distinct change in emphasis, from a perspective that indeed stressed both birth control and population control (and both for explicitly eugenic purposes) yet did so according to a vision of women's "liberation" (false though it was)— Sanger's bid to revolutionize intimate life — to a perspective that goes straight to numbers and profits. As Frances Hand Ferguson said,

> But then, we always said, "Children by choice and not by chance," that was the great slogan in the old days. Now I think it's much more, "Stop at two, don't be selfish, think what you're doing to the world at large." I think what brought that whole overpopulation, that sort of push, that emphasis, has been the men. Since the men got in, the emphasis has changed.[42]

The move from "maternal health into big business" was completed by the takeover of Planned Parenthood by the men.[43] Of course, it was never simply a matter of "maternal health," except as defined and measured by the sexual-lifestyle predilections of "fit" women. But even this eugenically vitiated view of female autonomy — autonomy for "fit" women only — had to give way before a literally androcentric misogyny: from one control ideology to an even more total one.

A by-product of the shift to male domination was a change in rhetoric: the male activists brought a much more explicitly militant perspective to population control than was evident before. The Clarence Gambles of the control movement always used this sort of language, saying, for example, that the various contraceptive methods formed an "armamentarium needed by the physician seeking to protect underprivileged patients against the chance of conception."[44] By the 1960s, however, warlike rhetoric moved center stage. For example, in 1963, Dr. John Rock, a researcher who was important in the development of the birth-control pill, without a trace of irony called for a new "Manhattan Project" to research contraceptive development, as did Hugh Moore.[45] Echoing this language, a USAID/India staff memorandum in 1968 called for a research effort similar to "the intensive and coordinated research and development effort which solved the critical problem of controlled nuclear explosion," but this time devoted to the supposedly explosive problem of Indian fertility. Likewise, Lenni Kangas, a USAID population manager in the Philippines, said in one interview that "ordering contraceptives is like ordering bullets for war. You don't want to run out." Indeed, Kangas was photographed tossing pills and condoms out of a helicopter into the jungle below as if they were bombs.[46] Reimert T. Ravenholt, Kangas's boss in the population department of USAID, referred to the newly developed prostaglandin abortifacient as "heavy artillery," while spending about $5 million on testing that abortifacient in Africa and Asia, because, as he admitted, such tests "couldn't be legally conducted in the U.S."[47] As Andrea Tone has observed, "Presidents John F. Kennedy, Lyndon Johnson, and Richard Nixon — who in 1969 unveiled his five-year plan to make contraceptives available to all low-income families — were less sexual revolutionaries than cold warriors who endorsed family planning for political reasons that played well economically at home."[48] (Though Tone here seems to betray some naivete about how the sexual revolution in fact relates to social control.)

Such a violent attitude toward the fertility of the poor could not help but infiltrate the developing world, especially given that the Population Council and USAID actively recruited Third World elites to come to America for demographic fellowships in the hopes that they might then return to their countries, take high positions in government, and ideologically infiltrate the native culture.[49] An example of a thoroughly indoctrinated native elite is Harvard-educated Dr. D. N. Pai, the director of family planning in Bombay in the 1970s, who advocated a compulsory sterilization program. He told the *New York Times* in 1976:

> If some excesses appear, don't blame me.... You must consider it something like a war. There could be a certain amount of misfiring out of enthusiasm. There has been pressure to show results. Whether you like it or not, there will be a few dead people.[50]

Of course, many feminists have refused to accept that a "few" dead women and girls is a necessary fact of demographic life. A critical examination of the situation reveals that it is the predisposition to view female fertility as the enemy in a war, and not that fertility itself, that necessitates the sacrifice of a few peasants on the altar of demographic reduction.

The language of the battlefield persists, although it has been used more circumspectly. A more recent example is the word choice of a researcher in 1982, who was writing about the potential role of an anti-pregnancy "vaccine"; he said that it would be an "antigenic weapon" against "the reproductive process, a process which left unchecked threatens to swamp the world."[51] Not surprisingly, the vaccine was tested by the Population Council in India, a paradigm case, as the population controllers see it, of "the reproductive process … left unchecked."[52]

Despite the brutal misogyny inherent in the warlike rhetoric of men like Moore, PPFA was willing to let him and others mold the agenda of the organization, casting doubt on the sincerity of its commitment to women. Mary Steichen Calderone, the medical director of PPFA from 1953 to 1964, claimed that "the only time I've ever really met sexist attitudes in all of my not-so-long career" was when she was refused a pay raise which would have put her salary on a par with the male employees at PPFA.[53] Such sexism has thoroughly infected the attitudes of PPFA, IPPF, and other population-control organizations. For example, the attitude toward women of the bureaucrats committed to population control at USAID is that they are primarily to be regarded as "at-risk reproducers," as uteri which may inconveniently fill with children too often for the comfort of what many State Department types insist to be America's interests.[54] Petchesky notes that birth control is an industry managed by the medical profession, pharmaceutical concerns, insurance companies, and population-control groups—all male-dominated sectors, which view population control as the solution to poverty and "social instability."[55] So hypothetical concerns regarding national security and economics systematically trump any solicitude for the individual woman's health needs.[56]

A grotesque example of such misogynistic disregard is the behavior of Reimert Ravenholt, director of USAID's Population Services from 1966 to 1979. As the fifth chapter detailed, Ravenholt's zeal to promote birth-control pills in developing countries was such that he supported their distribution by paramedical personnel and hoped that they might even be sold over the counter.[57] He was constantly offending people with his sexism and combativeness.[58] He flooded less-developed countries with substandard contraceptives, including high-estrogen birth-control pills, unsafe Dalkon Shield IUDs, and Depo-Provera (over a decade before it was approved for use in America).

For example, when high-estrogen birth-control pills were determined by the FDA to be unsafe in 1970, one pharmaceutical company, Syntex, decided to dump its supply with the one buyer likely to purchase unsafe contraceptives with few questions asked: the United States government.

Syntex offered USAID a discount, and the agency began to distribute the dangerous pills instead of safer ones. The decision was rationalized by Dr. Malcolm Potts, a prominent contraceptive researcher who was IPPF's medical director from 1969 to 1978 and subsequently director of the International Fertility Research Program, an organization that has been aptly described as arising from "the union between U.S. foreign policy objectives and the corporate drive to expand contraceptive markets overseas."[59] Potts offered the following sound bite to help sell the pills, which could cause painfully swollen breasts: "It makes your breasts more beautiful and that is good for everyone — including the tailors who have to make bigger brassieres."[60] Potts claimed that the pill had minimal health risks and decried the regulation of oral contraception in the U.S. and United Kingdom as "a lot of pompous nonsense."[61] He also touted the benefits of the injectable contraceptive Depo-Provera for some American "subgroups," suggesting that targeting certain groups in America for Depo use, along with the developing world, would help to answer any accusations of a double standard.

> I'd like to suggest that, even among the vast population of the United States, you can find subgroups of people who have the same problems as people in the Third World. They may not be so large, but you know you have several million immigrants from Mexico, who bring with them the same health problems, the same cultural assumptions, the same need for fertility regulation as they had in Mexico. I think that if the FDA were to turn its attention to the needs of some of the subgroups within the United States, we would not be faced with the situation in which we can be accused of having a dual standard of medical practice and drug regulation around the world. If you look hard enough in the States, I think you can find the same type of population — as I say, it may not be very large — as one finds in the north of Thailand.[62]

Such a statement is not so surprising when one learns that Potts, as late as 1988, was editing the annual proceedings of the Eugenics Society in England. (It should also not be surprising to learn that both IPPF and UNFPA were among the earliest distributors of Depo.)

Another contraceptive, the Dalkon Shield IUD, was reported to be unsafe as early as 1971, only a few months after its commercial release. By the time its manufacturer, A. H. Robins, stopped marketing it in 1974, the device had caused at least 18 deaths and over 200,000 cases of severe uterine infection in the United States; the problem eventually led to a lawsuit filed by over 300,000 women, ending in a $2.5 billion settlement that forced the sale of the company in 1988.[63] Realizing early on that their product had a problem, in 1972 Robins' executives turned to Ravenholt, not one to let a few dead and damaged women get in the way of population control. The Shield was offered to USAID at a 48% discount, but with a catch: the devices were provided in an unsterilized condition. No IUD manufacturer would dream of marketing unsterilized IUDs in wealthy countries, because one of the greatest risks of IUD use is the possibility of uterine infection, yet the wombs (and the lives) of women and girls in developing countries were apparently more disposable than those of richer women.

In defense of such racist misogyny, officials of control organizations have tended to beg the question by insisting that pregnancy is more dangerous in Third World countries than in the United States, so that the use of any contraceptive, no matter how dangerous, provides health benefits.[64] In defending the distribution of contraceptives without the safeguards of adequate medical supervision, Frances Ferguson explained how, for Planned Parenthood, the pill and the IUD

> have changed the whole concept of birth control. And where now of course, internationally — although you can't do it in this country — we have started distribution of [oral] contraceptives outside the clinic, it is called community-based distribution.... [O]ur philosophy there is that even though the pill may have some bad effects on some people and the doctors can't always find it when they prescribe the pill — the people who are given the pill are told to report back if they have troubles — that anyway, the dangers of the pill aren't as great as the danger of having an unwanted child.[65]

At least two fallacies are operative in such reasoning. First, it embraces a consequentialist or cost-benefits analysis that assumes that the effect of an additional child in the "over-populated" world outweighs the possible ill effects of a contraceptive to an individual woman. (Population control is an absolute value, trumping any other concern, even that of women's health.) Beyond the falsity of this underlying assumption, there is a second fallacy in the comparison itself: instead of comparing the health effects of, in this case, the pill to the effects of another, perhaps less dangerous, contraceptive, which would be logically coherent, Ferguson assumes it is either a simple method (the pill or the IUD) or no contraceptive at all.

Two more fallacies seem to be operative to the extent that Ferguson is depending on standard birth-control rhetoric about the dangers of childbirth. It is fallacious to assume that childbirth is always more dangerous than any contraception — especially given the toxic nature of the contraceptives under consideration. Such an assumption betrays an attitude that views the female reproductive system as haphazard, chaotic, alien, as if it does not quite work the way it ought, or as if it is not quite natural for the female body to bear children: some control, any control, is better than nothing. The final fallacy has to do with another false comparison in Ferguson's last sentence: it is assumed that the alternative to dangerous childbirthing conditions is not the logical opposite — namely, *safer* childbirthing conditions — but rather no childbirth at all, as guaranteed by a potentially unsafe contraceptive. Surely, if population-control advocates were really concerned about women's health in childbirth, they would concentrate their efforts on increasing prenatal care and equipping health-care centers, midwives, and obstetric personnel in developing countries with the resources necessary to improve overall childbirthing safety. Instead, population-control agencies such as IPPF offer contraceptives — a "solution" that not only might be dangerous to women's health but also happens to conform to Planned Parenthood's demographic goals.[66] After all, improved maternal health care runs exactly counter to those goals, being what Sanger would call a matter of dysgenic altruism.

In addition to this sort of specious reasoning, Ravenholt, in responding to critics of his dumping of the unsterilized Dalkon Shield, outrageously argued that the infections killing off women in poor countries were due to the women's own promiscuity. He also noted that the Lippes Loop, another IUD that Alan Guttmacher in particular pushed, was also initially provided in an unsterile form — an admission not likely to reassure the women concerned.[67] After the Shield's recall in America, USAID was also forced to recall its own unused stocks, which groups like IPPF had warehoused, but the damage had already been done: some 440,000 women throughout the world were using the device, and even five years after the recall, population-control advocates admitted that the Shield was still being inserted in places like India and Pakistan.[68]

Ravenholt managed to commit these kinds of atrocities with a remarkable degree of freedom. When really pushed, Ravenholt justified his obsession with population control at the expense of women's health by invoking the classic male rationale for hindering other people's reproduction: it is good for business. He told one newspaper that population control enabled "the normal operation of U.S. commercial interests around the world.... The self-interest thing is the compelling element."[69]

Female Experimentation and Puerto Rico

The concrete effects of the misogynist population-control mindset are unfortunately numerous. In its desire to promote demographic reduction, Planned Parenthood has countenanced both the subtle imperialism of breaking down cultural mores as well as the more obvious injustice of testing dangerous contraceptives on Third World women without informed consent. The driving motive for the development of the birth-control pill, for example, was demographic reduction, not the liberation of women, as John Rock and Gregory Pincus, two of the main devisers of the pill, have admitted; the latter was also directly interested in eugenics, as his letter to Pearl quoted in chapter three shows.[70]

Sanger herself, with her wealthy friend Katharine Dexter McCormick, provided the impetus for the development of oral contraceptives, and both were driven by the supposed world-population crisis, by their own admission: Sanger told McCormick that "the world and almost our civilization for the next twenty-five years is going to depend upon a simple, cheap, safe contraceptive to be used in poverty stricken slums, jungles and among the most ignorant people."[71] Indeed, the development of the pill was a dream come true for Sanger, who back in 1928 had urged the development of methods "that will be so simple, so safe, so convenient and so cheap that the popularization of their use among poor and ignorant people will be a comparatively easy matter."[72] Sanger adds at the end a more complete rationale for her program:

> Believing as I do that hap-hazard, uncontrolled parentage leads directly and inevitably to poverty, over-crowding, delinquency, defectiveness, child labor, infant mortality, international friction and war, and believing further that the development of more perfect contraceptive methods and the better understanding of the various problems of Birth Control are necessary if these evils are to be stamped out, I hope that the program I have outlined in the foregoing pages may be carried out....[73]

Sanger here lays out the demographic rationale for a "simple method," that is, one that even the "unfit" could not foul up. Originally, the diaphragm was the contraceptive of choice for Sanger (as it still is for educated women who want a barrier method that can be controlled by them with no change in body chemistry). She was roundly criticized by other birth controllers and professional eugenicists for advocating a relatively complex method of birth control that could not easily be used by the "unfit," but she held her ground, insisting that (especially at the time) the diaphragm was the most reliable method. An additional advantage in Sanger's eyes was that the dissemination of the diaphragm required a clinic system, medical involvement to provide instruction in its use and controller supervision. But by the late 1920s, realizing the limits of the clinic system in reaching her target population, she began (as the statements quoted above show) to seriously consider other methods, the demographic exigencies becoming especially clear as she became more focused on international work.[74] The diaphragm was simply too awkward for use by women in, say, India, who might not be willing to put up with its cumbersome mechanism and who perhaps would not have the privacy to insert it surreptitiously. A birth-control pill, however, could be taken easily by anyone at any time, and no husbands would need be the wiser. Unfortunately for the women on whom the pill has been pushed, the radical alteration of body chemistry that the pill produces is not without its dangers, and the early experimental versions of the pill were even more toxic for the women who were targeted to be test subjects.

Given the basic eugenic attitude underlying the drive for population control, it is hardly surprising that the poor have been the population on whom most contraceptive experimenting has been done. They are often not told that the "contraceptive" pill they have been given is a placebo (this has happened at Planned Parenthood clinics).[75] In one test, the investigator defended his methodology by saying, "If you think you can explain a placebo test to women like these, you have never met Mrs. Gomez from the West Side."[76] The rationale for the testing being done primarily on Third World women, according to a government-funded professional, is that "dealing with the domestic problem would create controversy ... therefore programs using overseas countries as laboratories" are preferred.[77] The difficulty in finding female subjects on which to test the early birth-control pills frustrated McCormick immensely; she complained to Sanger that what Pincus really needed was "a 'cage' of ovulating females to experiment with," leading Pincus to suggest that they use mental patients at the Massachusetts State Hospital — a plan that was indeed carried out.[78]

Clarence Gamble had already dealt with this difficulty in finding a large pool of fertile women on which to test his various contraceptive ideas. Gamble recognized that the dispossessed were the ideal experimental population. Accordingly, Gamble initiated tests of the oral contraceptive in Puerto Rico precisely because the Puerto Ricans were unlikely to be able to protest any abuses. Gamble was involved in the territory long before Pincus and Rock were looking for subjects in the fifties: he went there both to promote contraception and sterilization as well as to test various contraceptives on the local populace, including one attempt to test methods of sterilization involving x-rays and intrauterine cautery, that is, the burning of the Fallopian tubes (accessed through the uterus) in order to build up enough scar tissue to prevent the passage of the egg.[79] One Puerto Rican elite, Mrs. Carmen Rivera de Alvardo, a social worker in Puerto Rico paid by Gamble until 1939, recalled his contribution by saying, "I think that your participation has been wonderful to the development of the work.

Sorry to say I doubt very much that any Puerto Rican would have done the same."[80] In this judgment she was undoubtedly correct.

The island was targeted by more mainstream groups, namely, Dickinson's Committee on Maternal Health and the Rockefeller Foundation, as early as the 1930s, to serve as a living laboratory. One Rockefeller official wrote in an internal memo, "Puerto Ricans are coming into New York City at the rate of 15,000 a week.... This is simply one aspect of the problems which exist in Puerto Rico of overpopulation."[81] Yet at this time, fertility was at a relatively low 1.5 percent on the island, while it was around 2.7% in the Caribbean in general.[82] The research process was sped up when IPPF held its Western Hemisphere meeting in San Juan in 1955. At the meeting (dominated, not surprisingly, by discussions of population control), Dr. Adaline Pendelton Satterthwaite, who worked at Ryder Memorial Hospital, met Clarence Gamble and others. In an interview with Satterthwaite, James Reed observed, "They must have been delighted to have gotten ahold of you ... have all those patients, have a real, live working physician ... after all, Dr. Gamble never had a patient, and here he had somebody with 800, 900 possible subjects a year."[83] Satterthwaite's situation was indeed ideal for Gamble and the others: she was a white, American, Protestant doctor who worked in a large hospital that served the native population, and she subscribed fully to the population-control ideology, so much so that after she left Puerto Rico she abandoned full-time medical practice to work with the Population Council.

The first field tests of oral hormonal contraceptives in Puerto Rico began in 1956 under the supervision of Dr. Edris Rice-Wray, utilizing as subjects some women living in a housing development in a slum clearance area called Rio Piedras.[84] Soon a second trial began in Umacao in 1957 under Satterthwaite's supervision. Not long thereafter, Pincus and the birth-control organizations, pharmaceutical companies, and the Population Council were all knocking at her door, enlisting her to test the birth-control pill and the IUD on Puerto Ricans.[85] In the end, the tests of the pill and the IUD at Ryder would involve 1,700 women.[86]

So far from being driven by concern for women's health, these experiments warranted the methodological assessment made by Dr. Herbert Ratner, editor of the peer-reviewed journal *Child and Family*. As he put it, the 1957 testing of Enovid, the first birth-control pill, by Searle, was quite flawed from the test subject's perspective: "When they did the basic studies in Puerto Rico their real interest was in effectiveness and they took safety for granted. As a result, the studies were extremely poor from the point of view of safety."[87] Unfortunately, safety was not the guiding "point of view" under which the scientists labored.[88] Rice-Wray complained to

Gregory Pincus that the high-estrogen pills were causing side effects, such as nausea and headaches, but Pincus dismissed her concerns as inventions: "Most of them happen because women expect them to happen."[89] Even Satterthwaite has admitted, "[Y]ou can't get around the fact that in those days, indeed, there was not the type of careful control on human experimentation that there is today."[90]

By the late 1960s, studies were beginning to suggest that the pill could increase a woman's risk of fatal blood clots four- to ninefold.[91] Other problems found to result from the hormones include bloating, headaches (sometimes migraines), depression, weight gain, ovarian cysts, and loss of libido. In 1970, Senate hearings on the safety of the pill chaired by Democrat Gaylord Nelson were held, leading to an FDA-written package insert detailing potential side effects, problems that Searle had attempted to hide even from doctors. The insert was opposed by both drug makers and the American Medical Association. As one doctor put it during the Nelson hearings, "If you tell [women] they might get headaches, they will."[92]

Pill-pushing abuses in impoverished countries can still be found today. In the early 1980s, the packet insert for the Mala birth-control pill, produced in India, told its users that "there is no harm by this pill," a statement even the most rabid population controller would be hesitant to make. In fact, in 1993 the U.S. Office of Technology found that product labeling on most drugs manufactured in America and sold in other countries "diverged significantly and seriously from the standard" information given out in America, especially when it came to oral contraceptives.[93] But the U.S. government has agencies that are not so interested in telling the truth: a confidential letter from USAID to IPPF urged the latter to stop using the word "contraindications" in its manuals because "it may have very negative connotations and a major inhibitory effect." USAID insisted instead that birth-control workers talk up supposed benefits of using the pill, including the familiar refrain that the risks of pregnancy are greater than the risks of the pill.[94]

The "Perfect Contraceptive": The Development of the IUD

We have already seen how dangerous the population-control establishment's disregard of women's health could be in the case of the Dalkon Shield IUD disaster. Unfortunately, as with the pill, so too was the development of the IUD guided from the beginning by demographic, not feminist, concerns, leading the developers to publicly insist on the device's safety despite the evidence they had already gathered of its potential health dangers. As Brown and Moskowitz have put it, a "demographic imperative made it especially important for national leaders and international donors that high levels of continuous contraceptive practice be achieved."[95] That is, the pill did not represent the attainment of the population-control holy grail of a "simple method" (despite Sanger's hopes), because the user has to be sufficiently motivated to take the medication every day. This means that the pill is a woman-controlled, not a doctor-controlled, method (recall the reasons quoted in chapter one for supporting the IUD according to PPFA's president Alan F. Guttmacher). Another mechanism was needed, one that would render a woman infertile day in and day out, regardless of the woman's motivation. The quest for this method led to the IUD.

The Population Council can claim credit for the development of the IUD (though its wide dissemination came about through Planned Parenthood's vast delivery and propaganda system). In the late 1920s, the German obstetrician Grafenberg revealed that rings made of silkworm gut and wire inserted in the uterus prevented conception.[96] Papers published in 1959 by Israeli and Japanese researchers revived interest in the subject, so the Population Council began in 1961 to give grants in support of IUD research, first to Lazar C. Margulies and Jack Lippes (the latter connected with a Planned Parenthood clinic in New York). In 1962, a conference on the IUD, convened partly at Guttmacher's urging, instigated more interest in the topic. By 1964, the Council had already dispersed some $2 million toward IUD research, and its testing in 1968, directed by Christopher Tietze, included over 30,000 women.

A memo from Sheldon Segal to various people involved in the IUD program at the Population Council reveals, already in 1963, some evidence that IUD wearers in Puerto Rico suffered from endometriosis and had abnormal Pap smear results at a higher rate than did the control group. One doctor described the test group's tissue as "horrendous."[97] In an internal memo written probably in 1964, Christopher Tietze said that the IUD investigators had been unable to gather sufficient statistics on the incidence of cervical cancer to follow up on the abnormal Pap smears.[98] Despite these problems, the PPFA Medical Committee (which included Tietze) confidently stated that there was "no scientific evidence" of cancer.[99]

Even more, the PPFA Committee felt justified in saying as early as July 1964 that IUDs "are both safe and effective."[100] The incidence of pelvic infection was held to be "low," and doctors were told that they need not wear sterile gloves during insertion. The Committee estimated that fewer than 2% of the "candidates for intrauterine contraception" needed to be turned down on account of contraindications.[101] Yet Tietze admitted privately that, due to the fact that the freestanding clinics participating in his studies might not test for pelvic inflammatory disease, there was perhaps a "serious underreporting of PID."[102] The purpose of the Committee's sanitized review was to encourage PPFA affiliates to promote this device among their patients. After all, the IUD was, in the opinion of the Medical Committee, close to being the "ideal contraceptive," since it was "safe, effective, inexpensive, acceptable to the patient and easy to use."[103] A year later, despite evidence of pregnancies occurring with the device in utero (a condition that happened as frequently as 7.5 percent of the time with the stainless-steel ring) leading to a miscarriage rate "significantly higher than normal," the Medical Committee continued to recommend the use of IUDs by PPFA affiliates.[104] The IPPF Medical Committee advised its affiliates to tell their patients that pregnancy might occur with the IUD in place, but that the "baby is *never* affected, nor is the delivery."[105] At the same time, Alan F. Guttmacher, by then president of PPFA, claimed that "infrequent" pregnancies occurred with an IUD in place and that the result was a normal pregnancy, in which "the child is unaffected."[106] Yet, in 1966, Christopher Tietze blithely acknowledged in a letter that even dangerous "ectopic pregnancies are by no means rare," occurring, in fact, about once every 23 pregnancies with the IUD in situ.[107] Later cases of uterine infection causing birth defects in Dalkon Shield users tragically showed just how unfounded Guttmacher's assertions were.

Other common and observable problems include perforations of the uterus. In one clinic alone, as many as 30 perforations occurred by 1966, about 1 in 170 IUD insertions,[108] while many more undiagnosed cases were acknowledged. One doctor said that "fortunately, or perhaps unfortunately, perforations with Lippes loop are generally silent."[109]

The promoters of the IUD found various ways to explain away indications of the device's danger. One doctor theorized that a "significant percentage" of the women coming to IUD clinics were already pregnant. The downside of this hypothetical situation, the physician claimed, would not be the IUD's causing a spontaneous abortion (with all the dangers that entails for the woman), but merely that "the IUD would get an undeserved reputation for causing bleeding."[110] For evidence of this claim, he enclosed a case study of a Pakistani woman from his clinic in Lahore who, at 4 feet 8 inches and 80 pounds, was considered in "good health" when she came into the clinic in late 1962. By the time she was finished with her IUD experience, almost two years later, she had lost ten more pounds and quite a bit of blood, had spontaneously aborted, had had her womb curetted, and had undergone minor surgery to have her Lippes Loop taken from her womb, after it had come loose from its embedded position in her uterine wall.[111]

Similar rationalizing came from Tietze, the man in charge of gathering statistics concerning IUD safety at the National Committee on Maternal Health (which was by the 1960s a fully funded subsidiary of the Population Council). He argued that pelvic inflammatory disease (PID) occurred more commonly among women "of low socioeconomic status," and therefore was not due to IUD use, even though he acknowledged that there were no available statistics to support this claim.[112] (This approach would be echoed a decade later by spokesmen for A. H. Robins, who claimed that women using the Dalkon Shield developed PID because of sexually transmitted diseases contracted due to promiscuity.)[113] He supported the inclusion of women with a history of PID in the initial IUD trials, building PID into the sample and therefore immunizing the study's results from criticism on that score. He did this even though the device might seriously aggravate the disease, because he argued PID "has a strong tendency to recur, with or without" the IUD.[114] This seriously jeopardized these women's health, but it was important for Tietze to defuse the PID question because, as the Population Council's committee on IUDs recognized, it was "a question ... on which the method will stand or fall in the eyes of the profession."[115]

Of course, one need not concoct such absurd hypotheses to explain the elevated rates of PID accompanying IUD use. Surprisingly for a device that has been used for decades, no one is entirely sure what the IUD does to the uterus, but the available evidence seems to show that the IUD works precisely by irritating the uterine lining, perhaps causing a low-level and chronic uterine infection. Women are certainly not adequately informed about how this device works, nor are they informed that the IUD frequently if not always functions not as a contraceptive but as an abortifacient. (Some argue that it secretes agents that work as spermicides, but this seems unlikely to be its main mechanism, given the effect that it has on the uterine wall.) The constant irritation of the uterine lining is likely to be how the device achieves its "contraceptive" effect, rendering the uterine lining inhospitable for a newly conceived embryo. For this reason, the device is promoted by some family-planning groups for use as "emergency contraception" *up to seven days after intercourse.* This makes sense only if its insertion can prevent implantation or dislodge an already implanted embryo.[116]

Beyond the (deliberate?) unclarity that surrounds the mechanics of IUD functioning, an additional problem with the device that birth controllers gloss over is the pain caused in insertion and removal. One physician, Major Russel J. Thomsen, testified to a House committee in 1973 that he regularly saw women faint during IUD insertion and removal. One doctor said that inserting the Dalkon Shield had to be "the most traumatic manipulation ever perpetrated upon womanhood." (It should be noted that Dalkon Shield insertion and removal was exceptionally painful compared to other IUDs, in part because of the former's unusual design, which is said to imitate a bug: five legs on either side, around a central "eye." The ten legs bite into the uterine wall.) In response to such complaints, Shield inventor Hugh Davis retorted that a woman feeling pain just needed a "stiff drink."[117]

Others in the control movement, though, did acknowledge some of the IUD's negatives. Nevertheless, utilitarian disregard for personal dignity, disdain for female fertility, and demographic zealotry demand that these negatives be put in the proper perspective, as Dr. J. Robert Willson made clear at the Population Council's First International Conference on Intra-Uterine Contraception held in New York City in 1962:

> They [IUDs] are horrible things, they produce infection, they are outmoded and not worth using ... [but] suppose one does develop an intrauterine infection and suppose she does end up with a hysterectomy and bilateral salpingoophorectomy [the removal of the ovaries and Fallopian tubes]? How serious is that for the particular patient and for the population of the world in general? Not very.... Perhaps the individual patient is expendable in the general scheme of things, particularly if the infection she acquires is sterilizing but not lethal.[118]

It is clear that the promotion of the IUD had everything to do with its demographic potential, not its benefit to the women subjected to it. When what is at stake is the control of female fertility for demographic reasons, any inconvenient facts such as potential health risks to women have to be glossed over in public, and IUD promoters did not flinch from out-and-out deception; for example, a lawyer representing an IUD manufacturer revealed that he was told in 1975 to destroy documentation that might give evidence of the Dalkon Shield's danger, testimony that indicates how potentially flawed contraceptive research can be, given the ideological fervor involved.[119] Alan Guttmacher noted that "we in America are primarily interested in IUDs as a means of population control in huge population groups. Any technique that would slow down or complicate insertion, when you are trying for mass population control, would be an important deterrent," even if such a technique were safer than the IUDs, which can be inserted speedily.[120] Note that no pretense of empowering women or safeguarding their health is put forward: PPFA's Guttmacher honestly acknowledges that efficiency in enacting massive population control programs is the prime motive factor. In a letter to PPFA activists and donors, Guttmacher also listed the following *advantages*, which most feminists view as precisely the reasons why the IUD is *not* good for women.

> 1) A woman simply has to be motivated sufficiently to have the device inserted. Nothing else has to be done to prevent pregnancy. To conceive, she must return to the physician to have the IUD removed. A patient may actually forget its presence since it works without her cooperation. 2) Like the pill, the IUD possesses the great psycho-sexual advantage of being "coitus independent." It is inserted at a time remote from the act of sexual intercourse. 3) The IUD is cheap. One of the best is manufactured for 5½¢; it markets for more. 4) It may remain in the uterus indefinitely.[121]

The fact that the woman is dependent on doctors to remove the device, doctors who may prefer her to keep the device in place, indicates a serious problem with the IUD and, indeed, with any device that is heavily physician-dependent for its discontinuation. Cases have been reported in places such as India and China where the health-care professionals, under pressure to meet quotas, have refused to remove long-term contraceptive devices. As I will show, long-term devices that "work without" the woman's "cooperation" are still heavily promoted for lower-income women whose fertility is considered a problem by the men who set demographic targets.

The Population Council has continued to maintain its interest in discovering contraceptives to be used, as the organization's internal budget report noted in 1979, "particularly in developing countries."[122] The Council was continuing to sponsor research in IUDs at that time, as well as a new method, referred to as a "subdermal implant," noting that all these methods "will provide contraception with much less attention on the part of the user than is the case with oral contraceptives."[123] The subdermal implant would be marketed later as Norplant.

Norplant and Other Methods to Colonize the Female Body

Norplant was developed by the Population Council, beginning in 1967, for purely demographic reasons. As was stated in chapter five, it entails the implanting of six rods, each containing 36 mg of progestin, under a woman's skin (usually in the upper arm). The rods are effective for five years. They cannot be left in the body indefinitely and must be removed by a doctor. According to the early internal documents of the Population

Council, Norplant had the "attractiveness of providing long-term contraceptive action without requiring attention except for the initial placement and eventual removal."[124] Like the IUD, Norplant was intended for use in the developing world. By 1977, the Population Council could tell its major donors that Norplant was in its final stages of development, and the Council showed its hand in this communiqué when it stressed that the device was being tested only in "poor urban and rural settings," in order to determine "the importance of this method for these societies."[125] Not surprisingly, Norplant was tested by Satterthwaite on her Puerto Rican patients.[126]

Unconscionable lapses attended Norplant testing on Third World women; for example, researchers from the Population Council wrapped up one study and left, neglecting to remove the Norplant rods from some 300 Brazilian women who had been test subjects.[127] Similarly, in Indonesia, 238 women, out of 813 participants, were "lost to follow-up," meaning that the women had perhaps moved or otherwise were unable to be found, with the Norplant capsules still in their arms.[128] Given the poor state of health care in many Third World countries and the unlikelihood of other medical personnel being trained or adequately equipped to remove the capsules, the cruelty of such insouciance must be acknowledged.

The health risks of the drug are also not completely known. For example, many women experience an increase in cholesterol levels, which may lead to stroke or heart attacks. The progestin released can enter into a mother's breastmilk, potentially posing great danger to her baby (and many of the Third World women who were conscripted into testing the drug were breastfeeding). Of course, Norplant has the same side effects as do other forms of hormonal contraception, such as the pill: headaches, weight gain, moodiness, and so forth. And then there is the question of removal: if one can get a doctor to take it out, he or she might not be able to extract it with skill. Sometimes scar tissue forms around the capsules, making removal quite difficult; sometimes the capsules migrate, forcing doctors to perform increasingly invasive surgery to remove them. Some women have suffered nerve damage; others have scars on their upper arms from the procedure.[129] As a result of all these problems, Norplant manufacturer Wyeth-Ayerst had to settle a $54 million class-action suit involving over 36,000 women.[130]

One woman gave the following statement in 2002:

> In April, 1993, I received a Norplant implant. The doctor warned me only of mild headaches and possibly a little weight gain. Immediately after the implant, I stopped having periods. I went from 89 lbs. to 170 lbs. in 2 months. In 1994, I began having extremely bad headaches and my vision rapidly deteriorated. Because of my deteriorating health, I had the Nor-

plant removed. I had to be cut 4 times to find all the tubes. I have never recovered.[131]

This woman also had problems with excessive hair growth, debilitating weakness, and daily seizures. She gave birth to a daughter, who also had significant health problems.

Despite extensive criticism by feminists and some in the Third World medical community, Norplant continues to be used and abused. Indonesia's government, which in some years purchased two-thirds of the world's Norplant, has relied heavily on the device to further its population-control goals, often requiring proof of its use in order to receive a job or a paycheck.[132] In December 1997, members of the Bangladeshi feminist group Naripokkho documented instances of poor women who, after having Norplant implanted without proper counseling, tried to get the implants removed and were refused. Earlier in the 1980s, Bangladeshi women had had great difficulty in getting the rods removed after suffering side effects, and the government claimed to have fixed the problem. But when Norplant shipments increased dramatically — in 1996, UNFPA sent 78,600 sets to Bangladesh, and USAID chipped in an additional 2,000 — the same problems occurred all over again.[133] Such recidivistic disregard for women's health and dignity can be traced to the population-control-above-all-else ethos of the Bangladesh program; the director of the Norplant program in the country said:

> It has been found by researchers that contraceptive pills containing progestin and more commonly used other reversible methods necessitate continuous motivational involvement by the user. In a country like Bangladesh this fact is more true than in the developed world. It is, therefore, necessary to introduce methods in Bangladesh which can continue to be effective for long periods without continuous motivation by Family Planning Workers. Norplant is perhaps the most effective method which is likely to prove successful here.[134]

IPPF has long been committed to Norplant as a method of population control in the developing world. In 1986, four years before FDA approval of the drug for use in the U.S., IPPF was already promoting the drug in countries where the lack of quality health care and the fervency of government-run population-control programs frequently exacerbate the dangers inherent in the drug.[135] In addition to irresponsible promotion of Norplant abroad, Planned Parenthood has been accused of negligence and misinformation in its dissemination of the device in the U.S.[136] One study of low-income Southern women receiving Norplant determined that the pre-insertion counseling was strongly directional in that it "minimized the possibility of adverse side-effects." One woman complained, "They don't jump to take it out but they sure do want to put it in."[137] A eleven-year-old girl who was repeatedly raped by her stepfather was implanted with the device after she told her mother about the rapes.[138] In this case, Norplant was used for the express purpose of covering up crimes against a female in order to continue them, an always dangerous possibility for non-user-controlled methods such as Norplant, the IUD, and sterilization (as well as for "incest" abortions done on minors). Not surprisingly, about half of the women in America who have used Norplant are on Medicaid. Here it is easy to see how Norplant, as a device that is beyond the immediate control of the woman using it, can be used to further the misogynistic and abusive aims of powerful persons who do not want the specter of the fertility of the poor haunting their comfortable lifestyles.[139]

Along these lines, just two days after the FDA's approval of Norplant in 1990, the *Philadelphia Inquirer* ran an editorial entitled "Poverty and Norplant — Can Contraception Reduce the Underclass?" which speculated about the benefits of providing incentives to welfare mothers to use Norplant.[140] One of its own columnists, Steve Lopez, noted, "What we have, basically, is the *Inquirer* brain trust looking down from its ivory tower and wondering if black people should be paid to stop having so many damn kids."[141] Eleven days later, after a firestorm of controversy, the newspaper printed an apology. The *Inquirer*'s dream was shared by many state legislators: soon after Norplant's approval, more than twelve states from 1991 to 1993 introduced legislation that would have mandated Norplant use for an assortment of populations, including welfare recipients, convicted child abusers, and drug users. Fortunately, none of the bills passed.[142]

Like Norplant and surgical sterilization, the hormonal contraceptive shot Depo-Provera has been used against impoverished minority women for the purposes of domestic population control. Its injectable nature makes it easy to be given to an unaware woman, who might be told she is receiving some kind of immunization, and its lengthy effectiveness (3 months) makes it attractive to family planners. Depo's side effects are similar to those of other hormonal contraceptives. It has also been linked to increased rates of bone loss as well as to breast, endometrial and cervical cancers.[143] It can cause low birth weight in babies conceived while traces of the drug linger in their mothers' bodies, and it passes through breastmilk to nursing infants.[144]

The Institute for the Study of Medical Ethics began to collect case studies in California in the 1960s and 1970s when it became evident that many women were being given the drug without informed consent. Out of the over 150 women interviewed by the institute, 85 percent said they had not signed a consent form. Despite its experimental status, a random survey of gynecologists in the greater Los Angeles area indicated that about a third had administered Depo for contraceptive purposes.[145] A twenty-seven-year-old woman testified to severe depression, nausea, and bloating, leading her to discontinue use of the drug. A few years later, her daughter was born bleeding from the vagina, with enlarged breasts and a *linea negra*. Other young women received hysterectomies due to severe bleeding, infections, and enlarged uteruses.[146]

Depo's history has been marked by a prolonged controversy over its side effects. First tested in 1958 for treating miscarriage and endometriosis (for which problems it is now considered ineffective), the drug was first put up for approval by the manufacturer Upjohn as an injectable contraceptive in 1967. Upjohn's own tests done on beagles and monkeys indicated that it was a carcinogen, and the FDA resisted approving the drug. Upjohn insisted, however, that only large-scale human tests would indicate the drug's safety, thus essentially advocating that a questionable drug be put on the market in order to force women into serving as unwitting guinea pigs. Depo cheerleader Malcolm Potts has argued, "We're not going to know whether Depo-Provera is safe until a large number of women use it for a very large time"— by which he meant twenty to fifty years.[147] Only after such massive involuntary human experimentation is completed, Potts argued, can we know if Depo is, for example, a carcinogen. Legitimating this barbaric disregard for the health and dignity of women, the FDA's Obstetrics-Gynecology Expert Advisory Committee repeatedly recommended Depo for approval. A past director of the FDA's Bureau of Drugs, Dr. J. Krout, complained, "Most of the members of that [OB-GYN] committee are in the population control business."[148] One OB-GYN Committee member said in 1971 that the State Department was pushing for approval so that it could be used in the Third World. Indeed, Upjohn's 1979 annual report noted, "Foreign markets, including China and the Eastern European bloc account for roughly three-fourths" of its prostaglandin sales. "Enormous potential markets for contraceptives and abortifacients exist in India and China. In underdeveloped countries, where birth rates are high, large markets await social and scientific understanding of the advantages of birth control."[149] The FDA finally acquiesced to the pressure, not least that applied by IPPF and other population-control groups (who were already distributing millions of shots to Third World women) and approved the drug in 1992.[150]

On the way to this approval, Depo researchers did in fact violate the basic ethical canons of human experimentation. For example, one might note a Depo study done during the 1970s at Emory University's Grady Memorial Family Clinic, which looked at 4,400 mostly black women. In retrospect, the FDA determined that the study did not adhere to FDA experimental protocol; among the problems was that patients and staff were mostly not informed that the drug was not yet approved. Because of the absence of informed consent, the Emory University Institutional Review Board would not approve the study as "ethically acceptable." An FDA officer determined that the study was not adequately set up to investigate side effects and efficacy: "This was not any sort of scientific investigation. We really had a population of [minority] patients receiving treatment [i.e., contraception] ... approval of the study was really to allow them to continue receiving treatment."[151] Upjohn's representative on the FDA Board of Inquiry into the drug, Griff Ross, manifested similar attitudes when he urged that Depo be approved for use by drug abusers and the mentally disabled.[152]

Yet even the flawed consent mechanism of the Georgia study would be preferable to what happened to female wards of Illinois in the 1970s: the state Department of Children and Family Services allowed a special-education school to inject teenage girls without their consent. The Mary Lee School for Special Education gave girls shots if they refused to go on the pill or if they were "chronic runaways." The department's medical consultant, J. Keller Mack, said breezily, "If you didn't test the drug on somebody, you would never be able to put it on the market. I thought they might just as well test it on our Illinois girls as girls from anywhere else."[153] Dr. Mack never seemed to consider that any contraceptive drug-testing should be done only with consenting adults. The Illinois case is especially egregious given that Depo use might result in decreased bone density, which would be particularly harmful for growing adolescents.

Depo-Provera researchers, especially those hired by Upjohn, the drug's manufacturer, manifested the same kind of patronizing and dismissive attitude toward women in the test groups that was seen with those who researched the pill. For example, one nurse claimed that female patients complaining of headaches and mood swings were probably just scapegoating the drug: a little probing, she said, would reveal that other things in the women's lives had to be the cause.[154] Unfortunately, a woman who suffers Depo's side effects can only wait for the drug to leave her system; she cannot have it removed or stop taking a pill.

Beyond the health risks, the research abuses indicate that Depo-Provera's fundamental problem, as we saw with the IUD and Norplant, is that it aims to colonize the female body, subjecting its fertility to the control of medical personnel. The woman cannot suddenly opt out, nor is she usually given full disclosure of the drug's dangers. Nor are the women who are presented with this contraceptive "option" usually given any other choice.

Outside America, documented coercive use of the drug has occurred in Thailand, Mexico, India, Bangladesh, and South Africa.[155] In Thailand, for example, Depo was given to every women in the Kamput refugee camp as "a prerequisite to marriage."[156] But abuses are not restricted to developing countries. The National Women's Health Network has observed that a French study showed that minorities were disproportionately using Depo in comparison to native French women. "These results cannot be explained as merely the choice of the women involved," the NWHN pointed out. "A review of the records revealed that African[-born] women initially requested a method other than Depo-Provera more than twice as often as French women."[157] The non-native women, in other words, were being pressured into accepting the shots.

UNFPA and IPPF are the world's largest distributors of Depo-Provera, which has been pushed in many population-control programs.[158] Despite the ruthless disregard for women's health and dignity displayed by Upjohn in its drive to get Depo on the market, Planned Parenthood continues to collude with it, even accepting Upjohn's sponsorship of the 1996 PPFA annual conference, "One Vision, Many Voices." According to Felice Gonzales, the first vice chairperson of PPFA and emcee for the conference's opening ceremonies, the eightieth anniversary of Planned Parenthood again brought to mind the organization's origin in Margaret Sanger's activities and the "proud tradition of speaking up and speaking out on behalf of those who need us."[159]

The Disease of Being Female

The latest war against women and girls is being fought by means of sophisticated prenatal diagnostic techniques. Like genetic screening for eugenic purposes, this antenatal misogyny targets a certain genetic defect and seeks to eliminate persons who carry that defect — but this time the genetic "defect" is simply having two X chromosomes.

Called "sex-selection abortion," this practice utilizes prenatal genetic-screening methods such as amniocentesis or chorionic villus sampling (CVS) to determine which fetuses are female. According to many geneticists who agree to test for gender — and some 62 percent of geneticists either do so themselves or else would refer to another who does — the inevitable result is the abortion of a fetus with the "wrong sex." One genet-icist, John D. Stephens, who patented a technique that can test for gen-der quite early, noted that, if a fetus is aborted, it is "almost always a girl."[160]

The procedure is quite common in other countries, especially in those where population policies mean that families are faced with the pressure of having only one or two children. In those cases, parents choose abor-tion or infanticide for their daughters, rather than risk the financial bur-den of having only female children. And not only economic considerations are in play: conventional notions of the preferability of having boys are depressingly universal. A deep-rooted misogyny plus population control can mean that, if a couple is not allowed to bear many children, those they do have must be "perfect" — and that invariably means male.[161] Thus, as a United Nations Development Program report noted, there are some 100 million "missing women" in Southeast Asia alone over the last century, due to female infanticide and abortion, dowry-related deaths, and lack of med-ical care for women.[162] The 2001 census of India showed a decline from 945 to 927 in the ratio of females to every 1,000 males.[163] Baby girls are killed by strangulation, drowning, being buried alive, or starvation, while wealthier Indians simply utilize ultrasound and abortion to single out females: there are about 3,500 abortions of females a year in the city of Jaipur alone.[164] Those who are not killed can wind up in orphanages, where conditions tend to be substandard.

By 2001, advertisements promoting sex-selection procedures appeared in *The New York Times* and in the North American editions of *Indian Express* and *India Abroad*.[165] Yet Americans had already begun making use of the method. In observing this phenomenon, Charlotte Allen has remarked:

> As sex selection in America moves out of Third World ghettos and becomes an option for the control-obsessed upper middle class, it's worrying that nobody — not doctors, not genetics counselors, not abortion counselors, and not most feminists — seems willing to discourage the practice and some even encourage it.[166]

PPFA bears responsibility as a family-planning organization that implic-itly encourages the practice by its refusal to condemn it, taking an amoral, pragmatic approach from the very beginning. In 1975, the chairwoman of PPFA's medical committee foresaw that, as the reporter summarized it, "planned parenthood will increasingly connote planning the sex as well as the spacing of offspring." Instead of resisting this outcome on the basis of its preeminence among family-planning organizations and its claims to be a bulwark for women's rights, Planned Parenthood has capitulated; as one physician summarized, "[Sex selection] is here. We can't dismiss it out of hand. We ought to take it seriously; watch it; use it with care, discrimination, and due reflection on its potential outcomes—use it well."[167] How such a practice can be used well is not explained.

Planned Parenthood's capitulation to sex-selection abortion follows logically from its eugenic ideology. PPFA fostered the attitude that a person can and should have the "perfect" baby, free of all disease and defect. In a misogynist society, simply being a female is often taken to be a defect, and we have seen that the sex-selection procedure reflects this: the babies aborted are in fact disproportionately female. A love affair with control— with reproductive, population, and eugenic control—has led PPFA to participate in genetic screening for the purpose of sex selection, despite the lethal misogyny often involved. By countenancing sex selection, PPFA colludes with the denigration of the female. How is it that self-proclaimed feminists could come to this? First, women (especially poor women) having fewer babies is an absolute good for Planned Parenthood, even if the ones eliminated are overwhelmingly female. In addition, Planned Parenthood's global antinatal attitude easily dovetails with an anti-woman bias.

Why is this? As we have seen, Planned Parenthood and the other population controllers generally blame the female reproductive system for causing overpopulation and, thus, the majority of world evils, including war, poverty, and starvation. (And, as we shall see in the next chapter, Sanger initiated this line of thought in her *Woman and the New Race*.) Population-control zealots like the recently deceased Garrett Hardin readied themselves to fight an all-out war against female reproductive powers. Likewise, physician Warren Hern, another population-control and putative "reproductive rights" advocate (he is a vocal supporter of partial-birth abortion), argued that pregnancy ought to be viewed as a disease.[168]

For men like Hardin and Hern, as well as far too many women, nothing is more disgusting than a pregnant woman. Only when women physiologically ape men, with flattened-out hormonal rhythms and non-functional wombs, will they no longer be a threat. This kind of radical misogyny, more pervasive than is realized, especially values hormonal contraception, because this introjects within the female body the phallocratic template of childless sexuality and relieves men of having to deal with distasteful things such as menstruation. Early advertisements for Enovid, the first birth-control pill, made this bias explicit:

> *Unfettered.* From the beginning woman has been a vassal to the temporal demands—and frequently the aberrations—of the cyclic mechanism of

her reproductive system. Now to a degree heretofore unknown, she is permitted *normalization*, enhancement or suspension of cyclic function and procreative potential. This new method [of] control is symbolized in an illustration borrowed from ancient Greek mythology — Andromeda freed from her chains.[169]

In other words, only with the pill's engineered cycle is the female body "normal." There is a direct lineage here from Margaret Sanger, who, as we saw in the introduction and chapter one, had the key insight that birth control could simultaneously advance negative eugenics and the bourgeois paradigm of sex without commitment. The control of female fertility achieves eugenic-demographic aims while advancing this kind of sexuality. The female body needs to be fixed by technology, because nature did not quite get it right the first time.

Instead of challenging this resentment of the female body and offering a truly pro-woman philosophy as an alternative — a philosophy that would value female bodies, including their reproductive potential, rather than seeking to deform them, whether surgically or chemically — Planned Parenthood has played a significant role in perpetuating hegemonic, radically misogynist cultural biases. By nevertheless claiming to be pro-woman, it has also succeeded in infecting mainstream feminism with its dangerous orientation. When it comes to sex-selection abortion, as in other areas governed by Planned Parenthood's ideology of control, feminism has not had the courage it needs to stand up to rampant and even fatal misogyny.

Conclusion

The promotion of contraceptives as a simple solution to many complex problems, especially economic ones, reveals that the control movement defends the interests of a very definite social class, a self-anointed elite. Planned Parenthood's "strategy envisions the achievement of population limitation in America and abroad, and a corresponding reduction of instability, insecurity and hunger without substantial change in the distribution of power within social and economic institutions."[170] As a result, women and girls, especially the poor, continue to suffer at the hands of an unchallenged misogyny that considers their reproductive powers inherently problematic, if not repugnant, and disposable for the sake of the "greater good."

Why have businessmen jumped so enthusiastically onto the population-control bandwagon? Surely it would be in their financial self-interest to want the birth of *more* people, in order to increase the number of consumers. But the leaders of Planned Parenthood and other control groups shrewdly realized that they could argue that, in order to support the particular kind of middle- to upper-class consumerist lifestyle that supplies the market for certain types of businesses, consumers would need to have smaller families. Why? Because smaller families use proportionately less money for essentials and a lot more money on non-essentials, on self-gratifying luxuries. As Hugh Moore put it, "It isn't the number of people that counts, but *purchasing power*, which is higher in an economy with a stabilized population."[171] The Population Council realized from its inception that one necessary means for achieving its goals would be to implement "every possible way of making children expensive."[172] In like manner, the Chinese government has regaled its populace with such decidedly non-Marxist slogans as "With two children you can afford a 14-inch TV, with one child you can afford a 21-inch TV."[173] Thus, the oft-made claim that population-control groups are interested in protecting environmental resources is disingenuous at best and outright dishonest at worst. After all, who uses more resources and generates more waste, a childless American family or a six-child African family?

The businessmen funding and running population-control organizations were and are often the most egregious offenders in destroying the environment, and they have used the poor families in Asia and Africa as scapegoats for their own rapacity. What these businessmen want is the right kind of consumer for their goods, consumers who would value more cars and electronic goods and other luxuries instead of children. In other words, children are the primary competition that these businessmen must denigrate and ultimately negate, and the business-funded population-control ad campaigns bombarding Third World cultures pose the ultimate consumerist choice: which will you choose, progeny or purchasing power?[174] In promoting this consumerist ideology (one that Sanger's own version of the bourgeois lifestyle presaged), Planned Parenthood, among others, has allowed itself to become a tool of men more interested in profits than in people.

CHAPTER EIGHT

Beyond Control: Toward a New Feminism

"Within [woman] is wrapped up the future of the race — it is hers to make or mar."— Margaret Sanger, 1920[1]

"More and more it seems that women themselves are coming to regard their wombs as a burden they have been lumbered with on behalf of the race.... If men flee the female, we will survive, but if women themselves treat femaleness as a disease we are lost indeed."— Germaine Greer, 1999[2]

The women's movement has made great advances in calling attention to systematic misogyny. Because of the universal prevalence of the dark reality that it exposes, feminism bids fair to be the premiere liberation movement of our age, achieving a universality that could surpass that of all other movements. However, the eugenic "feminism" of Margaret Sanger and her organizations is antithetical to a liberating feminism, not in the least because eugenics has little use for the dignity of the embodied person. As far as eugenics goes, embodiment is a problem to be solved technologically: the bodies of the "unfit" must be controlled; the bodies of the "fit" are to be liberated from constraints on the maximization of pleasure. (There is here operative a basic attitude of *ressentiment* toward the limitations of embodiment: having a body is a condition that supposedly restricts freedom by binding the individual to a particular time and place, that is, to a particular context and community —

and, in the worst-case scenario, to the exigencies of female physiology.)

Eugenicists yearn for the cool rationality of the machine and the unfettered freedom of the titan, to realign the future of the race by "rational" social control through the bare exercise of the power they believe is their due. Sex and all things sexual in particular must be "rationalized": hence the involvement of many eugenicists in sexology and marriage counseling, beginning with Havelock Ellis. And so the problem of embodiment invariably becomes the problem of the female body and of female fertility. The rational removal of the possibility of haphazard procreation opens up the space for pleasure, they believe, which should be earnestly pursued with the help of sex manuals and "sexperts." Sex for a eugenicist might be about pleasure or bonding or romantic love or some such, but in any case it has little to do with the naked facticity of the female body with all of its uncouth emissions and embarrassing bulges, and the more of the brute femaleness (or, better, non-maleness) of such a body that can be neutralized, the better. Sex, in other words, should be mostly about recreation and not procreation: "bodies and pleasures," as Michel Foucault has asserted, and the less specifically male or female the bodies in question are rendered, the greater the supposed range of possible pleasures. But as many feminists have noted, the project of neutering sex/gender is usually a Trojan horse for a secret masculinity. In the demystifying light of a true feminism, the true stakes are revealed: (polymorphous, technologically liberated) "bodies" are really masculine or at least non-feminine bodies, and "pleasures" are whatever enjoyments become possible when female otherness no longer intrudes. Ironically, however, when the specificity of bodies evaporates, the field of possible pleasures, supposedly extending into an open horizon of polymorphous experiences, dissolves into an unrelenting sameness, testified to by the increasingly frantic attempts by Sanger and her lovers to squeeze out new thrills from their couplings. The specificity of bodies, it seems, has something to do with the specificity (that is, the non-sameness, the freshness, the iconicity) of pleasures. Whose bodies? Which pleasures? Anonymity in sex has been tried over and over again, but no amount of experimenting or tinkering makes it anything but radically exploitative and therefore boring, reducing otherness to self-sameness: bodies are not interchangeable like spare parts of a machine.

Nevertheless, Sanger wished to experience bodily pleasures in this atomistic, depersonalized way, fleeing the hard contours of embodiment; she wished, as the romantic vision in *Woman and the New Race* shows, to be freed from the encumbrances of the female body. The development of hormonal contraception, in particular, realized her vision. Recall the early ad for Enovid that championed the pill's ability to render a woman "*unfettered*" from her slavery to the "demands of the cyclic mechanism of her reproductive system" through the "*normalization*" of her body — by means of an artificial cycle.[3] The free woman, according to the ideology of control, is the engineered and infertile woman. She is, in the end, the controlled woman.

Instead of accepting this radical misogyny, feminism should value the female body as something with a unique dignity. Whenever feminism denigrates this body, it destroys an irreplaceable foundation stone of feminism's universality, the shared, specific experience of the dignity and vulnerability of female embodiment.[4] It also thereby trivializes the damage done to women and girls through violence perpetrated on their bodies.

Despite feminism's emancipatory potential, the history of Western feminism is far from unsullied. As we have seen and as other feminist scholars have pointed out, the birth-control movement is implicated in many oppressive ideologies, including eugenics.[5] Unfortunately, these tendencies are not simply regrettable past problems, since the organizations involved in eugenic population control, including the Planned Parenthood Federation of America, the Population Council, and the Pathfinder Fund, are still important players on the world scene and are still considered valuable allies by many feminists. Why have some feminists turned a blind eye to the eugenic histories of supposed allies, when surely eugenics represents, in a paradigmatic way, the dehumanization of the vulnerable (and especially of women) that feminism should oppose?

This chapter will examine the possibilities of discovering and overcoming blind spots within the women's movement, in order to safeguard an internally consistent feminism that can work for the liberation of all women. In the first section, I will summarize Sanger's eugenically compromised feminism by analyzing her account of female nature as found in her rhetorically powerful 1920 book, *Woman and the New Race*. In the second, I will present the current situation. Lastly, I will argue for some solutions: how can those interested in furthering women's liberation develop an approach to protecting the lives and health of women and girls, especially those in the developing world, without inflicting on them a culturally conditioned alienation from their bodies?

The Unfit and Fecund Woman

As we have noted, Margaret Sanger, the founder of the Planned Parenthood Federation of America and the International Planned Parenthood

Federation, has been hailed as a great feminist foremother, a pioneer in the work of female liberation. Yet her feminism might not be recognizable to women today. Intimately linked with her belief in the goodness and necessity of birth control was a eugenic desire to control the reproduction of the "unfit." Birth control was for "fit" women like herself, who wished to be freed from the difficulties of childbirth and child rearing in order to pursue a bourgeois, romantic vision of sexual freedom. But it was also for those women who were "unfit," who "recklessly" perpetuated their damaged genetic stock by irresponsibly breeding more children in an already overpopulated world. If the latter did not voluntarily embrace birth control, according to Sanger, it should be forced upon them.

As we have seen, population control was a natural extension of Sanger's eugenic desire for population "quality, not quantity"; she insisted, "a *qualitative* factor as opposed to a *quantitative* one is of primary importance in dealing with the great masses of humanity."[6] She was one of the first activists to extend the influence of eugenics by concentrating on population control (that is, facilitating "quality" by focusing on the "not quantity" side of the eugenic equation as applied to the fecund poor), and her organizations made sure she would not be the last. The fourth and fifth chapters showed that scientific demography had its ideological origins in eugenics. Demography's attitude toward people was also determined by the "quantity vs. quality" dichotomy. Thus, the concern for reducing the number of people born was interwoven with the eugenic desire to reduce the number of "*unfit*" people born.

How could such eugenic sentiments be advanced by a feminist? And how could organizations such as Planned Parenthood, whose ostensible purpose is the promotion of women's rights, support such activities? As surprising as it might be to those unaware of the seriousness of Sanger's commitment to eugenic ideology, many forms of feminism have not been immune to oppressive tendencies and to androcentric cooptations of the feminist ideal. In order to point out the warning signs of such cooptation, I will summarize the elements of the ideology that we have seen in Sanger's thought and then indicate how it is operative within much contemporary feminism.

We see in *Woman and the New Race* that underlying Sanger's promotion of birth control was her understanding of what she called the "sex servitude" of women.[7] The inferior place of woman was caused by her acceptance of the "chains" forged by "the maternal functions of her nature."[8] When "unenlightened" women participated in what she called the "wickedness of large families," they foisted upon the world hordes of "cheap" human beings.[9] Note that human beings (and, therefore, women) do not have an innate dignity. They are like a commodity that loses its value when the market is flooded. These worthless people in turn became the ignorant, idle, impoverished class.[10] Thus, "woman has, through her reproductive ability, founded and perpetuated the tyrannies of the Earth."[11]

If the cause of "war, famine, poverty and oppression of the workers"[12] is to be found in the woman's womb, then she cannot evade her responsibility: "The task is hers. It cannot be avoided by excuses, nor can it be delegated. It is not enough for woman to point to the self-evident domination of man. Nor does it avail to plead the guilt of rulers and the exploiters of labor.... In her submission lies her error and guilt."[13] As a result, "she incurred a debt to society. Regardless of her own wrongs, regardless of her lack of opportunity and regardless of all other considerations, *she* must pay that debt."[14] Nor can the payment of this debt be mere palliative action, such as programs of social and political amelioration. No, the fault lies in her womb, and there the price must be paid.[15]

Sanger's gnostically dualist view of women leads her to this conclusion. In opposition to "the chains of [woman's] own reproductivity," there exists "the feminine spirit"[16]: "...woman's desire for freedom is born of the feminine spirit, which is the absolute, elemental, inner urge of womanhood."[17] This spirit can be understood as a vitalist, quasi–Hegelian spirit of the race expressing itself within woman. It has as its proximate goal the freedom of individual women but its ultimate goal is "the birth of a new race."[18] Thus, the feminine spirit can express itself in a specific kind of motherhood that is not slavery, when motherhood is voluntary and produces "fit" children, while the "chief obstacles" to its expression are "the burden of unwanted children."[19]

It should be noted that Sanger here seems to leave open the possibility that the poor could enter the ranks of the fit, should the women of the lower economic classes conform to a certain lifestyle, living out the freedom of the feminine spirit. She believes, at least in 1920, that "free" women bring forth fit children, while "unfree" women can only bring forth the unfit — though "freedom" means "voluntary motherhood" and the bourgeois sexual lifestyle that implies. Though this is problematic enough, she has not at this point embraced a full-blown eugenic determinism when it comes to the poor, as she will eventually, in which the poor as such are unfit. See, for example, her 1939 letter to Frederick Osborn — discussed in the introduction — that insists that the poor as a class should have their fertility controlled; whether or not they are "free" is no longer a consideration.[20] In this book, however, it was Sanger's goal to be more radical than Marx in showing the way toward the emancipation of the working class, here by means of sexual as opposed to economic revolution, with the women who live according to the feminine spirit replacing the proletariat as the new revolutionary class. Birth control has the power to elevate the unfit to the level of the fit (though still their fertility will be under control). Thus, at least in this work, she is unwilling to call the underclass (or at least the working class) unfit *tout court*, although in an article written two years earlier she still held that other groups of people should not reproduce:

> By all means there should be no children when mother (or father) suffers from such diseases as tuberculosis, gonorrhea, syphilis, cancer, epilipsy [sic], insanity, drunkenness or mental disorders.... No more children should be born when the parents, though healthy themselves, find that their children are physically or mentally defective. No matter how much they desire children, no man and woman have a right to bring into the world those who are sure to suffer from mental or physical affliction. It condemns the child to a life of misery and places upon the community the burden of caring for them, probably of their defective descendants for many generations.[21]

But the kind of eugenic mobility made possible by "voluntary motherhood" is still open at least to the poor in 1920; only later does she doubt that any real improvement is possible.[22]

In *Woman and the New Race*, Sanger maintains that a motherhood freed from the burden of "enforced maternity" "works in wondrous ways. It refuses to bring forth weaklings.... It withholds the unfit, brings forth the fit; brings few children into homes where there is not sufficient to provide for them. Instinctively it avoids all those things which multiply racial handicaps."[23] The feminine spirit, Sanger contends, when freed from fear of unwanted children, will naturally channel itself into an appropriately eugenic maternity. This is due to Sanger's hyper-romantic idea of sexual love in which the free development of the personalities of the lovers always takes precedence over the responsibilities of parenting. Given this narcissism, few children can be accommodated, but after all, eugenic reproduction is by definition a matter of quality, not quantity: "In sharp contrast with these women who ignorantly bring forth large families and who thereby enslave themselves, we find a few women who have one, two or three children or no children at all. These women, with the exception of the childless ones, live full-rounded lives."[24] What does such a life look like? "Theirs is the opportunity to keep abreast of the times, to make and cultivate a varied circle of friends, to seek amusements as suits their taste and means, to know the meaning of real recreation. All these things remain unrealized desires to the prolific mother." They are, in other words, "fit mothers of the race, ... the courted comrades of the men they choose, rather than the 'slaves of slaves.'"[25]

Those who do not care for such a bourgeois life, who rather pursue true cultivation in the rhythms of — and not despite — a life of raising children, are by implication unfit. Sanger's vision of the life of mothers in large working-class families makes quite clear that she thought that large families make a woman unfit:

> Instead, such a mother is tired, nervous, irritated and ill-tempered; a determent, often, instead of a help to her children. Motherhood becomes a disaster and childhood a tragedy.... She is a breeding machine and a drudge — she is not an asset but a liability to her neighborhood, to her class, to society. She can be nothing as long as she is denied means of limiting her family.[26]

And such unfit women breed unfit children: "The most immoral practice of the day is breeding too many children.... Social workers, physicians and reformers cry out to stop the breeding of these, who must exist in want until they become permanent members of the ranks of the unfit."[27] As a result, birth control must be aimed at the unfit: "Birth control itself ... is nothing more or less than the facilitation of the process of weeding out the unfit, of preventing the birth of defectives or of those who will become defectives."[28]

Over and over again, Sanger comes back to the "responsibility" or the "duty" that this situation places upon woman. "Within her is wrapped up the future of the race — it is hers to make or mar."[29] As a result, birth control is strictly the woman's burden: "It is woman's duty as well as her privilege to lay hold of the means of freedom. Whatever men may do, she cannot escape the responsibility."[30] As she said in the first chapter of the book, woman's unfreedom is fundamentally caused by her maternal life, and only birth control can bring liberty; all other attempts at restructuring society or male behavior are merely superficial in comparison, including the struggle for suffrage and equal property rights (which she basically dismisses as epiphenomenal window dressing).[31] Woman must control her fertility for the sake of the race. In compensation, Sanger closely binds the eugenic task to the self-actualization of women: "If we are to make racial progress, the development of womanhood must precede motherhood in every individual woman."[32] If she suffers want or injustice, she has no one to blame but herself for not freeing her "feminine spirit" by controlling her body.

The dangerous results of this philosophy have been traced throughout this book, most clearly in the account of the population-control movement's scapegoating of the female body. And this philosophy has seeped into popular consciousness and even into feminism itself. The eagerness to blame women's problems on their reproducing is omnipresent, an atti-tude clearly on display during the debates on welfare reform and single motherhood. Concretely, it leads to the very situation Sanger agitated for: attempts to reduce poverty and to reform sexist attitudes are buried under the all-consuming obsession to contracept women. Many women do indeed experience great difficulties when it comes to raising children due, say, to poverty or to the evasion of paternal responsibility, but rarely do we attempt to solve those problems directly; rather, we attempt to elimi-nate her ability to have children. But a poor and exploited woman who is sterilized is still poor and exploited. But with our ideological blinkers, all we see as the source of such a woman's problems is her fertility. It is but a short step, even in the name of compassion, to the coerced or forced administration of birth control. If a woman's problems are caused by her fertility, and if she refuses to acknowledge this reality, it is for her own good, so the reasoning goes, to persuade or demand or force her to stop having children.

It could be argued, of course, that Sanger could not have foreseen the perpetuation of imbalances of sexual power when she agitated for change in the laws and attitudes concerning contraception. It is certainly true that she believed that she was fighting for the means of female empowerment; she wanted a *female* contraceptive pill precisely because she believed that it would place the reproductive control in the hands of women alone. Yet this fact itself shows that she considered contraception to be all about the control of the woman's body, whether by the woman herself or by those who know better than the woman. If a woman is not willing to internal-ize her slavery, plenty of others, including many women, are willing to force her to do it. As a result, we have the kind of situation Germaine Greer described recently: "More and more it seems that women themselves are coming to regard their wombs as a burden they have been lumbered with on behalf of the race…. If men flee the female, we will survive, but if women themselves treat femaleness as a disease we are lost indeed."[33]

Where Are We Now?

Recently, participants in both the population-control movement and the "new," supposedly benevolent, eugenics have claimed that the shift in institutional rhetoric from advocacy for overt coercion to the championing of individual rights shows how the old eugenic plans for societal control have been eliminated from the organizations that formerly espoused this ideology. Yet two objections arise against this sanguine view. First, as the sixth chapter on sterilization showed, active coercion persists to this day within population-control programs, whether overtly (as in China and Peru) or more quietly (as in the countries that still utilize coercive incentive policies). Secondly, as we saw with the "new eugenics," control need not be implemented through active coercion. Only a socially uncritical naivete could postulate that everything an individual does is truly free.[34] Libertarian individualism masks ideological conditioning.

Furthermore, a rhetorical commitment to "women's health," while sounding feminist, can be used strategically to mask misogynist policies.[35] Back in the 1960s, William Vogt, a past president of Planned Parenthood, explained the value of the language of maternal health as an ideological cover: "It seems to me that perhaps we could ... spread birth control under the guise of maternal health."[36] The official biography of Clarence Gamble shows that birth controller Gamble was also consciously aware of the propagandistic benefit of "health" language: "While population control might be a desirable and inevitable result, and he personally regarded genetic improvement of human stock as a desirable goal, he put his emphasis on the health of mother and family, aware that racial and national groups did not like to be told that it would be a better world if *they* cut down on *their* kind."[37] In addition, "health" was often evoked as a code word for eugenic concerns, as the name of eugenicist and birth controller Robert L. Dickinson's National Committee on Maternal Health indicates. But, as we have seen, the promotion of birth-control methods with dangerous side effects in the poorer countries of the world indicates the limits of the control movement's actual commitment to women's health. Greer foresaw this cooptation over twenty-five years ago, after the 1974 Bucharest population conference, and sounded a too-little-heeded alarm: "That any superpower should give the name women's liberation to the boot that he is preparing to place upon the necks of Third World women, ought to call forth the most appalling exhibition of women's rage that the world has yet seen."[38]

As Greer understood, proponents of the control ideology are not only not actually concerned about women's health, they also often view the female body with barely concealed disgust. Population controllers have not failed to express their hatred for the female reproductive system, referring to it in epidemiological terms. Warren Hern, a population-control activist and abortionist, asked, "Is pregnancy really normal?" and theorized that human population growth was "carcinogenic."[39] In 1971, Edgar Chasteen argued, "Our country and our world is presently engulfed by a *pregnancy epidemic* which threatens to destroy us all. Public health and safety is now in as much danger from the pregnancy epidemic as it was from smallpox in the eighteenth century, and the solution is the same: the development of effective immunization and the enactment of compulsory legislation."[40] Only minds thoroughly steeped in the control mentality could evince such grotesque misogyny.

Beyond the Control of Female Bodies: Some Proposals

What can the example of Sanger's advocacy of eugenic population control teach us? First of all, it should inspire a little soul-searching by contemporary feminists: whom do we choose as our allies, and why? Do we betray our responsibility to defend women and girls who need our support when we allow pragmatic considerations to keep us from looking too closely at our supposed "friends," such as Planned Parenthood and the other population-control organizations?

Secondly, it should bring home the fact that we must never allow the violation of the fundamental human rights of the marginalized and powerless for any supposed "greater good." The history of eugenics teaches us that a willingness to label some individuals as defective, to consider some humans as not possessed of inherent and inviolable dignity, especially threatens women and girls. The abuse of one group of people opens up the floodgates for the abuse of the rest because the powerful are capricious and we can all become inconvenient. But women and girls are especially vulnerable to the violence of the war against the weak. Eugenic contempt for the poor and for persons with disabilities is logically consistent with the forced sterilizations of women in the name of population control, practices which continue to this day. Whenever the ideology of the powerful carries the day, women always find themselves under the knife. Feminism must be especially vigilant in its attitudes towards the powerless and must never tolerate an occlusion of the inviolability of every human's fundamental rights, if it is to be true both to its internal emancipatory dynamism and to its mandate to protect women and girls. No true feminist can make peace with any assault on the powerless.

So what should be done? A few broad goals, backed up by some concrete proposals, come to mind. First of all, feminism should recommit itself to being a sign of contradiction. This means that, when the usual misogynist suspects—the self-anointed elites in the mainstream press, big business, Hollywood, the education establishment, the academy, as well as popular culture (the propaganda machine of these elites)—are advocating a certain ideology and plan of action, feminists should investigate the matter very carefully, with full critical consciousness, before jumping on the bandwagon. Should Ted Turner's biases set the agenda for the women's liberation movement? Whenever women are told to imitate men's own unfreedom, the liberation of either sex is not likely to follow. Women and girls, both here and abroad, desperately need the kind of counter-cultural witness that feminism could bring to lives in which abuse, poverty, and sexual wounding is too often suffered and then internalized as a result of the prevailing anti-woman ethos.

Secondly, all of us, women and men, who live comfortable lives in the West need to perform an examination of conscience concerning our susceptibility to ideologies that justify our lifestyles, especially ones that scapegoat the poor for their poverty. People in the developing world are immiserated and starving due to factors of immense complexity, including the fact that there are both right-wing and left-wing forces at play in the economic underdevelopment of the Third World. Nevertheless, we must seriously confront the fact that many components of the consumerist lifestyle are implicated, predisposing us to soothe our consciences with mythology. Why does it not seem obviously outrageous when simple-minded talking heads and editorialists tsk-tsk, insinuating that the real problem is that "those" people have too many babies when there is famine in Africa? Conjuring the bogeyman of overpopulation is one of the great mystifying strategies of our age. It is easier to destroy the ovaries and wombs of poor women than for us to change our lives.

Concretely, feminists must stop making deals with the devil. Planned Parenthood has a eugenic history and philosophy, in accord with which it has conducted a war against the fertility of poor women in particular. One of the main purposes of this book has been to bring this history to the light of day, so that feminists can realize that Planned Parenthood embodies an ideology that is not conducive to female liberation. One need only note the apologies it gives for brutally misogynistic regimes and population-control programs to realize the necessity of a clean break.

Contemporary feminism has a mission to fulfill in both developed and developing countries. Many women from developing countries might have a hard time recognizing the agenda of their wealthier sisters as harmonious with their own real needs. For example, Sanger was frustrated that many poor women in this country and abroad did not eagerly accept what was for her sexual liberation, and she felt it was necessary for society to force them to conform. The population-control movement has a similar attitude toward Third World women who do not wish to contracept, an additional justification for the attempts either to "motivate" women to use birth control by offering monetary incentives or to directly coerce. Insofar as the women's movement gives population-control institutions its support, it offers women only the false compensations of Sanger's ideology of control, an empty "liberation," if not outright oppression inflicted upon women whose real needs are thereby ignored.

The particular needs of women in wealthier countries should not be neglected. There feminism needs to champion the dignity of the female body, especially to those women who are starving, mutilating, and otherwise torturing themselves. In order to witness to this dignity, we must move away from the control paradigm. Bodies are not fundamentally alien matter needing to be controlled by detached and enlightened minds. The control ideology sets up a model of opposition between a woman and "her" body, as though it were slave property needing to be broken. Too many women in the developed world have internalized this ideology of control: Western females have a distant or even adversarial relation to their bodies, to such a degree that they do not even know how their ovulatory cycles work, much less how to live in harmony with their perplexing flesh. As Farida Akhter has observed,

> The demand of reproductive rights [as presently conceived by population controllers and many Western feminists] has a sharp bourgeois imprint. By it, we are demanding the individual right of women over their own bodies. It is an ownership concept we are importing. Implicitly, we are demanding that a woman should own individually the reproductive factory she is carrying within her own body.[41]

This sort of rights-language belongs to the basic conceptual armament of the ideology of control, which views the disruptive female anatomy as a problem to be managed, not as the material basis for, and expressive medium of, a life to be lived in full integrity. Respect for the inherent dynamisms of the body promotes human dignity. Indeed, this dignity is fatally threatened every time such respect is absent. To be free, women must live in harmony with the rhythms of their bodies, not in spite of them. Phallocentric propaganda would have girls and women assess themselves and their bodies according to the grotesque predilections of a masculine *libido dominandi*. The social regime determined by a bent masculine desire will begin to crumble only if women begin valuing the power and beauty of their fertile bodies rather than engaging in a strange attempt to "control" what is inseparable from their own selves.

Part of this process must include the foreswearing of the desire to internalize one's slavery, to conform to a deformed masculinity, with its peculiar conceptions of empowerment and liberation. The price of such capitulation was indicated in the previous chapter, which recounts how the takeover by men of the population-control organizations solidified the birth-control movement's basic eugenic attitude and radicalized it through the deployment of management techniques and new technology to control the fertility of poor women. Sanger had already promoted a variation of the deformed masculine (that is, phallocentric) model of unencumbered sexuality, according to which she used and disposed of men with the same callousness that marks many men's treatment of women. In this kind of sexual play, another person is objectified as a sexual toy — and nothing spoils the fun more than the conception of a child. For such a lifestyle, female fertility is a problem or a disease, and it must be controlled, usually by (literally) man-made pharmaceutical concoctions, preferably in the form of hormonal contraceptives. As Greer has observed,

> All the time women have been agitating for freedom and self-determination they have been coming more and more under a kind of control that they cannot even protest against. Feminists used to demand the right to control our own bodies; what we got was the duty to submit our bodies to control by others. Much of what is done to women in the name of health has no rationale beyond control.[42]

Indeed, we Western women have internalized a sexual regime that requires that we feel our bodies to be alien. We feel victimized by our strange changes; we accept artificial cycles, despite the attendant (and not fully researched) dangers and discomforts; and we try desperately to "control" our fertility with the assistance of profit-seeking pharmaceutical companies. In so doing, we offer up our bodies to be controlled by a sexual regime dictated by a deformed masculine desire. A fertile female body is a cipher to women and a threat to men. Feminism needs to provide the tools for women and girls to rebuild their fragile sense of self, so that they once again feel at home in their bodies. Among other things, feminists need to educate women and girls regarding their physiology and natural fertility cycles,[43] broadcast information concerning the side effects of hormonal contraception, and persevere in the role of gadflies to those cultural arbiters that set artificial standards of female beauty — standards that, if followed faithfully, would, for instance, render a woman infertile due to lack of sufficient body fat and that in fact cause massive psychic damage in women and girls as indicated by the epidemic of eating disorders. Young women especially need to be reminded that they do not have to subject their bodies to Norplant and IUDs just because many males want to treat them as sexual dolls.

All this does indeed mean that feminism must also shed its inhibitions concerning the defense and even the celebration of motherhood.

Feminists have justly critiqued the reductive calculation of a woman's worth in terms of cooking, cleaning, and childbearing. Yet, is getting a job simply a matter of liberation for women? Or is it more complicated than that? While there are still significant barriers to women's full participation in the working world, it is in fact the case that the current wage-structure tends to require two-income households: companies want to get twice as much work for basically the same pay. And households with few (or no) children tend to pursue a more materialistic, bourgeois lifestyle, almost invariably consuming more than large families. The hegemonic forces of our consumerist economy are behind the push to convince women that maternity is a burden and counterproductive for society. And these forces are projecting themselves into the developing world, seeking to reorient desire from family toward consumption. Consider population-control advertising prevalent in developing countries: typical is a picture of the unhappy, poor, and burdened family with six children and no pigs, juxtaposed with the happy, prosperous, and contentedly consuming family with two children and six pigs. Beyond the fact that human children are valued less than pigs in this schema, the message to the woman is clear: your mothering is a burden to you and a threat to the world, precisely Sanger's message in *Woman and the New Race*. To counter these messages, feminists need not and of course ought not begin advocating 1950s suburban housewifery. Yet we could point out that the either-or of work *or* motherhood is a relatively recent paradigm; that social structures (such as job-sharing between spouses) could be put into place that would make a working world that is inimical to the dynamisms of female fertility conform to motherhood instead of forcing the female body into the mold of a sterile masculinity; that the unpaid physical and intellectual labor of childrearing and household management is no less valuable than the work that brings with it society's seal of approval in the form of a paycheck; and that we must build vital urban public spaces that allow for meaningful mutual recognition, exploding the confines of both the isolated suburban home as well as the cubicle culture with its meager satisfactions.[44] The reform projects entailed would indeed be of immense complexity, so that one can understand the temptation to just pop a pill instead. But to capitulate to a social, economic, and sexual regime that demands the control of female fertility is to condemn women to severe exploitation, violence, and self-alienation.

This book has argued for Margaret Sanger's world-historical importance as the great institutionalizer of eugenic ideology. Her vision was realized through the control of female fertility as carried out by the organizations she founded. This book now ends with a proposal for a feminism freed from her eugenic and control-saturated view of women. The specifics of how feminism should shake off Sanger's legacy are debatable, but the historical truth of that legacy's destructive effects on women is not. Only by knowing this history can women recognize their unfreedom and reject the eugenic model of progress forced onto them by the control movement. The great tragedies of our failed and ongoing experiments with eugenic control — the maimed and dead women, men, and children — cannot be erased, but perhaps from the memory of these victims will arise a new feminism.

Appendix 1

List of Abbreviations

PPFA, IPPF, and their institutional predecessors are in bold.

AAAS: American Association for the Advancement of Science
ABCL: American Birth Control League
AES: American Eugenics Society
APSL: American Philosophical Society Library
AQV: Anticoncepcion Quirurgica Voluntaria
AVS: Association for Voluntary Sterilization
AVSC: Association for Voluntary Surgical Contraception
BCCRB: Birth Control Clinical Research Bureau; also known as the Clinical Research Bureau
BCFA: Birth Control Federation of America
BCR: *Birth Control Review*
BEMFAM: [IPPF Brazilian affiliate] Sociedade Civil Bem-Estar Familiar no Brasil
CBD: Charles Benedict Davenport
CESA: Committee to End Sterilization Abuse
CJG: Clarence J. Gamble
CMH: Committee on Maternal Health
CVS: chorionic villus sampling
EES: Eugenic Education Society
ERA: Eugenics Research Association
ERO: Eugenics Record Office

ES: [English] Eugenics Society

FO: Frederick Osborn

FPA: [IPPF's Chinese affiliate] Family Planning Association

HBAA: Human Betterment Association of America

HEW: [Department of] Health, Education, and Welfare

HGP: Human Genome Project

ICPD: International Conference on Population and Development [Cairo, 1994]

ICPP: International Committee on Planned Parenthood

IHS: [Federal] Indian Health Services

IPPF: International Planned Parenthood Federation

IUD: intrauterine device

IUSSP: International Union for the Scientific Study of Population

JDR3: John D. Rockefeller 3rd

KAP: knowledge, attitude, practice [surveys]

MMF: Milbank Memorial Fund

MS: Margaret Sanger

MSP-LC: Margaret Sanger Papers, Library of Congress

MSP-SSC: Margaret Sanger Papers, Sophia Smith Collection

NCFLBC: National Committee for Federal Legislation on Birth Control

NCMH: National Committee on Maternal Health

NGO: non-governmental organization

NPG: negative population growth

NWHN: National Women's Health Network

PAA: Population Association of America

PAC: Population Action Committee

PBO: Planned Birth Office [in China]

PC: Population Council

PID: pelvic inflammatory disease

PPFA: Planned Parenthood Federation of America

PPLM: Planned Parenthood League of Massachusetts

PP-WP: Planned Parenthood-World Population

PRB: Population Research Bureau

PRI: Population Research Institute

RAC: Rockefeller Archive Center

RF: Rockefeller Foundation

RG: Record Group

RLD: Robert Latou Dickinson

RP: Raymond Pearl

SMBG: Sarah Merry (Bradley) Gamble

SSC: Sophia Smith Collection

SSSB: Society for the Study of Social Biology

UNFPA: United Nations Fund for Population Activities, now the United Nations Population Fund

USAID: United States Agency for International Development

WHO: World Health Organization

WPEC: World Population Emergency Campaign

ZPG: Zero Population Growth

APPENDIX 2

Chronology

Dates concerning the founding of the institutional predecessors of Planned Parenthood are in bold.

1879: Margaret Sanger (MS) is born Margaret Higgins in Corning, New York

1902: MS marries Bill Sanger

1914: MS founds the magazine *Woman Rebel* but flees to Europe a few months later when charged under the federal Comstock postal laws

1914–1915: MS lives in England studying with the Neo-Malthusians and visits Dutch birth-control clinics

1916: MS founds America's first birth-control clinic in Brownsville, New York, and is almost immediately arrested; Planned Parenthood understands the founding of this clinic to mark the beginning of its history, thereby identifying itself with the succession of organizations MS goes on to found

1921: MS founds the American Birth Control League (ABCL) and organizes the First American Birth Control Conference in New York; she divorces Bill Sanger; the Eugenics Society of the United States of America chartered

1922: MS marries millionaire James Henry Noah Slee and begins publishing the *Birth Control Review*

1923: MS opens the Birth Control Clinical Research Bureau (BCCRB) in New York City; the Eugenics Society of the U.S.A. changes name to the American Eugenics Society (AES)

1927: United States Supreme Court decision *Buck v. Bell* legitimizes state eugenic sterilization laws

256

1928: MS resigns as president of the ABCL

1929: MS resigns as publisher of the *Birth Control Review*; she founds the National Committee for Federal Legislation on Birth Control (NCFLBC)

1933: Merger between NCFLBC, ABCL, and the American Eugenics Society (to be named the Council on Population Policy) proposed and studied but does not occur; Harry Laughlin's Model Sterilization Law passed in Nazi Germany

1936: Second Circuit Court of Appeals ruling *United States v. One Package Containing 120, More or Less, Rubber Pessaries to Prevent Conception* allows the promotion and distribution of contraceptives under the Comstock laws; the NCFLBC disbands

1939: Sanger's old ABCL reunites with the BCCRB and forms the Birth Control Federation of America (BCFA); Sanger does not lead the BCFA

1942: BCFA changes name to the Planned Parenthood Federation of America (PPFA)

1948: MS founds the International Committee on Planned Parenthood (ICPP)

1952: John D. Rockefeller 3rd initiates the Population Council; ICPP changes name to the International Planned Parenthood Federation (IPPF)

1954: Hugh Moore publishes a pamphlet entitled "The Population Bomb"

1960: Enovid, the first birth-control pill, brought to market in the United States

1962: Alan F. Guttmacher assumes presidency of PPFA and holds it until his death

1966: MS dies

1967: United States Congress earmarks Title X money for population-control activities, to be spent by the United States Agency for International Development (USAID)

1969: United Nations Fund for Population Activities (UNFPA), later called the United Nations Population Fund, established

1971: Dalkon Shield IUDs sold in the United States

1973: United States Supreme Court *Roe v. Wade* decision legalizes abortion for all nine months of pregnancy (given the expansive definition of "health" in the companion case, *Doe v. Bolton*)—search-and-destroy eugenic abortions now possible; AES changes its name to the Society for the Study of Social Biology (SSSB)

1974: Guttmacher dies; Third World nations protest population-control activities at the World Population Conference organized by the U.N. in Bucharest; Dalkon Shield pulled from the market after numerous complaints; federal appellate court decision *Relf v. Weinberger* leads to more regulation of sterilization of Medicaid patients

1979: China launches its "one-child" population-control policy

1984: President Ronald Reagan institutes the "Mexico City Policy," which requires non-governmental organizations to abstain from performing or promoting abortion abroad, should they wish to receive federal funding; most Planned Parenthood organizations working abroad refuse U.S. funding

1985: Congress passes Kemp–Kasten Amendment, which denies federal funding to organizations that are involved in coercive population-control programs (including coerced abortion or sterilization); Reagan administration determines that UNFPA involvement in China's program disqualifies it from receiving funding

1986: IPPF begins promoting Norplant in Third World countries

1990: Norplant approved for use in the United States

1992: Depo-Provera approved for use in the United States

1993: President Bill Clinton rescinds the Mexico City Policy and reinstates funding for international Planned Parenthood organizations; his administration asserts that UNFPA is not directly involved in coercion under Kemp–Kasten and should be eligible for federal funding again

1994: International Conference on Population and Development organized by the U.N. in Cairo

2001: President George W. Bush reinstates Mexico City Policy

2002: Bush administration determines that UNFPA's involvement in China violates Kemp–Kasten and withholds federal funds

Chapter Notes

Introduction: Taking Sanger Seriously

1. Margaret Sanger (henceforth MS) to Vera Houghton, 5/10/55, Margaret Sanger Papers, Sophia Smith Collection (henceforth MSP-SSC), Smith College, Northampton, Massachusetts.

2. Germaine Greer, *The Whole Woman* (New York: Alfred A. Knopf, 1999), 114.

3. It is a truism of contemporary hermeneutics that facts are not self-interpreting and that there is no view from nowhere. This situatedness applies to the historian also. Therefore, on the one hand, the researcher has the obligation to ensure that his or her perspective does not obfuscate the matter at hand: there are truths to be discovered, else all is ideology. On the other hand, it must be acknowledged that this situatedness can be a strength, if it is attuned to the reality under investigation. My perspective is that of a feminist (that is, one with a special commitment to furthering justice for women), and I believe that this viewpoint is best able to pierce the ideologies that disguise the history of misogynistic oppression.

4. I do not intend, by criticizing Sanger, to place myself in the camp of someone like George Grant, whose writings on Sanger have allowed ideological zeal to lead him away from historical truth. For example, in his book *Grand Illusions* (Franklin, Tenn.: Highland Books, 1998), 75, he calls Sanger an anti–Semite, when there is no evidence for this claim and actually some counter-evidence, considering that her first husband, William Sanger, was Jewish!

5. I will support these claims in the remaining chapters; see especially chapter one (on Sanger's negative eugenics) and chapter six (on her support of the forced sterilization of some groups of people).

6. MS to Vera Houghton, 5/10/55, MSP-SSC.

7. I recognize that "control" is not a purely negative concept, especially in the case of "self-control" and other virtues. It will be made clear, however, that Sanger's advocacy of negative eugenics had little to do with these positive connotations and much more to do with forcible, violating, heteronomous control, that is, control used against women and other powerless persons for eugenic ends. Sanger herself complained that too often "self-control" was simply repression; see, for example, her presentation, redolent of a pansexual vitalism, of the sexual drive as an overwhelming brute force that cannot be controlled through abstinence in Margaret Sanger, "The Need for Birth Control in America," in *Birth Control: Facts and Responsibilities*, ed. Adolf Meyer, M.D. (Baltimore: Williams and Wilkins Co., 1925), 11–49, here 42.

8. However, I will take issue with many forms of birth control, namely, those that were developed for the purposes of population control and that are obviously harmful to women.

9. This ideology is succinctly voiced by a 1940s flyer from the Birth Control Federation of America: "MODERN LIFE IS BASED ON CONTROL AND SCIENCE. We control the speed of our automobile. We control machines. We endeavour to control disease and death. Let us control the size of our family to ensure health and happiness." Quoted in Linda Gordon, *Woman's Body, Woman's Right: Birth Control in America*, second ed. (New York: Penguin Books, 1990), 345.

10. Among the former, see most recently Edwin Black, *War Against the Weak: Eugenics and America's Campaign to Create a Master Race* (New York: Four Walls Eight Windows, 2003), especially 125–44. In the latter group, an important exception is Linda Gordon.

11. Donald T. Critchlow has basically the same criticisms that I do of Sanger scholarship. He notes, "By focusing on the social history of the birth-control movement and its rich legal history in the courts, scholars have tended to obscure the importance of eugenics in the movement" (Donald T. Critchlow, "Birth Control, Population Control, and Family Planning: An Overview," in *Politics of Abortion and Birth Control in Historical Perspective*, ed. Donald T. Critchlow [University Park: Pennsylvania State University Press, 1996], 5).

12. See, for example, Ellen Chesler, *Woman of Valor: Margaret Sanger and the Birth Control Movement in America* (New York: Simon & Schuster, 1992), 216–17.

13. James W. Reed, "The Birth Control Movement Before *Roe v. Wade*," in *Politics of Abortion and Birth Control in Historical Perspective*, 50.

14. In fact, Sanger's objection to positive eugenics was not enduring; on at least one occasion she advocated the increased fertility of the "fit," where she stated that among the ultimate objectives for her organization should be the desire "to raise the general level of intelligence of the nation's population" by encouraging "the increase of the birth rate where health, intelligence and favorable circumstances tend to promote desirable types or racial stock" ("Aims and Objectives," n.d. [1938?], MSP-SSC).

15. For the overlap between ABCL and AES board members, consult any issue of the *Birth Control Review* and *The Eugenics Review* in the 1920s.

16. This is Planned Parenthood's basic defense of its founder; see www.plannedparenthood.org.

17. A photo can be found in Chesler, 1992, figure 15.

18. See ibid., 300–3.

19. MS to Robert G. H. Tallman, 7/19/55, MSP-SSC.

20. MS to Frederick Osborn, 12/29/39, Planned Parenthood Federation of America Records (henceforth PPFA-SSC), Sophia Smith Collection, Smith College, Northampton, Massachusetts.

21. Carole R. McCann, *Birth Control Politics in the United States, 1916–1945* (Ithaca: Cornell University Press, 1994), 4, 19. McCann criticizes other historians of birth control for being focused on Sanger's "personality" and not sufficiently taking into account the "discursive horizons of her time." McCann has a confused notion of the nature of subjective agency in history; this mystification is necessary so that she may explain away the association of Sanger and the birth-control movement with eugenics. Among the historians McCann criticizes, she includes Linda Gordon and Ellen Chesler, framing her criticism this way: "Such a focus on Sanger tends to represent the development of the birth control movement as a consequence of Sanger's will as an autonomous individual, independent of the historical context in which she was situated" (4). I want to note how absurd is this criticism of Gordon and Chesler in particular. There are, to be sure, ideological weaknesses in both Gordon and Chesler (shared by McCann), especially the insistence on the centrality of sexual "liberation" to feminism, almost completely ignoring the phallocentric and misogynist nature of sexual "liberation" (though Gordon seems vaguely to recognize that something problematic is involved). But the works of Gordon and Chesler cited in this chapter are immensely rich historically, far more so than McCann's, and are indispensable for gaining historical insight into these periods of American history. The scholarly community owes a great debt to them.

22. See, for example, her treatment of Sanger's support of eugenic sterilization: "Sanger endorsed sterilization, *as did most of the nation*" (ibid., 117, italics mine).

23. Ibid., 16–18.

24. Margaret Sanger, "Birth Control and Racial Betterment," *Birth Control Review*, February, 1919, 11–12.

25. See the section on Osborn in the third chapter.

26. See Diane B. Paul, *The Politics of Heredity: Essays on Eugenics, Biomedicine, and the Nature-Nurture Debate,* ed. David Edward Shaner, Philosophy and Biology (Albany: SUNY Press, 1998), for essays on the variety of eugenic parties in America and England.

27. Margaret Sanger, "Hereditary Factor" (n.d.), Margaret Sanger papers, Library of Congress (henceforth MSP-LC), Washington, D.C., reel 131, cont. 203.

28. See, for example, McCann, n. 95, 127.

29. It is more generally acknowledged among feminist scholars, if not Planned Parenthood activists, that Sanger and many other early feminists were eugenicists (see many examples given in Angelique Richardson, "Biology and Feminism," *Critical Quarterly* 42 [3, 2000]: 35–63, and the detailed study in her *Love and Eugenics in the Late Nineteenth Century: Rational Reproduction and the New Woman* [New York: Oxford University Press, 2003]); indeed, a recent trend in feminist scholarship to which Carole McCann could be seen as belonging has attended to the eugenic narratives within early feminist thought and either critiqued or tried to make sense of early progressivist eugenic ideology. See Dana Seitler, "Unnatural Selection: Mothers, Eugenic Feminism, and Charlotte Perkins Gilman's Regeneration Narratives," *American Quarterly* 55 (March 2003), 61–88, for a summary of the scholarship and for an attempt to perform this task with regard to Gilman's fiction. In general, this scholarship assists our understanding of figures such as Sanger because it attempts to take them seriously, but its frequent refusal to critique the eugenic ideology of its subjects compromises its liberatory potential.

30. Sanger's many relationships, frequently with British bohemians, and the emotional romanticism that accompanied these entanglements are on frequent display throughout her letters.

31. Even before Sanger's activism, the wealthy tended to have fewer children than the poor. See Andrea Tone, *Devices and Desires: A History of Contraceptives in America* (New York: Hill and Wang, 2001) for a history of the contraceptive black market.

32. Sanger, "The Need for Birth Control in America," 13–14, italics hers. In this essay,

the meaning of "individual freedom" is obscure: freedom for what or for whom? The surrounding text gives a Neo-Malthusian reading of the increasing rationalization of eugenic control down through history, moving from the savage methods of infanticide to the civilized means of birth control, with an allusion to the uncontrollable "reproductive instinct" (14). Later statements refer to the sexual drive as "one of the strongest forces in Nature" (42). These hints, combined with the other preoccupations that come through in her writings as a whole, clarify that "freedom" means primarily the freedom to engage in sexual activity without having to have recourse to brutal eugenic controls.

33. Margaret Sanger, *Woman and the New Race* (New York: Blue Ribbon Books, 1920), 45.

34. McCann claims that Sanger was guided fundamentally by voluntarism (see McCann, 119), but this claim can be made only when one chooses to ignore the many passages in Sanger that put definite limits on the "freedom" being advocated. In the end, McCann does not take Sanger's own words sufficiently seriously.

35. Sanger, 1920, 4, 6.

36. Margaret Sanger, "The Need for Birth Control in America," 11–49.

37. Margaret Sanger, "Woman and War," *Birth Control Review,* June 1917, 5.

38. Margaret Sanger, *The Pivot of Civilization* (New York: Brentano's, 1922), 98.

39. Olive Byrne Richard with Jacqueline Van Voris, November 25, 1977, from "Transcript of an Interview with Olive Byrne Richard" (Sophia Smith Collection, Smith College, 1977), 7. Donald K. Pickens puts it succinctly when he says, "The world had a choice: Margaret Sanger wanted the choice to be birth control" (Donald K. Pickens, *Eugenics and the Progressives* [Vanderbilt: Vanderbilt University Press, 1968], 82).

40. Her niece, Olive Byrne Richard, noted that she was just "sort of patting little children on the head in passing.... I remember (strange that I should remember) she always burned the cocoa" (Richard with Van Voris, quoted in Chesler, 53).

41. MS to Frederick Osborn, 12/29/39, PPFA-SSC.

42. Richard Neuhaus, *In Defense of People: Ecology and the Seduction of Radicalism* (New York: The Macmillan Company, 1971), 189. On the links between racism and both

population control and eugenics, see Dorothy Roberts, *Killing the Black Body: Race, Reproduction, and the Meaning of Liberty* (New York: Pantheon Books, 1997).

43. I will primarily engage in historical analysis of Sanger's words and legacy, though an adequate historical analysis in this case must involve ideology critique. So, while there will be no *epoché* of theory in this book, explicit engagement with the theoretical debates of academic feminism remains outside the scope of this project.

44. Karl Barth, *Church Dogmatics*, vol. 3.4: *The Doctrine of Creation*, trans. G. W. Bromiley and T. F. Torrance (Edinburgh: T&T Clark, 2000), 424.

1. Woman and the New Race

1. Margaret Sanger, *Woman and the New Race* (New York: Blue Ribbon Books, 1920), 229.

2. Gisela Bock, "Racism and Sexism in Nazi Germany: Motherhood, Compulsory Sterilization, and the State," *Signs: Journal of Women in Culture and Society* 8, no. 3 (1983): 400–21, here 401.

3. See, for example, Amy Aronson, "Outrageous Acts and Bad, Bad Girls," *Ms.*, July/August 1998, 68–77, especially 75.

4. Gisela Bock, 1983; Gisela Bock, *Zwangssterilisation im Nationalsozialismus: Studien zur Rassenpolitik und Frauenpolitik*, Schriften des Zentralinstituts für sozialwissenschaftliche Forschung der Freien Universität Berlin, vol. 48 (Opladen: Westdeutscher Verlag, 1986).

5. As I pointed out in endnote 29 of the introduction, recent feminist scholarship has become less squeamish about pointing out and criticizing early feminism's eugenic commitment. In the case of Sanger, feminist disability scholarship has been more direct in addressing Sanger's reinscription of feminist thought within a eugenic discourse; as Licia Carlson observes, "Feminists such as Margaret Sanger ... exploited" so-called feebleminded women "for the advancement of their political agenda, and for the benefit of non-disabled women" ("Cognitive Ableism and Disability Studies: Feminist Reflections on the History of Mental Retardation," *Hypatia: A Journal of Feminist Philosophy* 16 [4, 2001]: 124–46).

6. Broadsheet (n.d.), MSP-SSC, (unfilmed), box 49, folder 1.

7. Margaret Sanger, *The Pivot of Civilization* (New York: Brentano's, 1922), 22.

8. Citizens Committee for Planned Parenthood, "The Quality of Life" (New York: Birth Control Federation of America, 1939), 33, MSP-SSC. In a speech entitled, "What Are People For? Population Versus People," Sir Julian Huxley told the Annual Luncheon of PPFA in 1959 that the population explosion presents an example of the necessity of "the passage of quantity into quality. Mere quantitative increase in human numbers is radically altering the quality of human life" (11/19/59, 1, PPFA-SSC). The Huxley example shows how the quality-vs.-quantity theme continued in Planned Parenthood after its founder had basically quit her active involvement, a fact that will be shown in more detail in the chapter on population control.

9. Stella Hanau to Raymond Pearl, 8/30/32, from Raymond Pearl papers (henceforth RP), American Philosophical Society Library, Philadelphia, Pennsylvania, "Margaret Sanger" folder. Likewise, Edna Rankin McKinnon, who worked for Sanger in Washington and for Sanger coworker and eugenicist Clarence Gamble in North Carolina, wrote a letter to the editor defending the American Birth Control League against accusations of atheism by saying: "No, the American Birth Control League has not and is not allied with atheistic movements or any movements other than health, eugenic and population groups" (Edna Rankin McKinnon to "Editor Nashville Journal," 12/10/38, MSP-SSC [unfilmed]).

10. Ellen Chesler, *Woman of Valor: Margaret Sanger and the Birth Control Movement in America* (New York: Simon & Schuster, 1992), 29.

11. Margaret Sanger, *An Autobiography* (Elmsford, New York: Maxwell Reprint Company, 1970), 29.

12. Chesler, 42.

13. I am much indebted to Chesler for the history of this period of Sanger's life: see ibid., 44–127.

14. Quoted in James Reed, *From Private Vice to Public Virtue: The Birth Control Movement and American Society Since 1830* (New York: Basic Books, 1978), 84.

15. Quoted in Chesler, 96.

16. See, for example, pages 1–8 of Sanger, *Woman and the New Race*.

17. See Chesler, 63. The Sachs incident is related in Sanger, 1970, 89–92, inter alia. Toward the beginning of the chapter of her 1938 autobiography in which the Sadie Sachs story is told, "The Turbid Ebb and Flow of Misery," Sanger honestly states her distaste for the poor, a standard component of the basic eugenic attitude: "I hated the wretchedness and hopelessness of the poor, and never experienced the satisfaction in working among them that so many noble women have found" (86–87). And describing the most impoverished stratum of the immigrant district, she writes, "The utmost depression came over me as I approached this surreptitious region. Below Fourteenth Street I seemed to be breathing a different air, to be in another world and country where the people had habits and customs alien to anything I had ever heard about" (88). No recognition here of the cultural and religious vitality of immigrant communities. With such an attitude, Sanger could not but draw a grotesque caricature of the poor that only the comfortable, especially the elite, could find plausible. (Unfortunately, there are too many, including Chesler [62], who indeed have read Sanger's account of tenement life without seeming to have any inkling how patently absurd it is.) For example, the destitute immigrant women of this district "seemed to slink on their way to market and were without neighborliness," and the men "were sullen and unskilled...." (87). Sanger has the men as shiftless and brutish and the women as desperate for abortion and contraception, seeming to know absolutely nothing about the way their bodies work. And there is not a little trading on the trope of the poor man's exceptional, and often inhuman, sexual rapacity (88). The caricature she draws is one specifically meant to convey, as in an allegory, the diagnosis that was gradually coming to her in this period of the fundamental cause of poverty: neither suffragism nor socialism nor syndicalism would get to the root cause. To her eyes, the problem was uncontrolled female fertility: "pregnancy was a chronic condition among the women of this class" (88).

18. Reed, 82–83; Chesler, 62–65.

19. Recently, Edwin Black takes the Sachs story at face value and argues that Sanger was moved by the incident to begin her crusade for women's health and rights (Edwin Black, *War Against the Weak: Eugenics and* *America's Campaign to Create a Master Race* [New York: Four Walls Eight Windows, 2003], 126). Like Gordon, Black clearly understands that Sanger is a eugenicist, but unlike Gordon he does not see an evolution from feminism to eugenics, rather he sees, correctly, that the two coexisted in Sanger. As a result, he has to wrestle with the question of how that is possible, and he resorts to observing that other feminists at Sanger's time held both positions (ibid., 127–28). Black's analysis would be helped at this point by an understanding of the degree to which feminism in general, and Sanger's feminism in particular, can be distorted by the ideology of control and thus made susceptible to eugenic deformation.

20. See, for example, Linda Gordon, *Woman's Body, Woman's Right: Birth Control in America*, second ed. [New York: Penguin Books, 1990], 120–122 and 274, for this argument that there was an earlier, reformist eugenics and then a later, conservative form. For Gordon's thesis of the "professionalization" of the birth-control movement, of a supposed shift from leftist concerns toward eugenics, note, for example, "Sanger, too, had always argued the 'racial' values of birth control, but as time progressed she gave less attention to feminist arguments and more to eugenic ones" (281).

21. Diane B. Paul, *Controlling Human Heredity: 1865 to the Present*, Atlantic Highlands, N.J.: Humanities Press, 1995, 44. Gordon does not even mention Weismann, seeming to link the rejection of Lamarckism solely with the rediscovery of Gregor Mendel's genetic research at the turn of the century (120–122). To be fair, when Gordon originally wrote her book, eugenic historiography had forgotten some of its insights into the appeal eugenics held for many on the left, an analysis of which could be found, for example, in Mark H. Haller, *Eugenics: Hereditarian Attitudes in American Thought* (New Brunswick, N.J.: Rutgers University Press, 1963) and Donald Pickens, *Eugenics and the Progressives* (Vanderbilt: Vanderbilt University Press, 1968). This insight into the connection between the left and eugenics has been brought back to light in, for example, Daniel J. Kevles, *In the Name of Eugenics: Genetics and the Uses of Human Heredity*, second ed. (Cambridge: Harvard University Press, 1985), as well as in the work cited above of Diane Paul's (91–96 are of particular relevance), as well

as in "Eugenics and the Left," *The Politics of Heredity: Essays on Eugenics, Biomedicine, and the Nature-Nurture Debate*, SUNY Series, Philosophy and Biology, ed. David Edward Shaner (Albany: SUNY Press, 1998), 11–36.

Paul is especially good on the pluralism of eugenics, carefully tracing the sometimes subtle, sometimes glaring variations of the eugenic ideology from one scientific camp to another, from one political group to another, from one country to another. She points out, for example, that though it is the case that utopians tended to find Lamarckism more congenial, assuming it to give greater latitude to reform initiatives by supposedly privileging environment over heredity, there were still Marxist scientists with enough integrity to resist capitulating to Lysenkoist obscurantism: "Weismann's doctrine of the continuity of the germ plasm, which by then was generally accepted by geneticists, was condemned as having racist and reactionary implications. But Marxist scientists who accepted Weismannism denied the charge that it would give comfort to enemies of the proletariat. A. S. Serebrovsky in the Soviet Union, H. J. Muller in the United States, and J. B. S. Haldane, a member of the Executive Committee of the Communist Party in Britain, followed [Alfred Russel] Wallace and advanced the counterclaim: not Weismannism but Lamarckism was reactionary, since it implied that working-class and colonial peoples, having lived in impoverished conditions, would now be genetically inferior to more powerful classes and nations" (44–45).

22. Paul, 1995, 92. The statement on the radicality of Goldman's pamphlet is to be found on Gordon, 220. Gordon wants to take the birth-control movement away from Sanger, whose eugenic commitment cannot be glossed over: instead, Goldman is the true initiator, and socialists were the indispensable movement personnel. Gordon correctly notes that it was socialist clubs and IWW locals that coalesced around Sanger after her *Woman Rebel* indictment, but there would have been nothing around which these other leftists could have coalesced without Sanger.

As Chesler correctly observes, Gordon and others believe "that Sanger saw birth control as a single issue early on and isolated herself from radical labor politics, but the facts substantially dispute this interpretation" (Chesler, 489). In chapter eight, we will look at the persistence of Goldman-inspired rhetoric, as inflected by Sanger's ideology of control, in Sanger's 1920 book, *Woman and the New Race*.

23. Gordon, 213.

24. *The Woman Rebel*, 1: 1 (March 1914), 1, 3, cited in Chesler, 98. Sanger describes her magazine as being dedicated to the interests of working women in her autobiography: Sanger, 1970, 106.

25. Sanger, 1970, 108. Chesler, 97, identifies the Sanger acquaintance who actually came up with the name.

26. *The Woman Rebel*, 1: 1 (March 1914), 1, 3, cited in Chesler, 98. The history of this period of Sanger's life is to be found in Chesler, 97–104.

27. Reed, 1978, 89.

28. Grant Sanger, M.D., interview with Ellen Chesler (henceforth Sanger and Chesler), Family Planning Oral History Project (M-138), August 1976, Schlesinger Library, Radcliffe Institute, 18.

29. Lyndsay Andrew Farrall, *The Origins and Growth of the English Eugenics Movement, 1865–1925* (New York: Garland Publishing, Inc., 1985), 220.

30. Havelock Ellis, "Birth Control in Relation to Morality and Eugenics," *Birth Control Review*, February 1919, 7–9, especially 8.

31. Ibid., 7.

32. Summarized in Kevles, 88.

33. Havelock Ellis, *Essays in War-Time: Further Studies in the Task of Social Hygiene* (Freeport: Books for Libraries Press, 1969), 241.

34. Ibid., 258, 274.

35. Ibid., 73.

36. The British Neo-Malthusians will be discussed in more detail in the fourth chapter on population control.

37. Neo-Malthusian League flier (n.d.), MSP-SSC (unfilmed).

38. National Committee, "Planned Parenthood U.S.A." pamphlet (1941?), MSP-SSC (unfilmed).

39. Chesler, 114.

40. Margaret Sanger, "The Need for Birth Control in America," in *Birth Control: Facts and Responsibilities*, ed. Adolf Meyer, M.D. (Baltimore: Williams and Wilkins Co., 1925), 11–49, here 44.

41. Ibid., 42. See also the sexology presented in *Woman and the New Race*, op. cit.

42. See Atina Grossmann, *Reforming Sex: The German Movement for Birth Control and Abortion Reform, 1920–1950* (New York: Oxford University Press, 1995) for Weimar, although she overstates the discontinuity between Weimar and the Nazi era.
43. Margaret Sanger, "Havelock Ellis— An Appreciation," *Birth Control Review,* February 1919, 6.
44. Reed, 94–96; Chesler, 112.
45. Sanger, 1970, 141. See also Sanger, 1970, 121–141 and Chesler, 112–125 for more details on Sanger's sojourn in England and her relationship with Ellis there.
46. Phyllis Grosskurth, *Havelock Ellis: A Biography* (New York: Alfred A. Knopf, 1980), 290.
47. Sanger, 1970, 189, 211–223.
48. Ibid., 224–30.
49. Ibid., 250.
50. Chesler, 244.
51. Ibid., 199–205.
52. Sanger, 1922, 279, 282.
53. American Birth Control League, "What We Stand For" pamphlet draft (1921?), MSP-SSC.
54. MS to anonymous, 4/12/23, MSP-SSC. Italics mine.
55. Ibid.
56. Middle Western States Birth Control Conference program, 1923, RP papers, "Margaret Sanger" folder.
57. Ibid., 3.
58. Chesler, 238.
59. "Certificate of Incorporation of National Committee on Federal Legislation for Birth Control, Inc.," 7/26/32, 1, MSP-SSC. Italics mine.
60. This kind of overlap between the causes of birth control, eugenics, abortion, sterilization and euthanasia was not unusual among progressives; other examples include Robert Latou Dickinson, Alan Guttmacher, Ruth Proskauer Smith, and Margaret Sanger herself. See Ian Dowbiggin, "'A Rational Coalition': Euthanasia, Eugenics, and Birth Control in America, 1940–1970," *Journal of Policy History* 14, no. 3 (2002): 223–60.
61. See "Francis Hand Ferguson," *The Complete Marquis Who's Who* (New York: Marquis Who's Who, 2003), accessed from the Biography Resource Center via the online resources of the Boston College library.
62. Frances Hand Ferguson, interview with James W. Reed (henceforth Ferguson and Reed), Family Planning Oral History

Project (M-138), June 1974, Schlesinger Library, Radcliffe Institute, 54.
63. Ibid., 58–59.
64. Chesler, 372–74.
65. Reminiscences of Mary Lasker, with John T. Mason, Jr., 1966, Columbia University Oral History Research Office, series I, vol. 3, 451.
66. See ibid., 392–95.
67. MS to Edna Rankin McKinnon, 3/29/49, Edna Bertha (Rankin) McKinnon papers (MC-325) (henceforth ERM), Schlesinger Library, Radcliffe Institute, Harvard University, box 6, folder 121.
68. "Minutes of the Executive Committee Meeting of the Birth Control Clinical Research Bureau," 10/13/38, 4, MSP-SSC.
69. Sanger, 1922, 12–13, 28, for example.
70. Quoted in Chesler, 393.
71. For this view as held by the Rockefellers, with religious overtones echoing "Manifest Destiny" rhetoric, see Albert F. Schenkel, *The Rich Man and the Kingdom: John D. Rockefeller, Jr., and the Protestant Establishment,* edited by B. J. Booten and F. S. Fiorenza, vol. 39, Harvard Theological Studies (Minneapolis: Fortress Press, 1995).
72. Chesler, 277; Dana S. Creel to John D. Rockefeller, Jr., 3/11/55, from RAC, Family Collection, RG 2 (Offices of the Messrs. Rockefeller), "Medical Interests," IPPF Subseries, box 5, folder 40. (John D. Rockefeller 3rd deliberately chose to write his name with Arabic, not Roman, numerals.) I will address in more detail the Rockefellers' eugenically motivated funding of population control in the fifth chapter.
73. Lawrence B. Dunham to Mr. Thomas M. Debevoise, 3/5/31, 1–2, from ibid., box 1, folder 1.
74. Leon F. Whitney to JDR, Jr., 1/28/25, 2, from RAC, Family Collection, RG2 (Offices of the Messrs. Rockefeller), "Cultural Interests," box 60, folder 599.
75. JDR, Jr., to Arthur Woods, 1/30/25, from ibid.
76. James W. Reed and Frances Hand Ferguson, "Schlesinger-Rockefeller Oral History Project, Frances Hand Ferguson, June 1974" (Radcliffe College, 1974), 30.
77. For an overview of Rockefeller funding of German eugenic research beginning in the 1920s, see Black, 279–308.
78. Stefan Kühl, *The Nazi Connection: Eugenics, American Racism, and German Socialism* (New York: Oxford University Press, 1994), 36.

79. Arthur W. Packard to JDR 3, 6/9/37, 2, from RAC, Family Collection, RG2 (Offices of the Messrs. Rockefeller), "Medical Interests," box 1, folder 1.

80. Arthur W. Packard to JDR, Jr., 3/13/47, from ibid., box 4, folder 32a.

81. Quoted in Reed, 1978, 109.

82. Grant Sanger with Jacqueline Van Voris, March 28, 1977, from "Transcript of an Interview with Grant Sanger" (Sophia Smith Collection, Smith College, 1977), 27.

83. Chesler, 225–26.

84. Gordon, 295.

85. Quoted in Farida Akhter, "The Eugenic and Racist Premise of Reproductive Rights and Population Control," *Issues in Reproductive and Genetic Engineering* 5, no. 1 (1992): 1–8, especially 8. The question of why a woman with a working-class background would develop such an antagonistic attitude to people of that same class is a vexed and important one, but finding an answer would require a more psychological and subjective approach to the historical data than I am interested in pursuing any further here.

86. Richard and Van Voris, 17.

87. Angela Y. Davis, *Women, Race, and Class* (New York: Vintage Books, 1983), 208.

88. Richard and Van Voris, 20.

89. See Gordon, 1990; Charles Valenza, "Was Margaret Sanger a Racist?" *Family Planning Perspectives* 17, no. 1 (1985): 44–46.

90. Black, 135.

91. See, however, endnote 14 from the introduction which cites some of her statements in support of positive eugenics.

92. Sanger also belonged to all the organizations that a good eugenic-minded progressive would join, as Ian Dowbiggin has masterfully shown, including pro-euthanasia organizations. See Dowbiggin, 2002. See also his "A Prey on Norman People: C. Killick Millard and the Euthanasia Movement in Great Britain, 1930–55," *Journal of Contemporary History* (36), no. 1 (2001): 59–85.

93. Chase, 2–3, 55, 72. See also Kenneth M. Ludmerer, *Genetics and American Society: A Historical Appraisal* (Baltimore: The Johns Hopkins University Press, 1972), 20–33.

94. L. J. Cole to MS, 1/15/24, 1, from MSP-LC, cont. 42, reel 28.

95. Soon after, Sanger devoted a whole issue of the *Birth Control Review* to the topic, stating, "Sterilization as well as Birth Control has its place as an aim of the Amer-ican Birth Control League" (Margaret Sanger, "Editorial," *Birth Control Review*, March 1928, 73).

96. For one historical analysis of eugenic racism, see Gregory Michael Dorr, "Assuring America's Place in the Sun: Ivey Foreman Lewis and the Teaching of Eugenics at the University of Virginia," *Journal of Southern History* 66, no. 2 (2000): 257–96.

97. This side includes feminist historians and thinkers such as Linda Gordon and Angela Y. Davis.

98. House Committee on Immigration and Naturalization, *Statement of Dr. Harry H. Laughlin*, 67th Congress, 3rd Session, November 21, 1922, 756, 725, quoted in Edwin Black, 191.

99. Black, 392–93. I am indebted to Diane Paul for an assessment of the extent of Laughlin's influence.

100. Ibid., 133–34; www.nyu.edu/projects/sanger/abcl.htm, accessed 12/18/03. This site lists most of the personnel and advisors connected to Sanger's organizations in their various incarnations.

101. Lothrop Stoddard, *The Rising Tide of Color Against White World Supremacy* (New York: Charles Scribner's Sons, 1926), 303, 306, quoted in Black, 133.

102. http://www.plannedparenthood.org/about/thisispp/sanger.html, accessed 12/20/03.

103. C. C. Little, D.Sc., "Natural Selection and Its Resulting Obligations," *Birth Control Review*, August 1926, 244.

104. Her 1938 proposal for the controversial "Negro Project" says provocatively, "The mass of Negroes, particularly in the South, still breed carelessly and disastrously, with the result that the increase among Negroes, even more than among whites, is from that portion of the population least intelligent and fit, and least able to rear children properly" ("Negro Project" proposal, 1938, MSP-SSC). Yet this sentence is a quote from a 1932 *Birth Control Review* article by black leader W. E. B. du Bois (W. E. B. du Bois, "Black Folk and Birth Control," *Birth Control Review*, vol. 22, no. 8 [May 1938]: 90).

105. MS to Clarence Gamble, 12/10/39, MSP-SSC.

106. MS to Gamble, 2/4/40, MSP-SSC.

107. MS to Gamble, 11/26/39, MSP-SSC.

108. Margaret Sanger, 1920, 27–28.

109. Black, 135. Black does not manage

to integrate recognition of Sanger's eugenics with what he perceives as a high-minded pursuit of women's liberation. He does not question the veracity of the Sachs story, for example, nor does he question what the story symbolizes: the primacy of women's health as Sanger's motivation (see 126–27). He argues convincingly *that* she is a eugenicist but does not present clearly *how* this fits into her total ideology, in which birth control plays a necessary role as a means of controlling female fertility and only secondarily as an instrument for promoting women's health. He leaves us with a study in unresolved contrasts.

110. Cited in Simone M. Caron, "Birth Control and the Black Community in the 1960s: Genocide or Power Politics?" *Journal of Social History* 31 (March 22, 1998): 545–70, here 551.

111. Grossmann, 154.

112. Report by Monika Simmel-Joachim and Elke Kiltz to the National Board of Pro Familia, May 16, 1984, quoted and translated in Grossmann, 211.

113. Ibid., 204.

114. Ibid., 210–11.

115. *Pro Familia Informationen* (internal section of *Sexualpädogik und Familienplannung*), June 1984, 21, quoted and translated in Grossmann, 211.

116. Sanger, 1922, 174–175.

117. Margaret Sanger, "An Answer to Mr. Roosevelt," *Birth Control Review*, December 1917, 12–14. It is true that she goes on to state a criticism of "eugenics," but only positive eugenics.

118. Sanger, 1970, 374–75.

119. Chesler, 1976, 17; Sanger, 1920, 229.

120. Margaret Sanger, "Mrs. Sanger's Nine Reasons Children Should Not Be Born," *Birth Control Review*, December 1924, 346.

121. Sanger, 1922, 274.

122. "Margaret Sanger Scores Crime Conference: Shows Definite Connection Between Birth Control and Crime," press release, 1953, MSP-SSC, reel 64.

123. Margaret Sanger, "A Program of Contraceptive Research," 6/5/28, 10, MSP-SSC.

124. Sanger, 1922, 25.

125. Ibid., 25, 98.

126. James W. Reed, 1974, 51, 52.

127. Margaret Sanger, "The Eugenic Value of Birth Control Propaganda," *Birth Control Review*, October 1921, 5.

128. Margaret Sanger, "The Need for Birth Control in America," in *Birth Control: Facts and Responsibilities*, ed. Adolf Meyer, M.D. (Baltimore: Williams and Wilkins Co., 1925), 11–49, here 48.

129. Margaret Sanger, "Is Race Suicide Probable?" *Collier's* 1925, 25.

130. Margaret Sanger, "Opening Remarks," the International Congress on Population and World Resources in Relation to the Family, at Cheltenham, England, 1948, 19–20, MSP-SSC (unfilmed), unprocessed papers, Acc. #98S-9 (Suhey collection).

131. Found on www.plannedparenthood.org/about/thisispp/sanger.html, accessed 9/97.

132. Kevles, 62. See also the comparison to stock breeders raising thoroughbreds by a Southern eugenicist in Edward J. Larson, *Sex, Race, and Science: Eugenics in the Deep South* (Baltimore: The Johns Hopkins University Press, 1995), 2.

133. Margaret Sanger, "We Must Build a Race of Thoroughbreds," unpublished manuscript, 1929, MSP-LC, cont. 131, reel 203.

134. Margaret Sanger, "Birth Control and Racial Betterment," *Birth Control Review*, February 1919, 11–12.

135. Ibid.

136. Ibid.

137. "Minutes of the Executive Committee Meeting of the Birth Control Clinical Research Bureau," 10/13/38, 4, MSP-SSC; see also National Committee for Planned Parenthood, BCFA, "A Practical Course of Action for Race Development in the United States through Promotion and Control of Its Population," n.d. (early 1940s?): "These and kindred educational services should also contribute much to further greater reproduction among the mentally and physically sound, the economically capable and the socially minded."

138. Margaret Sanger, "Aims and Objectives," memo, n.d. (1938?), 2, MSP-SSC.

139. National Committee for Planned Parenthood, "Still the Most Important Thing in the World" (New York: Birth Control Federation of America, 1941), 9, MSP-SSC (unfilmed).

140. Citizens Committee for Planned Parenthood, "The Quality of Life" (New York: Birth Control Federation of America, 1939), 20, MSP-SSC (unfilmed).

141. National Committee for Planned Parenthood, "We Believe…" (New York:

Birth Control Federation of America, 1941), 2, MSP-SSC (unfilmed).

142. Ibid.

143. Alan Valentine, "Address," 5/8/52, 2, PPFA-SSC. Valentine also cited colonialist reasons to suppress the reproduction of the rest of the world: "More than we realize, we Americans are only a minority in the world population. The traditions we cherish, the concepts we hold most dear, are little known and little valued in many other areas of the world. That minority which is our Western population is shrinking in proportion to the increases in human life elsewhere; that minority which is our Western civilization has lost ground all over the world in the last decade" (ibid., 2–3).

144. Ibid., 6.

145. MS to Clarence Gamble, 4/5/40, Clarence J. Gamble Papers (H MS c23) (hereafter CJG), Harvard Medical Library in the Countway Library of Medicine, Boston, Massachusetts, box 195, folder 3090.

146. See the section in the third chapter on C. P. Blacker, the leader of both the birth-control and the eugenics movements in England.

147. American Committee of the International Congress on Population and World Resources in Relation to the Family, "U.S. Experts on Population Problems Sail Today for Congress in England," press release, 1948, MSP-SSC (unfilmed), unprocessed papers, Acc. #98S-9 (Suhey collection).

148. Chesler, 407–10. For more on Dorothy Brush's eugenic commitments, see chapter three.

149. C. P. Blacker, "Proposed Formation of a British Advisory Committee," International Committee on Planned Parenthood, 1952, 1, from MSP-SSC (unfilmed).

150. Harriet Pilpel and T. O. Griessemer, "Redraft of Constitution of the International Planned Parenthood Federation," 12/8/53, 2, MSP-SSC.

151. See "Draft Constitution of the International Planned Parenthood Federation" (n.d.; 1/53?), 1, MSP-SSC; Beryl Suitters, *Be Brave and Angry: Chronicles of the International Planned Parenthood Federation* (London: International Planned Parenthood Federation, 1973).

152. MS to C. P. Blacker, 5/5/53, Wellcome Institute, London, Box 112, quoted in Black, 144.

153. *Medical News Letter* no. 3, Sept. 1961, 4, MSP-SSC.

154. Chesler, 417.

155. "Address by Margaret Sanger," 10/25/50, 3, MSP-LC, cont. 201, reel 130.

156. Ibid., 5–6.

157. Ibid., 5. See Sanger, 1922, 105–23 (her chapter on "The Cruelty of Charity") for more on her dislike of private and governmental spending programs on behalf of the poor.

158. Ibid., 6.

159. Chesler, 417–18.

160. Ibid., 457–58.

161. This connection will be examined in the fifth chapter.

162. Quoted in Donald T. Critchlow, *Intended Consequences: Birth Control, Abortion, and the Federal Government in Modern America* (New York: Oxford University Press, 1999), 19.

163. Medical and Scientific Committee of the Human Betterment Association of America, Inc., "To Protect the Adolescent Retarded" (New York: Human Betterment Association of America, 1960).

164. Ferguson and Reed, 37.

165. Ibid., 39.

166. Ruth Proskauer Smith, "Annual Business Meeting, 11/1/57, Report of the Executive Director," from CJG papers, box 231, folder 3565.

167. Alan F. Guttmacher, M.D., *Babies By Choice or By Chance* (Garden City: Doubleday and Company, 1959), 138.

168. Alan F. Guttmacher, "General Remarks on Medical Aspects of Male and Female Sterilization," in *Eugenic Sterilization,* ed. Jonas Robitscher (Springfield, Ill.: Charles C. Thomas, 1973), 52–60, especially 54.

169. Alan F. Guttmacher, M.D., "The Population Crisis and the Use of World Resources," in *The Population Crisis and the Use of World Resources,* ed. Stuart Mudd, World Academy of Art and Science (Bloomington: Indiana University Press, 1964), 268–273, especially 269, 270.

170. Alan F. Guttmacher, M.D., "Heredity Counseling: Diabetes, Pregnancy and Modern Medicine, A Genetic Misadventure," *Eugenics Quarterly,* September 1954, 191–192.

171. Guttmacher, 1964, 273.

172. Mrs. Alan F. Guttmacher, interview with James W. Reed (henceforth Guttmacher and Reed), Family Planning Oral History Project (M-138), November 1974, Schlesinger Library, Radcliffe Institute, 2.

173. Alan F. Guttmacher, M.D., "The Contraceptive Clinic and Preventive Medicine," Annual Meeting of the Birth Control Federation of America, New York, 1942, 7, MSP-SSC (unfilmed).

174. Alan F. Guttmacher, M.D., "Planned Parenthood/World Population/Annual Report 1963" (New York: Planned Parenthood Federation of America, 1963), 19.

175. Alan F. Guttmacher, M.D., "The Pill or the IUD?" *President's Letter*, January 26, 1965, 2–3.

176. Quoted in Andrea Tone, *Devices and Desires: A History of Contraceptives in America* (New York: Hill and Wang), 2001, 271.

177. David Dempsey, "The Fertility Goddess vs. the Loop: Dr. Guttmacher Is the Evangelist of Birth Control," *New York Times Magazine*, February 9, 1969, 32–40.

178. Guttmacher, 1959, 161–62.

179. Quoted in Barbara Seaman, *The Doctors' Case Against the Pill*, second ed. (Alameda: Hunter House, 1995), 24.

180. Quoted in ibid., 25.

181. Guttmacher, 1959, 182.

182. Guttmacher and Reed, 11.

183. Dempsey, 84.

184. Ibid.

185. "Compulsory Population Control Foreseen," *Medical World News*, June 6, 1969, 11.

186. Guttmacher to Osborn, 9/25/61, Frederick Osborn papers (henceforth FO), American Philosophical Society Library, Philadelphia, Pennsylvania, Guttmacher folder.

187. For example, PPFA celebrated its 75th anniversary in 1991, dating from the founding of the Brownsville clinic.

188. A case *could* be made for John D. Rockefeller 3rd, but it seems clear to me that Sanger's reach was far greater.

189. Nevertheless, PPFA continues to sanitize its founder's views through misleadingly selective quotation, an activity that would infuriate her. They do not, however, deny the most obvious of her eugenic views. See, for example, http://www.plannedparenthood.org/about/thisisppl/sanger.html, accessed 12/20/03.

190. Planned Parenthood Federation of America, Inc., "PPFA Issues Manual" (New York: Planned Parenthood Federation of America, Inc., 1986), 12.7.

191. Ibid.

192. International Planned Parenthood

Federation, "Planned Parenthood — a Duty and a Human Right," in *Proceedings of the Eighth International Conference of the International Planned Parenthood Federation*, ed. R. K. B. Hankinson, R. L. Kleinman, and Peter Eckstein (Santiago, Chile: International Planned Parenthood Federation, 1967), 238.

193. "Ethical Implications of New Technology for Reproductive Health Care," in *Planned Parenthood Federation of America*, conference in Los Angeles, tape transcript (1983), 28.

194. Ibid., 44.

195. Ibid., 51.

196. "PPFA Issues Manual," 3.24.

197. Steven A. Holmes, "Abortion Issue Divides Advocates for Disabled," *New York Times*, July 4, 1991, A11.

198. Gerard E. Sherry, "Lawsuit Questions Pasadena/Planned Parenthood Pact," *Our Sunday Visitor*, April 11, 1982, 10.

199. Family Planning Advocates of New York State, Inc., et al., "Spending to Save: A Special Budget Strategy for 1983" (New York City: 1983), 6–7.

200. Ibid., 14–15.

201. From PPFA's website, www.plannedparenthood.org/library/TEEN-PREGNANCY/Reducing.html, accessed 11/18/03. The web site cites a study by Patricia Donovan of the Alan Guttmacher Institute, formerly the research arm of PPFA.

202. Jacqueline Kasun, *The War Against Population: The Economics and Ideology of World Population Control*, second edition (San Francisco: Ignatius Press, 1999).

203. As with any libertarian ideology, what is at stake is the "freedom" of the powerful to live exploitative lifestyles. The possibility that a "choice," viewed critically in light of its total context, including the social forces involved, might in fact be a matter of propagandistic programming is dismissed by libertarians, because it is exactly their interests that are served by the status quo.

204. Ad for Planned Parenthood of Minnesota/South Dakota, *Burnesville/Lakeville Sun-Current*, 10/16/96; 18A.

205. See Carol Iannone, "Opinion: Legitimate Mothers," *First Things* 55, August/September (1995): 11–17.

206. Germaine Greer, *Sex and Destiny: The Politics of Human Fertility* (New York: Harper & Row, 1984).

207. "PPFA Issues Manual," 13.2.

208. It is a hallmark of the processes of ideological mystification to leave aside questions of why something is so, to fail to critically uncover the genealogy of a given fact. PPFA officials, in obfuscating Sanger's eugenic past, succumb to the illusion that only the outcome of Sanger's activity matters, while I would like to argue that one cannot correctly assess an outcome without understanding its genealogy through critical historical research. It does not occur to them that things could and perhaps should be otherwise, given that Sanger's approach was an ideological deformation of feminism.

2. Eugenics as the Control of Births

1. Margaret Sanger, "The Eugenic Value of Birth Control Propaganda," *Birth Control Review* 5, no. 10 (Oct. 1921): 5.

2. Frederick Osborn, "Notes on 'Paradigms or Public Relations: The Case of Social Biology,'" 2, 1/25/74, from FO papers, Notes on "Paradigms" folder. Many thanks to Diane Paul for providing this important reference and to APSL archivist Scott Dehaven for tracking down the text.

3. For example, Edwin Black's excellent *War Against the Weak: Eugenics and America's Campaign to Create a Master Race* (New York: Four Walls Eight Windows, 2003), which devotes a chapter (125–44) to Sanger. Yet he sees her primarily as a tragic example of eugenics perverting an otherwise noble cause. I think, instead, that Sanger's role on the eugenic stage is less that of a victim of an intellectual fashion and more that of a protagonist propelling the plot.

4. See chapter one for her statements in the 1930s accepting some kind of positive eugenics.

5. Diane B. Paul, *The Politics of Heredity: Essays on Eugenics, Biomedicine, and the Nature-Nurture Debate*, ed. David Edward Shaner, SUNY Series, Philosophy and Biology (Albany: SUNY Press, 1998), 95–115.

6. Although I am indebted to Paul's analysis, which has assisted greatly in clarifying my own thoughts, I do not share her skepticism about the possibility of providing at least a heuristic definition of eugenics in the hope of preventing abuses today. A comprehensive definition might well be incapable of doing justice to the heterogeneity of the movement, yet surely a beginning can be made in tracing out the main lines of an ideology that joined together the various self-described practitioners of eugenics in an identifiable movement with a high degree of cohesiveness, despite disagreement over emphases and political strategies. Eugenicists believed they were talking about a concept with meaning when they used the word "eugenics"; the task of the historian is to unearth what that meaning is.

7. This way of framing the question prescinds from a deeper analysis of the "neutrality" involved: does the proclamation of "choice" mean that the choices made are necessarily made without any external and perhaps unconscious pressure? I will examine these issues later in this chapter.

8. Daniel J. Kevles, *In the Name of Eugenics: Genetics and the Uses of Human Heredity*, second ed. (Cambridge: Harvard University Press, 1995), 291–301. See also his "Eugenics and Human Rights," *British Medical Journal* 319, no. 7207 (1999): 435–38.

9. Quoted in Paul, 1998, 124.

10. Barbara Katz Rothman, "From the SWS President: A Sociological Skeptic in the Brave New World," *Gender and Society* 12, no. 5 (October 1998): 501–4, here 501.

11. Ludmerer recognizes the commitment of geneticists to eugenics, estimating as many as half of the geneticists during the early part of the twentieth century were eugenicists, yet he still tends (somewhat inconsistently) to maintain the scientific naïveté of the movement; see Kenneth M. Ludmerer, *Genetics and American Society: A Historical Appraisal* (Baltimore: The Johns Hopkins University Press, 1972), 34–43.

12. A glaring exception to the movement's scientific respectability is the highly idiosyncratic and bias-laden work of the eugenic fieldworkers, as will be discussed below.

13. This is not to say that eugenics can be scientifically legitimated. Opposition to eugenics must include non-ideological presentation of the scientific facts. For example, intelligence is a far more complex phenomenon than eugenicists and genetic determinists are willing to allow. I only ob-

ject to relying *primarily* upon scientific argumentation in combating eugenics. Without an ethical orientation, scientific research is easily compromised by ideology, blocking access to the truth of the phenomenon under study.

14. Mark H. Haller, *Eugenics: Hereditarian Attitudes in American Thought* (New Brunswick, New Jersey: Rutgers University Press, 1963), 3.

15. Kevles has observed that eugenics was supported primarily by people who were "largely middle to upper middle class, white, Anglo-Saxon, predominately Protestant, and educated" (Kevles, 1995, 64). Support for eugenics crossed political lines, however, with advocates professing anything from conservatism to progressivism to Marxism. Eugenicists' class makeup, however, remained fairly uniform: understandably, eugenics never drew many adherents from poorer classes. For details on Galton's life, see Nicholas Wright Gillham, *A Life of Sir Francis Galton: From African Exploration to the Birth of Eugenics* (New York: Oxford University Press, 2001).

16. See Haller, 17.

17. Edward J. Larson, *Sex, Race, and Science: Eugenics in the Deep South* (Baltimore: The Johns Hopkins University Press, 1995), 18–19. For other biographical sketches of Galton and the early English eugenics movement, see also Paul, 1995; Kevles, 1995; and Haller.

18. Larson, 20–21; Haller, 77–78.

19. Kevles, 1995, 85, 221.

20. For a genealogy of the notion of "the unfit," see Elof Axel Carlson, *The Unfit: A History of a Bad Idea* (Cold Spring Harbor, N.Y.: Cold Spring Harbor Laboratory Press, 2001).

21. Kevles, 1995, 47.

22. Ibid., 51.

23. Diane B. Paul, *Controlling Human Heredity: 1865 to the Present*, ed. Margaret C. Jacob and Spencer R. Weart, The Control of Nature Series (Atlantic Highlands, New Jersey: Humanities Press International, 1995); Paul, 1998; see also Donald K. Pickens, *Eugenics and the Progressives* (Vanderbilt: Vanderbilt University Press, 1968).

24. Kevles, 1995, 101–7. See also Larson, 21–30. For the particular case of laws mandating eugenic sterilization, see chapter six.

25. Larson, 21–39.

26. Paul Popenoe and Roswell Johnson, *Applied Eugenics*, ed. Richard T. Ely, second ed., Social Science Textbooks (New York: Macmillan Company, 1933), 135.

27. Ibid., 136.

28. See ibid., 146–48.

29. Quoted in Haller, 65. For a contemporary parallel, see former *Science* editor Daniel Koshland's 1989 comment concerning the need to deal with homelessness by dealing with their genes, discussed on p. 84.

30. This pattern of wealthy patronage, as chapter five will show, held good also for the funding of the population-control movement, in both its scientific and institutional aspects.

31. Kevles, 1995, 54–55.

32. Paul, 1995, 10. The fifth chapter on population will show that the Rockefellers' contribution to eugenics did not end with their funding of the ERO.

33. Quoted in Kevles, 1995, 56. For more on Davenport and the ERO, see Garland E. Allen, "The Eugenics Record Office at Cold Springs Harbor, 1910–1940: An Essay in Institutional History" [reprinted as "Eugenics Comes to America"], in *The Bell Curve Debate: History, Documents, Opinions*, ed. Russell Jacoby; Naomi Glauberman (New York: Times Books, 1995), 441–75.

34. See, among others, the descriptions of the shoddiness of eugenic fieldwork in Paul, 1995, 50–61.

35. Kevles, 1995, 56.

36. Leon J. Kamin, "The Pioneers of IQ Testing," in *The Bell Curve Debate*, op. cit., 476–509, excerpted from Leon J. Kamin, *The Science and Politics of I.Q. Testing* (Potomac, Md.: Lawrence Erlbaum Associates, 1974).

37. Chase, 1980, 245.

38. Margaret Sanger, *The Pivot of Civilization* (New York: Brentano's, 1922), 175.

39. Ludmerer, 53–54. Ludmerer notes that Davenport's objections to birth control put him in the minority among eugenicists.

40. MS to Charles B. Davenport, 2/11/25, Charles Benedict Davenport papers (henceforth CBD), American Philosophical Society Library, Philadelphia, Pennsylvania, "Margaret Sanger" folder.

41. MS to Charles B. Davenport, 3/13/25 and 3/24/25; Davenport to MS, 3/26/25, ibid.

42. Margaret Sanger, "The Eugenic Value of Birth Control Propaganda," *Birth Control Review*, October 1921, 5.

43. Henry Pratt Fairchild, reprint from *The Living Age* (March 1940), 3, MSP-SSC (unfilmed).

44. Quoted in Linda Gordon, "The Politics of Population: Birth Control and the Eugenics Movement," *Radical America* 8, no. 4 (1974): 79.

45. American Eugenics Society, "Organized Eugenics" (New Haven: American Eugenics Society, 1930), 22, 31, MSP-SSC (unfilmed).

46. "BCFA, Inc" memo, 5/20/41, 1, from RAC, Family Collection, RG 2 (Offices of the Messrs. Rockefeller), Series "Medical," box 4, folder 30.

47. H. Curtis Wood, Jr., to John D. Rockefeller 3rd, 5/15/56, from ibid., box 4, folder 26.

48. See Licia Carlson, "Cognitive Ableism and Disability Studies: Feminist Reflections on the History of Mental Retardation," *Hypatia* 16, no. 4 (October 31, 2001): 124–146, for a philosophical/historical reflection on the role of women in the eugenics movement. She draws an interesting correlation (based on Rayna Rapp's work) between female eugenic fieldworkers of the early twentieth century and the preponderance of women in genetic counseling today.

49. See ibid., 71–79.

50. Paul, 1995, 54–57.

51. Josephine Donovan, *Feminist Theory: The Intellectual Traditions of American Feminism* (New York: Frederick Ungar Publishing Co., 1985), 31–64.

52. Linda Gordon, *Woman's Body, Woman's Right: Birth Control in America*, second ed. (New York: Penguin Books, 1990).

53. Originally named the Eugenic Society of the United States of America, it was incorporated as the AES in 1926 (Philip R. Reilly, *The Surgical Solution: A History of Involuntary Sterilization in the United States* [Baltimore: The Johns Hopkins University Press, 1991], 76).

54. Ibid., 76–77.

55. "American Birth Control League Minutes," 3/16/28, 2, MSP-SSC, reel 61.

56. Reilly, 77. See also Philip K. Wilson, "Harry Laughlin's Eugenic Crusade to Control the 'Socially Inadequate' in Progressive Era America," *Patterns of Prejudice* 36, no. 1 (2002), 49–67.

57. Barry Alan Mehler, "A History of the American Eugenics Society, 1921–40" (dissertation [University of Illinois at Urbana-Champaign], 1988), 82–83.

58. Frederick Osborn, "History of the American Eugenics Society," *Social Biology* 21, no. 2 (1974): 117.

59. Mehler, 110; Reilly, 76–79; and Leon Whitney, *Autobiography* (American Philosophical Society Library collections, n.d.), 219–20. See the next chapter for Osborn's role within the eugenics and birth-control movements.

60. Kevles, 1995, 69.

61. Chase, 1980, 351–52. For the eugenicists who participated in Sanger's organizations, see the mastheads of the *Eugenics News* and the Smith College Collection reel guide (www.upapubs.com/guides/sanger.htm).

62. American Eugenics Society, Inc., "Five-Year Report of the Officers: 1953–1957" (New York: The American Eugenics Society, Inc., 1958), 2, MSP-SSC (unfilmed).

63. Mehler, 97.

64. Henry Pratt Fairchild, *People: The Quantity and Quality of Population* (New York: Henry Holt and Company, 1939).

65. For more on the connection between eugenics and population control, see the fourth and fifth chapters.

66. Mehler, 339–40.

67. Note, 5/32, MSP-LC, cont. 33, reel 22; AES Board Meeting minutes, 1/9/35, MSP-LC, cont. 63, reel 44.

68. MS to Leon Whitney, 1/29/31, MSP-LC, ibid.

69. See, for example, the membership letters from the AES to MS in MSP-LC and MSP-SSC, through 1963; e.g., Frederick Osborn to MS, 2/16/55, MSP-SSC.

70. See Ludmerer, 87–113. Laughlin's motivation was in part racist: he wrote that America had to "keep the nation's blood pure by not marrying the colored races (Negroes and Southern Europeans)...." Quoted in Dorothy Roberts, *Killing the Black Body: Race, Reproduction, and the Meaning of Liberty* (New York: Pantheon, 1997), 72.

71. Paul, 1995, 72. The sixth chapter will examine in more detail the passage of sterilization laws, which represented the most important legislative victory (along with immigration legislation) for the organized eugenics movement.

72. For the AES's activities, especially concerning public education and propaganda, see Steven Selden, *Inheriting Shame: The Story of Eugenics and Racism in America*, ed. Jonas F. Soltis, Advances in Contemporary Educational Thought Series

(New York: Teachers College Press, 1999); Osborn, 1974, 118.

73. Gordon, 1990, 303–29.

74. Edgar Sydenstricker and G. St. J. Perrott, "Sickness, Unemployment and Differential Fertility," given at the American Conference on Birth Control and National Recovery, 1/17/34, 7, MSP-SSC (unfilmed).

75. Ibid. It should be noted that Sanger never worked as a professional social worker.

76. Arthur W. Packard to files, 4/16/40, RAC, Family, Medical Series, RG 2, box 4, folder 28.

77. Quoted in Ellen Chesler, *Woman of Valor: Margaret Sanger and the Birth Control Movement in America* (New York: Simon & Schuster, 1992), 343.

78. Guy Irving Burch, "Population Policy Vital to National Defense," n.d. (1943?), MSP-SSC (unfilmed).

79. Gordon, 1974, 95.

80. Speech, D. Kenneth Rose, 1/28/42, 4, MSP-SSC (unfilmed).

81. Ibid., 2.

82. Ibid., 5.

83. See Haller, 73.

84. Congressman Robert Allen, Democrat from West Virginia; quoted in Kevles, 1995, 97. For a discussion of eugenics and racism, see also Haller, 144–59.

85. See the more extensive discussion in the previous chapter.

86. Haller, 163–67; Kevles, 1995, 258–64.

87. Margaret Sanger, ed. *Proceedings of the World Population Conference* (London: Edward Arnold & Co., 1927). Sanger's involvement in promoting eugenic population control will be examined in detail in the fifth chapter.

88. See Kevles, 1995, 164–75; Haller, 183–84.

89. Mehler, 30.

90. Paul, 1998, 135; also Evelyn Fox Keller, "Nature, Nurture, and the Human Genome Project," in *The Code of Codes: Scientific and Social Issues in the Human Genome Project*, ed. Daniel J. Kevles and Leroy Hood (Cambridge: Harvard University Press, 1992), 280–99. See also Selden, 1999, 63–83, which analyzes the persistence of eugenic ideas in textbooks through the 1940s. The continuation of eugenic beliefs among prominent geneticists continued even in post-war Germany after the Nuremberg trials (Paul Weindling, "The Survival of Eugenics in 20th-Century Ger-

many," *American Journal of Human Genetics*, 52, no. 3 [1993]: 643–49), *pace* Kevles and others.

91. Ibid.; Haller, 183–84.

92. Sanger, *Pivot of Civilization*, 1922, 177.

93. Henry Pratt Fairchild, reprint from *The Living Age*, op. cit., 3. See also the PPFA press release, 1/27/44, MSP-SSC (unfilmed), regarding Fairchild's speech to PPFA entitled "Is Overpopulation a Threat to Permanent Peace?" in which he argues that the major problems confronting the world were due to overpopulation.

94. Alan Valentine, "Speech delivered at the Annual Dinner," 1/28/42, 1, MSP-SSC (unfilmed).

95. Ibid., 2. Ten years later, Valentine returned to the topic at PPFA's annual meeting ("Address" by Alan Valentine, Thirty-Second Annual Meeting Luncheon of the PPFA, 5/8/52, 2, PPFA-SSC).

96. Citizens Committee for Planned Parenthood, "The Quality of Life" (New York: Birth Control Federation of America, 1939), 20, MSP-SSC (unfilmed).

97. See the discussion in the previous chapter.

98. See Hannah M. Stone, "The Birth Control Clinic of Today and Tomorrow," *Eugenics* 1929, 9–11; and "The Birth Control Raid," *Eugenics* 2, no. 8 (1929): 24–27; Abraham Stone, "Hereditary Counseling: Eugenic Aspects of the Premarital Consultation," *Eugenics Quarterly*, March 1955, 51–52.

99. Paul, 1995, 124.

100. Richard Lynn, *Dysgenics: Genetic Deterioration in Modern Populations* (Westport: Praeger Publishers, 1996), 15.

101. Kevles, 1995, 120–29.

102. Allan Chase, quoted in Mehler, 112.

103. Ibid., 81–128; 244.

104. Ibid., 126.

105. Frederick Osborn, "Notes on 'Paradigms or Public Relations: The Case of Social Biology,'" 2, op. cit.

106. Kevles, 1995, 260. It should be remembered that "reform eugenicists" included such people as Osborn and C. P. Blacker, who opposed the more simple-minded, non-scientific brand of eugenics promoted by popularizers like Lothrop Stoddard and Harry Laughlin. For an analysis of Muller's communism, which did not hesitate to praise Stalin, see Paul, 1995, 117–20.

107. Ibid., 259–64. For Muller's explicit support of eugenics, which he was trying to rescue from Nazi-connected disrepute already by 1961, see "Human Evolution by Voluntary Choice of Germ Plasm," *Science* 134, no. 3480 (1961): 643–49.

108. Kevles, 1995, 262–63, 299.

109. Ibid., 267.

110. Quoted in Keller, 289.

111. Kevles, 1995, 140.

112. Ibid., 269–70.

113. Ibid., 271–75; see also William Shockley, "Sterilization — A Thinking Exercise," *The Stanford Daily*, April 12, 1974, 2.

114. Chase, 1980, 468–78; NAS report quoted in Keller, 287–88. Keller comments, "From these closing remarks of the NAS report, written in 1968, it would be tempting to conclude that, among geneticists, not much had changed since the 1920s..." (ibid.).

115. Riccardo Baschetti, "People Who Condemn Eugenics May Be in Minority Now," *British Medical Journal* 319, no. 7218 (1999): 1196.

116. For an overview of the history of the HGP, see Daniel J. Kevles, "Out of Eugenics: The Historical Politics of the Human Genome Project," in *The Code of Codes: Scientific and Social Issues in the Human Genome Project*, ed. Daniel J. Kevles and Leroy Hood (Cambridge: Harvard University Press, 1992), 3–36; and see also Horace Freeland Judson, "A History of the Science and Technology Behind Gene Mapping and Sequencing," from ibid., 37–80, for an introduction to the scientific side of the HGP.

117. C. Thomas Caskey, "DNA-Based Medicine: Prevention and Therapy," in *The Code of Codes*, op. cit., 116. For a nuanced ethical analysis, see Dorothy Nelkin, "The Social Power of Genetic Information," in ibid., 177–90. R. Alta Charo has given a feminist critique of the Human Genome Project in "The Human Genome Initiative, Women's Rights and Reproductive Decisions," *Reproductive Health Matters* 4 (1994): 80–86; and "Effect of the Human Genome Initiative on Women's Rights and Reproductive Decisions," *Fetal Diagnosis and Therapy* 8, Suppl. 1 (1993): 148–59.

118. Daniel Koshland, "Sequences and Consequences of the Human Genome," *Science* 246 (1989): 189, quoted in Robert Cook-Deegan, *The Gene Wars: Science, Pol-*itics, and the Human Genome (New York: W. W. Norton and Company, 1994), 246.

119. See, for example, Robert Plomin, "The Role of Inheritance in Behavior," *Science* 248, no. 4952 (1990), 187, quoted in Keller, 283.

120. Keller, esp. 288–91.

121. Judy Jones and Mairi Levitt, "Public Perception of Genetic Testing," *British Medical Journal* 319, no. 7220 (1999): 1283.

122. Richard J. Herrnstein and Charles Murray, *The Bell Curve: Intelligence and Class Structure in American Life* (New York: Free Press, 1994). For some of the many responses, see Russell Jacoby and Naomi Glauberman, *The Bell Curve Debate: History, Documents, Opinions* (New York: Times Books, 1995); Steven Fraser, *The Bell Curve Wars: Race, Intelligence, and the Future of America* (New York: Basic Books, 1995); Stephen J. Ceci, *On Intelligence: A Bioecological Treatise on Intellectual Development* (Cambridge: Harvard University Press, 1996); Claude S. Fischer, et al., *Inequality by Design: Cracking the Bell Curve Myth* (Princeton: Princeton University Press, 1996); Joe L. Kincheloe, et al., *Measured Lies: The Bell Curve Examined* (New York: St. Martin's Press, 1996); and Julian Simon, "Four Comments on *The Bell Curve*," *Genetica* 99, no. 2-3 (1997): 199–205.

123. Lynn, 1996, 45, 146–85.

124. Jacques Testart, "New Eugenics and Medicalized Reproduction," *Cambridge Quarterly of Healthcare Ethics* 4, no. 3 (1995): 305.

125. Geoffrey Sher and Michael A. Feinman, "The Day-to-Day Realities: Commentary on the New Eugenics and Medicalized Reproduction," *Cambridge Quarterly of Healthcare Ethics* 4 (1995): 314.

126. See also Glayde Whitney, "Reproductive Technology for a New Eugenics," *Mankind Quarterly* 60, no. 2 (1999): 179–92; Tony Fitzpatrick, "Before the Cradle: New Genetics, Biopolicy and Regulated Eugenics," *Journal of Social Policy* 30, no. 4 (Oct. 2001): 586–612.

127. Arthur Caplan, Glenn McGee, and David Magnus, "What Is Immoral About Eugenics?" *British Medical Journal* 319, no. 7220 (1999), 1284–85, would fall into this "libertarian" camp; in their opinion, as long as an individual makes a choice without obvious external force, that choice must be free.

128. Paul, 1998, 101–3.

129. See Dorothy Nelkin's thoughtful analysis of the role of genetic and standardized testing as means of wielding institutional power, in Nelkin, op. cit.

130. Beverly Beyette, "Better Brand of Soap," *Los Angeles Times*, June 2, 1999, www.latimes.com; Planned Parenthood Federation of America, "New Planned Parenthood Campaign Launches June 13 in New York Times," Press Release (New York City: Planned Parenthood Federation of America, 1999); Elizabeth Sobo, "Crooning for Contraception in Nigeria," *The Progressive*, September 1990, 26–28; Elizabeth Sobo, "Beyond Coercion: U.S. Government Funds Contraceptive Campaigns in Third World," *Columbia*, July 1991, 6–9. Note also Barbara Katz Rothman's comment: "My children will not be led to genetic technology in chains and shackles, or crowded into cattle cars. It will be offered to them. It will be *sold* to them" (Rothman, 502).

131. Regarding conscious propagandizing with antinatalist messages, see Judith Blake, "Judith Blake on Fertility Control and the Problem of Voluntarism," *Population and Development Review* 20, no. 1 (1994): 167–177. For a current example, consider the Midwestern PPFA affiliate's ad described in chapter one: "BABIES ARE LOUD, SMELLY AND EXPENSIVE." On the propagandistic tactics of eugenics, see the social analysis in Troy Duster, *Backdoor to Eugenics* (New York: Routledge, 1990).

132. Cara Warren and Catherine Dunne, "Lethal Autonomy: The Malfunction of the Informed Consent Mechanism Within the Context of Prenatal Diagnosis of Genetic Variants," *Issues of Law and Medicine* 14, no. 2 (Fall, 1998): 165–202.

133. There has been an explosion of literature on the subject of the "new" eugenics and human genome research; in addition to the literature cited above and below, see, among many others, Allen Buchanan, et al., *From Chance to Choice: Genetics and Justice* (New York: Cambridge University Press, 2000); Matt Ridley, "The New Eugenics: Better than the Old," *National Review*, July 31, 2000: 34–36; Sarah Cunningham-Burley and Mary Boulton, "The Social Context of the New Genetics," in *The Handbook of Social Studies in Health and Medicine*, ed. Gary L. Albrecht, et al. (London: Sage Publications Ltd., 2000): 173–87; Richard Lynn, *Eugenics: A Reassessment* (Westport, Ct.: Praeger, 2001); Anne Kerr and Tom Shakespeare, ed., *Genetic Politics: From Eugenics to Genome* (Cheltenham: New Clarion Press, 2002); Peter Augustine Lawler, "Libertarian Fantasy and Statist Reality," *Society* (November/December, 2002): 81–84; Peter Augustine Lawler, "The Utopian Eugenics of Our Time (Symposium)," *Perspectives on Political Science* 32, no. 2 (Spring 2003): 68–77.

134. For a perspective on the resurgence of eugenics in the early 1970s, see Ludmerer, 177–201. Other reflections on this subject (among many others) include Pauline M. H. Mazumdar, *Eugenics, Human Genetics, and Human Failings: The Eugenics Society, Its Sources and Critics in Britain* (New York: Routledge, 1992), 256–58; and Duster. For a comparison of our times with those of the earliest eugenicists, see Garland E. Allen, "Is a New Eugenics Afoot?" *Science* 294, no. 5540 (Oct. 5, 2001): 59–61.

135. R. F. Antonak, et al., "Influence of Mental Retardation Severity and Respondent Characteristics on Self-Reported Attitudes toward Mental Retardation and Eugenics," *Journal of Intellectual Disability Research* 39, no. 4 (1995): 316–325.

136. Millard, 444. See also Lynn, 50–58, for another statement about "genetic deterioration."

137. Alan F. Guttmacher, "Heredity Counseling: Diabetes, Pregnancy and Modern Medicine, A Genetic Misadventure," *Eugenics Quarterly*, September 1954, 191.

138. Thus, disability activists have critiqued the emphasis on testing for the purpose of identifying persons with disabilities, arguing that it frequently serves the purpose not of rehabilitation but of marginalization and quality control: Bernadette Baker, "The Hunt for Disability: The New Eugenics and the Normalization of School Children," *Teachers College Record* 104, no. 4 (June 2002): 663–703; and Sharon L. Snyder and David T. Mitchell, "Out of the Ashes of Eugenics: Diagnostic Regimes in the United States and the Making of a Disability Minority," *Patterns of Prejudice* 36, no. 1 (2002): 79–103.

139. Kathleen O. Steel, "Road That I See: Implications of New Reproductive Technologies," *Cambridge Quarterly of Healthcare Ethics* 4, no. 3 (1995): 351. Among the groups protesting eugenic policies aimed at persons with disabilities is Not

Dead Yet, accessible at www.acils.com/Not DeadYet.

140. Reilly, 83.

141. American Eugenics Society, Inc., "Five-Year Report of the Officers: 1953–1957," op. cit., 10.

142. Osborn, 1974, 122.

143. Quoted in Paul, 1998, 136.

144. Ibid. The Pioneer Fund has generated a small cottage industry of historiography and institutional response: see John Sedgwick, "Inside the Pioneer Fund," in *The Bell Curve Debate: History, Documents, Opinions*, ed. Russell Jacoby, Naomi Glauberman (New York: Time Books, 1995): 144–61; Richard Lynn, *The Science of Human Diversity: A History of the Pioneer Fund* (Lanham, Md.: Rowman and Littlefield, 2001); William H. Tucker, *The Funding of Scientific Racism: Wickliffe Draper and the Pioneer Fund* (Chicago: University of Illinois Press, 2002); and Michael G. Kenny, "Toward a Racial Abyss: Eugenics, Wickliffe Draper, and the Origins of the Pioneer Fund," *Journal of the History of the Behavioral Sciences* 30 (3, 2002): 259–283.

145. Paul, 1998, 137.

146. Quoted in ibid., 138; italics mine.

147. For a brief history of genetic medical discoveries, including amniocentesis, and the concomitant ethical questions, see Caskey, 112–25.

148. Paul R. Billings, et al., "Discrimination as a Consequence of Genetic Testing," *American Journal of Human Genetics* 50, no. 3 (1992): 476.

149. Marvin R. Natowicz, Jane K. Alper, and Joseph S. Alper, "Genetic Discrimination and the Law," *American Journal of Human Genetics* 50, no. 3 (1992): 466.

150. See ibid.; Kenneth L. Garver and Bettylee Garver, "Eugenics, Euthanasia and Genocide," *Linacre Quarterly* 59, no. 3 (1992): 24–51; Henry T. Greely, "Health Insurance, Employment Discrimination, and the Genetics Revolution," in *The Code of Codes*, op. cit., 264–80.

151. Billings, 481. See also Caskey, 124.

152. Paul, 1995, 131–32.

153. A new wrinkle in the current negative eugenic theorizing is to postulate criminality as a kind of disease (echoing earlier eugenic discourse on the subject) that is endemic in the "unwanted"; thus, Stephen Levitt and John Donohue have postulated that the drop in crime in the 1990s was due to the legalization of abor-

tion in the 1970s; for summaries and reaction, see Karen Brandon, "Stopping Crime Before It Starts," *Boston Globe*, August 8, 1999, A10; Marie McCullough, "Study Links Crime Rate's Fall, Legalized Abortion," *Philadelphia Inquirer*, August 11, 1999, wysiwyg://12/http://www.phillynews.com:80/inquirer/99/August/11/front_page/ABOR11.htm, accessed August 17, 1999; and Abraham McLaughlin, "A Jarring Theory for Drop in US Crime," *Christian Science Monitor*, August 11, 1999, http://www.csmonitor.com/durable/1999/08/11/p1s4.htm, accessed August 17, 1999. Due to limits of space, I will not address this subject.

154. Keller, especially 296.

155. Quoted in Paul, 1998, 148.

156. Walter Glannon, "Genes, Embryos, and Future People," *Bioethics* 12, no. 3 (1998): 187–211.

157. See Millard.

158. Clare Williams, Priscilla Alderson, and Bobbie Farsides, "Is Nondirectiveness Possible within the Context of Antenatal Screening and Testing?" *Social Science and Medicine* 54, no. 3 (Feb. 2002): 339–47.

159. Other coercive policies along these lines include pressure from insurance companies on parents to abort a disabled child; if the parents do not abort, some companies have threatened not to cover the child once he or she is born (Garver, 41–42; Billings, 480).

160. Judith A. Boss, "How Voluntary Prenatal Diagnosis and Selective Abortion Increase the Abnormal Human Gene Pool," *Birth* 17, no. 2 (1990): 77.

161. Quoted in Paul, 1998, 106; Nelkin, 182. Nelkin points out that Shaw fallaciously "is adapting a public health model to genetic disease."

162. Helga Kuhse and Peter Singer, *Should the Baby Live? The Problem of Handicapped Infants* (New York: Oxford University Press, 1985), 8.

163. Quoted in Judy Rebick, "Body Politics: The Attack of the Tomato People," *Herizons* 15, no. 2 (Oct. 31, 2001): 47.

164. See Rayna Rapp, *Testing Women, Testing the Fetus: The Social Impact of Amniocentesis in America* (New York: Routledge, 1999), 53–62.

165. Quoted in ibid., 106.

166. Ibid., 134. See also Garland E. Allen, "The Social and Economic Origins of Genetic Determinism: A Case History of the American Eugenics Movement, 1900–1940

and Its Lessons for Today," *Genetica* 99, no. 2-3 (1997): 77–88.

167. Glenn McGee, *The Perfect Baby: A Pragmatic Approach to Genetics* (Lanham, Md.: Rowman & Littlefield, 1997), 93.

168. Kuhse and Singer, 1985.

169. H. E. Jordan, "The Place of Eugenics in the Medical Curriculum," in *Problems in Eugenics* (London: Eugenics Education Society, 1912), 398, quoted in Ludmerer, 71.

170. See chapter 13, "Playing God: Genes, Clones, and Luck," in Ronald Dworkin, *Sovereign Virtue: The Theory and Practice of Equality* (Cambridge, Mass.: Harvard University Press, 2000). Dworkin's discussion of the two principles of "ethical individualism" is on 448–449. His treatment of prenatal testing and abortion, including his musings as to what makes a "successful" human life and what kind of fetal life would not make the cut is on 431–432. It should be noted that, at this point, he also voices an objection to sex-selection as a motive for abortion, but insists that the state has no right to protect victims of such a motive. It might also be of interest to note that Dworkin does not dismiss mandatory genetic testing out of hand, saying that it may "sometimes" be necessary for a pregnant woman to submit to genetic testing of her fetus (450). He presents this as a case when the rights of the fetus (say, to receive gene therapy) might outweigh those of the mother, but in fact both the rights of the mother and those of her fetus are threatened in a eugenic regime: we have already seen that Dworkin does not think that individuals with Down syndrome, for example, would have a "successful" human life. If one thinks this through, it will be clear what kind of so-called recommendations a mother would receive from genetic counselors and doctors in Dworkin's brave new world of mandatory testing. At the conclusion of the chapter (452), Dworkin reveals that the principle of autonomy mandates that "scientists and doctors" be given wide latitude in their pursuit of the genetic transformation of humanity. Adam Wolfson helpfully, and fairly accurately, cuts through Dworkin's clever camouflaging of the radicality of his position in "Politics in a Brave New World," *The Public Interest* 142 (winter, 2001): 31–43, here 34.

171. Keller, 296.

172. For the eugenic history of the usage of "quality of life" constructs in judging the value of individual lives (and the results on health care that can follow), see Tom Koch, "Life Quality vs the 'Quality of Life': Assumptions Underlying Prospective Quality of Life Instruments in Health Care Planning," *Social Science and Medicine* 51 (2000): 419–27.

173. See, similarly, Alasdair MacIntyre, *Dependent Rational Animals: Why Human Beings Need the Virtues*, The Paul Carus Lectures 20 (Chicago: Open Court, 1999); Hans S. Reinders, *Future of the Disabled in Liberal Society: An Ethical Analysis*, Revisions (South Bend, Ind.: University of Notre Dame Press, 2000).

3. Eugenicists, Coworkers, Friends

1. Quoted in James Reed, *From Private Vice to Public Virtue: The Birth Control Movement and American Society Since 1830* (New York: Basic Books, 1978), 109.

2. For example, eugenicists Edward East and Raymond Pearl worked often with Sanger, recognizing that she was likely to get things done, although they sometimes derided her behind her back; see the East correspondence in the Raymond Pearl papers.

3. Though in Robert Latou Dickinson's case, Sanger barely tolerated his activities early on, but the two became closer as their respective roles within the movement were further differentiated.

4. Sarah Lewit Tietze and Christopher Tietze, M.D., interview with James W. Reed (henceforth Tietze, Tietze and Reed), Family Planning Oral History Project (M138), December 1975–January 1976, Schlesinger Library, Radcliffe Institute, 7.

5. Frederick Osborn, "History of the American Eugenics Society," *Social Biology* 21, no. 2 (1974): 115–126.

6. Quoted in Barry Alan Mehler, "A History of the American Eugenics Society, 1921–40" (Ph.D. diss., University of Illinois, 1988), 110.

7. Ibid., 111. Fairfield Osborn was one of the founders of the Museum of Natural History in New York.

8. Kenneth M. Ludmerer, *Genetics and American Society: A Historical Appraisal*

(Baltimore: The Johns Hopkins University Press, 1972), 174.

9. Mehler, 113.

10. He called Fairfield a "racist" and doubted the scientific value of the work put out by the Cold Spring Harbor lab and its leaders, Harry Laughlin and Charles Benedict Davenport (Frederick Osborn, interview with Isabel Grossner, Carnegie Corporation Project Interview, 1967, Oral History Research Office Collection, Columbia University, New York, 1–2).

11. Ibid., 119, 408.

12. Leon F. Whitney, *Autobiography*, n.d., 219, Leon F. Whitney collection (henceforth LFW), American Philosophical Society Library, Philadelphia, Pennsylvania.

13. Yet it should not be forgotten that Osborn remained concerned about the greater fertility of Native Americans and Mexicans, and he continued to believe in some form of immigration restriction, especially for people coming from "south of the Rio Grande" (quoted in Mehler, 219).

14. Ludmerer, 174–77.

15. Mehler, 269–95; Frederick Osborn, "The Eugenic Hypothesis," *The Eugenics Review*, July 1952, 97–100; Frederic Osborn and Carl Jay Bajema, "The Eugenic Hypothesis," *Social Biology* 19, no. 4 (1972): 337–345.

16. Frederick Osborn, "The Quality of the American Population," *Journal of Contraception*, February (1939): 32.

17. Ibid., 31.

18. Ibid., 33.

19. Frederick Osborn, "The Protection and Improvement of Man's Genetic Inheritance," in *The Population Crisis and the Use of World Resources*, ed. Stuart Mudd, World Academy of Art and Science (Bloomington: Indiana University Press, 1964), 308.

20. Diane B. Paul, *Controlling Human Heredity: 1865 to the Present*, ed. Margaret C. Jacob and Spencer R. Weart, The Control of Nature (Atlantic Highlands, New Jersey: Humanities Press International, 1995), 121.

21. Dictation, "Conference on Population Problems," 6/20/52, 15, from RAC, Family Collection, RG 5 (John D. Rockefeller 3rd), series 1, sub-series 5, box 85, folder 720.

22. See the next chapter on population control for details.

23. Osborn to JDR3, 6/14/56, from RAC, Family Collection, RG 5 (John D. Rockefeller 3rd), series 1, sub-series 5, box 81, folder 679.

24. See James W. Reed and Frances Hand Ferguson, "Schlesinger-Rockefeller Oral History Project, Frances Hand Ferguson, June 1974," (Radcliffe College, 1974), 28.

25. For example, see the program for "Toward a Rational World Population Policy," 10/23/61, MSP-SSC (unfilmed).

26. Program for "Planned Parenthood's Contribution to the Future of America," The Annual Luncheon, 5/7/53, Waldorf-Astoria, New York City, MSP-SSC (unfilmed).

27. Note, Osborn to MS, 1958, with the 1958 Population Council Annual Report, MSP-SSC (unfilmed).

28. D. Kenneth Rose to Raymond Pearl, 10/17/40, and Pearl to Rose, 10/22/40, RP papers.

29. "Birth Control's Opportunity to Strengthen our Human Resources — Our Population," first draft, 7/6/40, from MSP-SSC (unfilmed).

30. "Our Human Resources," January 1941, draft, from PPFA-SSC, box 98, folder 5; resulting document in PPFA-SSC, box 34, "Population" folder.

31. Alan F. Guttmacher, "The Contraceptive Clinic and Preventive Medicine," at the Annual Meeting, Birth Control Federation of America, New York, 1942, 5, MSP-SSC (unfilmed).

32. Carl J. Bajema, ed., *Eugenics: Then and Now*, ed. David L. Jameson, 14 vols., Benchmark Papers in Genetics, vol. 5 (Stroudsburg: Dowden, Hutchinson & Ross, 1976), 269.

33. Osborn, 1974, 117.

34. Minutes of the Board of Directors, 11/17/72, AES papers, SSSB Minutes folder.

35. JDR3 told a Population Council supporter that "everyone is terribly pleased" by the job that Osborn was doing as the head of the Council (JDR3 to Alan Gregg, 11/4/53, from RAC, Family Collection, RG 5 [John D. Rockefeller 3rd], series 1, sub-series 5, box 81, folder 265).

36. The AES papers are full of references to fellowships given to various young scholars interested in such eugenic chestnuts as differential fertility; many of these were funded by the Population Council. The papers clearly show the continued presence of active eugenicists within academia in the 1960s and 1970s. See, for example, the Carl J. Bajema file in the AES papers.

37. Osborn to JDR3, from ibid., series 3, sub-series 4, box 72, folder 490.

38. Frank W. Notestein, "Demography in the United States: A Partial Account of the Development of the Field," *Population and Development Review* 8, no. 4 (1982): 685–86.

39. Quoted in Richard A. Soloway, *Demography and Degeneration: Eugenics and the Declining Birthrate in Twentieth-Century Britain* (Chapel Hill: University of North Carolina Press, 1990), 32.

40. Lyndsay Farrall, cited in Pauline M. H. Mazumdar, *Eugenics, Human Genetics, and Human Failings: The Eugenics Society, Its Sources and Critics in Britain* (New York: Routledge, 1992), 8.

41. Ibid., 23.

42. Ibid., 47. For more on the early history of the ES, see ibid., 7–57; Soloway, 1990.

43. Quoted in Soloway, 1990, 204.

44. Clarence Gamble to Robert Latou Dickinson, 7/24/48, Robert Latou Dickinson Papers (B MS c72) (henceforth RLD), Boston Medical Library in the Countway Library of Medicine, Boston, Massachusetts, box 1, folder 48.

45. Mazumdar, 204–7.

46. Ibid., 208.

47. Ibid., 243.

48. Beryl Suitters, *Be Brave and Angry: Chronicles of the International Planned Parenthood Federation* (London: International Planned Parenthood Federation, 1973), 174–75.

49. Soloway, 1990, 189, 193–225.

50. Daniel J. Kevles, *In the Name of Eugenics: Genetics and the Uses of Human Heredity*, second ed. (Cambridge: Harvard University Press, 1995), 172.

51. Mazumdar, 247–48; Soloway, 1990, 204.

52. Suitters, 171–72.

53. Soloway, 1990, xvii.

54. C. P. Blacker, "Obituary: Margaret Sanger," *The Eugenics Review* 58, no. 4 (1966), 179.

55. C. P. Blacker, "Proposed Formation of a British Advisory Committee" (London: International Committee on Planned Parenthood, 1952), 2, MSP-SSC (unfilmed).

56. See, e.g., the documents in PPFA-SSC, box 40, file 9.

57. G. Aird Whyte to MS, 3/24/55, 2, in MSP-SSC.

58. Suitters, 171.

59. Mazumdar, 255.

60. Robert Latou Dickinson, "Suggestions for a Program for American Gynecology," *Transactions of the American Gynecological Society* 45 (1920), 1–13, quoted in Reed, 1978, 165.

61. Ibid., 167.

62. Ibid., 148–52.

63. Ibid., 168.

64. Mary Steichen Calderone, M.D., interview with James W. Reed (henceforth Calderone and Reed), Family Planning Oral History Project (M-138), August 1974, Schlesinger Library, Radcliffe Institute, 3.

65. Ellen Chesler, *Woman of Valor: Margaret Sanger and the Birth Control Movement in America* (New York: Simon & Schuster, 1992), 273.

66. Ibid., 275.

67. Ibid., 276.

68. Ibid., 184.

69. RLD to JDR3, 2/7/34, RAC, Family Collection, RG2 (Offices of the Messrs. Rockefeller), "Medical Interests," box 2, folder 7.

70. Memo, "National Committee on Maternal Health, Inc.: History," 7/5/42, from ibid.

71. American Eugenics Society, "Organized Eugenics" pamphlet, 3, MSP-SSC (unfilmed).

72. Caroline Hadley Robinson, *Seventy Birth Control Clinics: a Survey and Analysis Including the General Effects of Control on Size and Quality of Population* (Baltimore: Williams and Wilkins Company, 1930), 101–2.

73. Ibid., 100.

74. Ibid., 50–1.

75. Dennis Hodgson, "The Ideological Origins of the Population Association of America," *Population and Development Review* 17, no. 1 (1991), 24.

76. Ibid., 2. See also chapter one of this book.

77. Ibid.

78. Birthright Constitution, CJG papers, box 230, folder 3553. For more on the history of Birthright, see chapter six on sterilization.

79. Philip R. Reilly, *The Surgical Solution: A History of Involuntary Sterilization in the United States* (Baltimore: The Johns Hopkins University Press, 1991), 89.

80. "Minutes of Executive Committee Meeting of Birthright, Inc.," 1/18/46, CJG papers, box 230, folder 3549.

81. Reilly, 89.

82. Program, MSP-SSC (unfilmed), box 13, folder 8.

83. Doone Williams and Greer Williams, *Every Child a Wanted Child: Clarence James Gamble, M.D. and His Work in the Birth Control Movement*, ed. Emily P. Flint, The Countway Library Associates Historical Publication, vol. 4 (Boston: The Francis A. Countway Library of Medicine, 1978), 177.

84. Stuart Mudd to "Sarah and Dick," 9/15/70, 1, Sarah Merry (Bradley) Gamble papers (MC 368) (henceforth SMBG), Schlesinger Library, Radcliffe Institute, Harvard University, box 14, folder 274. Mudd also shared the Gambles' eugenic values; see Stuart Mudd, "Citizenship and Birth Control," n.d., reprinted by the ABCL, from Emily Borie (Hartshorne) Mudd papers (T-149) (henceforth EBHM), Schlesinger Library, Radcliffe Institute, Harvard University, carton 18, folder 821.

85. Gamble's parents gave him a million dollars when he turned twenty-one. See Williams, 19–22.

86. See Williams, 51–55, for an account of the accident.

87. See the summary of Gamble's early biography in Reed, 1978, 227–31. For more detail, see Williams, 68–76.

88. Reed, 1978, 233.

89. Williams, 273.

90. Ibid., 91, 106–7. See also Reed, 1978, 239–46.

91. Chesler, 1992, 391.

92. Ibid., 422.

93. Reed, 1978, 234.

94. Williams, 192. For details concerning the conflicts between the original sole author of the biography on the one hand and the Gamble family and friends on the other, see the letters in SMBG, box 14, folder 241.

95. Stuart Mudd to Sarah and Richard Gamble, 9/15/70, memoir, 1, from SMBG, box 14, folder 274. Strangely enough, Stuart's wife Emily said almost the identical thing in a tribute to Sarah and Clarence Gamble: "[T]wo Pathfinders produce five — all of one color — the five add four who by joint effort produce, in the brief span of twelve years, 15 additions. In Jim's terms and his son's mathematics, this would be 55 pregnancies per 100 couple years — a figure twice that of the National Birth Rate. Might we dare to suggest that the Path itself is developing an internal, unpublicized — but let us hastily add — carefully

planned population explosion!" (From "Tribute to Sarah Gamble, by Emily Mudd," November 1965, Pathfinder Fund Advisory Council meeting, SMBG, box 27, folder 562).

96. Williams, 180.

97. Ibid., 175.

98. Ibid., 181–82.

99. Clarence Gamble to "Dear Sir," 11/15/45, MSP-SSC (unfilmed).

100. Williams, 179.

101. Ibid., 174–76.

102. Ibid., 179.

103. James Reed's comment, in Tietze and Reed, 34.

104. The Mudds shared his concern. Emily Mudd was a large donor to the Association for Voluntary Sterilization (a later avatar of the eugenic group Birthright) and considered H. Curtis Wood, also involved with the American Eugenics Society, a friend and colleague. See SMBG, box 7, folder 331.

105. Reilly, 133.

106. AVS, "Minutes," 4/11/47, SMBG, box 7, folder 331.

107. Clarence J. Gamble, "Eugenic Sterilization in the United States, 1948," *Eugenical News* 34, no. 1-2 (1949): 1.

108. Clarence J. Gamble, "Preventive Mental Hygiene in Alabama," *Journal of the Medical Association of Alabama* 19, no. 6 (1949): 162. Segregation by sex was considered to be the alternative to eugenic sterilization, because it would still prevent the "unfit" from becoming parents, but most eugenicists dismissed it as being too costly.

109. For the full history of this event, see Williams, 128–48; Edward J. Larson, *Sex, Race, and Science: Eugenics in the Deep South* (Baltimore: The Johns Hopkins University Press, 1995), 155–56; Reilly, 134–39.

110. Anne Lamb, paper, "How Planned Parenthood Functions in a Public Health Program," 1/20/46, 2, PPFA-SSC.

111. Reed, 253–54. For Gamble's own summary of his work up to 1939, see CJG to D. Kenneth Rose, 2/11/39 and 3/1/39, CJG, box 134, folder 2334.

112. Clarence J. Gamble, "Better Human Beings Tomorrow," *Better Health*, October 1947, 14, 15.

113. Reilly, 134. Ironically, despite the enormous amounts of time, energy, and money that Gamble devoted to the cause of eugenic sterilization, his official biography is silent on the issue, perhaps indicating

awareness on the part of his family that this side of Gamble's control activism was not publicly palatable. For more on the North Carolina sterilization program, see the differing views of Johanna Schoen, "Between Choice and Coercion: Women and the Politics of Sterilization in North Carolina, 1929–1975," *Journal of Women's History* 13 (1, 2001): 132–56; and Katherine Castles, "Quiet Eugenics: Sterilization in North Carolina's Institutions for the Mentally Retarded, 1945–1965," *Journal of Southern History* 68 (4, 2002): 849–78. See also Edwin Black, *War Against the Weak: Eugenics and America's Campaign to Create a Master Race* (New York: Four Walls Eight Windows, 2003), 421–22, for the involvement of the Wake Forest medical genetics department in eugenic sterilizations.

114. Ferguson and Reed, 26–27.

115. Reed, 1978, 241–46.

116. Edna Rankin McKinnon, interview with "DW," "Interview with Edna Rankin McKinnon re: family planning career, 1970's," 67, ERM papers, box 41, folder 69.

117. An example of the "living laboratory" attitude toward contraceptive research is evident in the letter of Kathryn Trent of the Gamble-funded Mountain Maternal Health League, in Berea, Kentucky. In describing its purposes, she gave the first one as: "To serve as a laboratory in which a simple and inexpensive contraceptive method and procedure might be tested through a statistical study" (Kathryn Trent to D. Kenneth Rose, 10/4/44, RAC, Family Collection, RG2 [Offices of the Messrs. Rockefeller], "Medical Interests," box 1, folder 2).

118. Edna Rankin McKinnon, interview with "DW," op. cit., 14–15.

119. Williams, 149–50.

120. Ibid., 185.

121. Calderone and Reed, 8.

122. This pragmatic attitude, namely, that PPFA and IPPF had to offer more than simple methods if contraception in general was to be acceptable, is seen also in people like Christopher Tietze, who worked first with Gamble and with Planned Parenthood. Tietze seemed not to express any moral reservations regarding simple methods but rather pragmatic ones. As James Reed expressed it in an interview with Tietze, "This correspondence between you and Dr. Gamble is very interesting because he really is interested in the cheapest method that he can find, and he doesn't think you can afford to go first-class, so to speak, and I think your argument was that you don't have much choice. You have to have a little better method or we're going to waste our time on this stuff" (Tietze and Reed, 12–13).

123. James W. Reed, "The Birth Control Movement Before *Roe v. Wade*," in *Politics of Abortion and Birth Control in Historical Perspective*, ed. Donald T. Critchlow (University Park: Pennsylvania State University Press, 1996), 36.

124. Memo, Vera Houghton to members of the IPPF Executive Committee, 1/7/54, quoting MS, letter to IPPF, 11/10/53, MSP-SSC.

125. MS to "Sarah and Clarence," 12/18/56, SMBG papers, box 27, folder 560.

126. Williams, 241; see 227–304 for Gamble's conflicts with the IPPF.

127. Ibid., 305–11.

128. Emily Hartshorne Mudd, interview with James W. Reed (henceforth Mudd and Reed), Family Planning Oral History Project (M-138), August 1974, Schlesinger Library, Radcliffe Institute, 230.

129. Williams, 425.

130. Ibid., 435–36.

131. See Barbara Ehrenreich, Mark Dowie, and Stephen Minkin, "The Charge: Gynocide; the Accused: The U.S. Government," *Mother Jones*, November 1979, 26–37 for the details of USAID's dumping.

132. Mudd and Reed, 232.

133. R. T. Ravenholt to Stuart Mudd, 12/22/69, 1, from EBHM papers, carton 11, folder 480.

134. Stuart Mudd to Sarah and Richard Gamble, 9/15/70, memoir, 1, from SMBG, box 14, folder 274.

135. United Nations Population Fund, "U.S. Population NGO, Philippine Parliamentarian to Receive 1996 United Nations Population Award" (New York: UNFPA, 1996).

136. Ferguson and Reed, 23.

137. Richard Gamble to Emily Mudd, 11/1/76, 1–2, from EBHM papers, carton 11, folder 491.

138. Williams, 196.

139. John Robinson, "On Nantucket, Style Is Still What Counts," *Boston Globe*, August 17, 1993, E49.

140. Anita Diamant, "Aftermath," *Boston Globe Magazine*, April 9, 1995, 26.

141. Vera Houghton to MS, 8/27/54, 1–2, MSP-SSC.

142. Chesler, 1992, 365.

143. Ibid., 410.

144. Dorothy Brush, "The Brush Foundation," *Eugenics*, February 1929, 17.

145. T. Wingate Todd, *The Herald's Staff: An Account of the Brush Inquiry* (Cleveland: Brush Foundation, 1929), 4.

146. Brush Foundation, "Race Betterment: A Symposium," in *Symposium on Race Betterment*, ed. Jerome C. Fisher, Brush Foundation Publications, No. IV (Dayton, Oh.: Brush Foundation, 1929), 7.

147. Ibid.

148. Ibid., 14.

149. Ibid., 24.

150. Ibid.

151. American Eugenics Society, Inc., "Five-Year Report of the Officers: 1953–1957" (New York: The American Eugenics Society, Inc., 1958), 2, from MSP-SSC (unfilmed), box 48, folder 2.

152. "AVS Holds National Conference on Voluntary Sterilization and World Starvation," *Association for Voluntary Sterilization, Inc., News*, Spring 1968, 1, 4, 7, from MSP-SSC (unfilmed), box 48, folder 11.

153. MS to Mrs. Charles Brush, Jr., 6/27/28, MSP-LC, cont. 68, reel 44.

154. Virginia R. Wing to MS, 12/4/30, ibid.

155. Clarence J. Gamble to Dorothy Brush, 12/7/57, CJG papers, box 150, folder 2515.

156. Brush Foundation, "The Brush Foundation: 1928–1980" (Cleveland: The Brush Foundation, 1981), 5. An earlier annual report explains in more detail what that entailed: "In 1948, the foundation provided the bulk of the funds necessary to establish the IPPF central office at 69 Eccleston Square, London. A subsidy (recently increased) toward operating expenses has been made annually. In 1952 and 1955, the foundation contributed modestly to two of IPPF's five international conferences—those held in Bombay and Tokyo. To the extent of an annual $10,000, the foundation underwrites the IPPF monthly bulletin, 'Around the World News of Population and Birth Control' (started in January 1952). The founder's daughter-in-law volunteered her services as editor during the first five years" (Brush Foundation, "The Brush Foundation, Cleveland, Ohio, 1928–1958" [Cleveland: Brush Foundation, 1958], 15).

157. Ibid., 5, 11, 15.

158. Brush to Anne Kennedy, 3/28/57, MSP-SSC (unfilmed), box 27, folder 2.

159. Copy, 40–41, in MSP-SSC (unfilmed), box 40, folder 9.

160. Ibid., 41–42.

161. Stephen G. Greene, "Philanthropy's Population Explosion," *Chronicle of Philanthropy*, May 31, 1994, 8.

162. Brush Foundation, "The Brush Foundation: Quadriennial Report, 1993–1996" (Cleveland: The Brush Foundation, 1997).

163. The Brush Foundation's involvement with abortion-rights groups also raises the problem, curiously ignored by all but a few feminists, of the ease with which abortion can be used as a weapon against disenfranchised women, especially in totalitarian countries such as China (see the section on China in the sixth chapter).

164. Brush's role in the eugenics movement was more that of an enthusiastic follower than an organizational leader, so her position within the movement has been somewhat neglected by eugenic historical scholarship. Sanger herself, as I have noted earlier, was not an original eugenicist, and eugenic historiography has often focused on those scientists and scholars who were most properly considered original "eugenicists," much as only a scientist, not a layperson, today would earn the title "geneticist." Yet the scholarship has perhaps neglected to note how Sanger's influence has been much more enduring than that of the professional eugenicists, warranting her more attention in scholarly examinations of the eugenic phenomenon.

165. Chesler, 1992 goes as far as to say: "Only a handful of avowed eugenicists ... were ever willing to associate with her publicly" (217). This statement does not take into account the over twenty "avowed eugenicists" on the advisory board of fifty for the American Birth Control League in the 1920s and the numerous others who spoke at her conferences, took leadership roles in her organizations, and otherwise "associated with her publicly."

166. Hannah Stone wrote two articles for *Eugenics*, the AES magazine, in 1929: "The Birth Control Raid," 2 (no. 8), 24–27; "The Birth Control Clinic of Today and Tomorrow," 2 (no. 5), 9–11. For Dorothy Bocker's involvement with eugenic statistical studies, see chapter four.

4. Quality, Not Quantity

1. Margaret Sanger, *Pivot of Civilization* (New York: Brentano's, 1922), 22.

2. Garrett Hardin, *The Ostrich Factor: Our Population Myopia* (New York: Oxford University Press, 1999), 61.

3. On a small scale, there is the work of the Brush Foundation (detailed in the previous chapter), run at one time by close Sanger friend Dorothy Brush. Its goals, according to its annual report from as recently as 1981, are "to improve the quality and reasonably limit the number of those born into the world"—again, the theme of quality, not quantity (Brush Foundation, "The Brush Foundation: 1928–1980" [Cleveland: The Brush Foundation, 1981], 5).

4. Hardin, op. cit., 61, 99–106, 163.

5. For an analysis of Hardin's eugenic beliefs as expressed in his writings, see Eric B. Ross, *The Malthus Factor: Population, Poverty and Politics in Capitalist Development* (New York: Zed Books, 1998), 73–78.

6. For a feminist analysis of Malthus, see, among other works, Asoka Bandarage, *Women, Population and Global Crisis: A Political-Economic Analysis* (London: Zed Books, 1997), 27–112.

7. T. R. Malthus, *An Essay on the Principle of Population*, ed. Raymond Geuss and Quentin Skinner, trans. Donald Winch, Cambridge Texts in the History of Political Thought (Cambridge: Cambridge University Press, 1992 [reprinted from 1803 edition]), 29.

8. Ibid., 17–19. A geometric series increases like this: 1, 2, 4, 8, etc., while an arithmetic series looks like this: 1, 2, 3, 4, etc.

9. Ibid., 21–23.

10. He said in the appendix to the 1817 edition of his work, "Indeed, I should always particularly reprobate any artificial and unnatural modes of checking population, both on account of their immorality and their tendency to remove a necessary stimulus to industry" (ibid., 368–69).

11. Ibid., 23.

12. Ibid., 25.

13. Donald Winch, introduction, in ibid., xvi; see also 213.

14. Ibid., 103.

15. Ibid., 249; Hardin quotes this passage favorably in Hardin, 1999, 100–101.

16. Allan Chase, *The Legacy of Malthus: The Social Costs of the New Scientific Racism* (Chicago: University of Illinois Press, 1980), 75.

17. Ibid.

18. Some anti-Malthusians argue that the "Green Revolution" has been more destructive than beneficial to agriculture; for this viewpoint, see the Marxist argument in Ross, 137–99. He observes that Malthus's theorizing was driven by a desire to justify private property.

19. Glenn Hodges, "When Good Guys Lie: Misleading the Public Is No Way to Make the World a Better Place," *Washington Monthly*, January 11, 1997, 30–39, here p. 39.

20. Margaret Sanger, ed., *The Case for Birth Control* (New York: Margaret Sanger, 1917), 43–92.

21. Margaret Sanger, "Opening Remarks," in *International Congress on Population and World Resources in Relation to the Family*, Cheltenham, England, 1948, 6. An earlier draft of this talk spoke in more detail: "That year was momentous in my life, and I think it safe to say that the knowledge I stored away in my studies at the British Museum—studies directed by my good friends Havelock Ellis, H. G. Wells, Edward Carpenter, C. V. Drysdale, Alice Vickery, the faithful followers of Malthus under the name of the New Malthusian—these studies served me well during the next ten years of writing, speaking, organizing and setting up Leagues and Clinics" (ibid., 3). Both drafts are from MSP-SSC, unprocessed, Acc. #98S-9, box 1 (Suhey collection).

22. Undated broadsheet, Malthusian League, MSP-SSC (unfilmed).

23. Richard A. Soloway, *Demography and Degeneration: Eugenics and the Declining Birthrate in Twentieth-Century Britain* (Chapel Hill: University of North Carolina Press, 1990), 61.

24. "International Neo-Malthusian and Birth Control Congress," 1922, RP papers, ABCL folder.

25. See Chesler, 1992, 235–36.

26. "Requested Statement for Times," 3/24/25, RP papers, ABCL folder.

27. *Medical and Eugenic Aspects of Birth Control*, ed. Margaret Sanger, 4 vols., The Sixth International Neo-Malthusian and Birth Control Conference, Reports and Papers, vol. 3 (New York: The American Birth Control League, Inc., 1926).

28. Havelock Ellis, in ibid., 1–18, here p. 18.

29. S. Adolphus Knopf, M.D., "Birth Control: A Social, Religious and Medical Issue," in ibid., 195–226, here p. 204.

30. Ibid., 246.

31. Birth Control International Information Centre, "A Statement of Policy" (London: Birth Control International Information Centre, 1928?), 2.

32. After the conference, Sanger shored up eugenic support for population control by writing to the dean of American eugenics at that time, Charles Benedict Davenport, to thank him for attending: "I wish personally to express my thanks to you for attending the Conference and the valuable contribution to the subject your presence gave. It is my sincere hope that the Population Union, of which Dr. Raymond Pearl is the Chairman and Dr. F.A.E. Crew is the Secretary, will prove to be a medium for solving the many population problems with which the world is confronted" (MS to C. B. Davenport, 11/9/27, CBD papers, "Margaret Sanger" folder).

33. C. Langford, "The Eugenics Society and the Development of Demography in Britain: The International Population Union, the British Population Society and the Population Investigation Committee," in *Essays in the History of Eugenics: Proceedings of a Conference Organised by the Galton Institute, London, 1997*, ed. Robert A. Peel (London: Galton Institute, 1998), 81–111, describes the overlap between Great Britain's Eugenics Society and the British chapter of the IUSSP (the British Population Society).

34. Frank Lorimer, "The Role of the International Union for the Scientific Study of Population," in *Forty Years of Research in Human Fertility: Retrospect and Prospect*, ed. Clyde V. Kiser (Carnegie Endowment International Center, New York City: Milbank Memorial Fund, 1971), 86–105, here p. 87.

35. Ibid., 93, 94.

36. Ibid., 89.

37. Ibid., 94.

38. Stefan Kühl, *The Nazi Connection: Eugenics, American Racism, and German National Socialism* (New York: Oxford University Press, 1994), 27–36.

39. Frank Lorimer, "The Development of Demography," in *The Study of Population: An Inventory and Appraisal*, ed. Philip M. Hauser and Otis Dudley Duncan (Chicago: University of Chicago Press, 1959), 124–179, here p. 164.

40. Dennis Hodgson, "The Ideological Origins of the Population Association of America," *Population and Development Review* 17, no. 1 (1991): 1–34, here pp. 2, 28.

41. Quoted in ibid., 9, 25. Accordingly, the PAA meeting in 1933 had as its theme "Who Shall Inherit America?" and the topics included "Is the quality of our population on the downgrade?" Among the speakers was Frank Notestein, while Frank Lorimer and Louis Dublin led the discussion (ibid., 27).

42. Frank W. Notestein, "Reminiscences: The Role of Foundations, the Population Association of America, Princeton University and the United Nations in Fostering American Interest in Population Problems," in *Forty Years of Research in Human Fertility: Retrospect and Prospect*, ed. Clyde V. Kiser, Milbank Memorial Fund Quarterly (Carnegie Endowment International Center, New York City: Milbank Memorial Fund, 1971), 67–85, here pp. 70–71.

43. Memo for the files, Arthur W. Packard, 5/31/34, and handwritten notes on letter from Frank Lorimer to "Members of the Population Association," 12/9/34, both in RAC, Family Collection, RG2 (Offices of the Messrs. Rockefeller), "Medical Interests," PAA subseries, box 2, folder 14. A letter from Frederick Osborn to Packard asking for money for the PAA touched on the same theme (Frederick Osborn to Packard, 12/21/34, 2, from ibid.).

44. Notestein, 1971, 71.

45. James Reed, *From Private Vice to Public Virtue: The Birth Control Movement and American Society Since 1830* (New York: Basic Books, 1978), 212.

46. Frank W. Notestein to Richard Demuth, from RAC, Special Collection (Population Council), series IV3B4, sub-series 5, box 101, folder 1902.

47. JDR3 to J. George Harrar, 9/27/63, from RAC, Family Collection, RG 5 (John D. Rockefeller 3rd), series 1, subseries 5, box 82, folder 681.

48. Lasker Foundation Award Speech, 10/25/50, 2, 4, MSC-LC, cont. 201, reel 130.

49. Michael S. Teitelbaum, "Some Genetic Implications of Population Policies," in *Population Growth and the American Future, Research Reports*, ed. C. F. Westoff and R. Parke, Jr. (1972), 493–503, here p. 493. Likewise, the prologue to an AES conference insisted, "It is worth documenting

some aspects of the quantity problem because it is intimately related to the quality problem" (Irving I. Gottesman and L. Erlenmeyer-Kimling, "A Foundation for Informed Eugenics," *Social Biology* 18, no. Supp. 2 [1971]: S1-S8, here S2). And in 1959, a mainstream text on population studies noted that the "primary objective of demographic research is to furnish an inventory of quantitative *and qualitative* population changes," in harmony with the eugenic aim of "genetic studies ... to search for the basic causes" (Franz J. Kallmann, M.D., and John D. Rainer, M.D., "Genetics and Demography," in *Study of Population: An Inventory and Appraisal*, ed. Philip M. Hauser and Otis Dudley Duncan [Chicago: University of Chicago Press, 1959], 759–790, here 759, emphasis mine).

50. I do not mean to imply that all eugenicists were interested in population control and vice versa, but the number of eugenicists involved in the founding of the population-control movement is so great as to make any hard-and-fast distinction between the two movements historically impossible. Nor I do mean to tar all contemporary population-control proponents with the eugenic brush; many would not accept articulated eugenic propositions. The problem arises when eugenic doctrines go undercover and reappear as a bigotry that is not really explicit but is present nonetheless in, say, bureaucratic elitism or a North Atlantic elitism vis-à-vis the developing world. The recognition of such ideological permutations requires knowing and understanding historical facts.

51. Garrett Hardin, "Parenthood: Right or Privilege?," *Science* 169, no. 3944 (1970): 427. It should be noted that Hardin combines his outrageous misogynism with a call for free access to birth control and abortion (he was also a cofounder of the National Abortion Rights Action League), another indication that those embracing the ideology of control consider these methods necessary for their plans. (See Garrett Hardin, "Choices of Parenthood," *Science* 170, no. 3955 [1970]: 259–60.)

52. Hardin, "Parenthood: Right or Privilege?" 427.

53. Garrett Hardin, "The Tragedy of the Commons," *Science* 162, December 1968: 1243–1248.

54. Garrett Hardin, *The Ostrich Factor:*

Our Population Myopia (New York: Oxford University Press, 1999), 78.

55. Bernard Berelson and Jonathan Lieberson, "Government Efforts to Influence Fertility: The Ethical Issues," *Population and Development Review* 5, no. 4 (1979): 581–614, here 596.

56. Bernard Berelson, "Beyond Family Planning," *Science*, 163 (Feb. 7, 1969), 533.

57. Berelson and Lieberson, 591.

58. F. T. Sai and K. Newman, "Ethical Approaches to Family Planning in Africa," Working Paper, Population and Human Resources Department, World Bank, Washington, D.C., December 1989, 11, quoted in Betsy Hartmann, "Population Control as Foreign Policy," *CovertAction* 39, Winter (1991-1992): 26–30, here 29.

59. Betsy Hartmann, *Reproductive Rights and Wrongs: The Global Politics of Population Control* (Boston: South End Press, 1995), 66. For more on the UNFPA and IPPF's defense of the brutal Chinese program, which uses not only incentives and disincentives but also outright force, see chapter six

60. Tietze and Reed, 58–59.

61. Quoted in Hartmann, 1995, 72.

62. Carl Jay Bajema, "The Genetic Implications of Population Control," *BioScience* 21, January 1971: 71–75, here p. 75.

63. Frederick Osborn, "Population: An International Dilemma," in *The Conference Committee on Population Problems — 1956–1957*, ed. Frederick Osborn (New York: Princeton University Press, 1958), vii–97, here p. 87.

64. Ibid., 77–78.

65. Ibid., 87–88.

66. Adam Miller, "Professors of Hate," in *The Bell Curve Debate: History, Documents, Opinions*, ed. Russell Jacoby; Naomi Glauberman (New York: Times Books, 1994), 162–78, here p. 171.

67. As of 1997, India's population per square mile is estimated to be 843; the same figure for the Netherlands is 1,195 (Jacqueline Kasun, *The War Against Population: The Economics and Ideology of World Population Control*, second edition [San Francisco: Ignatius Press, 1999], 69).

68. Linda Gordon, "The Politics of Population: Birth Control and the Eugenics Movement," *Radical America* 8, no. 4 (1974): 61–97, here p. 85.

69. Notestein, 1971, 68. Scripps reportedly "invited Thompson to accompany him

on his yacht for a trip to the Far East and the South Sea Islands" before setting up the Foundation, thereby demonstrating that the fertility and lifestyle of the poor appears quite alarming when juxtaposed with the creature comforts of a well-turned-out yacht.

70. Kenneth M. Ludmerer, *Genetics and American Society: A Historical Appraisal* (Baltimore: The Johns Hopkins University Press, 1972), 20; Lorimer, 1959, 162.

71. Frederick Osborn, "American Foundations and Population Problems," in *U.S. Philanthropic Foundations: Their History, Structure, Management, and Record*, ed. Warren Weaver (New York: Harper and Row, 1967), 365–374, here p. 366. Among the articles published by Thompson and Whelpton include Thompson's "Traits, Factors, and Genes" in the 1957 *Eugenics Quarterly*, and Whelpton and Kiser's *Social and Psychological Factors Affecting Fertility*, in four volumes published by the Milbank Memorial Fund from 1943 to 1954 (Kallmann and Rainer, 789–90).

72. Population Council, Inc., "Reports of the Executive Officers for the Period November 5, 1952 to December 31, 1955" (New York: Population Council, Inc., 1956), 33, MSP-SSC.

73. Brush Foundation, "The Brush Foundation, Cleveland, Ohio, 1928–1958" (Cleveland: Brush Foundation, 1958), 6, MSP-SSC; Notestein, 1971, 69, 77.

74. Clyde V. Kiser, "The Work of the Milbank Memorial Fund in Population Since 1928," in *Forty Years of Research in Human Fertility: Retrospect and Prospect*, ed. Clyde V. Kiser, Milbank Memorial Fund Quarterly (Carnegie International Endowment Center, New York City: Milbank Memorial Fund, 1971), 15–66, here p. 18.

75. Dorothy G. Wiehl, respondent, in ibid., 63.

76. Kiser, 19.

77. Ibid., 20.

78. See American Eugenics Society, Inc., "Five-Year Report of the Officers: 1953–1957" (New York: The American Eugenics Society, Inc., 1958), 2, MSP-SSC.

79. Kiser, 20.

80. The minutes for that meeting describe the decision: "Mr. Kingsbury further reported that he and Mr. Sydenstricker had recently spent a day going over the records of Mrs. Sanger's birth control clinic in this City [New York], and that there was such excellent material available that Mr. Sydenstricker, through the Research Division of the Fund, had suggested a comparative study, in order to check with the clinic at Johns Hopkins" (ibid., 21–22).

81. "Meeting of National Council of American Birth Control League, Inc.," 1/22/24, 1, MSP-SSC.

82. MS to Pearl, 5/24/23, RP papers, Sanger folder. In the end, Pearl did not use the eugenic data compiled by Sanger's clinic due to Bocker's hesitance to release patient records to Pearl for his free use; nevertheless, the project indicates the willingness on Sanger's part to participate in demographic eugenics. Pearl ended by using data from Mississippi for his study from 1931 to 1938 for Milbank.

83. Gar Allen, "The Work of Raymond Pearl: From Eugenics to Population Control," *Science for the People* 12, no. 4 (1980): 22–28; Elazar Barkan, *The Retreat of Scientific Racism* (New York: Cambridge University Press, 1992).

84. Frederick Osborn, "History of the American Eugenics Society," *Social Biology* 21, no. 2 (1974): 115–126, here p. 118.

85. Frank W. Notestein, "Demography in the United States: A Partial Account of the Development of the Field," *Population and Development Review* 8, no. 4 (December 1982): 651–87, here p. 655.

86. Kiser, 23.

87. Quoted in Barkan, 213–17.

88. Pearl to East, 5/7/25, RP papers, East folder.

89. Guttmacher and Reed, 4.

90. Phyllis Tilson Piotrow, *World Population Crisis: The United States Response*, Praeger Special Studies in International Economics and Development, Law and Population Book Series, vol. 4 (New York: Praeger Publishers, 1973), 8.

91. James W. Reed, "The Birth Control Movement Before *Roe v. Wade*," in *Politics of Abortion and Birth Control in Historical Perspective*, ed. Donald T. Critchlow (University Park: Pennsylvania State University Press, 1996), 22–52, here p. 39.

92. Kiser to Osborn, Memo: "Highlights of the Work of the Milbank Memorial Fund in the Field of Population," 2/1/65, 4, AES papers, APS, Milbank Memorial Fund folder.

93. Osborn to L. E. Burney, MMF executive director, 2/3/71, 1, ibid.

94. Frederick Osborn to Frank Boudreau, MMF Director, n.d. (1958?), 1, ibid.

95. Osborn to Morris Lewis (BCFA), 1/11/41, PPFA-SSC.

96. Notestein, 1971, 73; Lorimer, 1971, 91.

97. Lorimer, 1971, 92, 96.

98. Lorimer, 1959, 163.

99. Ibid., 165, emphasis mine. He once indicated the practical results of this vision of demography when he spoke to a eugenics meeting about the need to evaluate public programs in light of their eugenic effect on population (Osborn, 1974, 120).

100. Frank Lorimer, "Draft Report," June 1956, 3, from RAC, Special Collection (Population Council), series IV3B4, subseries 5, box 97, folder 1797. Guttmacher proffered Puerto Ricans sterilized at Mount Sinai Hospital as an example of contraceptive measures carried out on such "deviates."

101. Lorimer, 1959, 145.

102. American Eugenics Society, Inc., "Five-Year Report of the Officers: 1953–1957," (New York: The American Eugenics Society, Inc., 1958), 2–3, from MSP-SSC (unfilmed), box 48, folder 2.

103. Peter Bachrach and Elihu Bergman, *Power and Choice: The Formulation of American Population Policy* (Lexington: Lexington Books, 1973), 77.

104. Ibid., 79.

105. Edwin Black, *War Against the Weak: Eugenics and America's Campaign to Create a Master Race* (New York: Four Walls Eight Windows, 2003), 137–40.

106. Davenport to Leon Whitney, 4/5/28, cited in ibid., 140.

107. See Black, 141–42 for a brief history of this attempted merger seen from the point of view of the professional eugenicists involved. McCann emphasizes the initiatory role of the ABCL's Eleanor Jones in 1933 and highlights the fact that it was to be a merger that dissolved into a federation. However, she ignores Fairchild's call for the new group in 1931 and minimizes Sanger's role, who was involved in the discussions (by invitation of Fairchild and others) by 1933. See McCann, 181.

108. Barry Alan Mehler, "A History of the American Eugenics Society, 1921–40" (Ph.D. diss., University of Illinois, 1988), 96.

109. Henry Pratt Fairchild to Harry Perkins, 2/9/33, cited in Black, 141.

110. Ruth Topping to ABCL Board of Directors Meeting, "Memorandum on Proposed Merger," 3/2/33, 2, PPFA-SSC.

111. Henry Pratt Fairchild to Mrs. F. Robertson Jones, 4/7/33, PPFA-SSC.

112. Mrs. F. Robertson Jones to Henry Pratt Fairchild, 4/17/33, PPFA-SSC.

113. Ruth Topping to F. R. Jones, "Interview with Frederick Osborn" memo, 4/19/33, PPFA-SSC.

114. Ruth Topping, "Meeting" memo, 6/7/33, 2, PPFA-SSC.

115. "Council on Population Policy" minutes, 3/27/34, PPFA-SSC.

116. Black, using a slightly different set of documents than I have, observes that Henry Pratt Fairchild believed that Margaret Sanger's involvement in the scheme was sufficient to kill it, from Fairchild to Harry F. Perkins, 3/8/33, Vermont Public Records, cited in Black, 141.

117. Ibid., 3.

118. "Minutes of Conference on Coordination," 2/15/34, 1, PPFA-SSC.

5. Money Means Power

1. See also James W. Reed, "The Birth Control Movement Before *Roe v. Wade*," in *Politics of Abortion and Birth Control in Historical Perspective*, ed. Donald T. Critchlow (University Park: Pennsylvania State University Press, 1996), 22–52.

2. Frederick Osborn, "American Foundations and Population Problems," in *U.S. Philanthropic Foundations: Their History, Structure, Management, and Record*, ed. Warren Weaver (New York: Harper and Row, 1967), 373.

3. Peter Bachrach and Elihu Bergman, *Power and Choice: The Formulation of American Population Policy* (Lexington: Lexington Books, 1973), 77; Osborn, 1967; John Sharpless, "World Population Growth, Family Planning, and American Foreign Policy," in *The Politics of Abortion and Birth Control in Historical Perspective*, 72–102.

4. Quoted in Oscar Harkavy, *Curbing Population Growth: An Insider's Perspective on the Population Movement*, ed. Kenneth C. Land, Plenum Series on Demographic Methods and Population Analysis (New York: Plenum Press, 1995), 10.

5. Gar Allen, "The Work of Raymond Pearl: From Eugenics to Population Control," *Science for the People* 12, no. 4 (1980): 22–28, here 26.

6. Donald P. Warwick, *Bitter Pills:*

Population Policies and Their Implementation in Eight Developing Countries (Cambridge: Cambridge University Press, 1982), ix-xi.

7. Donald P. Warwick, "The Politics of Population Research with a UN Sponsor," in *The Research Relationship: Practice and Politics in Social Policy Research*, ed. G. Clare Wenger, Contemporary Social Research Series (Boston: Allen and Unwin, 1987), 167–184; see p. 183.

8. Warwick, 1982, 44.

9. Ibid., 106–107.

10. Peter J. Donaldson, *Nature Against Us: The United States and the World Population Crisis, 1965–1980* (Chapel Hill: University of North Carolina, 1990), 111.

11. Quoted in ibid., 101. Most of the time, however, outright physical violence was not necessary to produce the results he desired. Ravenholt, according to a pro–population control writer, "supported numerous research studies that produced much of the evidence on which this and many other studies of population and family planning programs are based." A colleague said, "He knew he was right so there had to be some data there somewhere" (ibid., 102). Such an attitude is not, needless to say, one of scientific objectivity.

12. Quoted in Julian L. Simon, "The Population Establishment, Corruption, and Reform," in *Population Policy: Contemporary Issues*, ed. Godfrey Roberts (New York: Praeger, 1990), 39–58, especially 43.

13. Donald P. Warwick, "The KAP Survey: Dictates of Mission versus Demands of Science," in *Social Research in Developing Countries: Surveys and Censuses in the Third World*, ed. Martin Blumer and Donald P. Warwick, Social Development in the Third World (New York: John Wiley and Sons Limited, 1983), 349–363.

14. Quoted in ibid., 350; italics mine.

15. Ibid., 351.

16. Ibid., 354–55.

17. Simon, 1990, 36–57.

18. From Mahumud Mamdani, *The Myth of Population Control: Family, Caste and Class in an Indian Village* (New York: Monthly Review Press, 1972), 19, quoted in Betsy Hartmann, *Reproductive Rights and Wrongs: The Global Politics of Population Control*, second ed. (Boston: South End Press, 1995), 60.

19. E. J. Stanley to T. O. Griessemer, 2/10/66, from RAC, Special Collection (Population Council), series IV3B4, subseries 5, box 101, folder 1893.

20. These examples are not isolated. One survey of population education in college courses determined that three kinds of faculty members are likely to incorporate pro–population control material into their courses: purists, propagandists, and popularizers. The first type consists of demographers who present the material more or less in a scientific way; the second group are those who have "little or no graduate training in demography, but substitute concern for the competence they lack"; and the third are those who have no training whatsoever but bring an evangelical zeal to the task of indoctrinating the younger generation. The last group incorporates whatever propaganda is "stuffed several times weekly into the mailbox of every professor remotely concerned with demography — ephemera from birth-control leagues, conservationist groups, advocates of zero population, and anti-industrialists of every description" (Theresa F. Rogers, "Attention to Population on Campus," mimeo [New York: Columbia University, Bureau of Applied Social Research, 1974], quoted in William Petersen, "Malthus and the Intellectuals," *Population and Development Review* 5, no. 3 [1979]: 469–478, here 476–77).

21. Kingsley Davis, "Population Policy: Will Current Programs Succeed?" *Science* (November 10, 1967): 158, 730–739.

22. Bachrach and Bergman, 33, 36. See also the article by Davis's wife and fellow demographer Judith Blake, who advocates basically the same cultural transformation (Judith Blake, "Judith Blake on Fertility Control and the Problem of Voluntarism," *Population and Development Review* 20, no. 1 [1994]: 167–177).

23. Quoted in Hartmann, 1995, 71.

24. Stephen G. Greene, "Philanthropy's Population Explosion," *Chronicle of Philanthropy*, May 31, 1994, 6–8, here 6.

25. Ibid.

26. Bachrach and Bergman, 43.

27. Quoted in Evelyn Fox Keller, "Nature, Nurture, and the Human Genome Project," in *The Code of Codes: Scientific and Social Issues in the Human Genome Project*, ed. Daniel J. Kevles and Leroy Hood (Cambridge: Harvard University Press, 1992), 281–99, on p. 284.

28. Osborn, 1967, 367.

29. Reed, 1996, 40.

30. JDR3 to JDR, Jr., 3/17/34, 2–3, from RAC, RF, RG2, Medical, box 1, folder 1.

31. Notestein, 1971, 78–79.

32. The story is related in Donald T. Critchlow, *Intended Consequences: Birth Control, Abortion, and the Federal Government in Modern America* (New York: Oxford University Press, 1999), 21.

33. Memo, Donald H. McLean to files, 6/25/52, from RAC, Family, RG 5, series 1, sub-series 5, box 81, folder 674.

34. Dictation, "Conference on Population Problems," 6/22/52, 53, from RAC, Family, RG 5, series 1, subseries 5, box 85, folder 721.

35. Phyllis Tilson Piotrow, *World Population Crisis: The United States Response*, Praeger Special Studies in International Economics and Development, Law and Population Book Series, vol. 4 (New York: Praeger Publishers, 1973), 12.

36. "Summary Report," John Hajnal (n.d.; probably August 1952), 3, from RAC, RG2, Medical Series, Birth Control Sub-series, box 1, folder 4.

37. Linda Gordon, "The Politics of Population: Birth Control and the Eugenics Movement," *Radical America* 8, no. 4 (1974): 61–96, on 83.

38. "Proposed Establishment of Population Council," 10/7/52, 5, from RAC, Family, RG 5, series 1, subseries 5, box 82, folder 682.

39. "Proposed Establishment of Population Council," 11/20/52, 5, from ibid.

40. Hajnal, "Summary," 4.

41. Dictation, "Conference on Population Problems," 6/22/52, 40–41, op. cit., folder 722.

42. JDR3 to J. George Harrar, 9/27/63, 1, from RAC, Family, RG 5, series 1, sub-series 5, box 82, folder 681.

43. "Conference on Population Problems," 6/22/52, op. cit., 25, 27.

44. Donald T. Critchlow, "Birth Control, Population Control, and Family Planning: An Overview," in *Politics of Abortion and Birth Control in Historical Perspective*, 1–21, here 9; John Sharpless, "World Population Growth, Family Planning, and American Foreign Policy," in ibid., 72–102, here 80; Osborn, 1967, 369.

45. JDR3 to Frederick Osborn, 6/12/39, from RAC, Family, RG 5, series 1, sub-series 5, box 60, folder 600.

46. JDR3 to Osborn, 4/4/38, from ibid.

47. Notestein, 1971, 80.

48. *Reminiscences of John D. Rockefeller 3rd*, Columbia University Oral History Project, part I (1964), 265, from RAC, Family, series 3, subseries 8, box 104, folder 868. Interestingly, a Rockefeller staff member edited out some of the eugenic language from the interview transcript.

49. Population Council, Inc., "Reports of the Executive Officers for the Period November 5, 1952 to December 31, 1955" (New York: Population Council, Inc., 1956), 9, MSP-SSC (unfilmed).

50. "Minutes of the Board of Trustees of the Population Council, Inc.," 3/11/54, 6–8, from RAC, Family, RG 5, series 1, sub-series 5, box 82, folder 684.

51. "Members of the Informal Twin Study Group," n.d. (11/56?), from RAC, Special Collections (Population Council), series IV3B4, sub-series 2, box 40, folder 568; Diane B. Paul, *The Politics of Heredity: Essays on Eugenics, Biomedicine, and the Nature-Nurture Debate*, ed. David Edward Shaner, Philosophy and Biology (Albany: SUNY Press, 1998), 61, 65.

52. Frederick Osborn, "Memorandum on Development of Twin Study," 11/11/54, from RAC, Special Collections (Population Council), series IV3B4, sub-series 2, box 40, folder 569.

53. Osborn to Lewontin, 5/10/66, AES papers, Carl J. Bajema file.

54. Population Council, "Annual Report," 1955–60, 32–33, MSP-SSC (unfilmed).

55. Frederick Osborn, "History of the American Eugenics Society," *Social Biology* 21, no. 2 (1974): 115–126, here 122.

56. American Eugenics Society, Inc., "Five-Year Report of the Officers: 1953–1957," 1958, 9, MSP-SSC (unfilmed).

57. Carl Jay Bajema to Frederick Osborn, 12/31/65, 1–2, AES, APS, Carl J. Bajema folder.

58. Carl Jay Bajema to Dr. David Sills, Population Council, 12/21/71, from ibid.

59. Irving I. Gottesman and L. Erlenmeyer-Kimling, "A Foundation for Informed Eugenics," *Social Biology* 18, no. Supp. 2 (1971): S1-S8, on S1.

60. Ibid., S7.

61. Harriet Pilpel, "Family Planning and the Law," *Social Biology* 18, no. Supp. 2 (1971): S127–S133.

62. "Association for Voluntary Sterilization, 2nd International Conference, 2/25–3/1/73," 2, Harriet Pilpel papers (un-

processed, accession number 82-M123) (henceforth HP), Schlesinger Library, Radcliffe Institute, Harvard University, folder 7. Elsewhere, among examples of "innovative approaches" to population control, she cites the fact that "in Korea a new and desirable apartment house is reserved for people who have had a vasectomy" and praises the fact that "the Constitution of Rio de Janeiro calls for the state government to give special attention to 'family planning and the development of a eugenic awareness of the family'" ("Morality, Medicine, Freedom & Population: a talk for the World Population Society, Washington, D.C. November 20, 1975," 7, 8, HP papers, folder 24). Her son believes that Pilpel rejected eugenic sterilization by the end of her life.

63. Christopher Tietze, "An Outline for an Experiment in Population Control," 10/30/46, in RAC, Family, RG 2, Medical series, Birth Control subseries, box 2, folder 1.

64. James W. Reed, Sarah Lewit Tietze, and Christopher Tietze, M.D., "Schlesinger-Rockefeller Oral History Project, Interview with Sarah Lewit Tietze and Christopher Tietze, M.D., December 1975–January 1976" (Cambridge: Radcliffe College, 1976), 22. For more details on the misogynistic motivation for IUD development, see the seventh chapter on women's rights and health.

65. Lynette J. Dumble, "Population Control or Empowerment of Women?" *Green Left*, November 2, 1994, 15.

66. Population Information Programs, "Decisions for Norplant Programs," *Population Reports*, November 1992, 1–32, on 9.

67. Ibid.

68. Barbara Mintzes, Anita Hardon, and Jannemieke Hanhart, eds., *Norplant: Under Her Skin* (Delft: The Women's Health Action Foundation, 1993), 7, 19. The seventh chapter will address Norplant and other dangerous contraceptives in more detail.

69. Quoted in Warwick, 1982, 165.

70. Hartmann, 1995, 169, 211.

71. "Population Control: Implications, Trends and Prospects," in *Pakistan International Family Planning Conference*, ed. Nafis Sadik (Dacca, Pakistan: Pakistan Family Planning Council, 1969), 258–260, on 259.

72. Memo, Sheldon J. Segal to Frank W. Notestein, 4/20/64, from RAC, Special Collections (Population Council), series IV3B4, sub-series 2, box 4, folder 38.

73. Sheldon J. Segal, "Norplant Developed for All Women, Not Just the Well-to-Do," *New York Times*, January 6, 1991, E18.

74. "Minutes for Drafting the American Ideas of a Constitution for the IPPF," 6/24/1953, 3, MSP-SSC.

75. Critchlow, 1999, 31.

76. Ibid., 32.

77. Allan Chase, "Passing the Word on Sterilization: 1937 to 1977," *Medical Tribune*, September 21, 1977, 1, 16, 28.

78. Ibid., 16; see also the literature in CJG papers, box 231, folder 3572.

79. James W. Reed and Frances Hand Ferguson, "Schlesinger-Rockefeller Oral History Project, Frances Hand Ferguson, June 1974" (Cambridge: Radcliffe College, 1974), 20.

80. Critchlow, 1999, 32.

81. Reed and Ferguson, 32.

82. *The Population Bomb: Is Voluntary Human Sterilization the Answer?* (New York: Hugh Moore Fund, n.d.), 11, MSP-SSC (unfilmed).

83. Lader, 1971, 100–101.

84. Ibid., 31.

85. Reed and Ferguson, 46.

86. Quoted in Critchlow, 1999, 32.

87. The seventh chapter will be devoted to this topic.

88. "A Symposium on Population," *Journal of Contraception*, February, 1939: 38–40, here 40.

89. "The Population Council: A Twenty-Five Year Chronicle, 1952–1977," 2/78, 46, from RAC, Family, RG 5, series 3, sub-series 4, box 72, folder 490.

90. "Resolution," 3/35, MSP-SSC.

91. Critchlow, 1999, 42–43.

92. Bachrach and Bergman, 79.

93. Gordon, 1974, 84.

94. Critchlow, 1999, 69.

95. Piotrow, 132.

96. Ibid., 169.

97. Ibid., 91.

98. Hartmann, 1995, 255.

99. Thomas Shapiro, *Population Control Politics: Women, Sterilization, and Reproductive Choice* (Philadelphia: Temple University Press, 1985), 91–92.

100. John Elliott, "'Genocide' Charged by Indian M.D. Investigator," *Medical Tribune*, August 24, 1977, 1, 8, here 8.

101. Ellen Barry, "Eugenics Victims Are Heard at Last," *Boston Globe*, August 15, 1999, B1, B6; Ellen Barry, "Pages from Past

Breed Uneasiness," *Boston Globe*, August 7, 1999, A1, B4.

102. Asoka Bandarage, *Women, Population and Global Crisis: A Political-Economic Analysis* (London: Zed Books, 1997), 83.

103. Hartmann, 1995, 212.

104. Alexander Cockburn, "Norplant and the Social Cleansers, Part II," *The Nation*, July 25–August 1, 1994, 116–17.

105. Ibid.

106. Ibid., 95–99.

107. Draper to William Rogers, 4/19/65, from RAC, Special Collections (Population Council), series IV3B4, sub-series 5, box 101, folder 1908.

108. Draper to William Rogers, 5/17/65, from ibid.

109. Glycon de Paiva and Paolo C. A. Antunes to Draper, 5/14/65, from ibid.

110. Bernadine and Charles Zukowski to Richard Gamble, 8/25/74, 3, SMBG papers.

111. Piotrow, 125.

112. "Harvard Seminar with Jack Sullivan," Center for Population Studies, notes by Sarah Bradley Gamble, 2/5/75, 1, from SMBG papers.

113. Piotrow, 132–39.

114. Ibid., 154.

115. "Plans for the World Population Conference," 1/6/53, from RAC, Family, RG 5, series 1, sub-series 5, box 84, folder 706.

116. Piotrow, 204–19.

117. Notestein, 1971, 78.

118. Piotrow, 212–16.

119. Dana S. Creel to John D. Rockefeller, Jr., 3/13/55, 3, from RAC, RG 2, Medical, box 5, folder 40.

120. Piotrow, 160.

121. Donaldson, 1990, 111.

122. Paul Wagman, "U.S. Program to Sterilize Millions," *St. Louis Post-Dispatch*, April 22, 1977, 1, 10, here 10. This strategy has been again acknowledged recently by Nafis Sadik, former executive director of UNFPA.

123. Reed and Ferguson, 30.

124. Wagman, 10.

125. "India," *Eugenics Review* 6, no. 3 (1964): 177.

126. Hartmann, 1995, 251. Regarding the incentive programs, Mary Lasker expressed a typical preoccupation with India's population when she complained, "India has never been noted for its outstanding support on a practical level of birth control methods, except in Madras where they're doing operations on men to make them permanently sterile. They give a cash sum to encourage men who have had more than an x-number of children to have this operation done, and so far as I know they've only done about 20 or 30 or 40 thousand operations. This isn't going to make a real dent in the population of India." For Lasker, as for so many population controllers, the only problem with coercive methods is their relative inefficacy (Reminiscences of Mary Lasker, with John T. Mason, Jr., 1966, Columbia University Oral History Research Office, series I, vol. 3, 451).

127. Piotrow, 180.

128. Ibid.

129. Hartmann, 1995, 251–52.

130. Quoted in Reed, 1974, 103.

131. Lewis M. Simmons, "Compulsory Sterilization Provokes Fear, Contempt," *Washington Post*, July 4, 1977, A1, A16, A17.

132. Alaka M. Basu, "Family Planning and the Emergency: An Unanticipated Consequence," *Economic and Political Weekly*, March 9, 1985, 422–425, on 422; Molly Moore, "Teeming India Engulfed by Soaring Birthrate," *Washington Post*, August 21, 1994, A1. Invariably, to Western eyes, India is "teeming."

133. Iris Kapil, "Case for Injectible Contraceptive," *Economic and Political Weekly*, May 11, 1985, 854–856, here 854.

134. Moore, 1994.

135. Gargi Parsai, "New Approach to Population Control Decried," *The Hindu*, June 13, 1999, www.indiaserver.com:80/thehindu/1999/06/12/stories/0212000i.htm, accessed 6/17/99.

136. "Centre not for Coercion in Population Control," *The Hindu*, June 12, 2001, www.hinduonnet.com/thehindu/2001/06/12/stories/02120005.htm, accessed 11/12/03.

137. Stephen G. Greene, "Ted Turner Maps Out His Sphere of Influence," *Chronicle of Philanthropy*, June 4, 1998, 9–10, 12, on 10.

138. Ibid., 12.

139. Turner Foundation web site, www.turnerfoundation.org/turner/pop96-2.html, accessed 1/6/2000.

140. Greene, 8.

141. "Turner: In His Own Words," *PRI Review*, Jan./Feb. 1997, 12–13, on 13.

142. Thomas Goetz, "Billionaire Boys' Cause: Can Three of the World's Richest Men Put Overpopulation Back on the Public Agenda?" *Village Voice*, Oct. 7, 41–43.

143. Ibid.

144. Tracey C. Rembert, "Conversations: Ted Turner: Billionaire, Media Mogul ... and Environmentalist," *E/The Environmental Magazine*, January-February 1999, www.emagazine.com/January-february_1999/0199conversations.html, accessed 5/18/99. Turner goes on to say that he personally thinks the world should have "somewhere between 40 and 100 million people," which would necessitate the elimination of over 98% of the world's people. In this, he echoes Garrett Hardin, who argued for 100 million people in 1996 (Interview, *Skeptic* 4, no. 2 [1996]: 42–46).

145. Ron Popeski, "Ted Turner Owns Nearly 1.5 Percent of New Mexico," *Reuters*, Sept. 25, 1996.

146. Bailey, 2.

147. Krista West, "The Billionaire Conservationist," *Scientific American* 287, no. 2 (August 2002): 34–35.

148. James E. Larcombe, "Living Large: Big Sky Plus Big Land Equals Big Money," *Denver Rocky Mountain News*, Sept. 28, 1997, 18A.

149. Perhaps this is why, as one article noted, he favors environmental groups in the immediate vicinity of his sprawling ranches: to get his money, "environmentalists must put up with Turner's quirks. He gives preference to groups in Montana, New Mexico, and other states where he owns ranches" (Scott Allen, "Ted Turner: Media Mogul on Course to Be One of Movement's Top Funders," *Boston Globe*, Oct. 19, 1997, A31).

150. Betsy Pisik, "He Gave at the U.N.," *Washington Times*, April 27, 1998, A14.

151. Goetz, 1.

152. Ibid., 3.

153. Warwick, 1982, 32.

154. Frederick S. Jaffe to Bernard Berelson, 3/11/69.

155. Quoted in Germaine Greer, *Sex and Destiny: The Politics of Human Fertility* (New York: Harper & Row, 1984), 388.

156. Maurice King and Charles Elliott, "To the Point of Farce: a Martian View of the Hardinian Taboo — the Silence that Surrounds Population Control," *British Medical Journal* 315, no. 7120 (1997): 1441–43.

157. Quoted in Harkavy, 73.

158. Hartmann, 1995, 81.

159. *Report of the International Conference on Population and Development, 5–13 September 1994*, A/Conf.171/13, October 18, 1994, www.un.org/popin/icpd/conference/offeng/poa.html, accessed on 8/7/02.

160. For critiques of the continuing post–Cairo cooptation of feminist language for the purposes of population control, see the essays in *Dangerous Intersections: Feminist Perspectives on Population, Environment, and Development; a Project of the Committee on Women, Population, and the Environment*, ed. Jael Silliman and Ynestra King (Boston: South End Press, 1999).

161. Quoted in Hartmann, 1995, 109.

162. Charles and Bernadine Zukowski to "Dick" Gamble, 8/30/74, from SMBG papers, box 27, folder 569.

163. Memo, George Zeidenstein to JDR3, 11/16/76, from RAC, Family, RG 5, series 3, sub-series 4, box 72, folder 486.

164. Zeidenstein memo, 11/16/76, from ibid. Feminist Betsy Hartmann has argued that the language of women's rights and health mouthed by population-control agencies and organizations is simply the expedient cooptation of feminist language for oppressive purposes (Betsy Hartmann, "Population Control as Foreign Policy," *CovertAction* 39, Winter [1991-1992]: 26–30).

165. For a critique of the pro–population control ideology within the Cairo draft plan, see S. Grimes, "The Ideology of Population Control in the UN Draft Plan for Cairo," *Population Research and Policy Review* 13, no. 3 (1994): 209–24.

166. UNFPA, *Coming Up Short: Struggling to Implement the Cairo Programme of Action*, report, May 13, 1997.

6. "Sterilize All the Unfit!"

1. Margaret Sanger, "The Function of Sterilization," *Birth Control Review* 10, no. 10 (October 1926): 299.

2. Quoted in Thomas M. Shapiro, *Population Control Politics: Women, Sterilization, and Reproductive Choice* (Philadelphia: Temple University Press, 1985), 117.

3. Dan Balz, "Sweden Sterilized Thousands of 'Useless' Citizens for Decades," *Washington Post*, August 29, 1997, A1.

4. Ibid.

5. See Gunnar Broberg and Nils Roll-Hansen, eds. *Eugenics and the Welfare State: Sterilization Policy in Denmark, Sweden, Norway, and Finland* (East Lansing: Uni-

versity of Michigan Press, 1996) for essays on the implication of the various Scandinavian countries in eugenics in general and sterilization in particular.

6. This has been true especially in Latin American countries, where sterilization is seen as emasculating the man. For example, in Peru, during the recent sterilization campaigns, women are "always" the targets, according to one witness (Angela Franks and David Morrison, Interview, July 1998).

7. Paul Popenoe and Roswell Johnson, *Applied Eugenics*, ed. Richard T. Ely, second ed., Social Science Textbooks (New York: Macmillan Company, 1933), 138–49.

8. Philip R. Reilly, *The Surgical Solution: A History of Involuntary Sterilization in the United States* (Baltimore: The Johns Hopkins University Press, 1991), 101.

9. Clarence J. Gamble, "Eugenic Sterilization in the United States, 1948," *Eugenical News* 34, no. 1-2 (1949): 1. See also the estimate in Popenoe and Johnson's eugenics textbook, in which it states that the cost to the state of identifying and treating the various types of "deficients" was around $5 billion. They also state that most of those unemployed during the Great Depression in 1929 would "probably" never find employment again, thereby blaming the systemic economic problems of the Depression on the supposed mental deficiency of those who suffered because of them (Popenoe and Johnson, 134, 136).

10. Birthright, "...Unto the Third and Fourth Generation" (Princeton: Birthright, Inc., 1949).

11. Reilly, 98.

12. For women's experience under the Nazis, see Gisela Bock, "Racism and Sexism in Nazi Germany: Motherhood, Compulsory Sterilization, and the State," *Signs: Journal of Women in Culture and Society* 8, no. 3 (1983): 401.

13. Ibid., 413.

14. Reilly, 109.

15. Bock, 1983, 417–18.

16. For brief summaries of American eugenic ideas and practices that were taken up by the Nazis, see Paul Crook, "American Eugenics and the Nazis: Recent Historiography," *European Legacy* 7 (3, 2002): 363–81 and Peter Quinn, "Race Cleansing in America," *American Heritage* 54 (1, 2003): 34–43. For detailed expositions, see Stefan Kühl, *The Nazi Connection: Eugenics, American Racism, and German National Socialism*

(New York: Oxford University Press, 1994) and Edwin Black's magisterial *War Against the Weak: Eugenics and America's Campaign to Create a Master Race* (New York: Four Walls Eight Windows, 2003).

17. For the impact of Nazi policies on the deaf in particular, see Horst Biesold, *Crying Hands: Eugenics and Deaf People in Nazi Germany*, trans. William Sayers (Washington, D.C.: Gallaudet University Press, 2002).

18. Reilly, 107.

19. As Gisela Bock notes, "'Inferiority' as a social category and reality also includes women as a social group next to ethnic and other similar social-cultural forms of inferiority" (Gisela Bock, *Zwangssterilisation im Nationalsozialismus: Studien zur Rassenpolitik und Frauenpolitik*, Schriften des Zentralinstituts für sozialwissenschaftliche Forschung der Freien Universität Berlin, vol. 48 [Opladen: Westdeutscher Verlag, 1986], 369, my translation).

20. *Buck v. Bell* (274 US 200., 1927).

21. Quoted in Allan Chase, *The Legacy of Malthus: The Social Costs of the New Scientific Racism* (Chicago: University of Illinois Press, 1980), 316.

22. Unfortunately, the *Buck* decision was neither the first nor the last time the Supreme Court would hallow assaults against the dignity of marginalized persons—from *Dred Scott* to *Korematsu* and beyond.

23. Stephen Jay Gould, *The Mismeasure of Man*, second ed. (New York: W. W. Norton and Company, 1996), 365–66.

24. Black, 400.

25. William Branigan, "VA Apologizes to the Victims of Sterilization," *Washington Post*, May 3, 2002, B1. Another victim of the Virginia law, Raymond Hudlow, mourned, "I hope it never again happens to any other child. It is horrible. You have no children. No family." Virginia formally apologized to the victims in 2002.

26. J. David Smith, "*The Bell Curve* and Carrie Buck: Eugenics Revisited," *Mental Retardation* 33, no. 1 (1995): 60. As does Edwin Black, Stefan Kühl details the many organizational connections between Nazi Germany and various American sterilization groups, including the Human Betterment Foundation and Birthright's Marian S. Norton Olden in Stefan Kühl, 1994.

27. Reilly, 95.

28. J. D. Robitscher, M.D., ed., *Eugenic Sterilization* (Springfield: Charles C. Thomas, 1973), 118–119.

29. For example, Alan Guttmacher acknowledged, "As a physician in private practice I have done occasional sterilizations on adolescent females brought to me by their parents for sterilization because of serious mental retardation" (in ibid., 54).

30. American Academy of Pediatrics Committee on Bioethics, "Sterilization of Women Who Are Mentally Handicapped," *Pediatrics* 85, no. 5 (1990): 868–871.

31. Maj. Gerard S. Letterie, M.C., U.S.A. and William F. Fox, Jr., J.D., "Legal Aspects of Involuntary Sterilization," *Fertility and Sterility* 53, no. 3 (1990): 391–398.

32. J. D. Zumpano-Canto, M.P.H., "Nonconsensual Sterilization of the Mentally Disabled in North Carolina: An Ethics Critique of the Statutory Standard and Its Judicial Interpretation," *Journal of Contemporary Health Law and Policy* 13, no. 79 (1996): 91.

33. Thomas E. Elkins and H. Frank Andersen, "Sterilization of Persons with Mental Retardation," *Journal of the Association for Persons with Severe Handicaps* 17, no. 1 (1992): 23.

34. Ellen Brantlinger, "Professionals' Attitudes Toward the Sterilization of People with Disabilities," *Journal of the Association for Persons with Severe Handicaps* 17, no. 1 (1992): 9.

35. Ibid., 11.

36. Shapiro, 89–90.

37. Ibid.

38. Angela Y. Davis, *Women, Race, and Class* (New York: Vintage Books, 1983), 216–17.

39. Quoted in Shapiro, 90.

40. Davis, 217.

41. Shapiro, 90–92.

42. Davis, 218. For a summary, see Sally J. Torpy, "Native American Women and Coerced Sterilization: On the Trail of Tears in the 1970s," *American Indian Culture and Research Journal* 24, no. 2 (2000): 1–22; also see Nancy L. Gallagher, *Breeding Better Vermonters: The Eugenics Project in the Green Mountain State* (Hanover, N.H.: University Press of New England, 1999) for the use of sterilization to attack the local Abenaki Indians.

43. Relf v. Weinberger et al. (1974).

44. See also Chase, 1980, 16–19.

45. Helen Rodriguez-Trias, "The Women's Health Movement: Women Take Power," in *Reforming Medicine: Lessons of the Last Quarter Century*, ed. Victor W.

Sidel and Ruth Sidel (New York: Pantheon Books, 1984), 120.

46. Shapiro, 143–48.

47. Shapiro, 105. See 94–107 for his argument. See also the series of articles by Allan Chase in 1977: "American Indian Women Not Fully Informed, GAO Study Finds," *Medical Tribune*, August 10, 1977, 1, 6; "MDs Helped Explode Early Conceptual Bias, and Yet...," *Medical Tribune*, September 14, 1977, 1, 21, 22; "Passing the Word on Sterilization: 1937 to 1977," *Medical Tribune*, September 21, 1977, 16, 28; "Pro-Hysterectomy Stance, Consent 'Failings' Hit," *Medical Tribune*, August 24, 1977, 1, 8; and "Today's Treatment of the Poor Linked to Early Eugenics Movement," *Medical Tribune*, September 7, 1977, 1, 22.

48. Shapiro, 90.

49. See Davis, 220; Shapiro, 111–15; Linda Gordon, *Woman's Body, Woman's Right: Birth Control in America*, second ed. (New York: Penguin Books, 1990), 441.

50. Shapiro, 92–94.

51. Dr. Ralph C. Wright, quoted in Lara V. Marks, *Sexual Chemistry: A History of the Contraceptive Pill* (New Haven: Yale University Press), 2001, 132.

52. Robert E. McGarrah, Jr., "Voluntary Female Sterilization: Abuses, Risks, and Guidelines," *The Hastings Center Report* 4, no. 3 (1974): 6.

53. David Dempsey, "The Fertility Goddess vs. the Loop: Dr. Guttmacher Is the Evangelist of Birth Control," *New York Times Magazine*, February 9, 1969, 32; and Alan F. Guttmacher, *Babies By Choice or By Chance* (Garden City: Doubleday and Company, 1959), 42, 46.

54. Quoted in Shapiro, 117.

55. Margaret Sanger, *The Pivot of Civilization* (New York: Brentano's, 1922), 101–2.

56. Margaret Sanger, "The Function of Sterilization," *Birth Control Review*, October 1926, 299.

57. Margaret Sanger, "A Plan for Peace," *Birth Control Review*, April 1932, 107.

58. Margaret Sanger, "Birth Control and Racial Betterment," *Birth Control Review*, February 1919, 11–12.

59. Margaret Sanger, "Lasker Foundation Award Speech," 10/25/50, from MSP-LC, cont. 201, reel 130.

60. Gamble to MS, 11/1/50, CJG, box 195, folder 3096.

61. Shapiro, 56; Ellen Chesler, *Woman*

of Valor: Margaret Sanger and the Birth Control Movement in America (New York: Simon & Schuster, 1992), 380. See also chapter three, which details Gamble's eugenic beliefs.

62. Mary Antoinette Cannon, *Outline for a Course in Planned Parenthood* (New York: Planned Parenthood Federation of America, 1945?), MSP-SSC (unfilmed).

63. Shapiro, 146.

64. Reilly, 133–46.

65. H. Curtis Wood, Jr., "The Physician's Responsibility in the Decline of National Intelligence" (Princeton: Birthright, Inc., n.d.).

66. Ibid., italics his.

67. Shapiro, 56–57.

68. Guttmacher is listed as residing in Baltimore, but he took over the Department of Obstetrics and Gynecology at Mount Sinai Hospital in New York in 1952, so the pamphlet must have originated before that time. The same pamphlet lists Sheldon C. Reed of Minneapolis on the board of directors. Reed was famous for writing a book on mental retardation in the 1960s, with Elizabeth Reed as co-author, arguing that mental retardation was mostly due to genetic factors, a common eugenic thesis that has not been accepted by the majority of mental disability professionals. This book was nevertheless later used in *The Bell Curve* in order to show the need for eugenic action.

69. Ruth Proskauer Smith to Clarence Gamble, 4/1/58, CJG papers, box 231, folder 3566.

70. H. Curtis Wood and Alan F. Guttmacher, n.d. (1958?), HBAA letter, CJG papers, ibid.

71. Alan F. Guttmacher, "The Population Crisis and the Use of World Resources," in *The Population Crisis and the Use of World Resources*, ed. Stuart Mudd, World Academy of Art and Science (Bloomington: Indiana University Press, 1964), 268–273, here 272–73.

72. See Shapiro, 58–59.

73. Ellen Brantlinger, "Professionals' Attitudes Toward the Sterilization of People with Disabilities," *Journal of the Association for Persons with Severe Handicaps* 17, no. 1 (1992): 14–15.

74. See, for example, Wang Wei, Head of the Delegation of the People's Republic of China at the World Population Conference, "Chinese Statements on Population at Bucharest, 1974, and Mexico City, 1984," *Population and Development Review* 20, no. 2 (1994): 449–459. China did support family planning and encouraged decreased fertility, but without the forceful planned approach that characterized later policy (John S. Aird, "Coercion in Family Planning: Causes, Methods, and Consequences," in *China's Economy Looks Toward the Year 2000*, ed. Congress of the United States Joint Economic Committee [Washington, D.C.: U.S. Government Printing Office, 1986], 184–221).

75. Steven W. Mosher, *A Mother's Ordeal: One Woman's Fight Against China's One-Child Policy* (New York: HarperPerennial, 1993), 224–40.

76. Michael Weisskopf, "China Orders Sterilization for Parents," *Washington Post*, May 28 1983, A1; Tyrene White, "Two Kinds of Production: The Evolution of China's Family Planning Policy in the 1980s," in *The New Politics of Population: Conflict and Consensus in Family Planning*, ed. Jason L. Finkle and C. Alison McIntosh, Population and Development Review, A Supplement to vol. 20, 1994 (New York: The Population Council, 1994), 146.

77. Weisskopf, 1983.

78. Quoted in John S. Aird, *Slaughter of the Innocents: Coercive Birth Control in China* (Washington, D.C.: AEI Press, 1990), 32. This volume traces the development of the Chinese policy, relying on previously untranslated Chinese documents.

79. White, 1994, 147.

80. Aird, 1986, 194.

81. Ibid., 184.

82. Susan Greenhalgh and Jiali Li, "Engendering Reproductive Policy and Practice in Peasant China: For a Feminist Demography of Reproduction," *Signs: Journal of Women in Culture and Society* 20, no. 3 (1995): 624.

83. White, 153–54.

84. Susan Greenhalgh, Zhu Chuzhu, and Li Nan, "Restraining Population Growth in Three Chinese Villages, 1988–93," *Population and Development Review* 20, no. 2 (1994): 601–41, here 386.

85. Newspaper accounts of coercion and human-rights abuses include: George Archibald, "House Panel Hears Firsthand of Forced Abortions in China," *Washington Times*, July 20, 1995, A12; Carroll J. Doherty, "Population Funds Entangled in China's Alleged Abuses," *Congressional*

Quarterly, June 5, 1993, 1429–1430; Celia W. Dugger, "Dozens of Chinese from 1993 Voyage Still in Jail," *New York Times*, February 3, 1997, A1, B5; Jim Kennet, "Stung by Coercion Controversy, China Defends Population Goals," *Family Planning World*, July/August 1993, 1; Nicholas D. Kristof, "China Issues Rebuttal to Human Rights Critics," *New York Times*, November 3, 1991, A12; Toni Marshall, "U.S. Called Too Easy on China: Rep. Smith Slams Rights Report, Says It Plays Down Abuses," *Washington Times*, February 4, 1998, A13; Stephen W. Mosher, "How China Uses U.N. Aid for Forced Abortions," *The Wall Street Journal*, May 13, 1985; Steven W. Mosher, "'One Family, One Child': China's Brutal Birth Ban," *Washington Post*, October 18, 1987, D1; Steven W. Mosher, "China's Grim One-Child Rule Get [*sic*] Worse," *Washington Times*, April 5, 1995, A19; Julian L. Simon, "China's Family-Planning by Coercion," *Washington Post*, March 10, 1993, A19; Patrick E. Tyler, "Birth Control in China: Coercion and Evasion," *New York Times*, June 25, 1995, A1, A8. An earlier turning point in bringing the Chinese humanitarian abuses to American public attention had come with Michael Weisskopf's three-part expose on the one-child policy: "One Couple, One Child, Part 1," *Washington Post*, January 6, 1985, A1, A30; "One Couple, One Child, Part 2," *Washington Post*, January 7, 1985, A1, A20; and "One Couple, One Child, Part 3," *Washington Post*, January 8, 1985, A1, A10.

86. See Mosher, 1995; Harry Wu, testimony to the U.S. House Committee on International Relations, October 17, 2001; from www.pop.org/china/Wu.htm.

87. Wu, 2001; Yemlibike Fatkulin, testimony to the U.S. House Committee on International Relations, October 17, 2001; from www.pop.org/china/fatkulin.htm.

88. Wu, 2001; Fatkulin, 2001.

89. Department of State, *Country Reports on Human Rights Practices for 1993* (Washington, D.C.: U.S. Government Printing Office, 1994), 610. Other observers estimate that the legal endorsement of eugenics began by at least 1984 (see Nicholas Eberstadt's testimony, U.S. House Subcommittee on International Operations and Human Rights of the Committee on International Relations, *Coercive Population Control in China* [Washington, D.C.: U.S. Government Printing Office, 1995], 100).

90. "'Better' Babies in China," *Washington Post*, January 2, 1993, A20.

91. Steven Mufson, "China Plans to Restrict 'Inferior' Births," *Washington Post*, December 23, 1993, A1, A28; Reuters, "China Seeks to Prevent Birth of 'Inferior' Children," *Washington Times*, December 21, 1993, A14.

92. UPI, "China Says New Birth Law Not Like Hitler's," December 29, 1993.

93. "North American Initiative Denounces Chinese Policy," *The Arc Today*, Spring 1994, 3–4. For more details on the Chinese eugenic law and the nation's attitudes toward disability, see Frank Dikotter, *Imperfect Conceptions* (New York: Columbia University Press, 1998); and Xun Zhou, "The Discourse of Disability in Modern China," *Patterns of Prejudice* 36, no. 1 (2002), 104–12.

94. Charlene L. Fu, "China — Eugenics," *Associated Press*, October 27, 1994; Jane Macartney, "New Chinese Law Urges Abortion in Cases Where Fetus Is Abnormal," *Washington Times*, June 1, 1995, A1; A. H. Bittles and Y. Chew, "Eugenics and Population Policies," *Human Biology and Social Inequality*, Society for the Study of Human Biology Symposium Series, vol. 39, edited by S. S. Strickland and P. S. Shetty (New York: Cambridge University Press, 1998), 272–87.

95. Greenhalgh, 1995, 627; "Women in China Becoming Harder to Find," March 8, 2002, Zenit News.

96. Michael Weisskopf, "One Couple, One Child, Part 3," A1, A10. Many female children are also abandoned to orphanages, which are essentially "dying rooms." See Human Rights Watch/Asia, "China: Chinese Orphanages: A Follow-Up" (New York: Human Rights Watch/Asia, 1996); Human Rights Watch/Asia, *Death by Default: A Policy of Fatal Neglect in China's State Orphanages* (New York: Human Rights Watch, 1996).

97. Elisabeth Rosenthal, "Bias for Boys Leads to Sale of Baby Girls in China," *New York Times*, July 20, 2003, http://www.nytimes.com/2003/07/20/international/asia/20CHIN.html?ei=5062&en=9c147d05.4, accessed 7/22/03.

98. "China's Gender Imbalance Stems from 'Family Planning' Policy," Cybercast News Service, April 6, 2001.

99. Greenhalgh, 1995, 635.

100. Tom Carter, "One Town's 'Mon-

ster' Tells a Tale of Horror," *Washington Times*, June 11, 1998, from www.washtimes.com.

101. Mindy Belz, "Monster by Day, Mother by Night," *World*, June 27, 1998, 14.

102. Ibid.

103. Ibid.

104. Carter, 2–3.

105. Josephine Guy, testimony to U.S. House Committee on International Relations, October 17, 2001; from www.pop.org/main.cfm?EID=304, accessed 3/18/2002. The full report can be found at www.pop.org/main.cfm?EID-312. For additional evidence on destruction of property, see Wu's interview with Chinese cadre Zhou Guilan, attachment 2 in Wu, 2001.

106. "The PRC Law of Population," published 12/29/01, cited in "Peru: UNFPA Supported Fujimori's Forced Sterilization Campaigns," *PRI Weekly Briefing* July 22, 2002, vol. 4, no. 17, 2–3.

107. For a detailed history of the controversy up to 1989, see Barbara B. Crane and Jason L. Finkle, "The United States, China, and the United Nations Population Fund: Dynamics of US Policymaking," *Population and Development Review* 15, no. 1 (1989): 23–59.

108. Cited in Aird, 1990.

109. Ibid., 173–74.

110. Belz, 15–16. For other recent testimony of human-rights abuses arising from China's policies, see Dele Olojede, "China Upholds Firing for Pregnancy," *Boston Globe*, November 22, 1998, A8; Jennifer Lin, "China Wrestles with Issue of Abandoned Children," *Boston Globe*, December 17, 1998, A34.

111. www.unfpa.org/regions/apd/countries/china.htm.

112. See, for instance, the same rhetoric regarding the Gao testimony in "Family Planners Punished, Papers Say," *Washington Times*, June 14, 1998, A9.

113. "Congressional Hearing Shows UNFPA Involvement in Forced Abortions," *Cybercast News Service*, Oct. 18, 2001.

114. Nafis Sadik, "Population Prize Award Ceremony Speech," www.sfpc.gov.cn/EN/enews20020114-2.htm, accessed 8/3/02.

115. Ibid.

116. Aird, 1986, 213.

117. United Nations Population Fund, "Inventory of Population Projects in Developing Countries Around the World"

(New York: United Nations Population Fund, 1996), 93–95.

118. See the testimonies published in the 1999 report by the Center for Reproductive Rights and the Comité Latinoamericano y del Caribe para la Defensa de la Mujer, *Silence and Complicity: Violence Against Women in Peruvian Public Health Facilities*, www.reproductiverights.org/pub_bo_silence.html#online, accessed 2/7/2004.

119. Angela Franks and David Morrison, Interview, July 1998. Already in the late 1980s, USAID had been involved in a contraception-distribution program in Peru that offered only Norplant or sterilization (Dorothy Roberts, *Killing the Black Body: Race, Reproduction, and the Meaning of Liberty* [New York: Pantheon, 1997], 139).

120. Tim Johnson, "Sterilization Debate in Peru: Are Some Women Coerced?" *Miami Herald*, January 11, 1998, www.africa2000.com/INDX/herald.html, accessed 2/7/2004.

121. Steven W. Mosher, "In Peru, Women Lose the Right to Choose More Children," *Wall Street Journal*, February 27, 1998, A19; Steven Mosher, "USAID Supported Fujimori Sterilization Campaign; Seeks to Cover Up Involvement," *PRI Weekly Briefing* 5, no. 27 (Sept. 22, 2003).

122. Mosher, 1998.

123. Mosher, 2003.

124. Grover Joseph Rees, "Report on Staff Delegation to Peru," (Washington, D.C.: Subcommittee on Internal Operations and Human Rights, 1998), 11; United Nations Population Fund, 1996, 356.

125. Franks and Morrison.

126. Rees, 1998.

127. Jane Macartney, A1.

128. Catherine Edwards, "Poor Women Charge Forced Sterilization," insightmag.com, March 2000; from www.insightmag.com/archive/20003330.shtml, 3/18/2002.

129. AQV report, June 2000, cited in *PRI Weekly Briefing*, 7/22/2002, 1–2. The UNFPA support for the Chinese and Peruvian programs is not surprising when one considers the organization's willingness to work with oppressive regimes in order to further demographic reduction: in 1998, UNFPA accepted war criminal Slobodan Milosevic's invitation to bring sterilization and abortion to one ethnic minority only — the Kosovars. Indeed, it appears that UNFPA has learned a thing or two from its coworkers in China. Armed with a strategy

entitled "How to change the mentality of Kosovar women" (about family planning), UNFPA bullied its way into Kosovar hospitals, offering bribes such as appliances to gynecologists in exchange for their cooperation. Kosovar women showed so little inclination to change their mentality that they labeled the UNFPA "White Plague" (Josipa Gasparic, "Milosevic and the 'UN Butchers,'" from the Population Research Institute, *The Kosovo File*, 1999, from www.pop.org/kosovo/butcher.htm, accessed 3/18/2002; "UNFPA Bribes Kosovo Gynecologist," *PRI Weekly Briefing*, November 8, 1999, vol. 1, no. 23).

130. Mosher, 2002, op. cit.

131. Edwards, op. cit.

132. "Congress Calls on USAID to Investigate Family Planning Abuses," *PRI Weekly News Briefing*, March 31, 2000, vol. 2, no. 9; "Peru's Coercive Family Planning Programs and USAID Involvement," *PRI Weekly News Briefing*, March 6, 2000, vol. 2, no. 6.

133. "Almost 300,000 Peruvian Women Forcibly Sterilized Over 10 Years," Zenit News, September 7, 2001.

134. Aird, 1986, 205.

135. Women's reproductive desires are not necessarily connected to contraceptive availability, contrary to what PPFA and IPPF (following Margaret Sanger) have claimed. Women's independence of mind concerning the number of children they wish to have is evident especially in developing countries where First World influence and pressure has remained more muted (see Lant H. Pritchett, "Desired Fertility and the Impact of Population Policies," *Population and Development Review* 20, no. 1 [1994]: 1–55).

7. Selling Out the Sisterhood

1. Discussion at workshop, "Internal Strategies: Survival Issues for PPFA in the 80's," PPFA Annual Meeting, October 31, 1981.

2. Lawrence Lader, *Breeding Ourselves to Death* (New York: Ballantine Books, 1971), 10.

3. Germaine Greer says, concerning cosmetic surgery (although the point is

much the same for hormonal contraceptives), "If the woman-made woman is never good enough, the man-made woman is no better than a toy, built to be played with, knocked about and ultimately thrown away" (Germaine Greer, *The Whole Woman* [New York: Alfred A. Knopf, 1999], 38).

4. Farida Akhter, "The Eugenic and Racist Premise of Reproductive Rights and Population Control," *Issues in Reproductive and Genetic Engineering* 5, no. 1 (1992): 1–8, here 6.

5. Mary Steichen Calderone, M.D., interview with James W. Reed, Family Planning Oral History Project (M-138), August 1974, Schlesinger Library, Radcliffe Institute, 25.

6. Guy Irving Burch to Mrs. Stephen Whitney Bodgett, 1/6/40, MSP-SSC.

7. James Reed, *From Private Vice to Public Virtue: The Birth Control Movement and American Society Since 1830* (New York: Basic Books, 1978), 265.

8. "Minutes of the Meeting of the Joint Committee of the American Birth Control League and the Birth Control Clinical Research Bureau," 10/10/38, MSP-SSC.

9. Citizen's Committee for Planned Parenthood, "The Quality of Life" pamphlet (New York: Birth Control Federation of America, 1939), 11–12, MSP-SSC.

10. Ferguson and Reed, 45–46.

11. D. Kenneth Rose, "Excerpts from Address," 1/47, 1–3, MSP-SSC (unfilmed).

12. Ibid., 4–5.

13. MS to Edna Rankin MacKinnon, 3/29/49, ERM papers, box 6, folder 121.

14. MS to Eleanor E. Dewey, 7/16/54, MSP-SSC.

15. "Minutes of the Executive Committee Meeting of the Birth Control Clinical Research Bureau," 10/13/38, 4, MSP-SSC, italics mine.

16. William Vogt, "PPFA Program Suggestions for 1952–53," 5/8/52, 3, MSP-SSC (unfilmed).

17. Ferguson and Reed, 51.

18. Quoted in Donald P. Warwick, *Bitter Pills: Population Policies and Their Implementation in Eight Developing Countries* (Cambridge: Cambridge University Press, 1982), 168.

19. Quoted in ibid., 169.

20. Vogt, 1952, 3.

21. William Vogt, "National Progress Report," 5/5/54, MSP-SSC (unfilmed).

22. Moore was hardly alone in this sort of Malthusian reasoning. It has, for example, dominated the population policy of the U.S. government. See, for example, the declassified National Security Study Memorandum 200 (NSSM 200), "Implications of Worldwide Population Growth for U.S. Security and Overseas Interests," 12/10/74, and various declassified CIA and Department of Defense documents cited in Elizabeth Liagin, *Excessive Force: Power, Politics and Population Control* (Washington, D.C.: Information Project for Africa, 1995).

23. Peter Bachrach and Elihu Bergman, *Power and Choice: The Formulation of American Population Policy* (Lexington: Lexington Books, 1973), 47.

24. Ibid.

25. Lader, 1971, 11–14. The business community has also not been inattentive to explicitly eugenic ideas: after the 1975 release of E. O. Wilson's *Sociobiology*, a *Business Week* reporter wrote, "Competitive self-interest, the bioeconomists say, has its origins in the human gene pool." The quote appeared in a series of articles entitled "The Genetic Defense of the Free Market" (quoted in Dorothy Nelkin, "The Social Power of Genetic Information," in *The Code of Codes: Scientific and Social Issues in the Human Genome Project*, ed. Daniel J. Kevles and Leroy Hood [Cambridge: Harvard University Press, 1992], 177–90, here 181).

26. Bachrach and Bergman, 47.

27. Reminiscences of Mary Lasker, with John T. Mason, Jr., 1966, Columbia University Oral History Research Office, series I, vol. 3, 441–42.

28. Commerce and Industry Committee of PP/WP, "The Economic Challenges of Population Growth: A Statement of the Problem,"11/10/64, MSP-SSC (unfilmed).

29. Marriner S. Eccles, "Citizen Responsibility in the Population Crisis," 5/11/61, MSP-SSC (unfilmed).

30. Cass Canfield to "Dear Friend," Nov. 23, 1962, PPFA-WPEC letter, CJG papers, box 147, folder 2476.

31. "People and Profits: The American Businessman's Stake in Family Planning," n.d., 1, PPFA-SSC.

32. Ibid., 23, 27. Compare the similar reasoning in 1968 by Dr. Joseph Beasley, head of the Louisiana Family Planning Program and Planned Parenthood activist, who described a disabled, unmarried woman with three children to a journalist and then claimed that "the cost of that girl and her children to the State, not to mention the cost in human suffering, eventually will be $800,000. You could educate 500 normal persons at Louisiana State University for that amount" (quoted in Andrea Tone, *Devices and Desires: A History of Contraceptives in America* [New York: Hill and Wang, 2001], 262).

33. "People and Profits," 21. For a detailed refutation of the economic claims of the population controllers, see the work by economist Jacqueline Kasun, *The War Against Population: The Economics and Ideology of World Population Control*, second edition (San Francisco: Ignatius Press, 1999).

34. "People and Profits," 22.

35. Ibid., 2.

36. Ibid., 9, 10.

37. Ibid., 16.

38. Ibid., 29.

39. Ibid, 30, emphasis in the original.

40. Phyllis Tilson Piotrow, *World Population Crisis: The United States Response*, Praeger Special Studies in International Economics and Development, Law and Population Book Series, vol. 4 (New York: Praeger Publishers, 1973), 18. For example, Oscar Harkavy of the Ford Foundation was originally a professor at Syracuse University College of Business Administration; he admits, "My own background was in economics, finance, and statistics, with absolutely no training in such population-relevant subjects such as demography, sociology, or public health" (Oscar Harkavy, *Curbing Population Growth: An Insider's Perspective on the Population Movement*, ed. Kenneth C. Land, Plenum Series on Demographic Methods and Population Analysis [New York: Plenum Press, 1995], 30).

41. James W. Reed, "The Birth Control Movement Before *Roe v. Wade*," in *Politics of Abortion and Birth Control in Historical Perspective*, ed. Donald T. Critchlow (University Park: Pennsylvania State University Press, 1996), 22–52, here 43.

42. Ferguson and Reed, 17.

43. Ibid., 44.

44. Doone Williams and Greer Williams, *Every Child a Wanted Child: Clarence James Gamble, M.D. and His Work in the Birth Control Movement*, ed. Emily P. Flint, The Countway Library Associates Historical Publication, vol. 4 (Boston: The Francis

A. Countway Library of Medicine, 1978), 172.

45. Piotrow, 76; Lader, 1971, 64.

46. Peter J. Donaldson, *Nature Against Us: The United States and the World Population Crisis, 1965–1980* (Chapel Hill: University of North Carolina, 1990), 106.

47. "Harvard Seminar with Jack Sullivan," Center for Population Studies, notes by Sarah Merry Bradley Gamble, 2/5/75, 1, from SMBG papers.

48. Tone, 263.

49. Frederick Osborn, "Population: An International Dilemma," in *The Conference Committee on Population Problems — 1956–1957*, ed. Frederick Osborn (New York: Princeton University Press, 1958), vii–97, describes this strategy.

50. Quoted in Betsy Hartmann, *Reproductive Rights and Wrongs: The Global Politics of Population Control* (Boston: South End Press, 1995), 243–44.

51. Quoted in ibid., 280. In 1992, 16% of the World Health Organization's budget for contraceptive research went toward finding a contraceptive "vaccine," which would cause a woman's immune system to attack either her own pregnancy-related hormones or else the eggs, sperm or embryo. Even bracketing the ethical questions, many medical concerns arise in the face of this sort of method: what kind of autoimmune reactions might be triggered? And how long would the vaccine's potency last? (Asoka Bandarage, *Women, Population and Global Crisis: A Political-Economic Analysis* [London: Zed Books, 1997], 87; Roberts, 146).

52. "Population Council Program Budget, 1979," CBR-7, from RAC, Family (Joan Dunlop) Collection, RG 17H, box 9.

53. Calderone and Reed, 26.

54. Jane S. Jaquette and Kathleen A. Staudt, "Women as 'At Risk' Reproducers: Biology, Science, and Population in U.S. Foreign Policy," in *Women, Biology, and Public Policy*, ed. Virginia S. Shapiro, Sage Yearbooks in Women's Policy Studies (Beverly Hills: Sage Publications, 1985), 235–268, here 236.

55. Rosalind Pollack Petchesky, "'Reproductive Choice' in the Contemporary United States: A Social Analysis of Female Sterilization," in *And the Poor Get Children: Radical Perspectives on Population Dynamics*, ed. Karen L. Michaelson (New York: Monthly Review Press, 1981), 50–88, here 67.

56. John Sharpless, "World Population Growth, Family Planning, and American Foreign Policy," in *The Politics of Abortion and Birth Control in Historical Perspective*, ed. Donald T. Critchlow (University Park: Pennsylvania State University Press, 1996), 72–102, here 76.

57. Piotrow, 155.

58. Donaldson, 102.

59. Stephen Minkin, "Nine Thai Women Had Cancer. None of Them Took Depo-Provera. Therefore Depo-Provera Is Safe. This Is Science?" *Mother Jones*, November 1981, 34–39, 50–51, here 36.

60. Barbara Ehrenreich, Mark Dowie, and Stephen Minkin, "The Charge: Gynocide; The Accused: The U.S. Government," *Mother Jones*, November 1979, 26–37, here 33–34.

61. "Population Control: Implications, Trends and Prospects," in *Pakistan International Family Planning Conference*, ed. Nafis Sadik (Dacca, Pakistan: Pakistan Family Planning Council, 1969), 258–260, here 259.

62. Quoted in Ehrenreich, 36.

63. Ibid., 28; George F. Brown and Ellen H. Moskowitz, "Moral and Policy Issues in Long-Acting Contraception," *Annual Review of Public Health* 18 (1997): 379–400; see also Susan Perry and Jim Dawson, *Nightmare: Women and the Dalkon Shield* (New York: Macmillan, 1985), and Nicole J. Grant, *The Selling of Contraception: The Dalkon Shield Case, Sexuality, and Women's Autonomy* (Columbus: Ohio State University Press, 1992).

64. In Ehrenreich; see also David Dempsey, "The Fertility Goddess vs. the Loop: Dr. Guttmacher Is the Evangelist of Birth Control," *New York Times Magazine*, February 9, 1969, 32–36.

65. Ferguson and Reed, 26.

66. Arguments similar to Ferguson's are still given today concerning the likely health risks of new contraceptives, such as the anti-pregnancy "vaccine"; one Canadian official within the government's International Development Research Center stated that the vaccine's potential risks would still be "a significant improvement" in comparison to the risks that women in Africa face in childbirth (Stephen Dale, "Women: Anti-Fertility Vaccine Seen as Tool for Government," *Inter Press Service*, August 23, 1995, retrieved from www.elibrary.com).

67. Ehrenreich, 30.

68. Ibid.

69. Ibid., 31.

70. James Reed, *From Private Vice to Public Virtue: The Birth Control Movement and American Society Since 1830* (New York: Basic Books, 1978), 339; Loretta McLaughlin, *The Pill, John Rock, and the Church: The Biography of a Revolution* (Boston: Little, Brown and Company, 1982), 2, 104; James W. Reed, "The Birth Control Movement Before *Roe v. Wade*," in *Politics of Abortion and Birth Control in Historical Perspective*, 22–52, here 42. Sanger once suggested that Pincus work with a particular Swedish researcher, noting that the latter had "long had an eugenic attitude toward life" (MS to Katherine Dexter McCormick, 12/14/54, MSP-SSC).

71. McLaughlin, 96. Andrea Tone observes, "From the beginning, the Pill was intended to supply critical ammunition in the war against unwanted population growth in developing nations" (Tone, 207). See Lara V. Marks, *Sexual Chemistry: A History of the Contraceptive Pill* (New Haven: Yale University Press, 2001) for a detailed history of the development of the pill; pp. 13–40 focus on the population-control motives of the pill pushers.

72. Margaret Sanger, "A Program of Contraceptive Research," 6/5/28, 1, MSP-SSC.

73. Ibid., 10.

74. See Chesler, 295–99.

75. And the researchers involved tend to have a dim view of the intelligence of the poor, an elitist bigotry that leads to the violation of the most fundamental ethical norms of informed consent governing human experimentation. "Ethical Considerations Concerning Research on Human Subjects," *Family Planning Perspectives* 3, no. 3 (1971): 2–3.

76. Helen Rodriguez-Trias, "The Women's Health Movement: Women Take Power," in *Reforming Medicine: Lessons of the Last Quarter Century*, ed. Victor W. Sidel and Ruth Sidel (New York: Pantheon Books, 1984), 107–126, here 109.

77. Quoted in Bachrach and Bergman, 69.

78. Katherine Dexter McCormick to MS, 5/31/55, 1, MSP-SSC; McCormick to MS, "Conversation with Dr. Pincus, June 30, 1955," memo in letter, 7/5/55, MSP-SSC; see also Tone, 219–20.

79. See Clarence Gamble to "Dr. Bele-

val," 8/3/50, CJG papers, box 47, folder 770. Bonnie Mass relates the steep rate of sterilizations that occurred on the island from the 1930s to the 1960s: "By 1965, approximately 34 percent of women of child-bearing age had been sterilized, two thirds of whom were still in their early twenties." The pressure did not let up; in 1975, it was determined that both Ryder Memorial and Presbyterian Hospitals were heavily promoting sterilization, and the targets for "the operation," as it was commonly called, were acknowledged by government family-planning officials to be the poor and uneducated (Bonnie Mass, "Puerto Rico: A Case Study of Population Control," *Latin American Perspectives* 4, no. 4 [1977]: 66–81, here 72, 77).

80. Williams and Williams, 171.

81. Quoted in Donald T. Critchlow, "Birth Control, Population Control, and Family Planning: An Overview," in *Politics of Abortion and Birth Control in Historical Perspective*, 1–21, here 7.

82. Mass, 1977, 67.

83. Adaline Pendelton Satterthwaite, interviewed by James W. Reed (henceforth Satterthwaite and Reed), Family Planning Oral History Project (M-138), June 1974, Schlesinger Library, Radcliffe Institute, 19.

84. Williams and Williams, 319.

85. Ibid., 325.

86. Mass, 1977, 73.

87. Quoted in Barbara Seaman, *The Doctors' Case Against the Pill*, second ed. (Alameda: Hunter House, 1995), 184.

88. Historians of medicine have pointed out that the legal restrictions on human experimentation that we have today did not exist in the 1950s. Of course, this hardly exculpates the scientists who, before such legal restrictions were codified, conducted reckless and, in effect, involuntary human experimentation. The analysis presented here makes clear that the researchers of the pill were guided by demographic, not humanitarian, concerns. See Marks, 89–115, for a more sympathetic interpretation of the testing.

89. Tone, 223–24.

90. Satterthwaite and Reed, 24.

91. Tone, 244.

92. Ibid., 250.

93. Hartmann, 1995, 184; see Ehrenreich, 1974.

94. Hartmann, 1995, 200.

95. Ibid., 380.

96. Much of the information for this paragraph comes from "The Population Council: A Twenty-Five Year Chronicle, 1952–1977," 2/78, 36–47, from RAC, Family, RG 5, series 3, subseries 4, box 72, folder 490.

97. Memo by Sheldon J. Segal, 10/1/63, 1, from RAC, Special Collection (Population Council), series IV3B4, subseries 2, box 4, folder 38.

98. Christopher Tietze, "Preliminary Report on Long-Range Plans for the Clinical Investigation of Intra-Uterine Contraceptive Devices," n.d. (probably mid–1964), 5–6, from ibid., subseries 4b, box 95, folder 1772.

99. Memo from the Medical Committee of the Planned Parenthood Federation, 7/30/65, 2, from ibid., subseries 4b, box 94, folder 1765.

100. Memo from the Medical Committee of the Planned Parenthood Federation, 7/15/64, 1, in ibid., subseries 5, box 107, folder 1995.

101. Ibid., 2–3.

102. Tietze, "Preliminary Report on Long-Range Plans," op. cit., 4.

103. Memo, Medical Committee, 7/15/64, 3–4.

104. Memo, 7/30/65.

105. IUD Group of the IPPF Medical Committee, "Instructions in the Use of Intra-Uterine Contraceptive Devices," 7/65, 9, from ibid., subseries 4b, box 95, folder 1775. My italics.

106. Alan F. Guttmacher, "The Newest Birth Control Method: The Intrauterine Devices," supplement to President's Letter no. 4, 4/65, 2, from ibid., subseries 5, box 107, folder 1996.

107. Christopher Tietze to Captain Charles M. Rucker, 6/1/66, from ibid., subseries 4b, box 95, folder 1767. This of course is an astonishingly high rate, and quite unacceptable, given the danger an ectopic pregnancy poses to the woman's health, not to mention to the embryo.

108. Adaline P. Satterthwaite to Christopher Tietze, 6/21/66, from ibid., folder 1773.

109. Adaline P. Satterthwaite to Sheldon J. Segal, 6/21/66, 2, from ibid.

110. John C. Cobb to Sheldon J. Segal, 8/19/64, 1, from ibid., subseries 4b, box 94, folder 1764.

111. "Case Report on IUD Complication," 8/18/64, from ibid.

112. Tietze, n.d., 4.

113. Tone, 280.

114. Tietze, n.d., 5.

115. "Corrected Minutes: Committee on Intra-Uterine Devices," 7/18/63, from ibid., subseries 4b, box 94, folder 1763.

116. www.fwhc.org/birth-control/iud-info.htm, accessed February 19, 2004. For the seven-day limit, see www.emory.edu/WHSC/MED/FAMPLAN/emergencycopperT.html, accessed 3/9/2004.

117. Quoted in Tone, 278.

118. Quoted in Hartmann, 1995, 213.

119. Hartmann, 1995, 216.

120. Guttmacher to E. K. Winata, 7/6/65, from RAC, Special Collections (Population Council), series IV3B4, subseries 4b, box 95, folder 1772.

121. Guttmacher, 4/65, 1, from ibid.

122. "Population Council Program Budget, 1979," CBR-1.

123. Ibid., CBR-2.

124. Ibid.

125. Population Council, "Improved Methods of Fertility Control," 11/15/77, 2, from RAC, Family, RG 5, series 3, subseries 4, box 72, folder 487.

126. Satterthwaite and Reed, 32.

127. Seaman, 241; Hartmann, 1995, 210.

128. Hartmann, 1995, 210.

129. Dorothy Roberts, *Killing the Black Body: Race, Reproduction, and the Meaning of Liberty* (New York: Pantheon, 1997), 122–28.

130. "Norplant Nightmare: An American Victim of Family Planning," *PRI Weekly Briefing* 4, no. 13 (June 18, 2002).

131. Ibid.

132. Roberts, 139.

133. "Norplant Is Back in Bangladesh," *Ms.*, July/August 1998, 32.

134. 1987 statement by Dr. Halida Hanum Akhter, quoted in Roberts, 140.

135. "Norplant Comes of Age," *Population Reports*, series K, no. 4 (November 1992): 9.

136. Phyllis Orrick, "Raging Hormone," *New York Press*, Sept. 29-Oct. 5, 1993, 1–4.

137. Cited in Roberts, 129, 132.

138. "Norplant for Girl as Alleged Rapes Went On," *Washington Post*, August 18, 1995, A8.

139. Wishing to utilize such a weapon against the fertility of the poor, the Baltimore public-school district has begun to dispense Norplant among its teenaged women of color. One African-American minister in Baltimore, Rev. Melvin Tuggle,

has warned, "It begins to sound like social engineering, like it's a way to control the population of the undesirables" (Tim Larimer, "Arming Girls Against Pregnancy," *USA Weekend*, February 26–28, 1993, 22, 24, here 24).

140. "Poverty and Norplant: Can Contraception Reduce the Underclass?" *Philadelphia Inquirer*, December 12, 1990, 18-A. A similar opinion was published about a month and a half earlier ("Don't Knock Norplant," *Philadelphia Inquirer*, November 1, 1990, 22-A).

141. See Roberts, 106–7.

142. ACLU, "Norplant: A New Contraceptive with the Potential for Abuse," at accessed 6/18/2002.

143. For critique of the Chiang Mai, Thailand, study that claimed to disprove the risk of endometrial cancer, see Minkin, 1981.

144. "Depo-Provera: A New Contraceptive Option for Family Planners," *Contraceptive Technology Update*, vol. 14, no. 1 (Jan. 1993): 3.

145. "The Case Against Depo-Provera," *Multinational Monitor*, vol. 6, no. 2-3 (Feb./March 1985), 6.

146. Ibid., 18.

147. Minkin, 37.

148. "The Case Against Depo-Provera," 5. When it comes to approval of contraceptives and abortifacients, this endangering of the health of women and girls by FDA advisory committees is all too common, scientific and ethical probity being sacrificed in the quest to control female fertility. Needless to say, FDA approval certainly does not mean that a drug is safe for women.

149. Upjohn Company, *Annual Report*, 1979.

150. "FDA Approves Depo Provera, an Injectible Contraceptive," *Washington Post*, Oct. 30, 1992, A2.

151. "The Case Against Depo-Provera," 7. Despite its abuse of protocol and extremely flawed experimental design (there was an overall turnover rate of 75 percent among the test subjects, and the clinic did not notify the FDA of deaths and severe reactions, among other problems), the Grady study was frequently cited to justify Depo's safety.

152. "The Case Against Depo-Provera," 15.

153. Carolyn Toll, "Experimental Contraceptive Tested on State's Girl Wards," *Chicago Sun-Times*, Aug. 2, 1973, 38.

154. "Counseling Is Key to Handling Depo-Provera Side Effects," from ibid., 9.

155. Rogers, 145.

156. Minkin, 39.

157. "Depo-Provera: A New Contraceptive Option for Family Planners," 1993, 5.

158. Hartmann, 1995, 201.

159. Planned Parenthood Federation of America, 1996 Annual Conference, Nashville, Tennessee.

160. Charlotte Allen, "Boys Only," *The New Republic*, March 9, 1992, 16–18.

161. On the preference for boys and the consequent sex-ratio imbalance, see Hongyan Liu and Baochang Gu, "Preference of Rural Population on the Sex of Expected Children and Their Corresponding Behaviors," *Chinese Journal of Population Science* 10, no. 3 (1998): 199–209; Rongshi Li, "An Analysis of the Sex Ratio at Birth in Impoverished Areas in China," *Chinese Journal of Population Science* 10, no. 1 (1998); Monica Das Gupta, "'Missing Girls' in China, South Korea, and India: Causes and Policy Implications" (Cambridge, MA: Harvard University, Center for Population and Development Studies, 1998); James Lee and Feng Wang, "Malthusian Models and Chinese Realities: the Chinese Demographic System 1700–2000," *Population and Development Review* 25, no. 1 (1999): 33–65, 205, 207; Lena Edlund, "Son Preference, Sex Ratios, and Marriage Patterns," *Journal of Political Economy* 107, no. 6, pt. 1 (1999): 1275–304.

162. Hema Shukla, "Report: Infanticide Rises in India," *UPS*, May 18, 1995.

163. Rajani Bhatia, et al., "Sex Selection: New Technologies, New Forms of Gender Discrimination," Committee on Women, Population and the Environment, October 2003, www.cwpe.org/Materials%20on%20 Sex%20Selection/FactSheet.htm, accessed 2/7/2004.

164. For reports, see John-Thor Dahlburg, "The Fight to Save India's Baby Girls," *Los Angeles Times*, February 22, 1994, A1, A3; Suzanne Goldenberg, "Killing of Girl Babies a Fact of Life in India," *Washington Times*, November 18, 1995, A9;Susan Greenhalgh, Zhu Chuzhu, and Li Nan, "Restraining Population Growth in Three Chinese Villages, 1988–93," *Population and Development Review* 20, no. 2 (1994): 365–395; Susan Greenhalgh and Jiali Li, "Engender-

ing Reproductive Policy and Practice in Peasant China: For a Feminist Demography of Reproduction," *Signs: Journal of Women in Culture and Society* 20, no. 3 (1995): 601–641; Steven Mufson, "Chinese Orphans Reported Dying from Abuse," *Washington Post*, January 6, 1996, A1, A16; Michael Weisskopf, "One Couple, One Child, Part 3," *Washington Post*, January 8,1985, A1, A10; Margery Wolf, *Revolution Postponed: Women in Contemporary China* (Stanford: Stanford University Press, 1985).

165. Bhatia, op. cit.

166. Allen, 1992, 18. In contrast, see Mary Anne Warren, *Gendercide: The Implications of Sex Selection*, New Feminist Perspectives (Totowa, N.J.: Rowman & Allanheld, 1985), for an improbable defense of sex-selection abortion as a feminist activity.

167. David N. Leff, "Boy or Girl: Now Choice, Not Chance," *Medical World News* 16, no. 26 (1975): 45–56, here 48, 56.

168. Warren M. Hern, M.D., "Is Pregnancy Really Normal?" *Family Planning Perspectives* 3, no. 1 (1971): 5–9.

169. Cited in Marks, 132; italics mine.

170. Bachrach and Berman, 88.

171. Lader, 1971, 58.

172. "Summary Report," John Hajnal (n.d.; probably August 1952), 9, from RAC, RG2, Medical Series, Birth Control Subseries, box 1, folder 4.

173. "China's Gender Imbalance Stems from 'Family Planning' Policy," Cybercast News Service, April 6, 2001.

174. Of course, many economists have critiqued population-control–centered economics as bad science, pointing, for example, to the need for a large workforce to help run a prosperous economy and pay taxes (see Jacqueline Kasun, *The War Against Population: The Economics and Ideology of Population Control*, second ed. [San Francisco: Ignatius Press, 1999]). This is not to mention the fact that the more persons there are, the greater the probability of insights that lead to technological innovations. A thriving market economy need not be predicated on a self-gratifying consumerist desire. But pursuing these questions would take us too far afield. For the moment, the main point is that many businessmen see profits in competition with people.

8. Beyond Control

1. Margaret Sanger, *Woman and the New Race* (New York: Blue Ribbon Books, 1920), 93.

2. Germaine Greer, *The Whole Woman* (New York: Alfred A. Knopf, 1999), 47–48.

3. Cited in Lara V. Marks, *Sexual Chemistry: A History of the Contraceptive Pill* (New Haven: Yale University Press, 2001), 132, italics mine.

4. Elisabeth Friedman points out that "the omnipresence of violence in women's lives provides [feminists] with a unifying agenda" (Elisabeth Friedman, "Women's Human Rights: The Emergence of a Movement," in *Women's Rights, Human Rights: International Feminist Perspectives*, ed. Julie Peters and Andrea Wolper [New York: Routledge, 1995], 28–35, here 21).

5. See, for example, Angela Y. Davis, *Women, Race, and Class* (New York: Vintage Books, 1983); Linda Gordon, "The Politics of Population: Birth Control and the Eugenics Movement," *Radical America* 8, no. 4 (1974): 61–97; Linda Gordon, *Woman's Body, Woman's Right: Birth Control in America*, second ed. (New York: Penguin Books, 1990).

6. Margaret Sanger, *The Pivot of Civilization* (New York: Brentano's, 1922), 22.

7. Sanger, 1920, 1.

8. Ibid., 2.

9. Ibid., 57, 3.

10. Ibid., 3.

11. Ibid.

12. Ibid., 7.

13. Ibid., 6.

14. Ibid.

15. For similar eugenic philosophies found in other feminists of the time, see Angelique Richardson, "Biology and Feminism," *Critical Quarterly* 42 (3, 2000): 35–63.

16. Sanger, 1920, 9–12.

17. Ibid., 27–28.

18. Ibid., 226.

19. Ibid.

20. See Introduction.

21. Margaret Sanger, "When Should a Woman Avoid Having Children?" *Birth Control Review*, November 1918, 6–7.

22. In addition to the letter to Frederick Osborn cited above, see her Lasker Foundation Award Speech, October 25, 1950, in MSP-LC, quoted on p. 54. When scholars such as Linda Gordon and Angela Y. Davis

claim a shift from an early radical/socialist commitment to a later eugenic one, they perhaps have in mind this movement in Sanger's thought, which basically consigned the poor to the class of the "unfit" by the late 1920s. What they do not see, however, is that Sanger's commitment to eugenic birth control dates from her "education" in England in 1914 and 1915 with Havelock Ellis and the other Neo-Malthusians. In other words, her basic eugenic attitude perdures through the evolution in her thought about poverty.

23. Sanger, 1920, 45.
24. Ibid., 53.
25. Ibid., 55.
26. Ibid., 53.
27. Ibid., 57.
28. Ibid., 229.
29. Ibid., 93. See also p. 185: "When women have raised the standards of sex ideals and purged the human mind of its unclean conception of sex, the fountain of the race will have been cleansed. Mothers will bring forth, in purity and in joy, a race that is morally and spiritually free." Or p. 233: "This is the dawn. Womanhood shakes off its bondage. It asserts its right to be free. In its freedom, its thoughts turn to the race. Like begets like. We gather perfect fruit from perfect trees. The race is but the amplification of its mother body, the multiplication of flesh habitations— beautified and perfected for souls akin to the mother soul."
30. Ibid.
31. Ibid., 2.
32. Ibid., 229.
33. Greer, 47–48.
34. For proponents of this libertarian view, see, among others, Bernard Berelson and Jonathan Lieberson, "Government Efforts to Influence Fertility: The Ethical Issues," *Population and Development Review* 5, no. 4 (1979): 581–614; George F. Brown and Ellen H. Moskowitz, "Moral and Policy Issues in Long-Acting Contraception," *Annual Review of Public Health* 18 (1997): 379–400; Arthur L. Caplan, Glenn McGee, and David Magnus, "What Is Immoral About Eugenics?" *British Medical Journal* 319, no. 7220 (1999): 1284–85; Steve Connor, "Women Hold Key to Population Curb: The UN Says It Is Vital," *Independent*, August 18, 1994, www.elibrary.com; Nafis Sadik, "The Role of the United Nations: From Conflict to Consensus," in *Pop-*

ulation Policy: Contemporary Issues, ed. Godfrey Roberts (New York: Praeger, 1990), 193–209; Nafis Sadik, "Statement by Dr. Nafis Sadik to the 23rd General Population Conference of the International Union for the Scientific Study of Population" (Beijing: UNFPA, 1997); Sheldon J. Segal, "Norplant Developed for All Women, Not Just the Well-to-Do," *New York Times*, January 6, 1991, E18.

35. See Farida Akhter on this topic: "Women in the West began to talk about reproductive rights in various international conferences since the mid-eighties. Interestingly, they are raising the question of accessibility to contraceptives and their right to choose. Now if the women of Bangladesh are already inundated with contraceptives, why this demand? … Women in the West are making a demand for the right to choose while women in Bangladesh, for example, are offered a choice between the pill (almost always a brand of high dose), IUD (copper-T), injectables (Depo-Provera and Net-en), implants (Norplant), or forced sterilisation…. By reproductive rights, one always means, and has to 'believe' in, stopping the childbirth of a fertile woman. Therefore it is nothing but the slogan for population control in disguise" (Farida Akhter, "The Eugenic and Racist Premise of Reproductive Rights and Population Control," *Issues in Reproductive and Genetic Engineering* 5, no. 1 [1992]: 1–8, here 2, 5).

36. Dictation, "Conference on Population Problems," 6/21/52, afternoon session, 38, from RAC, Family Collection, RG 5, series 1, subseries 5, box 85, folder 721.

37. Doone Williams and Greer Williams, *Every Child a Wanted Child: Clarence James Gamble, M.D. and His Work in the Birth Control Movement*, ed. Emily P. Flint, The Countway Library Associates Historical Publication (Boston: The Francis A. Countway Library of Medicine, 1978), 234.

38. Germaine Greer, "On Population and Women's Right to Choose," in *Madwoman's Underclothes: Essays and Occasional Writings* (London: Picador, 1986), 192–94, here 194.

39. Warren M. Hern, M.D., "Is Pregnancy Really Normal?" *Family Planning Perspectives* 3, no. 1 (1971): 5–9; Warren M. Hern, "Is Human Culture Carcinogenic for Uncontrolled Population Growth and Ecological Destruction?" *Bioscience* 43, no. 11 (1993): 768–773.

40. Steven W. Mosher, "A 'Stick' in Time Saves Nine," *PRI Weekly Briefing*, March 2, 2001, 1–4.

41. Akhter, op. cit.

42. Germaine Greer, 1999, 114.

43. See Helen B. Holmes, Betty B. Hoskins, and Michael Gross, eds., *Birth Control and Controlling Birth: Women-Centered Perspectives*, Contemporary Issues in Biomedicine, Ethics, and Society (Clifton: The Humana Press, Inc., 1980), for the experiences of some women's- health communities that are doing just this. See also the feminist promotion of natural family planning or "fertility awareness" by Toni Weschler, *Taking Charge of Your Fertility: The Definitive Guide to Natural Birth Control and Pregnancy Achievement* (New York: Perennial/HarperCollins, 1995).

44. For some feminist meditations on the relations between motherhood and feminism, see, among others, the varied views of Germaine Greer, *Sex and Destiny: The Politics of Human Fertility* (New York: Harper and Row, 1984); Naomi Wolf, *Misconceptions: Truth, Lies, and the Unexpected on the Journey to Motherhood* (New York: Doubleday, 2001); and the marvelous work of Jean Bethke Elshtain in *Public Man, Private Woman: Women in Social and Political Thought*, second ed. (Princeton: Princeton University Press, 1981) and "The New Eugenics and Feminist Quandaries: Philosophical and Political Reflections," from *Power Trips and Other Journeys: Essays in Feminism as Civil Discourse* (Madison: University of Wisconsin Press, 1990), 89–104.

Works Consulted

Manuscript Collections

The Population Council papers were unprocessed and largely closed when this researcher accessed them; many records have since been opened. The Margaret Sanger–Sophia Smith Collection has been microfilmed and miscellaneous Margaret Sanger correspondence is currently being collected for filming under the direction of Esther Katz, Ph.D. and with the assistance of Cathy Moran Hajo and Peter C. Engelman, as part of the Margaret Sanger Papers Project, Department of History, New York University, New York, New York. A selection of documents taken from the microfilm of the Margaret Sanger Papers will be published as a four-volume series; at press time, the first volume has been released: *The Selected Papers of Margaret Sanger: The Woman Rebel, 1900–1928*, Selected Papers of Margaret Sanger, vol. 1, ed. Esther Katz, Cathy Moran Hajo, and Peter C. Engelman (Bloomington: University of Indiana Press, 2002).

American Birth Control League. Records. Houghton Library, Harvard University, Cambridge, Massachusetts.

American Eugenics Society. Records. American Philosophical Society Library, Philadelphia, Pennsylvania.

Brush, Dorothy Hamilton. Papers. Sophia Smith Collection, Smith College, Northampton, Massachusetts.

Calderone, Mary Steichen. Papers (MC 179). Schlesinger Library, Radcliffe Institute, Harvard University, Cambridge, Massachusetts.

Davenport, Charles Benedict. Papers. American Philosophical Society Library, Philadelphia, Pennsylvania.

Dickinson, Robert Latou. Papers (B MS c72). Boston Medical Library in the Countway Library of Medicine, Boston, Massachusetts.

Dunlop, Joan. Papers. Rockefeller Archive Collection, North Tarrytown, New York.

Eugenics Record Office. Records. American Philosophical Society Library, Philadelphia, Pennsylvania.

Gamble, Clarence J. Papers (H MS c23). Harvard Medical Library in the Countway Library of Medicine, Boston, Massachusetts.

Gamble, Sarah Merry (Bradley). Papers (MC 368). Schlesinger Library, Radcliffe Institute, Harvard University, Cambridge, Massachusetts.

Himes, Norman. Papers (B MS c77). Harvard Medical Library in the Countway Library of Medicine, Boston, Massachusetts.

Jennings, Herbert Spencer. Papers. American Philosophical Society Library, Philadelphia, Pennsylvania.

McKinnon, Edna Bertha (Rankin). Papers (MC-325). Schlesinger Library, Radcliffe Institute, Harvard University, Cambridge, Massachusetts.

Mudd, Emily Borie (Hartshorne). Papers (T-149). Schlesinger Library, Radcliffe Institute, Harvard University, Cambridge, Massachusetts.

Osborn, Frederick. Papers. American Philosophical Society Library, Philadelphia, Pennsylvania.

Pearl, Raymond. Papers. American Philosophical Society Library, Philadelphia, Pennsylvania.

Pilpel, Harriet. Unprocessed papers (accession number 82-M123). Schlesinger Library, Radcliffe Institute, Harvard University, Cambridge, Massachusetts.

Pincus, Gregory. Papers. Library of Congress, Washington, D.C.

Planned Parenthood Federation of America Library. Planned Parenthood Federation of America headquarters, New York, New York.

Planned Parenthood Federation of America. Records. Sophia Smith Collection, Smith College, Northampton, Massachusetts.

Population Council. Records. Rockefeller Archive Collection, North Tarrytown, New York.

Rockefeller Family Archives. Record Group 2 (Office of the Messrs Rockefeller), Rockefeller Archive Collection, North Tarrytown, New York.

_____. Record Group 5 (John D. Rockefeller 3rd Papers), Rockefeller Archive Collection, North Tarrytown, New York.

Sanger, Margaret. Papers. Library of Congress, Washington, D.C.

Sanger, Margaret. Papers. Sophia Smith Collection, Smith College, Northampton, Massachusetts.

Whitney, Leon F. Collection. American Philosophical Society Library, Philadelphia, Pennsylvania.

Interviews

Calderone, M.D., Mary Steichen. 1974. Interview with James W. Reed, August. Family Planning Oral History Project. Schlesinger Library, Radcliffe Institute, Harvard University, Cambridge, Massachusetts.

Clothier, M.D., Florence. 1974. Interview with James W. Reed, January. Family Planning Oral History Project. Schlesinger Library, Radcliffe Institute, Harvard University, Cambridge, Massachusetts.

Ferguson, Frances Hand. 1974. Interview with James W. Reed, June. Family Planning Oral History Project. Schlesinger Library, Radcliffe Institute, Harvard University, Cambridge, Massachusetts.

Guttmacher, M.D., Alan F. and Harriet F. Pilpel. 1970. Abortion and the Unwanted Child. *Family Planning Perspectives* 2 (2):16-24.

Guttmacher, Mrs. Alan F. 1974. Interview with James W. Reed, November. Family Planning Oral History Project. Schlesinger Library, Radcliffe Institute, Harvard University, Cambridge, Massachusetts.

Hardin, Garrett. 1992. Interview: Garrett Hardin. *Omni*, June, 55–63.

_____. 1996. Interview. *Skeptic* 4(2): 42–46.

Johnson, Douglas, and Nafis Sadik. 1989. Interview on *Nightwatch*, CBS, November 11. Should the U.S. Participate in the U.N. Population Fund? An Exchange Between Douglas Johnson, Legislative Director, National Right to Life Committee, and Nafis Sadik, Executive Director, United Nations Population Fund (UNFPA).

Lasker, Albert Davis. 1950. Interview with Allan Nevins and Dean Albertson. Reminiscences of Albert Davis Lasker. Oral History Research Office Collection, Columbia University, New York.

Lasker, Mary. 1966. Interview with John T. Mason, Jr. Reminiscences of Mary Lasker. Oral History Research Office Collection, Columbia University, New York.

Marston, Margaret Sanger, and Nancy Sanger Ivins. 1977. Interview with Jacqueline Van Voris, May. Sophia Smith Collection, Smith College, Northampton, Massachusetts.

McKinnon, Edna Rankin. 1972. "Interview with Edna Rankin McKinnon re: family planning career, 1970's." Edna Rankin McKinnon papers. Schlesinger Library, Radcliffe Institute, Harvard University, Cambridge, Massachusetts.

Morrison, David. 1998. Interview with author, telephone. Washington, D.C.

Mudd, Emily Hartshorne. 1976. Interview with James W. Reed, August. Family Planning Oral History Project. Schlesinger Library, Radcliffe Institute, Harvard University, Cambridge, Massachusetts.

Myers, M.D., Lonny. 1976. Interview with Ellen Chesler, September. Family Planning Oral History Project. Schlesinger Library, Radcliffe Institute, Harvard University, Cambridge, Massachusetts.

Osborn, Frederick. 1967. Interview with Isabel Grossner. Carnegie Corporation Project Interview. Oral History Research Office Collection, Columbia University, New York.

Richard, Olive Byrne. 1977. Interview with Jacqueline Van Voris, November. Sophia Smith Collection, Smith College, Northampton, Massachusetts.

Sanger, M.D., Grant. 1976. Interview with Ellen Chesler, August. Family Planning Oral History Project. Schlesinger Library, Radcliffe Institute, Harvard University, Cambridge, Massachusetts.

Sanger, Grant. 1977. Interview with Jacqueline Van Voris, March. Sophia Smith Collection, Smith College, Northampton, Massachusetts.

Satterthwaite, Adaline Pendelton. 1974. Interview with James W. Reed, June. Family Planning Oral History Project. Schlesinger Library, Radcliffe Institute, Harvard University, Cambridge, Massachusetts.

Tietze, M.D., Christopher, and Sarah Lewit Tietze. 1976. Interview with James W. Reed, January. Family Planning Oral History Project. Schlesinger Library, Radcliffe Institute, Harvard University, Cambridge, Massachusetts.

Organizational Magazines and Newsletters

The following are some newsletters and magazines put out by some of the organizations discussed in this book. They were consulted during the relevant time periods; for individual articles, please see the endnotes.

Association for Voluntary Sterilization, Inc., News
Birth Control Review
Eugenics
Eugenics Review
Family Planning News
Letter from the President (PPFA)
News Exchange from the Planned Parenthood Federation
Planned Parenthood News
Population Today

Magazines, Newspapers and Newswires

The following are magazines, newspapers and newswires that were consulted for historical and contemporary events. I am indebted to the Boston Women's Health Book Collective for many of these citations. News sections in the following journals were also used. For individual articles, please see the endnotes.

The ARC
Associated Press
Baltimore Sun
Boston Globe
British Medical Journal
Bulletin of Medical Ethics
Chicago Sun-Times
Christian Science Monitor
Chronicle of Philanthropy
Columbia
Columbia Journalism Review
Congressional Quarterly
Contraceptive Technology Update
Deseret News
Discover
E/The Environmental Magazine
Earth Times
Economic and Political Weekly
Environmental Action
Family Health International Network
Family Planning Perspectives
Family Planning World
Far Eastern Economic Review
Foundation News
GeneWatch
Green Left
The Guardian
Herizons
The Hindu
The Independent

Inter Press Service
The Lancet
Los Angeles Times
Medical Tribune
Medical World News
Miami Herald
Modern Healthcare
Mother Jones
Ms.
The Nation
National Catholic News Service
National Review
The Nation's Health
New York City Tribune
New York Times
New York Times Magazine
Newsday
Newsweek
Ob. Gyn News
Our Sunday Visitor
Panoscope: Southern Voices on Environment and Development
Philadelphia Inquirer
Political Environments
Population Research International (PRI) Review
PRI Weekly Briefing
The Progressive
Responsive Philanthropy
Reuters
Rocky Mountain News
St. Louis Post-Dispatch
Science
Scientific American
United Press International
USA Today
USA Weekend
Village Voice
Wall Street Journal
Washington Monthly
Washington Post
Washington Times
The Weekly Standard
Wisconsin State Journal
World
World Health

Internet News Sources and Subscription Services

The following were consulted during the relevant time periods; for individual articles, please see the endnotes.

www.elibrary.com
www.insightmag.com
www.zenit.org

Books, Pamphlets and Reports: Primary

American Eugenics Society. 1930. *Organized Eugenics.* Pamphlet. New Haven: American Eugenics Society.

_____. 1938. *Practical Eugenics: Aims and Methods of the American Eugenics Society.* Pamphlet. New York: American Eugenics Society.

_____. 1958. *Five-Year Report of the Officers: 1953–1957.* New York: The American Eugenics Society, Inc.

Bajema, Carl J., ed. 1976. *Eugenics: Then and Now.* Edited by D. L. Jameson. 14 vols. Vol. 5, *Benchmark Papers in Genetics.* Stroudsburg: Dowden, Hutchinson & Ross.

Benson, Marguerite. 1938. *Annual Report of the American Birth Control League for the Year 1938.* New York: American Birth Control League.

Birth Control International Information Centre. 1928? *A Statement of Policy.* Pamphlet. London: Birth Control International Information Centre.

Birthright, Inc. 1949. *...Unto the Third and Fourth Generation.* Pamphlet. Princeton: Birthright, Inc.

Brush Foundation. 1958. *The Brush Foundation, Cleveland, Ohio, 1928–1958.* Cleveland: Brush Foundation.

_____. 1981. *The Brush Foundation: 1928–1980.* Cleveland: The Brush Foundation.

_____. 1993. *The Brush Foundation, Cleveland, Ohio: Quadrennial Report, 1989–1992.* Cleveland: The Brush Foundation.

_____. 1997. *The Brush Foundation: Quadriennial Report, 1993–1996.* Cleveland: The Brush Foundation.

Cannon, Mary Antoinette. 1945? *Outline for a Course in Planned Parenthood.* New York: Planned Parenthood Federation of America.

Center for Reproductive Rights and the Comité Latinoamericano y del Caribe para la Defensa de la Mujer. 1999. *Silence and Complicity: Violence Against Women in Peruvian Public Health Facilities.* Report. www.reproductiverights.org/pub_bo_silence.html#online, accessed 2/7/2004.

Chesterton, G. K. 1922. *Eugenics and Other Evils.* New York: Cassell and Company.

Citizens Committee for Planned Parenthood. 1938. *The Most Important Thing in the World.* Pamphlet. New York: The Citizens' Committee for Planned Parenthood.

_____. 1939. *The Quality of Life.* Pamphlet. New York: Birth Control Federation of America.

Daly, Herman E., and John B. Cobb, Jr. 1994. *For the Common Good: Redirecting the Economy Toward Community, the Environment, and a Sustainable Future.* Second ed. Boston: Beacon Press.

Dennis, K. J. 1975. *Abortion, Babies and Contraception: The A, B, C of Eugenics.* Edited by Sir Duglad Baird, M.D. Southampton: University of Southampton.

Dryfoos, Joy G. 1961. *Social Change and Social Action: A Social Science Report on Some Techniques for Effecting Social Change.* New York: PPFA Social Research Committee.

Duvall, Elizabeth S., ed. 1967. *Hear Me for My Cause: Selected Letters of Margaret Sanger, 1926–1927.* Northampton, Massachusetts: Sophia Smith Collection.

Ellis, Havelock. 1969. *Essays in War-Time: Further Studies in the Task of Social Hygiene.* Freeport: Books for Libraries Press.

Ernst Wachsmuth and Company. 1955. *Planned Parenthood and the Businessman: A Study of Attitudes and Opinions Relating to the Planned Parenthood Program and Its Financial Support.* New York: Planned Parenthood Federation of America.

Ethics Committee (1986–87) of the American Fertility Society. 1987. "Ethical Considerations of the New Reproductive Technologies." *Fertility and Sterility* 49 (2):Supplement 1, I-7S.

Eugenics Society. 1975. *Quantity and Quality of the British Population: A Eugenics Society Discussion Paper.* London: The Eugenics Society.

_____. n.d. *Aims and Objects of the Eugenics Society.* London: Eugenics Society.

Fairchild, Henry Pratt. 1939. *People: The Quantity and Quality of Population.* New York: Henry Holt and Company.

Family Planning Advocates of New York State, Inc., et al. 1983. *Spending to Save: A Special Budget Strategy for 1983.* New York City.

Glass, D. V. 1940. *Population: Policies and Movements in Europe.* Oxford: Clarendon Press.

Grymes, Sandra. 1982? *A Preliminary Report on the Counseling Function in Affiliates of Planned Parenthood Federation of America, Inc.* New York: Planned Parenthood Federation of America.

Guttmacher, Alan F. 1959. *Babies By Choice or By Chance.* Garden City: Doubleday and Company.

_____. 1963. *Planned Parenthood/World Population/Annual Report 1963.* New York: Planned Parenthood Federation of America.

_____. 1973. *Pregnancy, Birth, and Family Planning: A Guide for Expectant Parents in the 1970s.* Third ed. New York: The Viking Press.

Hardin, Garrett. 1999. *The Ostrich Factor: Our Population Myopia.* New York: Oxford University Press.

Harkavy, Oscar. 1995. *Curbing Population Growth: An Insider's Perspective on the Population Movement.* Edited by K. C. Land, *Plenum Series on Demographic Methods and Population Analysis.* New York: Plenum Press.

Herrnstein, Richard J., and Charles Murray. 1994. *The Bell Curve: Intelligence and Class Structure in American Life.* New York: The Free Press.

Huq, Md. Majmul, and S. Ahmad. 1989. *Study of Compensation Payments and Family Planning in Bangladesh: A Synthesis.* Bangladesh: Ministry of Health and Family Planning.

International Conference on Population and Development. 1994. *Population and Development: Programme of Action Adopted at the International Conference on Population and Development,* Cairo, 5–13 September.

International Planned Parenthood Federation. 1959. *International Planned Parenthood Directory: World List of Family Planning Agencies.* London: International Planned Parenthood Federation.

_____. 1996. *Annual Report, 1995–1996.* London: International Planned Parenthood Federation.

Johnson, Stanley. 1970. *Life Without Birth.* Boston: Little, Brown and Company.

Kaeser, Lisa, Rachel Benson Gold, and Cory L. Richards. 1996. *Title X at 25: Balancing National Family Planning Needs with State Flexibility.* New York: Alan Guttmacher Institute.

Kallmann, M.D., Franz J., and John D. Rainer, M.D. 1959. Genetics and Demography. In *Study of Population: An Inventory and Appraisal,* edited by P. M. Hauser and O. D. Duncan. Chicago: University of Chicago Press.

Kammeyer, Kenneth C. W., ed. 1969. *Population Studies: Selected Essays and Research.* Edited by E. F. Borgatta, *Rand McNally Sociology Series.* Chicago: Rand McNally & Company.

Kennedy, David M. 1970. *Birth Control in America: The Career of Margaret Sanger.* Vol. 18, *Yale Publications in American Studies.* New Haven: Yale University Press.

Lader, Lawrence. 1971. *Breeding Ourselves to Death.* New York: Ballantine Books.

Laughlin, Harry H. 1922. *Eugenical Sterilization in the United Sates: A Report of the Psychopathic Laboratory of the Municipal Court of Chicago.* Chicago: Municipal Court of Chicago.

Lynn, Richard. 1996. *Dysgenics: Genetic Deterioration in Modern Populations.* Westport, Ct.: Praeger.

_____. 2001. *Eugenics: A Reassessment.* Westport, Ct.: Praeger.

Malthus, T. R. 1992 (reprinted from 1803). *An Essay on the Principle of Population.* Edited by Donald Winch. Edited by R. Geuss and Q. Skinner, *Cambridge Texts in the History of Political Thought.* Cambridge: Cambridge University Press.

Maremont, Arnold H. 1963. *Birth Control and Public Responsibility.* Pamphlet. New York: Planned Parenthood-World Population.

Medical and Scientific Committee of the Human Betterment Association of America, Inc. 1960. *To Protect the Adolescent Retarded.* Pamphlet. New York: Human Betterment Association of America.

Meier, Gitta. 1959. *The Effect of Unwanted Pregnancies on the Relief Load.* New York: Research Department, Planned Parenthood Federation of America.

Moran, Al, and Shirley Gordon. 1983. *Spending to Save: A Special Budget Strategy for 1983.* New York City: Planned Parenthood of New York City.

Mumford, Stephen D. 1996. *The Life and Death of NSSM 200: How the Destruction of Political Will Doomed a U.S. Population Policy.* Research Triangle Park, N.C.: Center for Research on Population and Security.

Murray, Charles. 1994. *Losing Ground: American Social Policy, 1950–1980.* 2nd ed. New York: Basic Books.

_____. 1997. *What It Means to Be a Libertarian: A Personal Interpretation.* New York: Broadway Books.

Myerson, Abraham, M.D., James B. Ayer, M.D., Tracy J. Putnam, M.D., Clyde E. Keeler, and Leo Alexander, M.D. 1936. *Eugenical Sterilization: A Reorientation of the Problem.* New York: The Macmillan Company.

National Clinic Service Division. 1941. *Directory of Clinics and Clinical Services.* New York: Birth Control Federation of America.

National Committee for Planned Parenthood. 1941a. *Population Problem.* Pamphlet. New York: Birth Control Federation of America.

_____. 1941b. *Still the Most Important Thing in the World.* Pamphlet. New York: Birth Control Federation of America.

_____. 1941c. *We Believe....* Pamphlet. New York: Birth Control Federation of America.

Newman, Horatio Hackett, ed. 1932. *Evolution, Genetics and Eugenics.* Third ed. Chicago: University of Chicago Press.

Osborn, Frederick. 1940. *Preface to Eugenics.* New York: Harper & Row.

Pearson, M.Sc., Roger. 1966. *Eugenics and Race.* Second ed. New York: Roger Pearson.

Piotrow, Phyllis Tilson. 1976. *Draper World Population Fund Report: Voluntary Sterilization.* Washington, D.C.: Draper World Population Fund.

Planned Parenthood Federation of America. 1950. *1950 Annual Report.* New York: Planned Parenthood Federation of America.

_____. 1986. *PPFA Issues Manual.* New York: Planned Parenthood Federation of America, Inc.

_____. 1990. *Mission and Policy Statements.* New York: Planned Parenthood Federation of America.

_____. 1996. *One Vision, Many Voices: 1995–1996 Annual Report.* New York: Planned Parenthood Federation of America.

_____. 1997. *1997 Plan of Action.* New York: Planned Parenthood Federation of America, Inc.

Planned Parenthood–World Population, ed. n.d.-a. *Birth Control Services in Tax-Supported Hospitals, Health Departments, and Welfare Agencies.* New York: Planned Parenthood–World Population.

_____. n.d.-b. *The Poverty of Abundance: American Business and the World Population Crisis.* Pamphlet. New York: Planned Parenthood-World Population.

Popenoe, Paul, and Roswell Johnson. 1933. *Applied Eugenics.* Edited by R. T. Ely. Second ed., *Social Science Textbooks.* New York: Macmillan Company.

Population Council, Inc. 1956. *Reports of the Executive Officers for the Period November 5, 1952 to December 31, 1955.* New York: Population Council, Inc.

_____. 1994. *Reconsidering the Rationale, Scope, and Quality of Family Planning Programs.* New York: The Population Council.

_____. 1996a. *Annual Report 1996.* New York: The Population Council.

_____. 1996b. *The Unfinished Transition.* New York: The Population Council.

PPFA Communication Division. 1994. *The Truth About Margaret Sanger.* New York: Planned Parenthood Federation of America.

Rees, Grover Joseph. 1998. *Report on Staff Delegation to Peru.* Washington, D.C.: Subcommittee on Internal Operations and Human Rights.

Robinson, Caroline Hadley. 1930. *Seventy Birth Control Clinics: A Survey and Analysis Including the General Effects of Control on Size and Quality of Population.* Baltimore: Williams and Wilkins Company.

Robitscher, J.D., M.D., ed. 1973. *Eugenic Sterilization.* Springfield: Charles C. Thomas.

Rockefeller Foundation. 1997. "The Rockefeller Foundation on the US Role in International Population Programs." *Population and Development Review* 23 (1):218–219.

Rose, D. Kenneth. 1939. *A Report with Recommendations to the Board of Directors of the Birth Control Fed of America, Inc.* New York: BCFA.

Ross, John A., W. Parker Mauldin, and Vincent C. Miller. 1993. *Family Planning and Population: A Compendium of International Statistics.* New York: UNFPA.

Sanger, Margaret. 1920. *Woman and the New Race.* New York: Blue Ribbon Books.

_____. 1922a. *The Pivot of Civilization.* New York: Brentano's.

_____. 1922b. *Woman, Morality, and Birth Control.* New York: The American Birth Control League, Inc.

_____. 1970. *An Autobiography.* Elmsford, New York: Maxwell Reprint Company.

Sanger, Margaret, ed. 1917. *The Case for Birth Control.* New York: Margaret Sanger.

Singer, Peter. 1981. *The Expanding Circle: Ethics and Sociobiology.* New York: Farrar, Straus, & Giroux.

Singer, Peter, and Helga Kuhse. 1985. *Should the Baby Live? The Problem of Handicapped Infants.* New York: Oxford University Press.

Stone, M.D., Abraham, Norman E. Himes, M.D., and Joseph J. Rovinsky, M.D. 1965. *Planned Parenthood: A Practical Guide to Birth-Control Methods.* Second ed. New York: Collier Books.

Todd, T. Wingate. 1929. *The Herald's Staff: An Account of the Brush Inquiry.* Cleveland: Brush Foundation.

United Nations Population Fund. 1996a. *Inventory of Population Projects in Developing Countries Around the World.* New York: United Nations Population Fund.

_____. 1996b. *U.S. Population NGO, Philippine Parliamentarian to Receive 1996 United Nations Population Award.* New York: UNFPA.

_____. 1997a. *The State of World Population 1997: The Right to Choose: Reproductive Rights and Reproductive Health.* New York: United Nations Population Fund.

_____. 1997b. *UNFPA Hails Ted Turner's Plan to Donate $1 Billion to United Nations.* New York: United Nations Population Fund.

United States Agency for International Development. 1997. "U.S. Funding for International Population Programs." *Population and Development Review* 23 (1): 213–217.

United States Department of State. 1994. *Country Reports on Human Rights Practices for 1993.* Washington, D.C.: U.S. Government Printing Office.

United States House of Representatives. 1995. *Congressional Record* 141 (53 [March 22]): H3428–3519.

United States House Subcommittee on International Operations and Human Rights of the Committee on International Relations. 1995. *Coercive Population Control in China.* Washington, D.C.: U.S. Government Printing Office.

United States National Security Council. 1974. *Implications of Worldwide Population Growth for U.S. Security and Overseas Interests.* Washington, D.C.: National Security Council.

United States Senate. 1995. *Congressional Record* 141 (141): S13370–S13371.

Upjohn Company. 1979. *Annual Report.* Kalamazoo, MI: Upjohn Company.

Westoff, Leslie Aldridge, and Charles F. Westoff. 1971. *From Now to Zero: Fertility, Contraception and Abortion in America.* Second ed. Boston: Little, Brown and Company.

Wood, Jr., M.D., H. Curtis. n.d. *The Physician's Responsibility in the Decline of National Intelligence.* Pamphlet. Princeton: Birthright, Inc.

Articles and Essays: Primary

Bajema, Carl Jay. 1971. "The Genetic Implications of Population Control." *BioScience* 21 (January): 71–75.

Berelson, Bernard. 1969. "Beyond Family Planning." *Science* 163 (February 7): 533.

_____. 1978. "1966–1977: A Look at the Record." *Family Planning Perspectives* 10 (1): 20–22.

_____, and Jonathan Lieberson. 1979. "Government Efforts to Influence Fertility: The Ethical Issues." *Population and Development Review* 5 (4): 581–614.

Blacker, M.D., C. P. 1964. "The International Planned Parenthood Federation: Aspects of Its History." *The Eugenics Review* 56 (3): 135–142.

_____. 1966a. "Contraception and the Catholic Theologians." *The Eugenics Review* 58 (2): 85–94.

_____. 1966b. "Obituary: Margaret Sanger." *The Eugenics Review* 58 (4): 179–181.

Blake, Judith. 1994. "Judith Blake on Fertility Control and the Problem of Voluntarism." *Population and Development Review* 20 (1): 167–177.

Brush, Dorothy. 1929. "The Brush Foundation." *Eugenics*, February, 17–19.

Cadbury, George W. 1964. "The Role of the International Planned Parenthood Federation." In *The Population Crisis and the Use of World Resources*, edited by S. Mudd. Bloomington: Indiana University Press.

Calderone, M.D., Mary Steichen. 1960. "Illegal Abortion as a Public Health Problem." *American Journal of Public Health* 50 (7): 948–954.

Caplan, Arthur L., Glenn McGee, and David Magnus. 1999. "What Is Immoral About Eugenics?" *British Medical Journal* 319 (7220): 1284–85.

Chez, Ronald A. 1971. "Mental Disability as a Basis for Contraception and Sterilization." *Social Biology* 18 (Supplement): S120–26.

Dice, Lee R. 1952. "Heredity Clinics: Their Value for Public Service and for Research." *American Journal of Human Genetics* 4 (1): 1–13.

Djerassi, Carl. 1970a. "Birth Control After 1984." *Science* 169 (3949): 941–951.

_____. 1970b. "Contraception 1984: Putting Something in the Water Supply." *Family Planning Perspectives* 2 (3): 29.

Ehrlich, Paul R., and Anne H. Ehrlich. 1990. "The Population Explosion: Why Isn't Everybody as Scared as We Are?" *The Amicus Journal* (Winter): 22–29.

Ellis, Havelock. 1917. "Birth Control and Eugenics." *Eugenics Review* 9: 32–41.

_____. 1919. "Birth Control in Relation to Morality and Eugenics." *Birth Control Review*, February, 7–9.

Fraser, M.D., Ph.D., G. R. 1972. "The Implications of Prevention and Treatment of Inherited Disease for the Genetic Future of Mankind." *J. Génét. Hum.* 20 (3): 185–205.

Gamble, M.D., Clarence J. 1947. "Better Human Beings Tomorrow." *Better Health*, October, 14, 25.

_____. 1949a. "Eugenic Sterilization in the United States, 1948." *Eugenical News* 34 (1–2): 1–5.

_____. 1949b. "Preventive Mental Hygiene in Alabama." *Journal of the Medical Association of Alabama* 19 (6): 160–162.

_____. 1949c. "Preventive Sterilization in 1948." *The Journal of the American Medical Association* 141 (11): 773.

_____. 1951. "Human Sterilization." *The American Journal of Nursing* 51 (10): 625–626.

Gottesman, Irving I., and L. Erlenmeyer-Kimling. 1971. "A Foundation for Informed Eugenics." *Social Biology* 18 (Supp. 2): S1–S8.

Guttmacher, Alan F. 1954. "Heredity Counseling: Diabetes, Pregnancy and Modern Medicine, A Genetic Misadventure." *Eugenics Quarterly*, September, 191–192.

_____. 1964. "The Population Crisis and the Use of World Resources." In *The Population Crisis and the Use of World Resources*, edited by S. Mudd. Bloomington: Indiana University Press.

_____. 1973a. "The Genesis of Liberalized Abortion in New York: A Personal Insight." In *Abortion, Society, and the Law*, edited by D. F. Walbert and J. D. Butler. Cleveland: The Press of Case Western Reserve University.

_____. 1973b. "General Remarks on Medical Aspects of Male and Female Sterilization." In *Eugenic Sterilization*, edited by J. Robitscher. Springfield, Ill.: Charles C. Thomas.

_____. 1973d. "Why I Favor Liberalized Abortion." *The Reader's Digest*, November, 143–147.

Hardin, Garrett. 1968. "The Tragedy of the Commons." *Science* 162 (December): 1243–1248.

_____. 1970a. "Choices of Parenthood." *Science* 170 (3955): 259–60.

_____. 1970b. "Parenthood: Right or Privilege?" *Science* 169 (3944): 427.

_____. 1970c. "Multiple Paths to Population Control." *Family Planning Perspectives* 2 (3): 24–26.

Hauser, Philip M. 1967. "Family Planning and Population Programs: A Book Review Article." *Demography* 4: 402–405.

_____. 1969. "Non-family Planning Methods of Population Control." In *Population Control: Implications, Trends and Prospects*, edited by N. Sadik. Islamabad: Pakistan Family Planning Council.

Hern, M.D., Warren M. 1971. "Is Pregnancy Really Normal?" *Family Planning Perspectives* 3 (1): 5–9.

_____. 1993. "Is Human Culture Carcinogenic for Uncontrolled Population Growth and Ecological Destruction?" *Bioscience* 43 (11): 768–773.

Huxley, Julian. 1963. "Eugenics in Evolutionary Perspective." *Perspectives in Biology and Medicine* 6 (2): 155–87.

Information Office of the State Council. 1996. "Chinese Government White Paper on Family Planning." *Population and Development Review* 22 (2): 385–390.

International Union for the Scientific Study of Population. 1948. "Constitution Adopted by the General Assembly of the Union in Washington, D.C., September 6–11, 1947." *Milbank Memorial Fund Quarterly* 26 (3): 317–22.

King, Maurice, and Charles Elliott. 1997. "To the Point of Farce: A Martian View of the Hardinian Taboo— the Silence that Surrounds Population Control." *British Medical Journal* 315 (7120): 1441–43.

Koshland, Daniel. 1989. "Sequences and Consequences of the Human Genome." *Science* 246 (October 13): 189.

Kuralt, Wallace. n.d. "Mecklenburg County: A Pilot 'Pill' Project for Welfare Recipients." In *Birth Control Services in Tax-Supported Hospitals, Health Departments and Welfare Agencies*, edited by P. P.-W. Population. New York: Planned Parenthood-World Population.

Lorimer, Frank. 1959. "The Development of Demography." In *The Study of Population: An Inventory and Appraisal*, edited by P. M. Hauser and O. D. Duncan. Chicago: University of Chicago Press.

_____. 1981. "How the Demographers Saved the Association." *Population Index* 47 (3): 488–94.

McNamara, Robert S. 1974. "The World Bank Perspective on Population Growth." In *The Dynamics of Population Policy in Latin America*, edited by T. L. McCoy. Cambridge: Ballinger Publishing Company.

Muller, Hermann J. 1961. "Human Evolution by Voluntary Choice of Germ Plasm." *Science* 134 (3480): 643–49.

Notestein, Frank W. 1970. "Zero Population Growth: What Is It?" *Family Planning Perspectives* 2 (3): 20–24.

_____. 1981. "Memories of the Early Years of the Association." *Population Index* 47 (3): 484–88.

_____. 1982. "Demography in the United States: A Partial Account of the Development of the Field." *Population and Development Review* 8 (4): 651–87.

Osborn, Frederick. 1939. "The Quality of the American Population." *Journal of Contraception* (February): 31–33.

_____. 1952. "The Eugenic Hypothesis." *The Eugenics Review*, July, 97–100.

_____. 1955. "Eugenics." *News of Population and Birth Control, IPPF*, November, 1.

_____. 1964. "The Protection and Improvement of Man's Genetic Inheritance." In *The Population Crisis and the Use of World Resources*, edited by S. Mudd. Bloomington: Indiana University Press.

_____. 1967. "American Foundations and Population Problems." In *U.S. Philanthropic Foundations: Their History, Structure, Management, and Record*, edited by W. Weaver. New York: Harper and Row.

_____. 1974. "History of the American Eugenics Society." *Social Biology* 21 (2): 115–126.

_____, and Carl Jay Bajema. 1972. "The Eugenic Hypothesis." *Social Biology* 19 (4): 337–345.

Paniagua, M.D., Manuel E., P. R. Rio, A. B. Piedras, Henry W. Vaillant, and Clarence J. Gamble, M.D. 1961. "Field Trial of a Contraceptive Foam in Puerto Rico." *JAMA* 177 (2): 125–129.

Peng, Yu. 1994. "China's Experience in Population Matters: An Official Statement." *Population and Development Review* 20 (2): 488–491.

Potts, Ph.D., Malcolm. 1975. "Natural Law and Planned Parenthood." *Mount Sinai Journal of Medicine* 42 (4): 326–334.

Pilpel, Harriet. 1971. "Family Planning and the Law." *Social Biology* 18 (Supp. 2): S127–S133.

Reed, Sheldon C., and Esther B. Nordlie. 1961. "Genetic Counseling: For Children of Mixed Racial Ancestry." *Eugenics Quarterly* 8 (3): 157–163.

Rock, M.D., John. 1961. "Population Growth." *JAMA* 177 (1): 58–60.

Sanger, Margaret. 1917a. "An Answer to Mr. Roosevelt." *Birth Control Review,* December, 12–14.

_____. 1917b. "Shall We Break This Law?" *Birth Control Review,* February, 4.

_____. 1917c. "Woman and War." *Birth Control Review,* June, 5.

_____. 1918a. "Editorial Comment." *Birth Control Review,* September, 9.

_____. 1918b. "When Should a Woman Avoid Having Children?" *Birth Control Review,* November, 6–7.

_____. 1919a. "Birth Control and Racial Betterment." *Birth Control Review,* February, 11–12.

_____. 1919b. "Havelock Ellis—An Appreciation." *Birth Control Review,* February, 6.

_____. 1919c. "Why Not Birth Control Clinics in America?" *Birth Control Review,* May, 10–11.

_____. 1921. "The Eugenic Value of Birth Control Propaganda." *Birth Control Review,* October, 5.

_____. 1924. "Mrs. Sanger's Nine Reasons Children Should Not Be Born." *Birth Control Review,* December, 346.

_____. 1925a. "The Case for Birth Control." In *Selected Articles on Birth Control,* edited by J. E. Johnsen. New York: H. W. Wilson Co.

_____. 1925b. "Is Race Suicide Probable?" *Collier's* 76 (August 15), 25.

_____. 1925c. "The Need for Birth Control in America." In *Birth Control: Facts and Responsibilities,* edited by Adolf Meyer, M.D. Baltimore: Williams and Wilkins Co.

_____. 1926b. "The Function of Sterilization." *Birth Control Review,* October, 299.

_____. 1927. "Editorial." *Birth Control Review,* December, 317–318.

_____. 1928. "Editorial." *Birth Control Review,* March, 73–74.

_____. 1932. "A Plan for Peace." *Birth Control Review,* April, 107–108.

_____. 1933. "An Open Letter to Social Workers." *Birth Control Review,* June, 140–141.

_____. 1960. "My Fight for America's First Birth Control Clinic." *Reader's Digest,* February.

Shockley, William. 1974. "Sterilization—A Thinking Exercise." *The Stanford Daily,* April 12, 2.

Sieverts, Steven, and Frederick S. Jaffe. 1970. "An Exchange: Steven Sieverts/Frederick S. Jaffe." *Family Planning Perspectives* 2 (2): 2–5.

Sun, Dong-Sheng. 1981. "Popularizing the Knowledge of Eugenics and Advocating Optimal Births Vigorously." Beijing: Jinan Army Institute. 1939. "A Symposium on Population." *Journal of Contraception* (February): 38–40.

Wei, Wang, and Head of the Delegation of the People's Republic of China at the World Population Conference. 1994. "Chinese Statements on Population at Bucharest, 1974, and Mexico City, 1984." *Population and Development Review* 20 (2): 449–459.

Books, Pamphlets and Reports: Secondary

Aird, John S. 1990. *Slaughter of the Innocents: Coercive Birth Control in China.* Washington, D.C.: AEI Press.

Alan Guttmacher Institute. 1979. *Abortions and the Poor: Private Morality, Public Responsibility*. New York: Alan Guttmacher Institute.

American Civil Liberties Union. 1994. *Norplant: A New Contraceptive with the Potential for Abuse*. www.aclu.org/issues/reproduct/norplant.html.

Apple, Rima D., ed. 1990. *Women, Health, and Medicine in America: A Historical Handbook*. New York: Garland Publishing, Inc.

Bachrach, Peter, and Elihu Bergman. 1973. *Power and Choice: The Formulation of American Population Policy*. Lexington: Lexington Books.

Bandarage, Asoka. 1997. *Women, Population and Global Crisis: A Political-Economic Analysis*. London: Zed Books.

Barkan, Elazar. 1992. *The Retreat of Scientific Racism*. New York: Cambridge University Press.

Bhatia, Rajani, Rupsa Millik, and Shamita Das Dasgupta. 2003. *Sex Selection: New Technologies, New Forms of Gender Discrimination*. Committee on Women, Population and the Environment, October. www.cwpe.org/Materials%20on%20Sex%20 Selection/FactSheet.htm, accessed February 7, 2004.

Biesold, Horst. 2002. *Crying Hands: Eugenics and Deaf People in Nazi Germany*. Trans. William Sayers. Washington, D.C.: Gallaudet University Press.

Black, Edwin. 2003. *War Against the Weak: Eugenics and America's Campaign to Create a Master Race*. New York: Four Walls Eight Windows.

Blank, Robert H. 1990. *Regulating Reproduction*. New York: Columbia University Press.

Board of Trustees, American Medical Association. 1992. "Requirements or Incentives by Government for the Use of Long-Acting Contraceptives." *Journal of the American Medical Association* 267 (13): 1818–1821.

Bock, Gisela. 1986. *Zwangssterilisation im Nationalsozialismus: Studien zur Rassenpolitik und Frauenpolitik*. Vol. 48, *Schriften des Zentralinstituts für sozialwissenschaftliche Forschung der Freien Universität Berlin*. Opladen: Westdeutscher Verlag.

Boston Women's Health Book Collective. 1992. *The New Our Bodies, Ourselves*. New York: Touchstone Books.

Brennan, William. 1995. *Dehumanizing the Vulnerable: When Word Games Take Lives*. Chicago: Loyola University Press.

Broberg, Gunnar, and Nils Roll-Hansen, eds. 1996. *Eugenics and the Welfare State: Sterilization Policy in Denmark, Sweden, Norway, and Finland*. East Lansing: University of Michigan Press.

Buchanan, Allen, Norman Daniels, Daniel Wikler, and Dan W. Brock. 2000. *From Chance to Choice: Genetics and Justice*. New York: Cambridge University Press.

Carlson, Elof Axel. 2001. *The Unfit: A History of a Bad Idea*. Cold Spring Harbor, N.Y.: Cold Spring Harbor Laboratory Press.

Ceci, Stephen J. 1996. *On Intelligence: A Bioecological Treatise on Intellectual Development*. Second ed. Cambridge: Harvard University Press.

Chadwick, Ruth F., ed. 1992. *Ethics, Reproduction and Genetic Control*. Second ed. New York: Routledge.

Chase, Allan. 1980. *The Legacy of Malthus: The Social Costs of the New Scientific Racism*. Chicago: University of Illinois Press.

Chesler, Ellen. 1992. *Woman of Valor: Margaret Sanger and the Birth Control Movement in America*. New York: Simon & Schuster.

Cook-Deegan, Robert. 1994. *The Gene Wars: Science, Politics, and the Human Genome*. New York: W. W. Norton and Company.

Corea, Gena. 1985. *The Mother Machine: Reproductive Technology from Artificial Insemination to Artificial Wombs*. New York: Harper & Row Publishers.

Critchlow, Donald T. 1999. *Intended Consequences: Birth Control, Abortion, and the Federal Government in Modern America.* New York: Oxford University Press.

Cromartie, Michael, ed. 1995. *The Nine Lives of Population Control.* Grand Rapids: Wm. B. Eerdmans Publishing Co.

Das Gupta, Monica. 1998. *"Missing Girls" in China, South Korea, and India: Causes and Policy Implications.* Cambridge, MA: Harvard University, Center for Population and Development Studies.

Davis, Angela Y. 1983. *Women, Race, and Class.* New York: Vintage Books.

Donaldson, Peter J. 1990. *Nature Against Us: The United States and the World Population Crisis, 1965–1980.* Chapel Hill: University of North Carolina Press.

Donovan, Josephine. 1985. *Feminist Theory: The Intellectual Traditions of American Feminism.* New York: Frederick Ungar Publishing Co.

Duster, Troy. 1990. *Backdoor to Eugenics.* New York: Routledge.

Elshtain, Jean Bethke. 1981. *Public Man, Private Woman: Women in Social and Political Thought.* Second ed. Princeton: Princeton University Press.

Farrall, Lyndsay Andrew. 1985. *The Origins and Growth of the English Eugenics Movement, 1865–1925.* New York: Garland Publishing, Inc.

Finkle, Jason L., and C. Alison McIntosh, eds. 1994. *The New Politics of Population: Conflict and Consensus in Family Planning.* Edited by E. P. Churchill. Vol. 20, *Population and Development Review supplement.* New York: The Population Council.

Fischer, Claude S., Michael Hout, Martín Sánchez Jankowski, Samuel R. Lucas, Ann Swidler, and Kim Voss. 1996. *Inequality by Design: Cracking the Bell Curve Myth.* Princeton: Princeton University Press.

Foucault, Michel. 1978. *History of Sexuality: An Introduction.* Translated by Robert Hurley. 3 vols. Vol. 1. New York: Vintage Books.

Fraser, Steven, ed. 1995. *The Bell Curve Wars: Race, Intelligence, and the Future of America.* New York: Basic Books.

Gallagher, Nancy L. 1999. *Breeding Better Vermonters: The Eugenics Project in the Green Mountain State.* Hanover, N.H.: University Press of New England.

Gillham, Nicholas Wright. 2001. *A Life of Sir Francis Galton: From African Exploration to the Birth of Eugenics.* New York: Oxford University Press.

Gordon, Linda. 1990. *Woman's Body, Woman's Right: Birth Control in America.* Second ed. New York: Penguin Books.

Gould, Stephen Jay. 1996. *The Mismeasure of Man.* Second ed. New York: W. W. Norton and Company.

Grant, Nicole J. 1992. *The Selling of Contraception: The Dalkon Shield Case, Sexuality, and Women's Autonomy.* Columbus: Ohio State University Press.

Greer, Germaine. 1984. *Sex and Destiny: The Politics of Human Fertility.* New York: Harper & Row.

_____. 1986. *Madwoman's Underclothes: Essays and Occasional Writings.* London: Picador.

_____. 1999. *The Whole Woman.* New York: Alfred A. Knopf.

Grosskurth, Phyllis. 1980. *Havelock Ellis: A Biography.* New York: Alfred A. Knopf.

Grossmann, Atina. 1995. *Reforming Sex: The German Movement for Birth Control and Abortion Reform, 1920–1950.* New York: Oxford University Press.

Haller, Mark H. 1963. *Eugenics: Hereditarian Attitudes in American Thought.* New Brunswick, New Jersey: Rutgers University Press.

Hardon, Anita, and Elizabeth Hayes, eds. 1997. *Reproductive Rights in Practice: A Feminist Report on Quality of Care.* New York: Zed Books Ltd.

Harr, John Ensor, and Peter J. Johnson. 1988. *The Rockefeller Century.* New York: Charles Scribner's Sons.

Hartmann, Betsy. 1995. *Reproductive Rights and Wrongs: The Global Politics of Population Control.* Second ed. Boston: South End Press.

Hasian, Marouf A., Jr. 1996. *The Rhetoric of Eugenics in Anglo-American Thought.* Edited by B. J. Craige, *The University of Georgia Humanities Center Series on Science and the Humanities.* Athens: University of Georgia Press.

Hawkins, Mary F. 1997. *Unshielded: The Human Cost of the Dalkon Shield.* Toronto: University of Toronto Press.

Hicks, Karen M. 1994. *Surviving the Dalkon Shield IUD: Women v. the Pharmaceutical Industry.* Edited by G. Bowles, R. Klein and J. Raymond, *Athene Series.* New York: Teachers College Press.

Holmes, Helen B., Betty B. Hoskins, and Michael Gross, eds. 1980. *Birth Control and Controlling Birth: Women-Centered Perspectives, Contemporary Issues in Biomedicine, Ethics, and Society.* Clifton: The Humana Press, Inc.

Human Rights Watch/Asia. 1996a. *China: Chinese Orphanages: A Follow-Up.* New York: Human Rights Watch/Asia.

_____. 1996b. *Death by Default: A Policy of Fatal Neglect in China's State Orphanages.* New York: Human Rights Watch.

_____. 1997. *China: Chinese Diplomacy, Western Hypocrisy and the U.N. Human Rights Commission.* New York: Human Rights Watch/Asia.

Jacoby, Russell, and Naomi Glauberman, eds. 1995. *The Bell Curve Debate: History, Documents, Opinions.* New York: Times Books.

Kamin, Leon J. 1974. *The Science and Politics of I.Q. Testing.* Potomac, Md.: Lawrence Erlbaum Associates.

Kasun, Jacqueline. 1999. *The War Against Population: The Economics and Ideology of Population Control.* Second ed. San Francisco: Ignatius Press.

Kerr, Anne, and Tom Shakespeare, eds. 2002. *Genetic Politics: From Eugenics to Genome.* Cheltenham: New Clarion Press.

Kevles, Daniel J. 1995. *In the Name of Eugenics: Genetics and the Uses of Human Heredity.* Second ed. Cambridge: Harvard University Press.

Kincheloe, Joe L., Shirley R. Steinberg, and Aaron D. Gresson, III, eds. 1996. *Measured Lies: The Bell Curve Examined.* New York: St. Martin's Press.

Kline, Wendy. 2002. *Building a Better Race: Gender, Sexuality, and Eugenics from the Turn of the Century to the Baby Boom.* Berkeley: University of California Press.

Kühl, Stefan. 1994. *The Nazi Connection: Eugenics, American Racism, and German National Socialism.* New York: Oxford University Press.

Larson, Edward J. 1995. *Sex, Race, and Science: Eugenics in the Deep South.* Baltimore: The Johns Hopkins University Press.

Liagin, Elizabeth. 1995. *Excessive Force: Power, Politics and Population Control.* Washington, D.C.: Information Project for Africa.

Ludmerer, Kenneth M. 1972. *Genetics and American Society: A Historical Appraisal.* Baltimore: The Johns Hopkins University Press.

Lynn, Richard. 2001. *The Science of Human Diversity: A History of the Pioneer Fund.* Lanham, Md.: Rowman and Littlefield.

Marks, Lara V. 2001. *Sexual Chemistry: A History of the Contraceptive Pill.* New Haven: Yale University Press.

Marshall, Robert, and Charles Donovan. 1991. *Blessed Are the Barren: The Social Policy of Planned Parenthood.* San Francisco: Ignatius Press.

Mazumdar, Pauline M. H. 1992. *Eugenics, Human Genetics, and Human Failings: The Eugenics Society, Its Sources and Critics in Britain.* New York: Routledge.

McCann, Carole R. 1994. *Birth Control Politics in the United States, 1916–1945.* Ithaca: Cornell University Press.

McGee, Glenn. 1997. *The Perfect Baby: A Pragmatic Approach to Genetics*. Lanham, Md.: Rowman & Littlefield.

McIntyre, Alasdair. 1999. *Dependent Rational Animals: Why Human Beings Need the Virtues*. Vol. 20, *The Paul Carus Lectures*. Chicago: Open Court.

McLaren, Angus. 1990. *A History of Contraception: From Antiquity to the Present Day*. Edited by P. Laslett, M. Anderson and K. Wrightson, *Family, Sexuality, and Social Relations in Past Times*. London: Basil Blackwell Ltd.

McLaughlin, Loretta. 1982. *The Pill, John Rock, and the Church: The Biography of a Revolution*. Boston: Little, Brown and Company.

Miller, Marvin D. 1996. *Terminating the "Socially Inadequate": The American Eugenicists and the German Race Hygienists, California to Cold Spring Harbor, Long Island to Germany*. Commack: Malamud-Rose.

Mintzes, Barbara, Anita Hardon, and Jannemieke Hanhart, eds. 1993. *Norplant: Under Her Skin*. Delft: The Women's Health Action Foundation.

Mosher, Steven W. 1990. *China Misperceived: American Illusions and Chinese Reality*. New York: Basic Books.

_____. 1993. *A Mother's Ordeal: One Woman's Fight Against China's One-Child Policy*. New York: HarperPerennial.

National Women's Health Network. 1995. *Taking Hormones and Women's Health: Choices, Risks and Benefits*. Washington, D.C.: National Women's Health Network.

Neft, Naomi, and Ann D. Levine. 1997. *Where Women Stand: An International Report on the Status of Women in 140 Countries, 1997–1998*. New York: Random House.

Neuhaus, Richard. 1971. *In Defense of People: Ecology and the Seduction of Radicalism*. New York: The Macmillan Company.

Neuhaus, Richard John, ed. 1990. *Guaranteeing the Good Life: Medicine and the Return of Eugenics*. Vol. 13, *Encounter Series*. Grand Rapids, Michigan: William B. Eerdmans Publishing Company.

Paul, Diane B. 1995. *Controlling Human Heredity: 1865 to the Present*. Edited by M. C. Jacob and S. R. Weart, *The Control of Nature Series*. Atlantic Highlands, New Jersey: Humanities Press International.

_____. 1998. *The Politics of Heredity: Essays on Eugenics, Biomedicine, and the Nature-Nurture Debate*. Edited by D. E. Shaner, *SUNY Series in Philosophy and Biology*. Albany: SUNY Press.

Pernick, Martin S. 1996. *The Black Stork: Eugenics and the Death of "Defective" Babies in American Medicine and Motion Pictures Since 1915*. New York: Oxford University Press.

Perry, Susan, and Jim Dawson. 1985. *Nightmare: Women and the Dalkon Shield*. New York: Macmillan.

Pickens, Donald K. 1968. *Eugenics and the Progressives*. Vanderbilt: Vanderbilt University Press.

Piotrow, Phyllis Tilson. 1973. *World Population Crisis: The United States Response*. Vol. 4, *Praeger Special Studies in International Economics and Development, Law and Population Book Series*. New York: Praeger Publishers.

Population Information Program of Johns Hopkins. 1987. "Hormonal Contraception: New Long-Acting Methods." *Population Reports*, March–April, K57–88.

_____. 1992. *Norplant at a Glance*. Baltimore: Johns Hopkins Center for Communication Programs.

_____. 1992. "Decisions for Norplant Programs." *Population Reports*, November, 1–32.

Proctor, Robert N. 1988. *Racial Hygiene: Medicine Under the Nazis*. Cambridge: Harvard University Press.

Rainwater, Lee, and Karol Kane Weinstein. 1960. *And the Poor Get Children: Sex, Contraception, and Family Planning in the Working Class*. Chicago: Quadrangle Books.

Ramsey, Paul. 1978. *Ethics at the Edges of Life: Medical and Legal Intersections.* New Haven: Yale University Press.

Reed, James. 1978. *From Private Vice to Public Virtue: The Birth Control Movement and American Society Since 1830.* New York: Basic Books.

Reilly, Philip R. 1991. *The Surgical Solution: A History of Involuntary Sterilization in the United States.* Baltimore: The Johns Hopkins University Press.

Reinders, Hans S. 2000. *Future of the Disabled in Liberal Society: An Ethical Analysis. Revisions.* South Bend, Ind.: University of Notre Dame Press.

Richardson, Angelique. 2003. *Love and Eugenics in the Late Nineteenth Century: Rational Reproduction and the New Woman.* New York: Oxford University Press.

Roberts, Dorothy. 1997. *Killing the Black Body: Race, Reproduction, and the Meaning of Liberty.* New York: Pantheon.

Ross, Eric B. 1998. *The Malthus Factor: Population, Poverty and Politics in Capitalist Development.* New York: Zed Books.

Rosser, Sue V. 1994. *Women's Health: Missing from U.S. Medicine.* Bloomington: Indiana University Press.

Schenkel, Albert F. 1995. *The Rich Man and the Kingdom: John D. Rockefeller, Jr., and the Protestant Establishment.* Edited by B. J. Booten and F. S. Fiorenza. Vol. 39, *Harvard Theological Studies.* Minneapolis: Fortress Press.

Seaman, Barbara. 1995. *The Doctors' Case Against the Pill.* Second ed. Alameda: Hunter House.

Selden, Steven. 1999. *Inheriting Shame: The Story of Eugenics and Racism in America.* Edited by J. F. Soltis, *Advances in Contemporary Educational Thought Series.* New York: Teachers College Press.

Shapiro, Thomas M. 1985. *Population Control Politics: Women, Sterilization, and Reproductive Choice.* Philadelphia: Temple University Press.

Solinger, Rickie. 2001. *Beggars and Choosers: How the Politics of Choice Shapes Adoption, Abortion, and Welfare in the United States.* New York: Hill and Wang.

Soloway, Richard A. 1990. *Demography and Degeneration: Eugenics and the Declining Birthrate in Twentieth-Century Britain.* Chapel Hill: University of North Carolina Press.

Stepan, Nancy Leys. 1991. *The Hour of Eugenics: Race, Gender, and Nation in Latin America.* Ithaca: Cornell University Press.

Suitters, Beryl. 1973. *Be Brave and Angry: Chronicles of the International Planned Parenthood Federation.* London: International Planned Parenthood Federation.

Talpade, Chandra, Ann Russo, and Lourdes Torres, eds. 1991. *Third World Women and the Politics of Feminism.* Bloomington: Indiana University Press.

Tone, Andrea. 2001. *Devices and Desires: A History of Contraceptives in America.* New York: Hill and Wang.

Tucker, William H. 2002. *The Funding of Scientific Racism: Wickliffe Draper and the Pioneer Fund.* Chicago: University of Illinois Press.

Ward, Martha G. 1986. *Poor Women, Powerful Men: America's Great Experiment in Family Planning.* Boulder: Westview Press.

Warwick, Donald P. 1982. *Bitter Pills: Population Policies and Their Implementation in Eight Developing Countries.* Cambridge: Cambridge University Press.

Williams, Doone, and Greer Williams. 1978. *Every Child a Wanted Child: Clarence James Gamble, M.D. and His Work in the Birth Control Movement.* Edited by E. P. Flint. Vol. 4, *The Countway Library Associates Historical Publication.* Boston: The Francis A. Countway Library of Medicine.

Wolf, Margery. 1985. *Revolution Postponed: Women in Contemporary China.* Stanford: Stanford University Press.

Wolf, Naomi. 2001. *Misconceptions: Truth, Lies, and the Unexpected on the Journey to Motherhood.* New York: Doubleday.

Articles and Essays: Secondary

1989-1990. "Mary Steichen Calderone." In *Who's Who of American Women.* Wilmette, Illinois: Macmillan.

2003. "Frances Hand Ferguson." In *The Complete Marquis Who's Who.* New York: Marquis Who's Who, 2003.

60 Minutes. 1984. "No Brothers, No Sisters." CBS News. Transcript, CBS Television Network.

Aird, John S. 1986. "Coercion in Family Planning: Causes, Methods, and Consequences." In *China's Economy Looks Toward the Year 2000*, edited by U.S. Joint Economic Commitee. Washington, D.C.: U.S. Government Printing Office.

Akhter, Farida. 1992. "The Eugenic and Racist Premise of Reproductive Rights and Population Control." *Issues in Reproductive and Genetic Engineering* 5 (1): 1–8.

Allen, Charlotte. 1992. "Boys Only." *The New Republic*, March 9, 16–18.

Allen, Gar. 1980. "The Work of Raymond Pearl: From Eugenics to Population Control." *Science for the People* 12 (4): 22–28.

Allen, Garland E. 1986 (reprinted in 1995). "The Eugenics Record Office at Cold Springs Harbor, 1910–1940: An Essay in Institutional History" [reprinted as "Eugenics Comes to America"]. In *The Bell Curve Debate: History, Documents, Opinions*, edited by R. J. N. Glauberman. New York: Times Books.

_____. 1997. "The Social and Economic Origins of Genetic Determinism: A Case History of the American Eugenics Movement, 1900–1940 and Its Lesson for Today." *Genetica* 99 (2–3): 77–88.

_____. 2001. "Is a New Eugenics Afoot?" *Science* 294 (5540 [Oct. 5, 2001]): 59–61.

American Academy of Pediatrics Committee on Bioethics. 1990. "Sterilization of Women Who Are Mentally Handicapped." *Pediatrics* 85 (5): 868–871.

Antonak, R. F., C. R. Fielder, and J. A. Mulick. 1993. "Scale of Attitudes Toward the Application of Eugenics to the Treatment of People with Mental Retardation." *Journal of Intellectual Disability Research* 37 (1): 75–83.

Antonak, R. F., J. A. Mulick, F. H. Kobe, and C. R. Fiedler. 1995. "Influence of Mental Retardation Severity and Respondent Characteristics on Self-Reported Attitudes Toward Mental Retardation and Eugenics." *Journal of Intellectual Disability Research* 39 (4): 316–325.

Baker, Bernadette. 2002. "The Hunt for Disability: The New Eugenics and the Normalization of School Children." *Teachers College Record* 104 (4, June): 663–703.

Bandarage, Asoka. 1994. "A New and Improved Population Control Policy?" *Political Environments* 1 (1): 10–15.

Banister, Judith. 1986. "Implications of China's 1982 Census Results." In *China's Economy Looks Toward the Year 2000*, edited by U.S. Joint Economic Committee. Washington, D.C.: U.S. Government Printing Office.

Basu, Alaka M. 1985. "Family Planning and the Emergency: An Unanticipated Consequence." *Economic and Political Weekly*, March 9, 422–425.

Beneria, Lourdes, and Gita Sen. 1981. "Accumulation, Reproduction, and Women's Role in Economic Development: Boserup Revisited." *Signs: Journal of Women in Culture and Society* 7 (2): 279–298.

Billings, Paul R., Mel A. Kohn, Margaret de Cuevas, Jonathan Beckwith, Joseph S. Alper, and Marvin R. Natowicz. 1992. "Discrimination as a Consequence of Genetic Testing." *American Journal of Human Genetics* 50 (3): 476–482.

Bittles, A. H., and Y. Chew. 1998. "Eugenics and Population Policies." In *Human Biology and Social Inequity*, edited by S. S. Strickland and P. S. Shetty. New York: Cambridge University Press.

Bock, Gisela. 1983. "Racism and Sexism in Nazi Germany: Motherhood, Compulsory Sterilization, and the State." *Signs: Journal of Women in Culture and Society* 8 (3): 400–421.

Boss, Ph.D., Judith A. 1990. "How Voluntary Prenatal Diagnosis and Selective Abortion Increase the Abnormal Human Gene Pool." *Birth* 17 (2): 75–79.

Brantlinger, Ellen. 1992. "Professionals' Attitudes Toward the Sterilization of People with Disabilities." *Journal of the Association for Persons with Severe Handicaps* 17 (1): 4–18.

Brown, George F., and Ellen H. Moskowitz. 1997. "Moral and Policy Issues in Long-Acting Contraception." *Annual Review of Public Health* 18: 379–400.

Bunch, Charlotte. 1995. "Transforming Human Rights from a Feminist Perspective." In *Women's Rights, Human Rights: International Feminist Perspectives*, edited by J. Peters and A. Wolper. New York: Routledge.

Carlson, Licia. 2001. "Cognitive Ableism and Disability Studies: Feminist Reflections on the History of Mental Retardation." *Hypatia: A Journal of Feminist Philosophy* 16 (4): 124–46.

Caron, Simone M. 1998. "Birth Control and the Black Community in the 1960s: Genocide or Powerpolitics?" *Journal of Social History* 31: 545–70.

Caskey, C. Thomas. 1992. "DNA-Based Medicine: Prevention and Therapy." In *The Code of Codes: Scientific and Social Issues in the Human Genome Project*, edited by D. J. Kevles and L. Hood. Cambridge: Harvard University Press.

Castles, Katherine. 2002. "Quiet Eugenics: Sterilization in North Carolina's Institutions for the Mentally Retarded, 1945–1965." *Journal of Southern History* 68 (4): 849–78.

Corea, Gena. 1980. "The Depo-Provera Weapon." In *Birth Control and Controlling Birth: Women-Centered Perspectives*, edited by H. B. Holmes, B. B. Hoskins and M. Gross. Clifton, N.J.: Humana Press.

Crane, Barbara B., and Jason L. Finkle. 1989. "The United States, China, and the United Nations Population Fund: Dynamics of US Policymaking." *Population and Development Review* 15 (1): 23–59.

Critchlow, Donald T. 1996. "Birth Control, Population Control, and Family Planning: An Overview." In *Politics of Abortion and Birth Control in Historical Perspective*, edited by D. T. Critchlow. University Park: Pennsylvania State University Press.

Crook, Paul. 2002. "American Eugenics and the Nazis: Recent Historiography." *European Legacy* 7 (3): 363–81.

Cunningham-Burley, Sarah, and Mary Boulton. 2000. "The Social Context of the New Genetics." In *The Handbook of Social Studies in Health and Medicine*, edited by Gary L. Albrecht, et al. London: Sage Publications Ltd.

De Konick, Maria. 1998. "Discours féministe et néo-malthusianisme: les effets pervers d'une mésalliance." *Cahiers Québécois de Démographie* 27 (2): 253–65, 336–7, 339.

Donaldson, Peter J., and Amy Ong Tsui. 1994. "The International Family Planning Movement." In *Beyond the Numbers: A Reader on Population, Consumption, and the Environment*, edited by L. A. Mazur. Washington, D.C.: Island Press.

Donovan, Patricia. 1996. "Taking Family Planning Services to Hard-to-Reach Populations." *Family Planning Perspectives* 28 (3): 120–26.

Dorr, Gregory Michael. 2000. "Assuring America's Place in the Sun: Ivey Foreman Lewis and the Teaching of Eugenics at the University of Virginia." *Journal of Southern History* 66 (2): 257–96.

Dowbiggin, Ian. 2001. "A Prey on Normal People: C. Killick Millard and the Euthanasia Movement in Great Britain, 1930–55." *Journal of Contemporary History* 36 (1): 59–85.

_____. 2002. "'A Rational Coalition': Euthanasia, Eugenics, and Birth Control in America, 1940–1970." *Journal of Policy History* 14 (3): 223–60.

Dunne, Cara, and Catherine Warren. 1998. "Lethal Autonomy: The Malfunction of the Informed Consent Mechanism Within the Context of Prenatal Diagnosis of Genetic Variants." *Issues of Law and Medicine*, October 1, www.elibrary. com.

Eberstadt, Nicholas. 1994. "Population Policy: Ideology as Science." *First Things* 40 (January): 30–38.

Edlund, Lena. 1999. "Son Preference, Sex Ratios, and Marriage Patterns." *Journal of Political Economy* 107 (6, pt. 1): 1275–304.

Elkins, Thomas E., and H. Frank Andersen. 1992. "Sterilization of Persons with Mental Retardation." *Journal of the Association for Persons with Severe Handicaps* 17 (1): 19–26.

Elshtain, Jean Bethke. 1990. "The New Eugenics and Feminist Quandaries: Philosophical and Political Reflections." In *Power Trips and Other Journeys: Essays in Feminism as Civil Discourse*. Madison: University of Wisconsin Press.

Filemyr, Ann. 1997. "Unmasking the Population Bomber: Analyzing Domination at the Intersection of Gender, Race, Class, and Ecology." *NWSA Journal* 9 (Sept.): 138–49.

Fitzpatrick, Tony. 2001. "Before the Cradle: New Genetics, Biopolicy and Regulated Eugenics." *Journal of Social Policy* 30 (4): 589–612.

Freed, Stanley A., and Ruth S. Freed. 1985. "Two Decades of Sterilisation, Modernisation, and Population Growth in a Rural Context." *Economic and Political Weekly*, December 7, 2171–2175.

Friedman, Elisabeth. 1995. "Women's Human Rights: The Emergence of a Movement." In *Women's Rights, Human Rights: International Feminist Perspectives*, edited by J. Peters and A. Wolper. New York: Routledge.

Friedman, J. M. 1991. "Eugenics and the 'New Genetics'." *Perspectives in Biology and Medicine* 35 (1): 145–154.

Garver, Kenneth L., and Bettylee Garver. 1992. "Eugenics, Euthanasia and Genocide." *Linacre Quarterly* 59 (3): 24–51.

Glannon, Walter. 1998. "Genes, Embryos, and Future People." *Bioethics* 12 (3): 187–211.

Goodman, Amy, et al. 1985. "The Case Against Depo-Provera." *Multinational Monitor*, February/March, 2–22.

Gordon, Linda. 1974. "The Politics of Population: Birth Control and the Eugenics Movement." *Radical America* 8 (4): 61–97.

Gray, Virginia. 1974. "Women: Victims or Beneficiaries of U.S. Population Policy." In *Political Issues in U.S. Population Policy*, edited by V. Gray and E. Bergman. Lexington: Lexington Books, D.C. Heath and Company.

Greely, Henry T. 1992. "Health Insurance, Employment Discrimination, and the Genetics Revolution." In *The Code of Codes: Scientific and Social Issues in the Human Genome Project*, edited by D. J. Kevles and L. Hood. Cambridge: Harvard University Press.

Greenhalgh, Susan, Zhu Chuzhu, and Li Nan. 1994. "Restraining Population Growth in Three Chinese Villages, 1988–93." *Population and Development Review* 20 (2): 365–395.

Greenhalgh, Susan, and Jiali Li. 1995. "Engendering Reproductive Policy and Practice in Peasant China: For a Feminist Demography of Reproduction." *Signs: Journal of Women in Culture and Society* 20 (3): 601–641.

Grimes, S. 1994. "The Ideology of Population Control in the UN Draft Plan for Cairo." *Population Research and Policy Review* 13 (3): 209–24.

Gu, Hongyan Liu; Baochang. 1998. "Preference of Rural Population on the Sex of Expected Children and Their Corresponding Behaviors." *Chinese Journal of Population Science* 10 (3): 199–209.

Gupta, Jyotsna A. 1993. "People Like You Never Agree to Get It: An Indian Family Planning Clinic." *Womenews*, 12–14.

Handwerker, Lisa. 1995. "Social and Ethical Implications of In Vitro Fertilization in Contemporary China." *Cambridge Quarterly of Healthcare Ethics* 4 (3): 355–363.

Hansen, Bent Sigurd. 1996. "Something Rotten in the State of Denmark: Eugenics and the Ascent of the Welfare State." In *Eugenics and the Welfare State: Sterilization Policy in Denmark, Sweden, Norway, and Finland*, edited by G. Broberg and N. Roll-Hansen. East Lansing: University of Michigan Press.

Hartmann, Betsy. 1991–1992. "Population Control as Foreign Policy." *CovertAction* 39 (Winter): 26–30.

_____. 1994. "Population Fictions: The Malthusians Are Back in Town." *Dollars and Sense*, September/October, 14–16.

Hassed, Susan J., Connie H. Miller, Sandra K. Pope, Pamela Murphy, J. Gerald Quick, and Christopher Cunniff. 1993. "Perinatal Lethal Conditions: The Effect of Diagnosis on Decision Making." *Obstetrics and Gynecology* 82 (1): 37–42.

Hauerwas, Stanley, and L. John Roos. 1974. "Ethics and Population Policy." In *Political Issues in U.S. Population Policy*, edited by V. Gray and E. Bergman. Lexington: Lexington Books, D. C. Heath and Company.

Hirsch, Jerry. 1997. "Some History of Heredity-vs-Environment, Genetic Inferiority at Harvard (?), and *The* (Incredible) *Bell Curve*." *Genetica* 99 (2–3): 207–24.

Hodgson, Dennis. 1991. "The Ideological Origins of the Population Association of America." *Population and Development Review* 17 (1): 1–34.

Holtzman, Neil A., and Mark A. Rothstein. 1992. "Eugenics and Genetic Discrimination" *American Journal of Human Genetics* 50 (3): 457–459.

Hunter, James Davison, and Joseph E. Davis. 1996. "Cultural Politics at the Edge of Life." In *The Politics of Abortion and Birth Control in Historical Perspective*, edited by D. T. Critchlow. University Park: Pennsylvania State University Press.

Jaquette, Jane S., and Kathleen A. Staudt. 1985. "Women as 'At Risk' Reproducers: Biology, Science, and Population in U.S. Foreign Policy." In *Women, Biology, and Public Policy*, edited by V. S. Shapiro. Beverly Hills: Sage Publications.

Jones, Clinton. 1974. "Population Issues and the Black Community." In *Political Issues in U.S. Population Policy*, edited by V. Gray and E. Bergman. Lexington: Lexington Books, D.C. Heath and Company.

Judson, Horace Freeland. 1992. "A History of the Science and Technology Behind Gene Sequencing and Mapping." In *The Code of Codes: Scientific and Social Issues in the Human Genome Project*, edited by D. J. Kevles and L. Hood. Cambridge: Harvard University Press.

Kaler, Amy. 1998. "A Threat to the Nation and a Threat to the Men: The Banning of Depo-Provera in Zimbabwe, 1981." *Journal of Southern African Studies* 24 (2): 347–76.

Kamin, Leon J. 1995. "The Pioneers of IQ Testing." In *The Bell Curve Debate: History, Documents, Opinions*, edited by R. J. N. Glauberman. New York: Times Books.

Kapil, Iris. 1985. "Case for Injectible Contraceptive." *Economic and Political Weekly*, May 11, 854–856.

Keller, Evelyn Fox. 1992. "Nature, Nurture, and the Human Genome Project." In *The Code of Codes: Scientific and Social Issues in the Human Genome Project*, edited by D. J. Kevles and L. Hood. Cambridge: Harvard University Press.

Kenny, Michael G. 2002. "Toward a Racial Abyss: Eugenics, Wickliffe Draper, and the Origins of the Pioneer Fund." *Journal of the History of the Behavioral Sciences* 30 (3): 259–283.

Kevles, Daniel J. 1992. "Out of Eugenics: The Historical Politics of the Human Genome." In *The Code of Codes: Scientific and Social Issues in the Human Genome Project*, edited by D. J. Kevles and L. Hood. Cambridge: Harvard University Press.

_____. 1999. "Eugenics and Human Rights." *British Medical Journal* 319 (7207): 435–38.

Kobe, Frank H., and James A. Mulick. 1995. "Attitudes Toward Mental Retardation and Eugenics: The Role of Formal Education and Experience." *Journal of Developmental and Physical Disabilities* 7 (1): 1–9.

Koch, Tom. 2000. "Life Quality vs the 'Quality of Life': Assumptions Underlying Prospective Quality of Life Instruments in Health Care Planning." *Social Science and Medicine* 51: 419–27.

Lawler, Peter Augustine. 2002. "Libertarian Fantasy and Statist Reality." *Society* (November/December): 81–84.

_____. 2003. "The Utopian Eugenics of Our Time (Symposium)." *Perspectives on Political Science* 32 (2, Spring): 68–77.

Letterie, Maj., M.C., U.S.A., Gerard S., and William F. Fox, Jr., J.D. 1990. "Legal Aspects of Involuntary Sterilization." *Fertility and Sterility* 53 (3): 391–398.

Levine, Carol. 1980. "Depo-Provera: Some Ethical Questions About a Controversial Contraceptive." In *Birth Control and Controlling Births*, edited by H. B. Holmes, B. B. Hoskins and M. Gross. Clifton: The Humana Press, Inc.

Li, Rongshi. 1998. "An Analysis of the Sex Ratio at Birth in Impoverished Areas in China." *Chinese Journal of Population Science* 10 (1).

Lombardo, Paul A. 1996. "Medicine, Eugenics, and the Supreme Court: From Coercive Sterilization to Reproductive Freedom." *Journal of Contemporary Health Law and Policy* 13 (1): 1–26.

Lunde, Anders S. 1981. "The Beginning of the Population Association of America." *Population Index* 47 (3): 479–84.

Luo, Lin, Shi-Zhong Wu, Xiao-Qin Chen, Min-Xhiang Li, and Thomas W. Pullum. 1996. "A Follow-up Study of First Trimester Induced Abortions at Hospitals and Family Planning Clinics in Sichuan Province, China." *Contraception* 53: 267–273.

Mass, Bonnie. 1977. "Puerto Rico: A Case Study of Population Control." *Latin American Perspectives* 4 (4): 66–81.

McGarrah, Jr., Robert E. 1974. "Voluntary Female Sterilization: Abuses, Risks, and Guidelines." *The Hastings Center Report* 4 (3): 5–7.

Michaelson, Karen L. 1981. "Population Theory and the Political Economy of Population Processes." In *And the Poor Get Children: Radical Perspectives on Population Dynamics*, edited by K. L. Michaelson. New York: Monthly Review Press.

Millard, M.D., Charles E. 1980. "The Effects of Modern Therapeutics on the Human Gene Pool." *Rhode Island Medical Journal* 63 (11): 443–450.

Miller, Adam. 1994. "Professors of Hate." In *The Bell Curve Debate: History, Documents, Opinions*, edited by R. J. N. Glauberman. New York: Times Books.

Nag, Moni. 1985. "Population in Asian Countries: Trends, Issues and Strategies." *Economic and Political Weekly*, January 12, 75–79.

Natowicz, Marvin R., Jane K. Alper, and Joseph S. Alper. 1992. "Genetic Discrimination and the Law." *American Journal of Human Genetics* 50 (3): 465–475.

Nelkin, Dorothy. 1992. "The Social Power of Genetic Information." In *The Code of Codes: Scientific and Social Issues in the Human Genome Project*, edited by D. J. Kevles and L. Hood. Cambridge: Harvard University Press.

Nuechterlein, James. 1998. "Infanticide for Beginners." *First Things* 79 (January): 12–13.

Oduyoye, Mercy Amba. 1989. "Poverty and Motherhood." In *Motherhood: Experience, Institution, Theology*, edited by A. Carr and E. S. Fiorenza. Edinburgh: T & T Clark.

Okeyo, Achola Pala. 1981. "Reflections on Development Myths." *Africa Report*, March-April, 7–10.

Palen, J. John. 1990. "Population Policy: Singapore." In *Population Policy: Contemporary Issues*, edited by G. Roberts. New York: Praeger.

Patterson-Keels, Lisa, Elizabeth Quint, Doug Brown, David Larson, and Thomas E. Elkins. 1994. "Family Views on Sterilization for Their Mentally Retarded Children." *Journal of Reproductive Medicine* 39 (9): 701–706.

Peck, Susan L. 1974. "Voluntary Female Sterilization: Attitudes and Legislation." *The Hastings Center Report* 4 (3): 8–10.

Petchesky, Rosalind Pollack. 1981. "Reproductive Choice in the Contemporary United States: A Social Analysis of Female Sterilization." In *And the Poor Get Children: Radical Perspectives on Population Dynamics*, edited by K. L. Michaelson. New York: Monthly Review Press.

Petersen, William. 1979. "Malthus and the Intellectuals." *Population and Development Review* 5 (3): 469–478.

Pitkin, M.D., Roy M. 1991. "Screening and Detection of Congenital Malformation." *American Journal of Obstetrics and Gynecology* 164 (4): 1045–1048.

Post, Stephen G. 1994. "Implantable Hormonal Contraceptives: Emerging Controversy." *Obstetrics and Gynecology* 84 (6): 1055–1057.

Pritchett, Lant H. 1994. "Desired Fertility and the Impact of Population Policies." *Population and Development Review* 20 (1): 1–55.

Quinn, Peter. 2003. "Race Cleansing in America." *American Heritage* 54 (1): 34–43.

Rao, Arati. 1995. "The Politics of Gender and Culture in International Human Rights Discourse." In *Women's Rights, Human Rights: International Feminist Perspectives*, edited by J. Peters and A. Wolper. New York: Routledge.

Ravindran, T. K. Sundari. 1993. "Women and the Politics of Population and Development in India." *Reproductive Health Matters* (1): 26–38.

Reed, James. 1996. "The Birth Control Movement Before *Roe v. Wade*." In *Politics of Abortion and Birth Control in Historical Perspective*, edited by D. T. Critchlow. University Park: Pennsylvania State University Press.

Richardson, Angelique. 2000. "Biology and Feminism." *Critical Quarterly* 42 (3): 35–63.

Richter, Gabriel. 1990. "Blindheit und Eugenik — Zwischen Widerstand und Integration." In *Aussondern — Sterilisieren—Liquidieren: die Verfolgung Behinderter im Nationalsozialismus*, edited by M. Rudnick. Berlin: Edition Marhold.

Rodrigues, Edna Thomaz. 1994. "Economic Development for the Few." In *We Speak for Ourselves: Population and Development*, edited by Pamos Institute: Pamos Institute.

Rodriguez-Trias, Helen. 1984. "The Women's Health Movement: Women Take Power." In *Reforming Medicine: Lessons of the Last Quarter Century*, edited by V. W. Sidel and R. Sidel. New York: Pantheon Books.

_____. 1994. "Women Are Organizing: Environmental and Population Policies Will Never Be the Same." *American Journal of Public Health* 84 (9): 1379–1382.

Rosen, Robyn L. 1998. "Federal Expansion, Fertility Control, and Physicians in the United States: The Politics of Maternal Welfare in the Interwar Years." *Journal of Women's History* 10 (3): 53–73.

Ross, Loretta. 1994. "Why Women of Color Can't Talk About Population." *The Amicus Journal* (Winter): 27–29.

Rothenberg, J.D., MPA, Karen H. 1997. "Genetic Accountability and Pregnant Women." *Women's Health Issue*, July/August, 215–219.

Rothman, Ph.D., Barbara Katz. 1990. "Commentary: Women Feel Social and Economic Pressures to Abort Abnormal Fetuses." *Birth* 17 (2): 81.

_____. 1998. "From the SWS President: A Sociological Skeptic in the Brave New World." *Gender and Society* 12 (5): 501–4.

Rudnick, Martin. 1990. "Zwangssterilisation — Behinderte und sozial Randstaendige, Opfer nazistischer Erbgesundheitspolitik." In *Aussondern — Sterilisieren — Liquidieren: die Verfolgung Behinderter im Nationalsozialismus*, edited by M. Rudnick. Berlin: Edition Marhold.

Sadik, Nafis. 1990. "The Role of the United Nations: From Conflict to Consensus." In *Population Policy: Contemporary Issues*, edited by G. Roberts. New York: Praeger.

Scheyer, M.D., Stanley C. 1970. "DHEW's New Center: The National Commitment to Family Planning." *Family Planning Perspectives* 2 (1): 22–25.

Schoen, Johanna. 2001. "Between Choice and Coercion: Women and the Politics of Sterilization in North Carolina, 1929–1975." *Journal of Women's History* 13 (1): 132–56.

Scrimshaw, Susan C., and Bernard Paquariella. 1970. "Obstacles to Sterilization in One Community." *Family Planning Perspectives* 2 (4): 40–42.

Sedgwick, John. 1995. "Inside the Pioneer Fund." In *The Bell Curve Debate: History, Documents, Opinions*, edited by R. J. N. Glauberman. New York: Time Books.

Seitler, Dana. 2003. "Unnatural Selection: Mothers, Eugenic Feminism, and Charlotte Perkins Gilman's Regeneration Narratives." *American Quarterly* 55 (March, 1): 61–88.

Sharpless, John B. 1993. "The Rockefeller Foundation, the Population Council, and the Groundwork for New Population Policies." *Rockefeller Archive Center Newsletter* (Fall): 1–4.

_____. 1996. "World Population Growth, Family Planning, and American Foreign Policy." In *The Politics of Abortion and Birth Control in Historical Perspective*, edited by D. T. Critchlow. University Park: Pennsylvania State University Press.

Sher, Geoffrey, and Michael A. Feinman. 1995. "The Day-to-Day Realities: Commentary on the New Eugenics and Medicalized Reproduction." *Cambridge Quarterly of Healthcare Ethics* 4: 313–15.

Simon, Julian L. 1990. "The Population Establishment, Corruption, and Reform." In *Population Policy: Contemporary Issues*, edited by G. Roberts. New York: Praeger.

_____. 1997. "Four Comments on *The Bell Curve*." *Genetica* 99 (2–3): 199–205.

Smith, J. David. 1994. "Reflections on Mental Retardation and Eugenics, Old and New: Mensa and the Human Genome Project." *Mental Retardation* 32 (3): 234–238.

_____. 1995. "*The Bell Curve* and Carrie Buck: Eugenics Revisited." *Mental Retardation* 33 (1): 60–61.

Snyder, Sharon L., and David T. Mitchell. 2002. "Out of the Ashes of Eugenics: Diagnostic Regimes in the United States and the Making of a Disability Minority." *Patterns of Prejudice* 36 (1): 79–103.

Steel, Kathleen O. 1995. "Road That I See: Implications of New Reproductive Technologies." *Cambridge Quarterly of Healthcare Ethics* 4 (3): 351–54.

Sullivan, Donna. 1995. "The Public/Private Distinction in International Human Rights Law." In *Women's Rights, Human Rights: International Feminist Perspectives*, edited by J. Peters and A. Wolper. New York: Routledge.

Teitelbaum, Michael S. 1972. "Some Genetic Implications of Population Policies." In *Population Growth and the American Future, Research Reports*, edited by C. F. Westoff and J. Parke, R.

Testart, Jacques. 1995. "New Eugenics and Medicalized Reproduction." *Cambridge Quarterly of Healthcare Ethics* 4 (3): 304–12.

Thomas, Susan L. 1998. "Race, Gender, and Welfare Reform: The Antinatalist Response." *Journal of Black Studies* 28 (4): 419–46.

Torpy, Sally J. 2000. "Native American Women and Coerced Sterilization: On the Trail of Tears in the 1970s." *American Indian Culture and Research Journal* 24 (2): 1–22.

Turney, Lyn. 1993. "Risk and Contraception: What Women Are Not Told About Tubal Ligation." *Women's Studies International Forum* 16 (5): 471–86.

Valenza, Charles. 1985. "Was Margaret Sanger a Racist?" *Family Planning Perspectives* 17 (1): 44–46.

Varky, George, and Charles R. Dean, Ph.D. 1970. "Planned Parenthood Patients: Black and White." *Family Planning Perspectives* 2 (1): 34–37.

Vieira, Elisabeth Meloni. 1994. "Female Sterilization." *Women's Global Network for Reproductive Rights*, 10–12.

Walters, Le Roy. 1997. "Some Ethical Questions in Research Involving Human Subjects." *Perspectives in Biology and Medicine* 20 (2): 193–211.

Wang, James, and Feng Lee. 1999. "Malthusian Models and Chinese Realities: The Chinese Demographic System 1700–2000." *Population and Development Review* 25 (1): 33–65, 205, 207.

Warwick, Donald P. 1974. "Ethics and Population Control in Developing Countries." *The Hastings Center Report* 4 (3): 1–4.

_____. 1983a. "The KAP Survey: Dictates of Mission versus Demands of Science." In *Social Research in Developing Countries: Surveys and Censuses in the Third World*, edited by M. Blumer and D. P. Warwick. New York: John Wiley and Sons Limited.

_____. 1983b. "The Politics and Ethics of Field Research." In *Social Research in Developing Countries: Surveys and Censuses in the Third World*, edited by M. Blumer and D. P. Warwick. New York: John Wiley and Sons Limited.

_____. 1987. "The Politics of Population Research with a UN Sponsor." In *The Research Relationship: Practice and Politics in Social Policy Research*, edited by G. C. Wenger. Boston: Allen and Unwin.

_____. 1990. "The Ethics of Population Control." In *Population Policy: Contemporary Issues*, edited by G. Roberts. New York: Praeger.

Weigel, George. 1995. "What Really Happened at Cairo." *First Things* 50 (February): 24–31.

Weindling, Paul. 1993. "The Survival of Eugenics in 20th-Century Germany." *American Journal of Human Genetics* 52 (3): 643–49.

Wessman, James W. 1981. "Neo-Malthusian Ideology and Colonial Capitalism: Population Dynamics in Southwestern Puerto Rico." In *And the Poor Get Children: Radical Perspectives on Population Dynamics*, edited by K. L. Michaelson. New York: Monthly Review Press.

White, Tyrene. 1994. "Two Kinds of Production: The Evolution of China's Family Planning Policy in the 1980s." In *The New Politics of Population: Conflict and Consensus in Family Planning*, edited by J. L. Finkle and C. A. McIntosh. New York: The Population Council.

Whitney, Glayde. 1999. "Reproductive Technology for a New Eugenics." *Mankind Quarterly* 60 (2): 179–92.

Williams, Clare, Priscilla Alderson, and Bobbie Farsides. 2002. "Is Nondirectiveness Possible within the Context of Antenatal Screening and Testing?" *Social Science and Medicine* 54 (3): 339–47.

Wilson, Philip K. 2002. "Harry Laughlin's Eugenic Crusade to Control the 'Socially Inadequate' in Progressive Era America." *Patterns of Prejudice* 36 (1): 49–67.

Winch, Donald. 1992. "Introduction." In *An Essay on the Principle of Population*, edited by D. Winch. Cambridge: Cambridge University Press.

Wolfson, Adam. 2001. "Politics in a Brave New World." *The Public Interest* 142 (winter): 31–43.

Zhou, Xun. 2002. "The Discourse of Disability in Modern China." *Patterns of Prejudice* 36 (1): 104–12.

Zumpano-Canto, J.D., M.P.H., Joe. 1996. "Nonconsensual Sterilization of the Mentally Disabled in North Carolina: An Ethics Critique of the Statutory Standard and Its Judicial Interpretation." *Journal of Contemporary Health Law and Policy* 13 (79): 79–111.

Conference Talks

1932. A Decade of Progress in Eugenics: Scientific Papers of the Third International Congress of Eugenics. Papers read at Third International Congress of Eugenics, August 21–23, at American Museum of Natural History, New York.

1969. Population Control: Implications, Trends and Prospects. Papers read at Pakistan International Family Planning Conference, January 28–February 4, at Dacca, Pakistan.

1983. Ethical Implications of New Technology for Reproductive Health Care. Papers read at Planned Parenthood Federation of America, October 19, at Los Angeles.

Association for Voluntary Sterilization. 1979. Voluntary Sterilization: A Decade of Achievement. Papers read at 4th International Conference on Voluntary Sterilization, May 7–10, at Seoul, South Korea.

Beardmore, J. A. 1973. Some Genetic Consequences and Problems of the New Biology. Paper read at Population and the New Biology: Proceedings of the Tenth Annual Symposium of the Eugenics Society, in London.

Brown, George F., Christopher J. Elias, Ann H. Leonard, Katie Early McLaurin, et al. 1994. Reproductive Health Approach to Family Planning. Paper read at Professional Development Day at the USAID Cooperating Agencies meeting, February 25, in Washington, D.C.

Brush Foundation. 1929. Race Betterment: A Symposium. Paper read at Symposium on Race Betterment, October 10, at Dayton, OH.

Buck, Pearl. 1942. Paper read at Annual Meeting, Birth Control Federation of America, January 28, at New York.

Burney, L. E. 1971. Foreword. Paper read at Forty Years of Research in Human Fertility: Retrospect and Prospect, May 5–6, at Carnegie International Endowment Center, New York City.

Cox, Peter R. 1973. The Galton Lecture 1973: Population Prospects and the New Biology. Paper read at Population and the New Biology: Proceedings of the Tenth Annual Symposium of the Eugenics Society, in London.

Cummings, Michele. 1979. Ethnicity and the Urban Poor: Some Implications for Family Planning. Paper read at Planned Parenthood National Executive Directors Council, Professional Staff Day, November 13, at Houston.

Ellis, Havelock. 1926. The Evolutionary Meaning of Birth Control. Paper read at The Sixth International Neo-Malthusian and Birth Control Conference, at New York.

Free, M. J., and G. W. Duncan. 1973. New Technology for Voluntary Sterilization. Paper read at Population and the New Biology: Proceedings of the Tenth Annual Symposium of the Eugenics Society of London, in London.

Guttmacher, Alan F. 1941. Maternal Health and the Nation's Strength. Paper read at Annual Meeting, Birth Control Federation of America, January 28, at New York.
_____. 1942. The Contraceptive Clinic and Preventive Medicine. Paper read at Annual Meeting, Birth Control Federation of America, January 30, at New York.
International Planned Parenthood Federation Central Medical Committee. 1975. Male and Female Sterilization. Paper read at IPPF Panel of Experts on Sterilization, April 19–20, at London.
Kiser, Clyde V. 1971. The Work of the Milbank Memorial Fund in Population Since 1928. Paper read at Forty Years of Research in Human Fertility: Retrospect and Prospect, May 5–6, at Carnegie International Endowment Center, New York City.
Knopf, M.D., S. Adolphus. 1926. Birth Control: A Social, Religious and Medical Issue. Paper read at The Sixth International Neo-Malthusian and Birth Control Conference, at New York.
Langford, C. 1998. The Eugenics Society and the Development of Demography in Britain: The International Population Union, the British Population Society and the Population Investigation Committee. Paper read at The History of Eugenics, The Galton Institute, at London.
Lorimer, Frank. 1971. The Role of the International Union for the Scientific Study of Population. Paper read at Forty Years of Research in Human Fertility: Retrospect and Prospect, May 5–6, at Carnegie Endowment International Center, New York City.
Notestein, Frank W. 1971. Reminiscences: The Role of Foundations, the Population Association of America, Princeton University and the United Nations in Fostering American Interest in Population Problems. Paper read at Forty Years of Research in Human Fertility: Retrospect and Prospect, May 5–6, at Carnegie Endowment International Center, New York City.
Osborn, Frederick. 1958. Population: An International Dilemma. Paper read at The Conference Committee on Population Problems—1956–1957, at New York.
Sadik, Nafis. 1997a. Statement by Dr. Nafis Sadik to the 23rd General Population Conference of the International Union for the Scientific Study of Population, at Beijing.
_____. 1997b. Statement by Dr. Nafis Sadik to the Geneva Forum of International Affairs, at Geneva.
_____. 2002. Population Prize Award Ceremony Speech, www.sfpc.gov.cn/EN/enews20020114-2.htm, at Beijing.
Sanger, Margaret. 1948. Opening Remarks. Paper read at International Congress on Population and World Resources in Relation to the Family, at Cheltenham, England.
Sanger, Margaret, ed. 1926a. *Medical and Eugenic Aspects of Birth Control*. 4 vols. Vol. 3, *The Sixth International Neo-Malthusian and Birth Control Conference, Reports and Papers*. New York: The American Birth Control League, Inc.
_____. 1926b. *Religious and Ethical Aspects of Birth Control*. 4 vols. Vol. 4, *The Sixth International Neo-Malthusian and Birth Control Conference: Reports and Papers*. New York: The American Birth Control League, Inc.
_____. 1927. *Proceedings of the World Population Conference*. London: Edward Arnold & Co.
Segal, Sheldon J. 1971. Contraceptive Technology: Current and Prospective Methods. Paper read at Forty Years of Research in Human Fertility: Retrospect and Prospect, May 5–6, at Carnegie Endowment International Center, New York City.

Dissertations

Mehler, Barry Alan. 1988. A History of the American Eugenics Society, 1921–40. Ph.D. diss., University of Illinois, Urbana-Champaign.

Testimony Before Congress

Guy, Josephine. 2001. Testimony before the U.S. House Committee on International Relations, October 17.

Mosher, Steven W. 2001. Testimony before the U.S. House Committee on International Relations, October 17.

Schneider, Mark. 1998. Testimony before the U.S. House Committee on International Relations, Subcommittee on International Operations and Human Rights, February 25.

Wu, Harry. 2001. Testimony before the U.S. House Committee on International Relations, October 17.

Index

A.H. Robins 215–16, 224
Abenaki tribe 167, 294n42
abortion 11, 24, 32, 35, 58, 61, 65, 94, 125, 156, 162, 175, 176, 189, 192, 194, 196, 198, 229, 257–58, 263n17, 265n60, 282n163, 285n51, 297n129; for disability ("search and destroy") 82–83, 88–93, 96, 124, 277n170; for sex selection 61, 62, 94, 194, 195, 232–35, 277n170, 304n166
abstinence 36, 259n7
Afghanistan 197
Aird, John S. 193, 198, 201, 295n74, n78, n80, n81, 297n108, n109, n116, 298n134
Akhter, Farida 204, 248, 266n85, 298n4, 306n41
Akhter, Halida Hanum 302n134
Alabama 116, 185
Alan Guttmacher Institute 269n201
alcoholism 40, 71, 105, 182, 242
Alderson, Priscilla 276n158
Allen, Charlotte 233, 303n160, 304n166
Allen, Garland E. 143, 271n34, 275n133, 276n166, 286n83, 287n5
Allen, Robert 273n84
Alper, Jane K. 276n149
Alper, Joseph S. 276n149
American Academy of Pediatrics 184, 294n30
American Association for the Advancement of Science (AAAS) 153
American Birth Control League (ABCL) 10, 15, 33–36, 37, 39, 41–44, 50, 60, 73, 75, 76, 90, 102, 112–13, 123, 133, 205,

256–57, 260n15, 262n9, 266n95, 287n107; proposed merger with American Eugenics Society 146–49
American Civil Liberties Union (ACLU) 303n142
American College of Obstetrics and Gynecology 184
American Eugenics Society (AES) 10, 11–12, 32, 35, 38, 59, 65, 73–77, 89, 99–104, 110, 111, 115, 123, 125, 141, 143–46, 154, 158–61, 207, 256–57, 260n15, 272n45, n53, n62, n69, n72, 276n141, 278n36, 279n71, 280n104, 282n151, n166, 284n49, 286n78, n84, 287n102; proposed merger with American Birth Control League 146–49
American Genetic Association 149
American Gynecological Society 109
American Medical Association 111, 221
American Museum of Natural History 100, 277n7
American Society of Human Genetics 93
amniocentesis 62, 90, 92, 124, 232, 276n147; *see also* abortion, for disability
anarchism 27–29
anti–Communism 52, 163–65, 166, 213
Anticoncepcion Quirurgica Voluntaria (AQV) Committee 200–1, 297n129
anti–Semitism 10, 42, 45, 81, 144, 181–82, 259n4
Antonak, R. F. 275n135
Antunes, Paolo C. A. 168, 291n109
Aronson, Amy 262n3

337

Association for the Study of Abortion 35
Association for Voluntary Sterilization
(AVS) 35, 123, 124, 161, 164, 186, 190,
280n104; see also Association for Vol-
untary Surgical Contraception,
Birthright, Engender Health, Human
Betterment Association of America
Association for Voluntary Surgical Con-
traception (AVSC) 190; see also Associ-
ation for Voluntary Sterilization;
Birthright; Engender Health; Human
Betterment Association of America
atheism 69, 262n9
Auccapina, Alejandra Aguirre 200

Bachrach, Peter 144, 154, 155, 287n103,
n3, 288n22, n26, 290n92, 299n23, n24,
n26, 301n77, 304n170
Bajema, Carl Jay 140, 160, 278n15, n32,
n36, 285n62, 289n57, n58
Baker, Bernadette 275n138
Ball, Phillip 58
Bandarage, Asoka 283n6, 291n102,
300n51
Bangladesh 204, 228, 232, 305n35
Baochang Gu 303n161
Barkan, Elazar 143, 286n83, n87
Barry, Ellen 290n101
Barth, Karl 20, 262n44
Baschetti, Riccardo 274n115
Basu, Alaka M. 291n132
Battle Creek Race Betterment Foundation
71
Baumgartner, Leona 172
Baur, Erwin 134
Beglio, Linda 203
Berelson, Bernard 139, 151, 175, 285n55,
n56, n57, 305n34
Bergman, Elihu 144, 154, 155, 287n103,
n3, 288n22, n26, 290n92, 299n23, n24,
n26, 301n77, 304n170
Bethune, Mary McLeod 42
Beyette, Beverly 275n130
Bhatia, Rajani 303n163, 304n165
Billings, Paul R. 276n148, n151, n159
birth control: coining of term 7, 29,
264n25; funding of 5, 36, 99, 165–73;
Sanger's preference for term 37; "simple method" of 58, 99, 108, 117–21, 192,
216, 218, 222, 281n117, n122 (see also
individual methods); testing of 117–21,
162, 177, 204, 213, 217–21, 222, 227,
229–31, 281n117, 301n75, n88, 303n151

Birth Control Clinical Research Bureau
(BCCRB) 11, 35, 36, 44, 50, 60, 75, 108,
109, 110, 113, 119, 125, 143, 205, 218,
256–57, 286n80, n82
Birth Control Federation of America
(BCFA) 31, 36–37, 43, 50, 57, 60, 76,
78, 80, 81, 102, 103, 144, 205, 207, 257,
260n9, 267n137, n139, n140, n141,
273n96, 298n9
Birth Control International Information
Centre 134, 284n31
Birth Control League of Massachusetts
73; see also Planned Parenthood League
of Massachusetts
birth control movement 25–29, 37–38,
65, 73, 75–76, 268n146; professionalization of 25, 263n19
Birth Control Review: contents of 30, 33,
39, 42, 43, 49, 73, 105, 147, 182, 187–88,
260n15, n24, 261n37, 266n95, n104;
founding and editing of 16, 33, 256;
Sanger's resignation from 35, 256; see
also Hanau, Stella
birth strike 27; see also syndicalism
birthright 111–12, 115–16, 123, 161, 181,
186, 188, 189–92, 279n78, 280n104,
293n10, n26; see also Association for
Voluntary Sterilization, Association for
Voluntary Surgical Contraception,
Engender Health, Human Betterment
Association of America
Black, Sir Douglas 93
Black, Edwin 45, 260n10, 263n19,
265n77, 266n90, n98, n99, n100, n101,
n109, 268n152, 270n3, 281n113,
287n105, n107, n109, n 116, 293n16,
n24, n26
Black, Eugene 209
Blacker, C. P. 53, 83, 93, 99, 104–7, 108,
125, 126, 268n146, n149, 273n106,
279n54, n55
Blaire, Beatrice 45
Blake, Judith 275n131, 288n22
blindness 182
Bobsein, Otto 29
Bock, Gisela 21, 195, 262n2, n4, 293n12,
n13, n15, n19
Bocker, Dorothy 109, 125, 143, 282n166,
286n82
Boss, Judith 276n160
Boulton, Mary 275n133
Bowman-Gray School of Medicine 90
Brandon, Karen 276n153

Brazil 168, 277, 290n62; BEMFAM 168
Bronk, Detlev 157, 158
Brown, George F. 222, 300n63, 305n34
Brownsville, New York clinic 11, 33, 60, 256, 269n187
Brush, Charles Francis 122
Brush, Charles Francis, Jr. 122
Brush, Dorothy 39, 53, 76, 98–99, 121–26, 146, 282n144, n156, n158, n164, 283n3
Brush Foundation 53, 122–25, 142, 146, 148, 282n146, n147, n148, n149, n150, n156, n157, n163, 283n3, 286n73
Bryn Mawr College 114
Buchanan, Allen 275n133
Buck, Carrie 183
Buck, Doris 183
Buck v. Bell 183, 256, 293n22
Buffett, Warren 175
Burch, Guy Irving 42, 77–78, 114–15, 135, 152, 163, 205–6, 273n78, 298n6
Bureau of Social Hygiene 156
Burt, Cyril 84
businessmen *see* male interest in movement
Byrne, Ethel Higgins 33, 39–40

Calderone, Mary Steichen 108–9, 118, 214, 279n64, 281n121, 298n5, 300n53
Caldwell, John 176
California 62, 83, 115, 121, 183, 189, 229
The Call 23
Campbell, Clarence G. 135
Campbell, Lorraine 121
Canfield, Cass 205, 210, 299n30
Caplan, Arthur 274n127, 305n34
Carlson, Elof Axel 271n20
Carlson, Licia 262n5, 272n48
Carnegie Institution 71, 150
Caron, Simone M. 267n110
Carpenter, Edward 283n21
The Case for Birth Control 132
Caskey, C. Thomas 84, 274n117, 276n147, n151
Castles, Katherine 281n113
Catholicism 16, 22, 34, 45, 105, 199
Ceci, Stephen J. 274n122
cervical caps 35, 36
Ceylon 165
charitable giving 41, 71, 86, 122, 181, 217, 241, 268n157
Charo, R. Alta 274n117
Chase, Allan 100, 271n37, 272n61,

273n102, n103, n104, 274n114, 283n16, n17, 290n77, n78, 293n21, 294n44, n47
Chasteen, Edgar 245–46
Chesler, Ellen 10–12, 24–25, 31–32, 36–37, 54, 260n12, n17, n18, n21, 261n40, 262n10, n12, n13, n15, 263n17, n18, 264n22, n24, n25, n26, n28, n39, 265n44, n45, n50, n51, n58, n64, n70, n72, 266n83, 267n119, 268n148, n154, n159, n160, 273n77, 279n65, n66, n67, n68, 280n91, n92, 282n142, n143, n165, 283n25, 294n61, 301n74
Chile 162
China 52, 61, 94, 109, 128, 162, 173, 175, 176, 178, 192–99, 230, 245, 258, 282n163, 295n74, n78, 296n89, n93, n96, 297n105, n107, n110, n112, n129, 303n161
Chira, Juan Rosa Ochoa 200, 232
chorionic villus sampling 62
Ciba Conference 81
Claremont College 154
Clayton, Will 209
Cleveland 122–23
Coale, Ansley J. 170
Cockburn, Alexander 291n104, n105, n106
coercion 6–9, 13, 15–17, 45, 47–48, 56, 58–62, 68, 71, 73, 81–82, 87–94, 101, 129, 137–41, 162–63, 171–73, 177, 181, 186, 190–201, 244, 246, 258, 270n7, 275n129, 295n74, n85; *see also* Ideology of Control; sterilization, coerced; sterilization, forced
Cole, Leon J. 34–35, 41, 76, 266n94
colonialism 133, 173, 264n21, 268n143
Committee of One Hundred 33, 212
Committee on Maternal Health *see* National Committee on Maternal Health
Committee on Women, Population and the Environment 292n160, 303n163
Committee to End Sterilization Abuse (CESA) 186
Communism *see* Socialism
Comstock laws 29, 35–36, 256, 257
condoms 19, 208, 213
conferences 6, 28, 33, 34, 48, 52–53, 57, 61, 73, 79, 106, 107, 122–23, 133, 154, 160, 161, 162, 232, 282n156, n165; American Conference of Birth Control and National Recovery 77–78, 273n74, n75; Conference on Population Prob-

lems 157–58; Fifth International Neo-Malthusian and Birth Control Congress 133; Fifth International Planned Parenthood Federation Conference 124; First American Birth Control Conference 42, 256; First International Conference on Intra-Uterine Contraception 222, 225; International Conference on Family Planning 140; Middle Western States Birth Control Conference 34–35, 265n55, n56; Second International Congress of Eugenics 75; Seventh International Birth Control Conference 123; Sixth International Conference on Planned Parenthood 106; Sixth International Neo-Malthusian and Birth Control Conference 73, 133–34; World Population Conference (Geneva) 35, 76, 79, 134–35, 284n32; see also United Nations

Conklin, Edwin Grant 112–13

Connor, Steve 305n34

Contraception see birth control; also individual types of contraception

Cook, Robert C. 76, 115, 146, 160

Cook-Deegan, Robert 274n118

Cooper, Theodore 92

Copeland, Lammot duPont 209

Corning, New York 22, 35, 256

Council on Population Policy 102, 129, 146–49, 257, 287n116

Cox, Nial Ruth 185

Crew, F. A. E. 284n32

Crick, Francis 80, 81

crime 15, 31, 34, 38, 45, 46, 47, 54, 70, 108, 140, 183, 188, 207, 218, 276n153

Critchlow, Donald T. 260n11, 268n162, 289n32, n44, 290n75, n76, n80, n86, n91, n94, 301n81

Cunningham-Burley, Sarah 275n133

Dahlburg, John-Thor 303n164

Dalkon Shield 214–17, 221, 223, 224, 225, 257–58; see also intrauterine device

Darwin, Charles 69

Das Gupta, Monica 303n161

Davenport, Charles Benedict 69–74, 135, 147, 271n33, n39, 278n10, 284n32

Davis, Angela Y. 40, 207, 266n87, n97, 294n38, n40, n42, n49, 304n5, n22

Davis, Hugh 225

Davis, Kingsley 155, 157, 176, 288n21, n22

Day, Rufus S., Jr. 124

deafness 182, 293n17

De Lapouge, Georges 133

demography 46, 79, 103, 107, 125, 128, 129, 141–46, 148, 150–52, 159, 240, 285n49, 287n99, 288n20, 299n40

Dempsey, David 269n177, n183, n184, 294n53, 300n64

Denmark 180

De Paiva, Glycon 168, 291n109

Depo-Provera 162, 168, 201, 214, 215, 229–32, 258, 303n148, n151, 305n35

depression 182, 221, 230

De Seynes, Philippe 170

developing world 52, 53, 59, 62, 87, 106, 107, 118, 120, 125, 128–29, 152–54, 161–63, 165, 169, 171, 173, 174, 176–78, 183, 199, 201–2, 208, 209, 211, 213–19, 226–28, 230, 232, 233, 236, 247–48, 250, 258, 285n50, 298n135, 301n71; see also poverty

diabetes 56, 67

Diamant, Anita 281n140

diaphragm 117–19, 218–19

Dice, Lee R. 90

Dickinson, Robert Latou 77, 99, 105, 108–12, 113, 115, 126, 148, 156, 220, 245, 265n60 277n3, 279n60, n61, n62, n63, n69

differential fertility 31, 39, 56–57, 77–78, 106–7, 110, 113–15, 119, 134, 141–43, 145, 151, 278n36; see also poverty

Dight, Charles Fremont 89

Dight Institute 89–90

disability and persons with 10, 13, 15–16, 19, 31, 34, 38, 40, 42, 43, 45–47, 49–52, 54–56, 58, 61–63, 66–68, 70, 73, 75, 79, 83–97, 103, 105, 116, 124, 140, 145, 161, 180–82, 184–87, 189–91, 194, 195, 207, 218, 231, 234, 246, 262n5, 272n48, 275n138, 276n159, 294n29, 295n68, 296n93, 299n32

disease metaphor 18, 68, 97, 169, 232, 234–35, 245–46, 276n153

DNA data banks 91

Dodge, Mabel 23–24

Dodge Foundation 99

Dominican Republic 208

Donaldson, Peter 152, 288n10, n11, 291n121, 300n46, n58

Donohue, John 276n153

Donovan, Josephine 272n51

Donovan, Patricia 269n201

Dorr, Gregory Michael 266n96

Dowbiggin, Ian 265n60, 266n92
Dowie, Mark 281n131, 300n60
Down syndrome 93, 96, 277n170
Draper, Wicliffe C. 90; *see also* Pioneer Fund
Draper, Gen. William H. 166, 168–70, 209
Draper Fund 99
Drysdale, Alice Vickery 30, 104–5, 132, 283n21
Drysdale, C. V. 133, 134, 283n21
Dublin, Louis 136, 284n41
Du Bois, W. E. B. 266n104
Dumble, Lynette J. 290n65
Dunne, Catherine 275n132
Durand, Celia 200
Duster, Troy 275n131, n134
Dworkin, Ronald 95–96, 277n170

East, Edward M. 73, 76, 79, 110, 144, 277n2
Eccles, Marriner S. 209, 210, 299n29
Eddy, James G. 89
Edlund, Lena 303n161
Ehrenreich, Barbara 281n131, 300n60, n62, n63, n64, n67, 301n93
Ehrlich, Paul 128, 132, 171
elitist bigotry 9, 25–27, 40, 41–45, 74, 131, 150, 182, 301n75
Elliott, Charles 176, 292n156
Elliott, John 290n100
Ellis, Henry Havelock 14, 30–33, 104–5, 132–34, 238, 264n30, n31, n33, n34, n35, 265n45, 283n21, n28, 305n22
Elshtain, Jean Bethke 306n44
embodiment 237–39
Emerson, Haven 109
Engender Health 123, 189–92, 200; *see also* Association for Voluntary Sterilization; Association for Voluntary Surgical Contraception, Birthright, Human Betterment Association of America
Enovid 220, 234, 257
environment vs. heredity 12–13, 25–26, 49, 68, 84–85, 100–101, 211, 264n21; *see also* twin studies
environmentalism 19, 100, 145, 153, 236, 292n149
epilepsy 40, 47, 70, 108, 182, 242
Erlenmeyer-Kimling, L. 284n49, 289n58, n59
Ernst, Morris 35

eugenic fieldworkers 71–72, 74, 270n12, 271n34, 272n48
"eugenic hypothesis" 100, 102, 160
Eugenic Society (ES) 30, 53, 104–7, 134, 215, 284n33
eugenics 1–2, 7–20, 24–28, 37–39, 65–97, 237–44, 262n9, 270n6, n13; in Canada 74; in England 14, 15, 22, 26, 28, 29–30, 53, 69–70, 74, 93, 104–7, 261n26, 264n36, 268n146; historiography on 65–67, 263n21, 282n164; *see also* left-wing eugenics; negative eugenics; new eugenics; positive eugenics; right-wing eugenics; Sanger, Margaret, eugenics of
Eugenics Education Society (EES) *see* Eugenics Society
Eugenics Record Office (ERO) 71–72, 182, 271n33
Eugenics Research Association 100, 147–49
euthanasia 35, 265n60, 266n92
Euthanasia Society of America 35
evolutionary theory 69

Fairchild, Henry Pratt 73, 76, 80, 103, 135, 147, 148, 272n43, n64, 273n93, 287n107, n109, n111, n116
family planning *see* birth control
Family Planning Association (FPA, Britain) 53
Family Planning Association (FPA, China) 198–99
famine 130–32, 134, 211
Farrall, Lyndsay 264n29, 279n40, n41, n42
Farsides, Bobbie 276n158
Fatkulin, Yemlibike 194, 296n87, n88
feebleminded 13, 34, 41, 54, 68–70, 86, 99, 105, 110, 111, 123, 143, 179, 181, 183, 187, 262n5
Feinman, Michael A. 274n125
female *see* women
feminism 5–9, 10, 12–20, 21, 24, 26, 27, 74, 97, 125, 138, 183, 189, 202, 235, 237–51, 260n21, 262n43, 306n44; as eugenic, 25–28, 237–39, 261n29, 304n15; *see also* Sanger, Margaret, feminism of; women
Feng Wang 303n161
Ferguson, Frances Hand 35–36, 47, 55, 76, 116–17, 121, 123, 140, 146, 164–65, 171, 206, 208, 212, 216–17, 265n60, n76, 268n164, n165, 278n24, 281n114, n136,

290n79, n81, n85, 291n123, 298n10, n17, 299n42, n43, 300n65, n66
fertility awareness method *see* natural family planning
Finland 180
Fischer, Claude S. 274n122
Fischer, Eugen 38, 134
Fisher, Irving 75
Fisher, Jerome C. 124
"fit" 10, 15, 16, 17, 21, 22, 31, 34, 40, 43, 49, 50, 51, 59, 70, 81, 82, 100, 110, 114, 116, 122, 142, 157, 187, 212, 237, 240, 260n14
Fitzpatrick, Tony 274n126
Flint, Emily 114
Flora Tristan Center for Peruvian Women 199
Florida 116
foam powder contraceptive 116–18
Food for Peace 164, 170–71, 200
food production 130–32, 167, 209
Ford Foundation 150–51, 158, 160, 168, 176, 299n40
Fosdick, Rev. Raymond B. 76
Foucault, Michel 238
France 28–29, 129
Fraser, Steven 274n122
free-love movement 27, 28; *see also* Sanger, Margaret, views on sexuality of; sex reformers; sexology
freedom *see* coercion; ideology of control
Freud, Sigmund 27
Freudianism 32
Friedman, Elisabeth 304n4
Fujimori, Alberto 199–201

Galton, Francis 69–70, 104, 112, 143, 145, 271n15
Gamble, Clarence 42, 43–44, 52, 53, 99, 105, 108, 112–21, 123, 124, 126, 135, 152, 156, 161, 164, 169, 181, 185, 188, 190, 212, 219, 220, 245, 262n9, 279n44, 280n85, n87, n95, n99, n107, n108, n111, n112, n113, 281n117, n122, n126, 282n155, 293n9, 294n60, 295n61, 301n79
Gamble, Judy 121
Gamble, Nicki Nichols 121
Gamble, Richard 121, 177, 281n137
Gamble, Sarah Merry (Bradley) 114, 280n95, 291n112, 300n47
Gandhi, Prime Minister Indira 171
Gao Xiao Duan 195–97, 297n112

Garver, Bettylee 276n150, n159
Garver, Kenneth L. 276n150, n159
Gates, Bill 175
General Electric Company 122
genetic counseling 61–64, 67, 84, 88–98, 103, 146, 233, 272n48, 275n129, 277n170
genetic discrimination 90–91
genetic load 83
genetics 67–71, 80–88, 90, 92, 100, 102–4, 124, 127, 146, 148, 154, 156, 159–60, 233, 263n21, 270n11, n13, 273n90, 274n114, 276n147, n161, 282n164, 284n49
genocide 68, 81, 194, 201; *see also* nazism; racism
Georgia 43, 116, 231
Germany *see* nazism; Weimar Republic; World War II
Gesell, Judge Gerhard 185–86
Gillham, Nicole Wright 271n15
Gilman, Charlotte Perkins 261n29
Glannon, Walter 92, 276n156
Global South *see* developing world
Goddard, Henry H. 72
Goetz, Thomas 291n142, 292n151, n152
Goldenberg, Suzanne 303n164
Goldman, Emma 27–30, 264n22
Gonzales, Felice 232
Gordon, Linda 25–29, 39, 141, 157, 166, 207, 260n9, n10, n21, 263n19, n20, n21, 264n22, n23, 266n84, n89, n97, 272n44, n52, 273n73, n79, 285n68, 289n37, 290n93, 294n49, 304n5, n22
Gosney, Ezra 71, 181, 189
Gottesman, Irving I. 284n49, 289n58, n59
Grady Memorial Family Clinic (Emory University) 231, 303n151
Grafenberg ring 222
Graham, Robert K. 83
Grant, George 259n4
Grant, Madison 79
Great Depression 75, 77–80, 106, 137, 147, 180–81, 205, 293n9; *see also* charitable giving; poverty
Greely, Henry T. 276n150
Greene, Stephen G. 282n161, 288n24, n25, 291n137, n138, n140
Greenhalgh, Susan 195, 295n82, n84, 296n95, n99, 303n164
Greer, Germaine 5, 64, 176, 201, 237, 244, 245, 249, 259n2, 269n206, 292n155, 298n3, 304n2, 305n33, n38, 306n42, n44

Griessemer, Thomas O. 53, 163, 268n150
Grosskurth, Phyllis 265n46
Grossmann, Atina 265n42, 267n111, n112, n113, n114, n115
Guttmacher, Alan F. 22, 55–60, 76, 88, 102, 103, 110, 123, 145, 146, 159, 161, 164, 169, 187, 190, 191, 217, 222, 223, 225–26, 257–58, 265n60, 268n167, n168, n169, n170, n171, 269n173, n174, n175, n178, n181, n186, 275n137, 278n31, 287n100, 294n29, 295n68, n70, n71, 302n106, n120, n121
Guttmacher, Mrs. Alan F. 56–57, 58, 144, 268n172, 269n182
Guy, Josephine 196, 198, 297n105

Haldane, J. B. S. 264n21
Hall, Prescott 79
Haller, Mark 263n21, 271n14, n16, n17, n18, n29, 273n83, n84, n86, n88, n91
Hanau, Stella 22, 262n9
Hand, Augustus 35–36
Hand, Learned 35–36
Hardin, Garrett 59, 127, 128, 138–39, 234, 283n2, n4, n5, n15, 285n51, n52, n53, n54, 292n144, n156
Harkavy, Oscar 287n4, 292n157, 299n40
Harlem 19
Harman, Moses 28
Harmsen, Hans 45–46
Harriman, Mrs. E. H. 71
Hartmann, Betsy 173, 285n58, n59, n61, 288n18, n23, 290n70, n98, 291n103, n126, n129, 292n158, n161, n164, 300n50, n51, 301n93, n94, n95, 302n118, n119, n127, n128, 303n158
Harvard College 114–15, 144, 213
Harvard Medical School 113
Hauser, Philip 170
Health Research Group 186
Hepburn, Katharine Houghton 35
Hern, Warren 234, 245, 304n168, 305n39
Herrnstein, Richard J. 274n122
Higgins, Anne 22–23
Higgins, Michael 22–23
Hodges, Glenn 283n19
Hodgson, Dennis 135, 279n75, n76, n77, 284n40, n41
Hofmann, Otto 183
Holmes, Justice Oliver Wendell 183
Holmes, Steven A. 269n197
Hongyan Liu 303n161
Hoover, President Herbert 165

How-Martyn, Edith 134
Human Betterment Association of America (HBAA) 55, 74, 123, 124, 163, 164, 188, 190–91, 268n163, 293n26, 295n70; *see also* Association for Voluntary Sterilization; Association for Voluntary Surgical Contraception; birthright; Engender Health
Human Betterment Foundation 71, 181
Human Betterment League 116
human dignity 9, 18, 41, 64, 68, 86, 88–89, 97, 101, 117–18, 129, 182–84, 189, 192, 204, 208, 225, 228, 230, 232, 240–41, 248, 293n22
Human Genome Project 67, 83–85, 273n90, 274n116, n117, 275n133
Huntington, Ellsworth 148
Huntington's disease 96, 182
Huxley, Aldous 174
Huxley, Sir Julian 262n8

Iannone, Carol 269n205
ideology of control 5, 7–9, 10–14, 18–20, 21–22, 26–30, 32, 34, 37, 41, 44–45, 48, 51, 54, 60–64, 66–67, 76, 79, 80, 82, 83, 85, 87, 88–89, 93, 97, 98, 99, 101–2, 104, 122, 124, 127–29, 137–41, 146, 148–49, 151–55, 156, 158, 170, 173–74, 176, 179–83, 193–95, 198, 201–2, 204, 207, 212, 234–35, 237–46, 259n3, n7, 260n9, 261n29, n32, n34, 262n43, 263n19, 264n22, 266n109, 269n203, 270n6, n13, 285n51, 292n165; *see also* coercion; control movement; women, control of fertility of
Illinois Birth Control League 110
immigrants 11, 23, 42, 44–45, 70, 77, 79, 82, 90, 111, 148, 215, 263n17
Immigration Restriction League 79
incentives/disincentives for birth-control use/sterilization 58–59, 84, 87–88, 139, 158–59, 171–72, 175–76, 187–88, 193, 196, 200, 229, 247, 285n59, 291n126; *see also* motivation
India 38, 52–53, 58–59, 94, 106–7, 109, 117–18, 121, 141, 154, 171–72, 177, 200, 213, 214, 217, 219, 221, 226, 230, 232, 233, 285n67, 291n126, n132
Indian Health Service (IHS) 167–68, 185
Indonesia 162, 176, 227–28
infant/child mortality 47, 142, 211, 218
infanticide 94, 95, 134, 193–95, 199, 233, 261n32

Inge, Dean William Ralph 105
Institute for the Study of Medical Ethics
    229–30
institutionalization (or "segregation") 41,
    70–71, 105, 123, 180–81, 187–89,
    280n108
insurance bias 90–91, 214, 276n159
intelligence 13, 37–38, 40, 43, 47, 50, 57,
    68, 69–72, 75, 78, 80, 83–85, 96, 107,
    114–16, 136, 144, 146, 158–60, 188, 190,
    260n14, 266n104, 270n13, 301n75; see
    also feebleminded; intelligence quo-
    tient tests; unfit
intelligence quotient (IQ) tests 72, 84,
    116; see also intelligence
International Fertility Research Program
    215
International Planned Parenthood Federa-
    tion (IPPF) 22, 35–36, 46, 53–54, 61,
    76, 87, 99, 104–7, 117–20, 122–24, 139–
    40, 152, 155, 162–63, 166, 168–71, 191,
    192, 195, 198–99, 203, 214–15, 217, 220,
    221, 223, 228, 230, 232, 257–58,
    269n192, 281n122, n126, 282n156,
    285n59, 298n135
International Union for the Scientific
    Investigation of Population Problems
    see International Union for the Sci-
    entific Study of Population (IUSSP)
International Union for the Scientific
    Study of Population (IUSSP) 135–36,
    145, 151, 156, 284n33
intrauterine devices (IUD) 19, 57–58,
    161–62, 193–94, 196, 198, 201, 214–17,
    220–27, 229, 231, 249, 257, 290n64,
    302n105, n111, 305n35; see also Dalkon
    Shield

Jaffe, Frederick S. 175–76, 292n154
Japan 11, 192
Jennings, Herbert Spencer 67
Jensen, Arthur R. 84
John Price Jones 36, 205
Johnson, Pres. Lyndon 166–68, 213
Johnson, Roswell 70–71, 271n26, 293n7,
    n9
Johnson, Tim 297n120
Jones, Eleanor Dwight 35, 147–48,
    287n107, n112
Jones, Judy 274n121
Jordan, David Starr 79
Jordan, H. E. 277n169
Judson, Horace Freeland 274n116

Kaiser Wilhelm Institute for Anthropol-
    ogy, Eugenics, and Human Heredity
    38
Kaiser Wilhelm Institute for Psychiatry
    38
Kallmann, Franz J. 285n49, 286n71
Kamin, Leon J. 271n36
Kangas, Lenni 213
KAP (Knowledge-Attitude-Practice) sur-
    veys 153–54
Kapil, Iris 291n133
Kasun, Jacqueline 269n202, 285n67,
    299n33, 304n174
Kaw tribe 167
Keller, Evelyn Fox 85, 92, 96–97, 273n90,
    274n110, n114, n119, n120, 276n154,
    277n171, 288n27
Kellogg, John H. 71
Kemp-Kasten Amendment 258
Kempf, Edward A. 49
Kennedy, Anne 124
Kennedy, Pres. John F. 213
Kenny, Michael G. 276n144
Kentucky 117, 281n117
Kershaw, Joseph 210–11
Kessel, Elton 120
Kevles, Daniel J. 67, 70, 75, 83, 263n20,
    264n32, 267n132, 270n8, 271n15, n17,
    n19, n21, n22, n24, n31, n33, n35,
    272n60, 273n84, n86, n88, n101, n106,
    274n108, n109, n111, n112, n113, n116,
    279n50
Kiltz, Elke 267n112, n113, n114
Kincheloe, Joe L. 274n122
King, Maurice 176, 292n156
Kingsburgy, John A. 143, 286n80
Kirk, Dudley 76, 145–46, 159, 161
Kiser, Clyde V. 76, 103, 143, 145–46,
    284n71, n74, n76, n77, n79, n86, n92
Knopf, S. Adolphus 35, 134, 284n29, n30
Koch, Tom 277n172
Korea 58, 290n62
Koshland, Daniel 84, 271n29, 274n118
Kraepelin, Emil 38
Krout, J. 230
Kühl, Stefan 265n78, 284n38, 293n26
Kuhse, Helga 276n162, 277n168

Lader, Lawrence 123, 203, 290n83, n84,
    298n2, 299n25, 300n45, 304n171
Lamarckism 25–26, 263n21; see also envi-
    ronment vs. heredity
Lamb, Anne 280n110

Lamont, Thomas S. 209
Langford, C. 284n33
Lantos, U.S. Rep. Tom 197
Larimer, Tim 303n138
Larson, Edward J. 70, 267n132, 271n17, n18, n24, n25, 280n109
Lasker, Albert 36
Lasker, Mary 36, 209–10, 265n65, n66, 291n126, 299n27
Lasker Award 54, 112, 188
Laski, Harold 183
Laughlin, Harry 19, 42, 65, 75, 77, 79, 111, 135, 182, 257, 266n98, n99, 272n70, 273n106, 278n10
Lawler, Peter Augustine 275n133
Lee, James 303n161
Leff, David N. 304n167
Left-wing eugenics 10, 25–26, 28, 67, 70, 263n20, n21, 264n22, 265n60, 266n92, 271n15; *see also* Goldman, Emma; socialism
Lenz, Fritz 38
Levitt, Mairi 274n121
Levitt, Stephen 276n153
Lewontin, Richard C. 160
Lieberson, Jonathan 285n55, n57, 305n34
Lippes, Jack 222
Lippes Loop 58, 217, 223–24
Little, Clarence Cook (C.C.) 43, 75, 148, 266n103
Long Island College hospital 108
Lopez, Steve 229
Lorimer, Frank 76, 135, 145, 146, 170, 284n34, n35, n36, n37, 39, n41, n43, 286n70, 287n96, n97, n98, n99, n100, n101
Ludmerer, Kenneth M. 266n93, 270n11, 271n39, 272n70, 275n134, 277n169, n8, 278n14, 286n70
Lynn, Richard 81, 85, 273n100, 274n123, 275n133, n136, 276n144
Lysenkoism 264n21

MacIntyre, Alasdair 277n173
Mack, J. Keller 231
Magnus, David 274n127, 305n34
Maher, Bill 94
male desire 24–25, 27, 243, 248–49
male involvement in movement 18, 36–37, 54, 55, 164–65, 168, 202, 203–17, 235–36, 304n174
Mallet, Sir Bernard 134
Malthus, Thomas R. 31, 67, 129–32,

133, 141, 156, 283n5, n6, n7, n8, n9, n10, n11, n12, n13, n14, n15, n16, n17, n18, 299n22; *see also* neo–Malthusians
Mamdani, Mahumud 288n18
Mann, Rabbi Louis L. 76
Margulies, Lazar C. 222
Marx, Karl 241
Marxism *see* socialism
Mary Lee School for Special Education 231
Mass, Bonnie 39, 301n79, n82, n86
Massachusetts State Hospital 219
maternal mortality 24, 50, 216–17; *see also* motherhood
May, Cordelia Scaife 158, 177
Mazumdar, Pauline 107, 275n134, 279n40, n41, n42, n45, n46, n47, n51, n59
McCann, Carole 12–13, 100, 260n21, n22, n23; 261n28, n29, n34, 287n107
McCormick, Fowler 209
McCormick, Katherine Dexter 119, 218–19
McCullough, Marie 276n153
McGee, Glenn 94–95, 274n127, 277n167, 305n34
McKinnon, Edna Rankin 117–18, 207, 262n9, 281n116, n118
McLaughlin, Abraham 276n153
McLaughlin, Loretta 301n70, n71
McNamara, Robert 171
Medicaid 164, 167, 185–86, 229, 258
medical establishment 10, 91, 95, 96, 99, 104, 108–12, 184–87, 205, 221, 226, 233, 277n170
Mehler, Barry Alan 80, 82, 272n57, n59, n63, 273n89, n102, n103, n104, 277n6, n7, 278n9, n13, n15, 287n108
Mellon Foundation, Andrew W. 150, 153
Mendel, Gregor 69, 263n21
Metropolitan Life Insurance Company 136
Mexico 82, 168, 185, 215, 232, 278n13
Mexico City Policy 258
Meyer, Adolf 15, 76, 110, 259n7
Miami University in Ohio 141, 146
Milbank Memorial Fund (MMF) 77, 99, 129, 135, 142–44, 146, 149, 151, 286n71, n82
Miller, Adam 285n66
Minkin, Stephen 281n131, 300n59, n60, 303n143, n147, n156
Minnesota Birth Control League 90

Mississippi 116, 286n82
Mitchell, David T. 275n138
Moore, Hugh 54, 123, 154, 163–65, 166,
191, 203, 206, 209–10, 213–14, 236, 257,
299n22
Moore, Molly 291n132, n134
Moran, Al 61, 203
Morgan, J. Pierpont 100
Morrison, David 199–201, 293n6,
297n119, n125
Mosher, Steven 192, 295n75, 296n85,
n86, 297n121, n122, n123, 298n130,
306n40
Moskowitz, Ellen H. 222, 300n63,
305n34
motherhood 6, 7, 15, 21, 23, 27, 29, 45,
63, 93, 240–43, 249–50, 277n170,
305n29, 306n44; see also maternal mortality; women
motivation for birth-control use 56, 57–
58, 161, 175–76, 193, 201, 208, 222, 228,
247; see also coercion; motivation;
propaganda
Motta, Yong 200
Mount Sinai Hospital 56, 287n100,
295n68
Mudd, Emily 76, 112–13, 120, 146,
280n95, n104, 281n128, n132
Mudd, Stuart 76, 112–14, 120, 280n84,
n95, n104, 281n134
Muller, Hermann J. 83, 264n21, 273n106,
274n107
Murray, Charles 274n122
Muslims 172
Myers, Lonny 45
Myrdal, Alva 165

Naripokkho 228
National Abortion Rights Action League
(NARAL) 285n51
National Academy of Sciences (NAS) 84–
85, 157, 274n114
National Association of Catholic Physicians 199
National Committee for Federal Legislation of Birth Control (NCFLBC) 35–
36, 60, 76–78, 114, 257
National Committee on Maternal Health
74, 108–11, 113, 117, 148, 156, 161, 220,
224, 245
National Women's Health Network
232
nationalism 50–52, 80–81, 103

Native American Women's Health Education Resource Center 168
Native Americans 82, 125, 167–68, 185,
278n13, 294n42
Natowicz, Marvin R. 276n149
natural family planning 306n43
nazism 10, 12, 20, 21, 38, 42, 45–46, 51,
76, 79, 81–82, 86–87, 92, 93, 103, 106,
134–35, 159, 181–84, 188, 257, 265n42,
n77, 273n90, 274n107, 293n12, n16,
n17; see also genocide; racism
negative eugenics 10–11, 14, 40–41, 46–47,
50, 57, 66, 70–73, 94, 106, 114, 134, 180,
202, 235, 259n5, n7, 276n153
Negro Project 43–44, 266n104; see also
racism; Sanger, Margaret, racism question concerning
Nelkin, Dorothy 97, 274n117, 275n129,
276n161, 299n25
Nelson, Gaylord 221
Neo-Malthusianism 22, 27–33, 54, 85,
104–6, 130, 132–35, 165, 167, 256,
261n32, 264n36, 304n22
Netherlands 141, 285n67
Neuhaus, Richard 261n42
"new eugenics" 68, 83–84, 86–97, 127,
244–45, 275n133, n134, 306n44
"new woman" 27, 261n29
New York City 23–27, 29, 61, 109, 186,
220, 256
Newman, K. 285n58
Nietzsche, Friedrich 27
Nixon, Pres. Richard 167, 213
Norplant 162–63, 168, 176, 201, 226–29,
231, 249, 258, 297n119, 302n139,
303n140, 305n35
North Carolina 43, 90, 113, 116, 118, 185,
188, 262n9, 280n113
Norway 180
Not Dead Yet 275n139
Notestein, Frank W. 104, 136, 137, 141–45,
156, 159, 170, 279n38, 284n41, n42,
n44, n46, 285n69, 286n73, n85,
287n96, 289n31, n47, 291n117
Nuremberg trials 183, 273n90

Office of Economic Opportunity 168,
210–11
Olden, Marion S. Norton 111, 115, 190,
293n26
Oliva, Angelica 62
Orrick, Phyllis 302n136
Osborn, Frederick 11–12, 13, 17, 19, 37, 59,

65–66, 75, 80, 82–85, 89, 93, 98–105,
106, 108, 125–26, 135–36, 141, 144, 145,
147–48, 150, 158–60, 204, 206–7, 240,
270n2, 272n58, n59, n69, 273n72,
n105, n106, 276n142, 277n5, 278n10,
n11, n13, n15, n16, n17, n18, n19, n23,
n27, n33, n35, 279n37, 284n43,
285n63, 286n71, n84, n93, n94,
287n95, n99, 287n2, n3, 288n28,
289n44, n52, n53, n55, 300n49
Osborn, Henry Fairfield 75, 80, 100,
277n7, 278n10
Ottensen-Jensen, Elise 52

Packard, Arthur W. 38–39, 78, 136,
266n79, n80, 273n76, 284n43
Pai, D. N. 213
Pakistan 58, 217, 223
Paley, William 131
Parkes, A. S. 53
Parsai, Gargi 291n135
Pathfinder Fund 113, 119–20, 124–25, 166,
169–70, 177, 191, 200, 280n95
Paul, Diane 26, 67, 70, 94, 261n26,
263n21, 264n22, 266n99, 270n2, n5,
n6, n9, 271n17, n23, n32, n34, 272n50,
n71, 273n90, n99, n106, 275n128,
276n143, n145, n146, n152, n155, n161,
278n20, 289n51
peace 163, 187–88, 209, 211, 241273n93
Pearl, Raymond 75, 79, 110, 135, 142–45,
151, 156, 218, 277n2, 278n28, 284n32,
286n82, n88
Pearson, Karl 74, 145
pelvic inflammatory disease (PID) 222–
25; *see also* intrauterine device
Pennsylvania 113, 146, 190
Pennsylvania Birth Control League
112–14
Perrott, G. St. J. 77–78, 273n74
Peru 199–201, 245, 293n6, 297n119, n129
pessaries *see* cervical caps
Petchesky, Rosalind Pollack 214, 300n55
Philadelphia Inquirer 229, 303n140
Philippines 150, 162, 213
Pickens, Donald 261n39, 263n21, 271n23
Pierson, Richard N. 112
pill 19, 53, 56–58, 119, 144, 162–63, 169,
201–2, 208, 213–22, 226–28, 231, 234–
35, 238–39, 244, 257, 301n70, n71, n88,
305n35
Pilpel, Harriet 53, 123, 161, 268n150,
289n61, 290n62

Pinchot, Gertrude Minturn 108
Pincus, Gregory 119, 144, 218–21,
301n70
Pioneer Fund 90, 189, 276n144
Piotrow, Phyllis Tilson 212, 286n90,
289n35, 290n95, n96, n97, 291n111,
n113, n114, n116, n118, n120, n127, n128,
299n40, 300n45, n57
The Pivot of Civilization 16, 22, 37, 46,
127, 187, 261n38, 262n7, 271n38,
273n92, 283n1, 294n55, 304n6
Planned Parenthood Federation of America (PPFA) 8, 9, 18–20, 22, 35–38, 42–
43, 47, 49, 52, 55, 57–59, 60–64, 74, 76,
79, 85–86, 87, 102, 111–13, 116–18, 120–
21, 123–24, 140, 146, 161, 163–70, 191,
203–11, 214, 222–26, 232, 233–36, 257,
260n16, 261n29, 262n8, 269n187, n189,
n190, n191, n196, n207, 270n208,
273n93, n95, 276n187, n189, 190, n191,
n201, n204, n207, 281n122, 298n1
Planned Parenthood League of Massachusetts (PPLM) 121, 190
Planned Parenthood–World Population
(PP-WP) 163–65, 210
Plomin, Robert 274n119
Popenoe, Paul 70–71, 189, 271n26, n27,
n28, 293n7, n9
Population Action Committee (PAC) 163
Population Action International (PAI)
163
Population Association of America (PAA)
76
The Population Bomb 164
"Population Coalition" 154–55
Population Communications International, Inc. 173
population control 5, 8, 16, 17, 19, 29, 30,
127–78, 192–202, 240, 243, 244, 250,
259n8, 261n42, 262n9; business concerns and 173; cultural opposition to
173; and development 177–78, 209–11;
in England 132–33; government funding of 165–73; rhetorical change concerning 177–78
Population Council 59, 99, 102, 104, 129,
135, 137, 139, 140, 142–44, 146, 150–51,
154–66, 168, 170, 175, 177, 209, 213–14,
220, 222–27, 236, 257, 278n35, n36
Population Crisis Committee *see* Population Action International (PAI)
"population explosion" 54, 56, 83, 140,
205, 210

Population Reference Bureau (PRB) 78, 114–15, 152, 160, 163
Population Research Institute (PRI) 196, 199–201
positive eugenics 10, 30–31, 40–41, 47, 49–50, 66, 70, 73, 83–84, 99, 106, 113–16, 134, 141, 147, 260n14, 266n91, 267n117, 270n4
Potts, Malcolm 215, 230
poverty 6, 12–19, 24, 28, 31, 34, 37–41, 43–45, 47–48, 56–59, 61–64, 70–71, 76, 77–78, 81–82, 84, 88, 90, 94, 97, 99, 105–7, 110–113, 116–19, 121, 125, 128–130, 133–35, 137, 138, 140, 142, 162–63, 166–68, 172, 174, 182, 185–87, 190–92, 195, 197, 199–201, 204, 209–14, 217–19, 227–29, 234–36, 240–42, 246, 261n31, 263n17, 264n21, 268n157, 271n15, 285n69, 301n75, n79, 302n139, 304n22; see also differential fertility; neo–Malthusianism; unfit
Prentice, Rockefeller 209
"prevention" rhetoric 40, 81, 84, 89, 92, 103, 123, 191, 206–7, 211
Princeton University 94–95, 112–15, 144, 156; Office of Population Research 144
PRISMA 200–1
Pro Familia 46
Progressive Era 23, 25, 74, 261n29; see also "new woman"
propaganda 13, 16, 23, 31, 38–39, 47–48, 71, 73, 87–88, 93, 100, 106, 111–12, 128, 133, 138–39, 159, 173–74, 180, 222, 250, 272n72, 288n20
Puerto Rico 56, 161, 217–21, 227, 287n100

Qian Xinzhong 197
quality of life 50, 95, 262n8, 277n170, n172
quality over quantity 13, 22, 34, 50–52, 54, 63, 76, 81, 103, 110, 127–28, 132–34, 136–37, 138, 140, 150, 154, 158–61, 165, 194, 206, 240, 262n8, 283n3, 284n41, 285n49
quotas for population control 171–72, 192–94, 196, 200–1, 226

"race suicide" 132, 141
racism 10, 12–13, 19, 22, 38, 40–46, 69, 76, 79, 82, 84, 91, 93–94, 99–100, 109–111, 133–34, 141, 144, 182, 184–86, 194, 199–201, 216, 232, 261n42, 264n22, 266n96, 271n15, 272n70, 273n84,

278n10; see also genocide; nazism; Negro Project; Sanger, Margaret, racism question concerning
Rainer, John D. 285n49, 286n71
Rapp, Rayna 93, 272n48, 276n164, n165, n166
Ratner, Herbert 220
Rau, Lady Rama 118
Ravenholt, Reimert T. 120, 152, 169–72, 213–17, 281n133, 288n11
Rebick, Judy 276n163
Reed, James 10–12, 24–25, 30, 108, 115, 119, 121, 205, 220, 260n13, 262n14, 263n18, 264n27, 265n44, n62, n76, 266n81, 267n126, 268n164, n165, n172, 277n1, n4, 278n24, 280n87, n88, n90, n93, n103, n111, 281n114, n115, n121, n122, n123, n128, n132, n136
Rees, Grover Joseph 199, 297n124, n126
Reilly, Philip R. 180, 184, 272n53, n54, n56, n59, 276n140, 279n78, 280n81, n105, n109, n113, 293n8, n11, n14, n18, n27, 295n64
Reinders, Hans S. 277n173
Reitman, Benjamin 28
Relf, Mary Alice 185–86
Relf, Minnie 185–86
Rice-Wray, Edris 220–21
Richard, Olive Byrne 16, 37, 40–41, 261n39, n40, 266n56
Richards, Alfred N. 113
Richardson, Angelique 261n29, 304n15
Ridley, Matt 275n133
Right-wing eugenics 25–26, 70, 206, 263n20, 271n15
Roberts, Dorothy 261n42, 272n70, 297n119, 300n51, 302n129, n132, n134, n137, 303n141
Robinson, Caroline Hadley 110–11, 279n71, n72, n73
Robinson, John 281n139
Robinson, William Josephus 27
Rock, John 119, 212, 218–19
Rockefeller, John D., III 37, 53, 74, 104, 109, 137, 156–59, 165, 170, 177–78, 209, 257, 265n72, 269n188, 271n32, 289n48
Rockefeller family and foundations 29, 37–39, 45, 46, 59, 71, 73–75, 78, 110, 135–37, 144, 150–51, 155–57, 161, 163, 220, 265n71, n72, n77
Rogers, Theresa F. 288n20
Rogers, William 168
Rongshi Li 303n161

Roosevelt, Franklin Delano 189
Roosevelt, Theodore 132
Rose, D. Kenneth 36, 78–79, 205–8,
  273n80, n81, n82, 278n28, 298n11, n12
Rose, Florence 44
Rosenthal, Elisabeth 296n97
Ross, Eric B. 283n5, n18
Ross, Griff 231
Rothman, Barbara Katz 68, 270n10,
  275n130
Royal College of Physicians 93
RU-486 162, 175
Rüdin, Ernst 38, 106
Runcis, Maija 179
Rushton, Philippe 141

Sachs, Jake 24–25, 30, 263n17, n19,
  267n109
Sachs, Sadie 24–25, 30, 263n17, n19,
  267n109
Sadik, Nafis 198, 291n122, 297n114, n115,
  305n34
Sai, Fred T. 285n58
Salas, Rafael 152, 197
Saleeby, Caleb W. 70
Salt-solution method of birth control 118
Sanger, Grant 30
Sanger, Margaret: death of 55; dehumanizing language of 48–49, 267n132;
  early career 22–33, 264n22, n24, n26,
  266n85 (*see also* Sachs, Jack *and* Sachs,
  Sadie); eugenics of 7–17, 19, 21, 25, 30,
  33–34, 37, 40–50, 53, 64, 66, 70, 71,
  72–74, 98–99, 100, 102, 125–26, 146–49,
  259n7, 260n14, 261n29, n32, 262n5,
  263n17, 265n60, 270n3; feminism of
  5–9, 11, 14–17, 21, 36–37, 65–66, 212,
  237–44, 262n5, 263n19, 270n208; historiography on 6–7, 10–13, 24–28, 122,
  125–26, 259n4, 260n10, n11, n21,
  261n29, 262n5, 263n19, n20, n21,
  264n22, 266n109, 270n3, 282n164 (*see
  also* Chesler, Ellen; Gordon, Linda;
  McCann, Carole; Reed, James); imprisonment of 33; influence of 5–6, 18–19,
  60, 66, 73, 128, 137–38, 204–5, 250–51,
  270n3, 282n164; last years 52–55;
  "Margaret" play 122; on population
  control 132–38; positive eugenics and
  49–50, 267n117, n137, 270n4; racism
  question concerning 41–46; resignation
  from ABCL and *Birth Control Review*
  35; strategy of 5–6, 15, 66; support for

abortion 11; support for sterilization 11,
  187–89, 259n5, 260n22, 266n95; views
  on sexuality of 9, 14–17, 18, 23–25, 29,
  30, 31–32, 237–44, 259n7, 261n30, n32,
  263n17; see also *Birth Control Review*,
  editing and founding of; ideology of
  control; *The Pivot of Civilization*;
  Woman and the New Race; *The Woman
  Rebel*
Sanger, William (Bill) 23, 29, 259n4
Satterthwaite, Adaline Pendelton 220–21,
  227, 301n83, n90, 302n108, n109, n126
Scaife, Mrs. Alan M. 158
Schenkel, Albert F. 265n71
schizophrenia 182
Schneider, Mark 201
Schoen, Johanna 281n113
Scripps Foundation for Research in Popu-
  lation Problems 141–42, 146, 148, 150,
  285n69
Seaman, Barbara 269n179, 301n87,
  302n127
Searle, G. D. 57–58, 220–21
Sedgwick, John 276n144
Segal, Sheldon 162–63, 177, 222, 290n72,
  n73, 302n97, 305n34
segregation *see* institutionalization
Seitler, Dana 261n29
Selden, Steven 272n72, 273n90
Serebrovsky, A. S. 264n21
sex education 5, 27, 29
sexology 14, 18, 31–32, 108, 238, 264n41
sexually transmitted diseases 105, 242
Shapiro, Thomas M. 186, 290n99, 292n2,
  294n36, n37, n39, n41, n46, n47, n48,
  n49, n50, n54, n61, 295n63, n67, n72
Sharpless, John 287n3, 289n44, 300n56
Shaw, Margery 93, 276n161
Sher, Geoffrey 274n125
Sherry, Gerard E. 269n198
Shockley, William 84–85, 274n113
Shukla, Hema 303n162
Simmel-Joachim, Monika 267n112
Simmons, Lewis M. 291n131
Simon, Julian L. 274n122, 288n12, n17,
  296n85
Sinding, Steven W. 155
Singer, Peter 94–95, 276n162, 277n168
Sinsheimer, Robert 83–85
Slee, J. Noah 33, 39, 256
Smith, Ruth Proskauer 190, 265n60,
  268n166, 295n69
Snyder, Sharon L 275n138

Sobo, Elizabeth 275n130
Social Science Research Council 156
socialism 5, 22–25, 27–29, 32, 40, 46, 52,
   70, 163, 165–66, 194, 183, 207, 236, 241–
   42, 263n17, 264n21, n22, 273n106,
   304n22; see also Goldman, Emma;
   Sanger, Margaret, early career; syndicalism
Society for the Study of Social Biology
   (SSSB) 104, 257
Solari, Luis 201
Soloway, Richard A. 106–7, 279n39, n42,
   n43, n49, n51, n53, 283n23
South Africa 232
South Carolina 116, 185
Spencer, Herbert 26, 67
sperm bank 83
Steel, Kathleen O. 89, 275n139
Stephens, John D. 233
sterilization 6–7, 11, 30–31, 33, 53–59, 66,
   71, 75, 77, 82, 86, 99, 110–12, 115–16,
   123, 125, 161, 164, 171–72, 179–202, 219,
   225, 256, 265n60, 280n108, n113,
   290n62, 293n6, 294n29; in Alabama
   185–86; in California 123, 189; in China
   192–99; coerced 61, 71, 83–85, 94, 103,
   167–68, 257; in England 105–6; forced
   7, 11, 41, 45, 61, 70, 101, 105, 129, 143,
   171–72, 176, 182–83, 188, 192–201, 213,
   229, 257, 259n5, 297n129; in Germany
   38, 45–46, 106, 181–83, 188, 257; in
   North Carolina 116, 281n113; in Peru
   199–201, 297n119; in Puerto Rico 56,
   301n27; in Virginia 183, 293n25; see
   also Sanger, Margaret, support for sterilization
Stoddard, Lothrop 42–43, 76, 79,
   266n101, 273n106
Stone, Abraham 81, 125–26, 273n98
Stone, Hannah 35, 81, 125–26, 273n98,
   282n166
Stopes, Marie 15
Strauss, Lewis 157
Stycos, J. Mayone 153–54
suffrage 11, 26, 243, 263n17
Suitters, Beryl 268n151, 279n48, n52, n58
Sweden 52, 165, 179–80, 184
Sydenstricker, Edgar 77–78, 142, 145,
   273n74, 286n80
syndicalism 27–29, 263n17; see also Goldman, Emma; socialism
syntex 214–15
syphilis see STDs

Taeuber, Irene 156
targets see quotas for population control
Teitelbaum, Michael 138, 284n49
Testart, Jacques 274n124
Thailand 215, 232, 303n143
Third World see developing world
Thompson, Warren S. 76, 78, 141–42,
   145–46, 285n69, 286n71
Thomsen, Major Russel J. 225
Three-in-One Oil Company 39
Tietze, Christopher 99, 108, 115, 139, 145,
   155, 161–63, 222–24, 277n4, 281n122,
   285n60, 290n63, n64, 302n98, n102,
   n107, n112, n114
Tietze, Sarah Lewit 277n4, 280n103,
   285n60, 290n64
Todd, T. Wingate 282n145
Tone, Andrea 213, 261n31, 269n176,
   299n32, 300n48, 301n71, n78, n89, n91,
   n92, 302n113, n117
Trent, Kathryn 281n117
tuberculosis 15, 143, 242
Tucker, William H. 276n144
Tuggle, Rev. Melvin 302n139
Turner, Ted 151, 173–75, 247, 292n144,
   n149
Turner Foundation 173
twin studies 84, 102, 159

Udall, Stewart 167
"unfit" 10–13, 15–17, 21, 31, 32, 35, 38,
   40–41, 43, 45–51, 66, 70–72, 79–80, 82–
   84, 86, 88, 99–101, 105–6, 109–10, 114,
   116, 122–23, 128, 134, 142–43, 180, 182–
   83, 187, 190–91, 218, 237, 239–44,
   266n104, 271n20, 280n108, 304n22
United Nations Children's Fund
   (UNICEF) 194
United Nations Educational, Scientific
   and Cultural Organization (UNESCO)
   135
United Nations Foundation 173
United Nations International Conference
   on Population and Development
   (ICPD, Cairo) 176–78, 195, 258,
   292n160, n164, n165
United Nations Population Division 142,
   170
United Nations Population Fund
   (UNFPA) 120, 139–40, 151–52, 162,
   170–72, 177–78, 191, 196–98, 200–1, 215,
   228, 232, 257–58, 285n59, 291n122,
   292n166, 297n129

United Nations World Population Conference (Bucharest 1974), 169, 177–78, 244, 258, 295n74
United Nations World Population Conference (Mexico City 1984), 295n74
United Nations World Population Conference (Rome 1954), 170
United Nations World Population Fund 135
United States Agency for International Development (USAID) 120, 139, 152, 155, 164, 168–172, 192, 199–201, 213–17, 221, 228, 257, 281n131, 297n119; *see also* Ravenholt, Reimert T.
United States Department of Health, Education and Welfare (HEW) 92
United States Department of State 166, 168, 230, 296n89
United States Food and Drug Administration 168, 214, 215, 221, 228–31, 303n148, n151
United States House Subcommittee on International Operations and Human Rights 199
United States Office of Population 169
United States Office of Technology 221
Upjohn 230–32
Uri, Constance Redbird 167, 185

vaccine (contraceptive) 214, 300n51, n66
vaccine rhetoric 115, 246
Valentine, Alan 52, 81–82, 268n143, n144, 273n94, n95
Valenza, Charles 49, 266n89
vasectomy 171–72, 187, 290n62
Virginia 116
Vogt, William 55, 132, 163, 208–9, 245, 298n16, n20, n21

Wagman, Paul 291n122, n124
Wallace, Alfred Russel 26, 264n21
Wallstrom, Margot 179
Wang Liancheng 192
Wang Wei 295n74
War on Poverty 52, 167
"war" rhetoric 212–14
Ward, Robert DeCourcy 79
Warren, Cara 275n132
Warren, Mary Anne 304n166
Warwick, Donald 151–52, 175, 287n6, 288n7, n8, n9, n13, n14, n15, n16, 290n69, 292n153, 298n18, n19
Watamull, Ellen 33

Watson, James 80
Waxman, Barbara Faye 62
Weaver, Warren 156
Weimar Republic 32, 38, 265n42, n77
Weindling, Paul 273n90
Weismann, August 26, 263n21
welfare programs 31, 54, 62–63, 70, 71, 75, 76, 77–78, 81, 92, 113, 116, 123, 128, 131, 136, 139, 140, 176, 179–80, 185–87, 206, 211, 229, 241–44, 268n157; *see also* birth control, funding of; Medicaid
Wells, H. G. 48, 283n21
Weschler, Toni 306n43
West Virginia 116, 273n84
Whelpton, Pascal K. 103, 135, 141–42, 160, 286n71
White, Tyrene 193, 295n76, n79, n83
Whitney, Glayde 274n126
Whitney, Leon F. 38, 75, 77, 100, 135, 147, 265n74, 272n59, 278n12
Whyte, G. Aird 107, 279n57
Wiehl, Dorothy G. 142, 286n75
Williams, Clare 276n158
Williams, Doone 115, 280n83, n85, n86, n87, n89, n94, n96, n97, n98, n109, 281n119, n120, n129, n130, n138, 299n44, 301n80, n84, n85, 305n37
Williams, Greer 115, 280n83, n85, n86, n87, n89, n94, n96, n97, n98, n109, 281n119, n120, n129, n130, n138, 299n44, 301n80, n84, n85, 305n37
Wilson, E. O. 299n25
Wilson, J. Robert 225
Wilson, Philip K. 272n56
Winch, Donald 283n13
Wing, Virgina R. 282n154
Wirth, Timothy E. 173
Wirtz, Willard 167
Wolf, Margery 304n164
Wolf, Naomi 306n44
Wolfson, Adam 277n170
Woman and the New Race 5, 14, 15–16, 21, 24, 47, 234, 236–44, 250, 261n33, n35, 262n16, 264n22, n41, 266n108, 267n119, 304n1, n7, n8, n9, n10, n11, n12, n13, n14, n16, n17, n18, n19, 305n23, n24, n25, n26, n27, n28, n29, n30, n31, n32
The Woman Rebel 29, 50, 264n22, n24, n26
women, bodies of 6, 9, 18, 19, 186–87, 202, 234–35, 238, 248–49; control of fertility of 6–9, 19, 29, 57, 63–64, 129, 138, 178, 201–2, 204, 231–23, 234–35,

259n7, 263n17 (*see also* coercion; ideology of control); demographic responsibility of 174, 205, 234; eugenic responsibility of, 15, 21, 61, 63, 93, 138, 195, 237–44, 305n29; "feminine spirit" of 241–43; health of 23–24, 50, 57, 117, 125, 195, 208, 212, 216–17, 222–25, 244–46, 262n9, 303n148, n151; as sterilization targets 180–81; violence against 239, 304n4; *see also* abortion, for sex-selection; infanticide

Wood, H. Curtis, Jr. 74, 164, 190–91, 272n47, 280n104, 295n65, n66, n70

Worlbring, Greg 93

World Bank 139, 171, 209

World Health Organization (WHO) 55, 300n51

World Population Emergency Campaign 54, 163, 206, 209–10; *see also* Moore, Hugh

World War I era 25, 28

World War II era 22, 39, 50–52, 79–82, 103

Wright, Helena 118

Wu, Harry 194, 195, 296n86, n87, n88, 297n105

Wulkop, Elsie 116

Wyeth-Ayerst 227

Yale University 115

Yerkes, Robert 72

zero population growth (ZPG) 128, 173, 212

Zukowski, Charles and Bernadine 177, 292n162